DICTIONARY OF
BOTANY

DICTIONARY OF
BOTANY

Edited by

Er. Haojam Rocky Singh
Richa Chowdhary

JNANADA PRAKASHAN **(P&D)**

in association with

THE GLOBAL OPEN UNIVERSITY

NAGALAND (INDIA)

Published by :
JNANADA PRAKASHAN (P&D)
4837/2, 24, Ansari Road, Daryaganj
New Delhi-110002
Phone : 011-23272047
Mobile : 9212137080
Email: jnanadabooksdelhi@yahoo.com
Website: www.jnanadabooks.com; text.ind.in

Assisted by :
TEXT BOOK PROMOTION SOCIETY OF INDIA
4837/2, 24, Ansari Road, Daryaganj
New Delhi-110002
Phone : 011-23272047
Mobile : 9212137080

First Edition: 2021
Dictionary of Botany
ISBN: 978-81-7139-465-4

Paper Quality: 80 gsm sunshine
Size: Demy
Pages: 432

Typesetting by :
Vardhman Computers
New Delhi-110017

Published by Mrs. S. Chowdhary for M/s. Jnanada Prakashan (P&D)
Daryaganj, Ansari Road, New Delhi-110 002 and *printed at* Balaji Offset,
Navin Shahdara, Delhi-110032.

PREFACE

Botany is the scientific study of plants and their life growth. It is a branch of biology. Plants are one of two major kingdoms of life forms. There are about 300,000 plant species on earth. Plants are the only life forms that can produce their own food using energy from sunlight through photosynthesis process. Plants produce almost all of the oxygen in the air that all living beings breathe. Plants are also vital source of food, paper and other resources that make life possible for Earth's animals.

Botany covers a wide range of scientific disciplines concerned with the study of plants, algae and fungi, including structure, growth, reproduction, metabolism, development, diseases, chemical properties, and evolutionary relationships among taxonomic groups. The study of botany began with early human efforts to identify edible, medicinal and poisonous plants, making it one of the oldest sciences. Today, botanists study over 550,000 species of living organisms.

A botanical dictionary is also commonly referred to as a plant dictionary or flower dictionary. Use this outdoor and indoor plant resource to look up words used to describe plants, flower parts, types of foliage, plant living processes and growing habits, as well as leaf shapes, and much more.

Dictionary of botany is an uptodate reference source for anyone with interest in plant science. The dictionary contains some 5300 lucidly written entries, drawn from major fields of pure and applied plant science.

Also covered are selected terms from the fields of agricultural botany, horticulture and microbiology.

Suggestions are welcome for improving the next edition of this important publication.

A: Abbreviation for adenine.

Abaxial: Describing the side of leaves, petals, etc. facing away from the stem or main axis, i.e. the lower surface.

Abc soil: Soil that has a surface layer, subsoil, and a lower layer of loose rock material is called this. The layers are said to be it's A, B, and C horizons.

Aberrant: This describes a plant or species that is different in some way from the group in which it is placed.

Abiotic: Absence of living organisms.

Abortive: Imperfectly developed; defective; barron.

Abruptly pinnate: This describes a pinnate leaf that ends without an odd leaflet or tendril. It ends in a matched pair of leaflets.

Abscise: To cut off; hence abscission, abscissive, abscissile.

Abscission: The normal shedding from a plant of an organ that is mature or aged, e.g. a ripe fruit, an old leaf.

Absidia: A zygomycete fungus. Reported to be allergenic. May cause mucorosis in immune compromised individuals. The sites of infection are the lung, nasal sinus, brain, eye and skin. Infection may have multiple sites.

Absorption: (a) The uptake into a plant of water, solutes, or other substances by either active or passive means. Entry invariably involves movement across cellular membranes. Active absorption, for example the uptake of a solute against an osmotic gradient, involves expenditure of energy. An example of passive absorption is the intake of water by plantroots, which is controlled by the rate of transpiration. (b) The retention of radiant energy by the pigments of a plant. About 80% of the incident visible light and about 10% of the infrared radiation falling on a leaf is absorbed. Generally, less than 2% of this is used in photosynthesis.

Acantha: A botanical word that refers to a spine, thorn or prickle.

Acaricide: A pesticide used to kill or control mites or ticks.

Acarpous: This describes a plant that is sterile.

Acaulescent: A plant that is stemless. The word Acauline is also used.

ACC synthase: Abbreviation for l-amino-cyclopropane-l-carboxylase. The enzyme catalyses the rate limiting step in the ethylene biosynthetic pathway, and is particularly significant in the fruit ripening process. Plants typically carry a number of distinct ACC synthase genes, which are differentially regulated in response to a variety of developmental, environmental and chemical factors.

Acceptor control: The regulation of the rate of respiration by the availability of ADP as a phosphate acceptor.

Accessory bud: A lateral bud occurring at the base of a terminal bud or at the side of an axillary bud.

Accessory flower parts: Sepal and petal organs found on flowers. The sepals and petals are not essential for pollination but may aid in attracting insects or other organisms.

Accessory fruit: A fruit, or group of fruits derived from one flower, in which the conspicuous, fleshy portion develops from the receptacle and is shed with the true fruit(s) attached.

Accessory transfusion tissue: In certain gymnosperms, e.g. Cycas, transfusion tissue that extends through the mesophyll from the midrib to the margin.

Acclimatization: The adaptation of a living organism (plant, animal or micro-organism) to a changed environment that subjects it to physiological stress. Acclimatization should not be confused with adaptation.

Accrescent: Growing after flowering or bud development has occurred, as the sepals in hypericum and bud scales in carya.

Accretive: Increasing or adding by growth; continued development within.

Accumbent: Lying against. Mainly used to describe the first sprouts of an embryo when they lie against the body of the seed.

Aceae: New Latin suffix, meaning "the plants of the nature of", which is used to form names of families of plants. Examples are Liliaceae, Rosaceae, etc.

Acellular: Tissues or organisms that are not made up of separate cells but often have more than one nucleus.

Acentric chromosome: Chromosome fragment lacking a centromere.

Acephate: A man-made, systemic insecticide that is used to control numerous pests such as aphids, scale and thrips, of most ornamental plants.

Acervate: Growing in heaps or in compact clusters.

Acetyl co-enzyme A (acetyl CoA): A compound formed in the mitochondria when an acetyl group (CH3CO-) - derived from breakdown of fats, proteins, or carbohydrates - combines with the thiol group (-SH) of co-enzyme A.

Aceus: Suffix meaning 'resembling', eg myrtaceus, foliaceus.

Achene: A dry, indehiscent fruit formed from a superior ovary of one carpel and containing one seed which is free from the pericarp (often applied, less correctly, to the one-seeded fruits of asteraceae).

Achenecetum: An aggregation of achenes, as in Ranunculus.

Acicula, acicle: A needle-shaped projection; hence acicular: needle-shaped.

Aciculate: Finely marked as with pin pricks, fine lines usually randomly arranged.

Acid A91: A substance that dissociates in water, releasing hydrogen ions.

Acid soil: Soil with a pH value of less than 7, or lacking in lime.

Acid-fast stain: A widely applied stain in bacteriology that is used to identify organisms that can retain a dye on washing with acid alcohol. One technique is to stain a bacterial smear withhot carbol fuchsin and, after rinsing with water, expose the smear to concentrated hydrochloric acid dissolved in water or ethanol. Following a second rinsing, the smear is counterstained with methylene blue. Acid-fast organisms retain the red colour of the carbol fuchsin while other organisms appear blue. Examples of acid-fast bacteria are species of the genus Mycobacterium.

Acidify: To lower the soil's pH to meet the level of acid soil.

Acinaceous: Consisting of or full of kernels.

Acinaciform: Shaped like a scimitar (usually describes a leaf shape). An acinaciform leaf has one edge convex and thin and the other edge straighter and thick. This term is also used to describe the shape of the pods of some beans.

Acinarious: Covered with little round, stalked, grape-like sacs, as in some algae.

ACP: Abbreviation for acyl carrier protein.

Acquired: Developed in response to the environment, not inherited, such as a character trait (acquired characteristic) resulting from environmental effect(s).

Acridine dyes: A class of positively charged polycyclic molecules that intercalate into DNA and induce frameshift mutations.

Acritarch: Small microfossil of unknown or varied biological affinity, consisting of a central cavity enclosed by a wall of single or multiple layers.

Acrocentric: A chromosome that has its centromere near the end.

Acrocidal capsule: One that dehisces through terminal slits, or fissures, as in staphylea.

Acrodromous: With two or more primary or strongly developed secondary veins diverging at or above the base of the blade and running in convergent arches toward the apex over some or all of the blade length, the arches not basally curved.

Acrogen: A plant that increases by growth at the summit or terminal buds only. The acrogens form a division of the Cryptogams, including ferns, fern allies, liverworts, and mosses.

Acropetal: Arising or developing in a longitudinal sequence beginning at the base and proceeding towards the apex. Opposite: basipetal.

Acroramous: Leaves terminal, near apex of branch

Acroscopic: The side of the organ directed towards the apex of the axis on which it is bourne.

Acrostichoid: Acrostichum-like, of exindusiate sori densly covering the lower surface of the frond, or large areas of it; the lamina may be contracted or not.

Actinodromous: With three or more primary veins diverging radially from a single point at or above the base of the blade and running toward the margin, reaching it or not.

Actinomorphic: Descriptive of a flower or set of flower parts which can be cut through the center into equal and similar parts along two or more planes; having radial symmetry.

Actinostele: A type of protostele that looks like a star in cross section. The walls of the stele are heavily reinforced with lignin and are relatively thick. Xylem occupies the center but the phloem occupies the indentations in the xylem. This generates the star-like pattern.

Activated charcoal: Charcoal that has been treated to remove hydrocarbons and to increase its adsorptive properties. It acts by condensing and holding a gas or solute onto its surface; thus inhibitory substances in nutrient medium may be adsorbed to charcoal included in the medium.

Activator: Any substances, such as microorganisms and nutrients, which are added to a compost pile to speed the breakdown of organic matter. Also called compost activator and compost inoculant.

Active transport: Transport across a cell membrane which requires energy generated by the hydrolysis of some energy carrier (usually ATP). The selective active transport of ions (usually sodium) out of the cell is often used as a secondary energy storage mechanism.

Acuminate: Tapering and drawn out into a narrow point.

Acute: Terminating in a distinct but not protracted point, the converging edges separated by an angle less than 90 degrees.

Acyl carrier protein (ACP): A class of molecules that bind acyl intermediates during the formation of long-chain fatty acids. ACPs are important because of their involvement in many of the reactions necessary for in vivo fatty acid synthesis.

Adaptation: Adjustment of a population to changes in environment over generations, associated (at least in part) with genetic changes resulting from selection imposed by the changed environment. Not acclimatization.

Adaxial: Describing the side of lateral organs facing toward the stem or main axis, i.e. The upper surface. Compare to abaxial.

Additive genes: A form of allelic interaction in which there is no dominance. The heterozygote is intermediate in phenotype between homozygotes for the alternative alleles. For multiple-gene traits, approximately equal contributions made by many loci.

Additive genetic variance: The net effect of the expresson of additive genes, and thus the chief cause of the resemblance between relatives. It represents the main determinant of the response of a population to selection. Formally, the variance of breeding values.

Additive: Something that is added to a fertilizer to improve its chemical or physical condition.

Adelphous: Means having stamens united into sets; used mostly in combination, as in monoadelphous.

Adenosine triphosphate (adenosine 5'-triphosphate) (ATP): A nucleotide of fundamental importance as the major carrier of chemical energy in all living organisms. It is also required for RNA synthesis since it is a direct precursor molecule. ATP consists of adenosine with three phosphate groups, linked together linearly. The phosphates are attached to adenosine through the 5'-hydroxyl of its ribose (sugar) portion. Upon hydrolysis, these bonds yield either one molecule of adenosine 5'-diphosphate (ADP) and the inorganic phosphate ion, or one molecule of adenosine 5'-monophosphate (AMP) and pyrophosphate; in both cases releasing energy that is used to power biological processes. ATP is regenerated by the phosphorylation of AMP and ADP.

Adenosine: A combination of adenine with D-ribose, a pentose sugar. The two molecules are linked by a â-glycosidic bond and together form a nucleoside . Adenine may alternatively combine with 2-deoxy-D-ribose, in which case the nucleoside is called deoxyadenosine. The latter is the form found in DNA, while adenosine is found in RNA, ATP, ADP, and AMP. Certain derivatives of adenosine (e.g. isopentenyl adenosine cr IPA) are cytokinins.

Adenovirus: One of a group of DNA-containing viruses found in rodents, fowl, cattle, monkeys, and man. In man they are responsible for respiratory-tract infections, but they have been exploited as a vector in gene therapy, especially for genes targeted at the lungs.

Adenylic acid: Synonym for adenosine monophosphate, a (ribo)nucleotide containing the nucleoside adenosine. The corresponding deoxyribonucleotide is called deoxyadenosine 5'-monophosphate or deoxyadenylic acid.

Adhesion: Two dissmiilar organs or parts touching each other, +/- adhesively but easily separated and not fused or grown together.

Adiaxial: On the side of a lateral organ towards the axis or stem.

Adnate: Fused to an organ of a different kind, e.g. applied to a stamen fused to a petal.

Adnation: Fusion of unlike parts such as the labellum (of an Orchid) with the column.

Adnexed: In botany, annexed or touching, but not attached.

Adoptive immunization: The transfer of an immune state from one animal to another by means of lymphocyte transfusions.

Adosculation: In botany, the fertilization of plants by the falling of the pollen on the pistils.

Adpressed: Lying close and flat against.

Adsorb: To accumulate on the soil's surface.

Adventitious buds: Buds appearing in an unusual place; for example, buds on leaves.

Adventitious roots: A root that grows from somewhere other than the primary root, for example, roots that arise from stems or leaves.

Adventitious: In botany, appearing in an abnormal or unusual position or place; occurring as a straggler or away from its natural position, such as roots on aerial stems.

Adventive: A plant that has been introduced, but isn't naturalized yet.

Aerating or Knee: Vertical or horizontal aboveground roots

Aerator sandals: Sandal-type shoes or spikes strapped onto regular shoes used to break up compacted soil in lawns.

Aerator: Any implement that is used to break up compacted soil and facilitate air and gas exchange.

Aerenchyma: Aerenchyma are parenchyma cells that are associated with an air space or surround open canals as in the air space of a monocot vascular bundle or the vallecular or carinal canal of a horsetail.

Aerial or Epigeous: Above the ground or water, in the air; aerial stem - an erect stem arising from a horizontal rhizome.

Aerial root: This is a root that grows from the stems or shoots of a plant and helps to sustain it by absorbing moisture from the air. Many Orchids and other tropical plants have aerial roots.

Aerobic respiration: A type of respiration in which foodstuffs are completely oxidized to carbon dioxide and water, with the release of chemical energy, in a process requiring atmospheric oxygen.

Aerobic: Active in the presence of free oxygen, e.g. aerobic bacteria that can live in the presence of oxygen.

Aerophores: An outgrowth of tissue concerned with gas exchange, often at the base of pinnae in ferns.

Aerophyllous: With aerial leaves.

Aestivation: The arrangement of sepals and petals or their lobes in an unexpanded flower bud.

Affinity chromatography: A method for purifying specific components in a solution by exploiting their specific binding to known molecule(s). The mixed solution is passed through a column containing a solid medium to which the binding molecule is covalently attached.

Affinity tag: An amino acid sequence that has been engineered into a protein to make its purification easier. The tag could be another protein or a short amino acid sequence, allowing purification by affinity chromatography. Synonym: purification tag.

Aflatoxins: A group of toxic compounds, produced by Aspergillus flavus, that bind to DNA and prevent replication and transcription. Aflatoxins can cause acute liver damage and cancer. A health hazard in certain stored foods or feed.

Agamogynous: Inflorescence with neuter flowers inside or above and pistillate outside or below (agamogynecephalous)

Agamous or neuter: Without sex; sexual organs abortive

Agar: A polysaccharide gelifying agent used in nutrient media preparations and obtained from Rhodophyta (red algae). Both the type of agar and its concentration can affect the growth and appearance of cultured explants.

Agarose gel electrophoresis: A method to separate DNA and RNA molecules on the basis of their size, in which samples are subjected to an electric field applied to a gel made with agarose.

Agarose: The main functional constituent of agar.

Aggregate: 1. A clump or mass formed by gathering or collecting units. 2. A body of loosely associated cells, such as a friable callus or cell suspension. 3. Coarse inert material, such as gravel, that is mixed with soil to increase its porosity. 4. A serological reaction in which the antibody and antigen react and precipitate.

Aggregate fruit: A cluster of fruits formed from the free carpels of one flower.

Agonist: A drug, hormone or transmitter substance that forms a complex with a receptor site. The formation of the complex triggers an active response from a cell.

Agrobacterium rhizogenes: A bacterium that causes hairy root disease in some plants. Similar to the crown gall disease caused by Agrobacterium tumefaciens, this is achieved by the mobilization of the bacterial Ri plasmid with the transfer to the plant of some of the genetic material from the plasmid. This process has been used to insert foreign genes into plant cells, but to a lesser extent than the Agrobacterium tumefaciens-mediated transformation system, because regeneration of whole plants from hairy root cultures is problematical.

Agrobacterium tumefaciens-mediated transformation: The process of DNA transfer from Agrobacterium tumefaciens to plants, that occurs naturally during crown gall disease, and can be used as a method of transformation.

Agrobacterium: A genus of bacteria that includes several plant pathogenic species, causing tumour-like symptoms.

Aianthous or semperflorous: With flowers appearing throughout the year

Air layering: This is a method of propagation in which roots are induced to form around a plant's stem. This is done by removing a very narrow strip of bark from around the branch or stem, about 8 to 12 inches from the tip of the shoot, or at that same distance from the tip, a cut can be made about a third way through the branch in an upward direction and a sliver of wood can be inserted into the cut to keep it open. Next, a bundle of moist sphagnum moss is tied securely around the cut area. The moss must always remain moist (this may be done by wrapping it in polyethylene film) and the roots of the plant somewhat dry. New roots will soon sprout from the incision. The new plant is then cut off below the moss, potted and kept in a humid atmosphere until it is established.

Air plant: An epiphyte. Many epiphytic Orchids and Bromeliads are popularly called air plants.

Airlift fermenter: A cylindrical fermentation vessel in which the cells are mixed by air introduced at the base of the vessel and that rises through the column of culture medium. The cell suspension circulates around the column as a consequence of the gradient of air bubbles in different parts of the reactor.

Albinism: Hereditary absence of pigment in an organism. Albino animals have no colour in their skin, hair and eyes. Albino plants lack chlorophyll.

Albino: 1. An organism lacking pigmentation, due to genetic factors. The condition is albinism. 2. A conspicuous plastid mutant involving loss of chlorophyll.

Albumen: In botany, any form of nutritive matter stored within the seed. Also called endosperm.

Aleurone: The outermost layer of the endosperm in a seed, and the site of enzymes concerned with endosperm digestion during seedling growth.

Algae: (singular Alga) A simple and primitive group of photosynthetic organisms formerly placed in the plant kingdom but now put in kingdom protista. Many are single-celled, but others are multicullular, including algae known as seaweeds.

Algal biomass: Single-celled plants (e.g. Chlorella spp. and Spirulina spp.) grown commercially in ponds to make feed materials for zooplankton, which are in turn harvested as feed for fish farms.

Alginate: Polysaccharide gelling agent.

Alkali soil: 1. Highly alkaline soil with a pH of 8.5 or higher. 2. Soluble salt or a mixture of soluble salts present in a soil.

Alkylating agent: A class of chemicals that transfer alkyl (methyl, ethyl, etc.) groups; for example to the bases in DNA. Some of these (especially ethyl methane sulphonate, abbreviated EMS) have been much used as mutagens.

Allagostemonous: Having stamens attached to petal and torus alternately.

Allautogamy: Cross- and self-fertilization in same plant, as in viola.

Allele: A variant form of a gene. In a diploid cell there are two alleles of every gene (one inherited from each parent, although they could be identical). Within a population there may be many alleles of a gene. Alleles are symbolized with a capital letter to denote dominance, and lower case for recessive. In heterozygotes with co-dominant alleles, both are expressed.

Allele-specific amplification (ASA): The use of the polymerase chain reaction at a sufficiently high stringency that only one allele is amplified. A powerful means of genotyping for single-locus disorders that have been characterized at the molecular level.

Allelic exclusion: A phenomenon whereby only one functional allele of an antibody gene can be assembled in a given B lymphocyte.

Allelochemicals: Compounds that have an allelopathic effect.

Allergen: An antigen that provokes an immune response.

Allogamy or Xenogamy: The process of cross-fertilization in which the pollen of one plant fertilizes the flower of another.

Allogenic: Differing at one or more loci, although belonging to the same species. Thus an organ transplant from one human donor to another is allogeneic, whereas a transplant from a baboon to a human would be xenogeneic.

Allometric: When the growth rate of one part of an organism differs from that of another part or of the rest of the body.

Allopatric speciation: Speciation occurring at least in part because of geographic isolation.

Allopatric: In the context of natural populations of animals or plants, inhabiting distinct and separate areas.

Allopolyploid: A polyploid organism with sets of chromosomes derived from different species. Opposite: autopolyploid.

Allosome: Synonym for sex chromosome.

Allosteric enzyme: An enzyme that has two structurally distinct forms, one of which is active and the other inactive. Active forms tend to catalyse the initial step in a pathway leading to the synthesis of molecules. The end product of this synthesis can act as a feedback inhibitor, converting the enzyme to the inactive form, thus controlling the amount of product synthesized. Synonym: allozyme.

Allosteric regulation: A catalysis-regulating process in which the binding of a small effector molecule to one site on an enzyme affects the activity at another site.

Allosteric site: That part of an enzyme molecule where the non-covalent binding of an effector molecule can affect the enzyme's catalytic activity.

Allosteric transition: A reversible interaction of a small molecule with a protein molecule, resulting in a change in the shape of the protein and consequent alteration of the interaction of that protein with a third molecule.

Allosyndesis: Pairing of chromosomes derived from different species. It is seen in some diploid hybrids and in segmental allopolyploids.

Allotetraploid: An allopolyploid having two different progenitor genomes.

Allotype: A classification of antibody molecules according to the antigenicity of the constant regions; a variation that is determined by a single allele.

Allozygote: A individual that is heterozygous for two different mutant alleles.

Alluvial: Soil composed of sand, clay or silt which has been dispersed by water.

Alluvium: Clay, silt, sand and/or gravel deposited on land by running water.

Aloe: Aloes are succulent, clumping plants with fleshy, toothed (non-fibrous) leaves. THere are about 300 species of aloe; they live in warm, dry habitats and most originated in northern Africa. Aloe vera is a popular plant whose gel-like sap is used as a medicinal salve; it is originally from northern Africa, the Cape Verde Islands, and the Canary Islands. Aloe vera has gray-green leaves and tubular yellow flowers that grow on a stalk that is up to 3 feet tall.

Alpine house: An unheated, well-ventilated greenhouse used for cultivating alpine and bulbous plants.

Alternaria: Conidia dimensions 18-83 x 7-18 microns. A very common allergen with an IgE mediated response. It is often found in carpets, textiles, and on horizontal surfaces in building interiors. Often found on window frames. Outdoors it may be isolated from samples of soil, seeds and plants. It is commonly found in outdoor samples. The large spore size 20 - 200 microns in length and 7 - 18 microns in sizes, suggests that the spores from this fungi will deposited in the nose, mouth and upper respiratory tract. It may be related to bakers asthma. It has been associated with hypersensitivity pneu-monitis (E). The species Alternaria alternata is capable of producing tenuazonic acid and other toxic metabolites which may be associated with disease in humans or animals. Common cause of extrinsic asthma (immeadiate-type hypersensitivity: type I). Acute symptoms include edema and bronchiospasms, chronic cases may develop pulmonary emphysema.

Alternate: Occurring one at a node; said also of members of adjacent whorls in the flower when any member of one whorl is in front of or behind the junction of two adjacent members of the succeeding whorl.

Alternation of generations: A life cycle in which there are two stages (a) a diploid, sporophyte stage which produces haploid spores by meiosis, and (b) a haploid, gametophyte stage which produces haploid gametes of two types, usually called male and female but technically microgametes and megagametes. The female gamete is fertilized to become a diploid zygote, which matures to become a diploid sporophyte, completing the cycle. Either the gametophyte or the sporophyte stage may be, and typically is, very small and remains attached to the other stage.

Alternative mRNA splicing: The inclusion or exclusion of different exons to form different mRNA transcripts from a single transcription unit.

Alu sequences: A highly repeated family of 300-bp long sequences dispersed throughout the human genome, so named because they are released by the digestion of genomic DNA with the restriction endonuclease AluI.

Aluminum: A silver-like metallic chemical element that can be found in soil.

Aluminum silicates: Compounds that contain aluminum, silicon and oxygen.

Aluminum sulfate: A colorless salt used as a soil amendment to increase soil acidity.

Alveolate: Deeply pitted so as to resemble a honeycomb, as are the surfaces of some seeds or achenes.

Amendment: Any conditioner or material (ie. Lime, gypsum, etc.) that is added or mixed into the soil to make in more productive.

Ament or Catkin: A catkin; a slim spike-like and usually pendent flower cluster like those found on Willow, Poplar and Birch trees. Aments are either male or female. Some plants produce both male and female aments; others produce male aments on one plant and female on another.

Amino acid: A compound containing both amino (-NH2) and carboxyl (-COOH) groups. In particular, any of 20 basic building blocks of proteins having the formula NH2-CR-COOH, where R is different for each specific amino acid.

Aminoacyl site (A-site): One of two sites on ribosomes to which the aminoacyl tRNA molecules can bind.

Aminoacyl tRNA synthetase: An enzyme that catalyses the attachment of an amino acid to its specific tRNA molecule.

Amitosis: A cell division (including nuclear division through constriction of the nucleus). That occurs without chromosome differentiation as in mitosis. The mechanism whereby the genetic integrity is maintained during amitosis is uncertain.

Ammonification: The act of forming ammonium compounds from organic material by various organisms.

Ammonium ion: A form that nitrogen takes in many commercial fertilizers.

Ammonium nitrate: 1. An organic fertilizer that will add nitrogen to the soil. 2. The form that nitrogen takes in numerous commercial fertilizers.

Ammonium sulfate: An inorganic fertilizer applied to soil (20.6 % N.).

Amniocentesis: A procedure for obtaining foetal cells for prenatal diagnosis by sampling the amniotic fluid from a pregnant mammal. Cells are cultured, and the karyotype is checked for known irregularities (e.g. Down's syndrome and spina bifida in humans).

Amnion: The thin membrane that lines the fluid-filled sac in which the embryo develops in higher vertebrates, reptiles and birds.

Amniotic fluid: Liquid contents of the amniotic sac of higher vertebrates, containing foetal, but not maternal cells.

Amorph: A mutation that abolishes gene function. Synonym: null mutation.

Amorphic or paleomorphic: Flowers without symmetry; usually with an indefinite number of stamens and carpels, and usually subtended by bracts or discolored upper leaves; e.g., Salix discolor, Echinops ritro (mostly fossil forms)

Amphibious: Capable of growing both in water and on land; growing with part of the plant in the water or mud and part in the air.

Amphicarpous: Refers to a plant that produces two classes of fruit that differ either in form or in time of ripening.

Amphidiploid: A plant derived from doubling the chromosome number of an interspecific F1 hybrid. Naturally found hybrids of this sort are referred to as allopolyploid.

Amphiflorous: Flowers above and below ground, as in amphicarpum.

Amphimixis: True sexual reproduction involving the fusion of male and female gametes and the formation of a zygote.

Amphiphloic siphonstele (solenostele): A cylindrical stele with a parenchymatous centre with phloem on both the inside and the outside.

Amphisarca: A berry-like succulent fruit with a crustaceous or woody rind, as in Lagenaria

Amphithecium: The outer, "ectodermal" cell layer of the sporophyte in basal plants.

Amphitropous: Having the seed embryo curved or coiled back along the supporting stalk so that its base and the opening of the pollen tube bend close to each other.

Ampicillin: A penicillin-type antibiotic that prevents bacterial growth by interfering with synthesis of the cell wall. Commonly used as a selectable marker in the creation of transgenic plants.

Amplexicaul: Nearly surrounding or embracing the stem, as the base of some leaves.

Amplicon: The product of a DNA amplification reaction.

Amplification: 1. Creation of many copies of a segment of DNA by the polymerase chain reaction. 2. Treatment (e.g. use of chloramphenicol) designed to increase the proportion of plasmid DNA relative to that of bacterial (host) DNA. 3. Evolutionary expansion in copy number of a repetitive DNA sequence through a process of repeated duplication.

Amplified fragment length polymorphism (AFLP): A type of DNA marker, generated by the PCR amplification of restriction endonuclease treated DNA. A small proportion of all restriction fragments is amplified in any one reaction, so that AFLP profiles can be analysed by gel electrophoresis. This has the important characteristic that many markers can be generated with relatively little effort.

Amplify: To increase the number of copies of a DNA sequence, either in vivo by inserting into a cloning vector that replicates within a host cell, or in vitro by polymerase chain reaction.

Ampulla: A small bladder of flask-shaped organ attached to the roots or immersed leaves of some aquatic plants, as in Nepenthes or Utricularia.

Amylopectin: A polysaccharide comprising highly branched chains of glucose residues. The water-insoluble portion of starch.

Amylose: A polysaccharide consisting of linear chains of 100-1000 glucose residues. The water-soluble portion of starch.

Anabolic pathway: A pathway by which a metabolite is synthesized; a biosynthetic pathway.

Anabolism: One of the two subcategories of metabolism, referring to the building up of complex organic molecules from simpler precursors.

Anadromic, anadromous: With the first subbranch of a lateral branch produced on the acroscopic margin, mostly of venation in bipinnate ferns.

Anaerobe: An organism that can grow in the absence of oxygen. Opposite: aerobe.

Anaerobic digestion: Digestion of materials in the absence of oxygen.

Anaerobic respiration: Respiration in which foodstuffs are partially oxidized, with the release of chemical energy, in a process not involving atmospheric oxygen. A notable example is in alcoholic fermentation, where sugar is metabolized into ethanol.

Anaerobic: Having very little or nooxygen levels. Some aquatic plants can grow anaerobically while producing new growth in water.

Anaerobiosis: Life in the absence of air or free oxygen; anaerobic respiration, respiration occurring in the absence of oxygen.

Analogous: Features of organisms or molecules that are superficially or functionally similar but have evolved in a different way or contain different compounds.

Analysis of variance: A statistical analysis by which F values (variance ratios) are composed in such a manner as to determine the probability that differences among populations or treatments are too large to be due to chance.

Anaphase: The stage of mitosis or meiosis during which the daughter chromosomes migrate to opposite poles of the cell (toward the ends of the spindle). Anaphase follows metaphase and precedes telophase.

Anastomosis: Fusion to form a network e.g. of veins in a leaf blade.

Anatomy: The branch of morphology that deals with the structure of plants, esp. the internal structure as revealed by the microscope.

Anatropous: With body completely inverted so that funiculus is attached basally near adjoining micropyle area.

Anchor gene: A gene that has been positioned on both the physical map and the linkage map of a chromosome, and thereby allows their mutual alignment.

Andragamous: Inflorescence with staminate flowers inside or above and neuter flowers outside or below (andragamocephalous)

Androdioecious: Having hermaphrodite (bisexual) flowers on one plant of a species and male flowers on another plant of the same species, but no corresponding form with only female flowers.

Androecium: Male reproductive organs of a plant; a collective term applied to all structures of the stamen whorl or whorls.

Androgen: Any hormone that stimulates the development of male secondary sexual characteristics, and contributes to the control of sexual activity in vertebrate animals. Usually synthesized in the testis.

Androgenesis: Male parthenogenesis, i.e. the development of a haploid embryo from a male nucleus. The maternal nucleus is eliminated or inactivated subsequent to fertilization of the ovum, and the haploid individual (referred to as androgenetic) contains in its cells the genome of the male gamete only.

Androgynal A392: Bearing staminate and pistillate flowers on the same parent stem.

Androgynecandrous: Inflorescence with staminate flowers above and below pistillate, as in the spikes of some species of carex

Androgynophore: A stalk bearing both the androecium and gynoecium of a flower above the level of insertion of the perianth.

Androgynous: Inflorescence with staminate flowers inside or above and pistillate outside or below (androgynecephalous)

Andromonoecious: Plant with staminate and perfect flowers.

Androphore: The stalk or column supporting the stamens of certain flowers usually formed by a union of the filaments, as in the Malvaceae and in many genera of Leguminosae.

Anemone centered: Flowers or flower heads in which the central petals or flowers (modified stamens) form a pincushion-like mound and the outer rim or petals or ray florets are flat and spreading, as in some chrysanthemums.

Anemophilous: Wind pollinated; refers to flowers that depend on the wind for pollination. Anemophilous flowers are ordinarily unnoticeably small, uncolored and don't secrete honey; however, they produce an abundance of pollen. Examples include the flowers of grasses, pines, sedges, etc.

Anemophily: Seed plants which are pollinated by wind are said to be anemophilous.

Aneuploid: An organism or cell having a chromosome number other than the normal somatic number. Aneuploid gametes have a chromosome number other than the normal haploid number. The condition is aneuploidy.

Angiocarpian: A plant that has its fruit enclosed in a husk.

Angiocarpous: Having a fruit enclosed within a distinct covering, as the filbert within its husk.

Angiogenesis: The formation and development of new blood vessels in the body, stimulated by growth factors, such as angiogenin. The process is required for the spread of malignant tumours.

Angiogenin: One of the human angiogenic growth factors. In addition to stimulating (normal) blood vessel formation, angiogenin levels are correlated with placenta formation and tumour growth.

Angiosperm: Any flowering plant that reproduces by seeds enclosed in a protective seed vessel. The term angiosperms is given to the larger of the two divisions of seed-bearing plants, in contrast to gymnosperms, which lack flowers and in which the seeds are naked (Examples are Coniferae, Cycadaceae, etc.)

Angiospermae: A major division of the plant kingdom, commonly called flowering plants as their reproductive organs are in flowers, having seeds which develop in a closed ovary made of carpels, a very reduced gametophyte, and endosperm develop from a triple fusion nucleus.

Angiospermous: Having seeds enclosed in a seed vessel, for example, this refers to the poppy, the rose, and most flowering plants, opposed to gymnospermous, or naked-seeded.

Angustiseptate: With narrow partitions.

Anhydrous: Dry or lacking water.

Animal cell immobilization: Entrapment of animal cells in some solid material in order to produce some natural product or genetically engineered protein. Animal cells have the advantage that they already produce many proteins of pharmacological interest, and that genetically engineered proteins are produced by them with the post-translation modifications normal to animals. However, because animal cells are much more fragile than bacterial ones, they cannot tolerate a commercial fermentation process.

Anion: An ion that is carrying a negative charge of electricity.

Anisocotylous: With unequal cotyledons.

Anisophyllous: Having the leaves of a pair of two different shapes and sizes, as in conifers and many aquatic plants.

Anneal: The pairing of complementary DNA or RNA sequences, via hydrogen bonding, to form a double-stranded polynucleotide. Opposite: denature.

Annotinal or Yearly: Appearing yearly.

Annual: Living one year or less. Winter Annual-Living less than one year but through the winter; germination usually in late fall, and usually flowering and fruiting in early spring.

Annual rings: Annual rings are the layers of wood laid down by the vascular cambium in a woody dicot or a gymnosperm. Because the vascular cambium is active in the spring through the fall, xylem cells are being added to the circumference of the xylem tissue. In the spring these cells grow fast and are large, however as the summer progresses into fall, the numbers of cells being produced slows down and finally stops. At the same time, the cells get smaller and smaller. The next spring when the vascular cambium breaks dormancy, the cells are large and fast-growing again. Thus, the difference in size between the small cells (summer wood) and the new spring cells (spring wood) forms a line between the spring and summer wood. This then marks the boundary of an annual ring.

Annular: Arranged in or forming a ring.

Annulus: Specialized structure of some fern sporangia that is involved in the opening of the sporangium. In some mosses, on drying out the cells of the annulus contract and the sporangium ruptures, releasing the spores. In others, the annulus bears the peristome teeth, which perform a similar function.

Anomalicidal or Rupturing Capsule: One that dehisces irregularly, as in Ammannia

Anomalous: Irregular; abnormal.

Anonymous DNA marker: A DNA marker detectable by virtue of variation in its sequence. The function (if any) of the sequence is unknown. Microsatellites and AFLPs are typical anonymous DNA markers.

Anoxia: Lack of oxygen or not enough oxygen.

Antagonism: An interaction between two organisms (e.g. moulds or bacteria) in which the growth of one is inhibited by the other. Opposite: synergism.

Antagonist: A compound that inhibits the effect of an agonist in such a way that the combined biological effect of the two becomes smaller than the sum of their individual effects.

Anterior: The lobes away from axis, toward the subtending bract, abaxial lobes; anterior ridges, lines, grooves the lines, grooves, ridges in or on the dorsal side, abaxial, within the perianth

Anther culture: The aseptic culture of immature anthers to generate haploid plants from microspores via androgenesis.

Antheridiophore: A stalk that bears an antheridium.

Antheridium: The male gametangium of certain algae, fungi, bryophytes, and vascular plants other than gymnosperms and angiosperms.

Antherocyte: A cell that differentiates into an antherozoid without further cell division. The antherozoid is usually released from the antherocyte after it has been discharged from the antheridium.

Anthesis: Stage or period during which the flower bud is fully open; flowering.

Anthocarp: A false fruit consisting of the true fruit and the base of the perianth, as in nyctaginaceae.

Anthocarpous: Having a body of combined floral and fruit parts, as in multiple fruits

Anthocyanin: A water-soluble blue, purple or red flavonoid pigments found in vacuoles of cells of certain plants.

Anthography: The description of flowers.

Antholeucin: The dissolved coloring matter in white flowers.

Anthophore: An elongated segment as the base of a flower, between the stem and the base of the petals, stamens, and pistil, as in pinks (Dianthus) or catch-fly (Silene). Also called anthophorum.

Anthophyte: A flowering plant, or any of its closest relatives, such as the Bennettitales, Gnetales, or Pentoxylales.

Anthoropic soil: Soil worked by humans in a way to produce new characteristics that make it different from the original natural soil.

Anthotaxis: Arrangement of sporophylls, primarily reproductive in function

Anthoxanthin: The yellow or orange coloring matter of yellow flowers and fruit.

Anti idiotype antibody: An antibody, produced by an organism, which specifically binds to the binding site of an antibody developed by that organism against a foreign antigen. Involved with the regulation of the immune response. Some allergic responses are in part due to the breakdown of this sort of regulation.

Anti terminator: A protein which enables RNA polymerase to ignore certain transcriptional stop or termination signals and thereby produce longer than normal transcripts.

Antiauxin: A chemical that interferes with the auxin response, sometimes by the prevention of auxin transport. Some antiauxins may promote morphogenesis in vitro (e.g. 2,3,5-tri-iodobenzoate (TIBA) and 2,4,5-trichlorophenoxyacetate (2,4,5-T)) and are therefore used to stimulate the growth of some cultures.

Antibiosis: The prevention of growth or development of an organism by a substance or another organism.

Antibiotic: A class of natural and synthetic compounds that inhibit the growth of, or kill some micro-organisms. Antibiotics are widely used medicinally to control bacterial pathogens, but resistance in bacteria to particular antibiotics is often rapidly acquired through mutation.

Antibiotic resistance: The ability of a micro-organism to disable an antibiotic or prevent its transport into the cell.

Antibiotic resistance marker gene (ARMG): Genes (usually of bacterial origin) used as selection markers in transgenesis, because their presence allows cell survival in the presence of normally toxic antibiotic agents. These genes were commonly used in the development and release of first generation transgenic organisms (particularly crop plants), but are no longer favoured because of perceived risks associated with the unintentional transfer of antibiotic resistance to other organisms.

Antibody (Ab): An immunological protein produced by the lymphocytes in response to contact with an antigen. Each antibody recognizes just one antigenic determinant of one antigen and acts by specifically binding to it, thus rendering it harmless. Those from the IgG antibody class are found in the bloodstream and used in immunoassay.

Antibody binding site: The part of an antibody that binds to the antigenic determinant.

Antibody class: The class to which an antibody belongs, depending on the type of heavy chain present. In mammals, there are five classes of antibodies: IgA, IgD, IgE, IgG, and IgM.

Antibody structure: Describes the molecular architecture of an antibody, which consists of two identical "light" chains and two identical "heavy" chains and has two antigen-binding sites. Each chain consists of a constant region which is thc same between antibodies of the same class and sub-class, and a variable region that is antibody-specific.

Antibody-mediated immune response: The synthesis of antibodies by B cells in response to an encounter of the cells of the immune system with a foreign antigen. Synonym: humoral immune response.

Anticlinal: The orientation of cell wall or plane of cell division perpendicular to the surface. Opposite: periclinal.

Anticoding strand: The DNA strand used as template for transcription. The resulting mRNA is complementary in sequence to that of the anticoding strand. Synonym: template strand.

Anticodon: The three nucleotide sequence in a trna molecule that base pairs with the complementary mrna codon for the amino acid carried by that specific trna.

Antigen (Ag): A macromolecule (usually a protein foreign to the organism), which elicits an immune response on first exposure to the immune system by stimulating the production of antibodies specific to its various antigenic determinants. During subsequent exposures, the antigen is bound and inactivated by these antibodies. Synonym: immunogen.

Antigenic determinant: The individual surface feature of an antigen, that elicits the production of a specific antibody in the course of the immune response. Each antigenic determinant, typically a few amino acids in size, causes the synthesis of a different antibody and thus exposure to a single antigen may result in the expression of a number of antibodies.

Antigenic switching: The altering of a micro-organism's surface antigens through genetic re-arrangement, to elude detection by the host's immune system.

Antihaemophilic globulin (AHG): One of the blood clotting factors, a soluble protein that causes the fibrin matrix of a blood clot to form. Used as a treatment for haemophilia, AHG is usually obtained from genetically engineered cell cultures.

Antimicrobial agent: Any chemical or biological agent that inhibits the growth and/or survival of micro-organisms. Antinutrient Compounds that inhibit the normal uptake or utilization of nutrients.

Antioxidant: Compounds that slow the rate of oxidation reactions.

Antiparallel orientation: The normal arrangement of the two strands of a double-stranded DNA molecule, and of other nucleic-acid duplexes (DNA-RNA, RNA-RNA), in which the two strands are oriented in opposite directions so that the 5'-phosphate end of one strand is aligned with the 3'-hydroxyl end of the complementary strand.

Antisense DNA: One of the two strands of double-stranded DNA, usually that which is complementary (hence "anti") to the mRNA, i.e. the non-transcribed strand. However, there is not universal agreement on this convention, and the preferred designations are coding strand for the strand whose sequence matches that of the mRNA, and non-coding strand or template strand for the complementary strand (i.e. the transcription template).

Antisense gene: A gene that produces an mRNA complementary to the transcript of a normal gene (usually constructed by inverting the coding region relative to the promoter).

Antisense RNA: An RNA sequence that is complementary to all or part of a functional mRNA molecule, to which it binds, blocking its translation.

Antisense therapy: The in vivo treatment of a genetic disease by blocking translation of a protein with a DNA or an RNA sequence that is complementary to a specific mRNA.

Antisepalous: Inserted in front of the sepals; opposite the sepals.

Antiseptic: Any substance that kills or inhibits the growth of disease-causing micro-organism (a micro-organism capable of causing sepsis), but is essentially non-toxic to cells of the body.

Antiserum: The fluid portion of the blood of an immunized animal (after coagulation of the blood), which retains any antibodies.

Antitranspirant: A compound designed to reduce plant transpiration. Applied to the leaves of newly transplanted trees, shrubs etc., or cuttings in lieu of misting. Can interfere with photosynthesis and respiration if the coating is too thick or is unbroken.

Antitropous: With radicle pointing away from hilum.

Antixenosis: The modification of the behaviour of an organism by a substance or another organism. Particularly used in the context of a plant's apparent resistance against insect feeding, when the insects are presented with a choice of plant genotypes.

Apatite: 1. The main mineral found in phosphate rock. 2. An inorganic compound found in bones; a component of the fertilizer, bone meal.

Apetalous: Having flowers without petals; having no corolla.

Apex: The portion of a root or shoot containing the primary or apical meristem.

Apheliotropic: Turning away from the light; applied to shoots or other parts of plants, as in roots that turn away from the sun; opposite heliotropic.

Aphyllopodic: Without blade-bearing leaves at base of plant.

Aphyllous: Without leaves; applied to flowering plants that are naturally leafless, such as many kinds of cactus.

Apical cell: A meristematic initial in the apical meristem of shoots or roots of plants.

Apical dominance: The phenomenon where growth of lateral (axillary) buds in a plant is inhibited by the presence of the terminal (apical) bud on the branch. Explained by the export of auxins from the apical bud.

Apical meristem: A region of the tip of each shoot and root of a plant in which cell division is continually occurring to produce new stem and root tissue, respectively. Two regions are visible in the apical meristem: An outer 1-4-cell layered region (the tunica), where cell divisions are anticlinal; and below the tunica, (ii) the corpus, where the cells divide in all directions, and increase in volume.

Apical or terminal: At or towards the tip of an organ or axis.

Apiculate: Terminated abruptly by a small, distinct point, an apiculus or apicule.

Apicule: A short, sharp point.

Apiculum: A short, abrupt, flexible point.

Apiculus: A short sharp point in which an organ may end; hence apiculate.

Apocarpous: Of a gynoecium, consisting of two or more carpels which are free from one another or almost so.

Apoenzyme: Inactive enzyme that has to be associated with a co-enzyme in order to function. The apoenzyme/co-enzyme complex is called a holoenzyme.

Apogamous: The nature of or characterized by apogamy.

Apogamy: Generally, the absence of sexual reproductive power, the plant perpetuating itself only by vegetative means, as buds, bulbs, etc.

Apomict: A plant that produces viable seed without fertilisation.

Apomixis: In general, reproducing without sexual reproduction; often used to denote seed production without a sexual process having been involved.

Apomorphy: A character state which is unique to a single, terminal taxon. Example among primates, complex grammar is an apomorphy of human beings. It is quite diagnostic of humans, but useless in determining phylogenetic relationships because it is not a shared, derived characteristic, or synapomorphy, of any larger group.

Apopetalous or choripetalous: With separate petals.

Apophyllous: Having distinct leaves, applied to a whorled flower with distinct sepals and petals; opposed to gamophyllous.

Apoptosis: The process of programmed cell death, which occurs naturally as a part of normal development, maintenance and renewal of tissue. Differs from necrosis, in which cell death is caused by external factors (stress or toxin).

Apospory: Producing gametophytes directly from a sporophyte without producing spores.

Appendage: That which is attached to something as a proper part of it; a subordinate, attached part of anything. Specifically, any subsidiary part added to another part, as hairs and glands to a stem or leaf.

Appendicular: Typical stamen with a variously-shaped or modified, protruding connective, as in Viola.

Applanate or plane: Flat, without vertical curves or bends.

Appressed or adpressed: Pressed closely to axis upward with angle of divergence 15° or less

Aptamer: A polynucleotide molecule that binds to a specific molecule, often a protein.

Aquaculture: Farming of aquatic organisms, including fish, molluscs, crustaceans and aquatic plants.

Aquatic vascular plants: Aquatic plants containing the conductive vascular tissue, phloem and xylem.

Aquatic: Plants that are naturally found growing in water at or above the surface of the soil. There are different types of aquatic plants. Some are emergent or only partially submerged, such as Cattails; some are completely submerged, such as Anacharis; some float with roots anchored to the soil under water, such as Water Lilies; some float freely with roots free in the water, such as water Hyacinths.

Aquifer: A water-bearing formation, usually underground, through which water can move easily.

Arabidopsis: A genus of flowering plants in the Cruciferae. A. thaliana is used in research as a model plant because it has a small fully sequenced genome, can be cultured and transformed easily, and has a rapid generation time.

Arachnoid: Like a cobweb; covered with or consisting of soft fibers or hairs so entangled as to give a cobwebby appearance.

Arbitrarily primed polymerase chain reaction (AP-PCR): An application of the polymerase chain reaction to generate DNA fingerprints. The technique uses arbitrary primers to amplify anonymous stretches of DNA.

Arbitrary primer: An oligonucleotide primer whose sequence is chosen at random, rather than one whose sequence matches that of a known locus. These primers therefore amplify DNA fragments which have not been pre-selected.

Arbor: A bower formed by trees, vines, or shrubs intertwined or trained over a latticework trellis, so as to make a leafy roof. They are usually provided with seats; any shaded walk. Arbors are used to provide support for plants, to create shade, or to frame a view.

Arboraceous: Pertaining to or of the nature of trees.

Arborescent: Resembling a tree (applied to non-woody plants attaining tree height and to shrubs tending to become tree-like in size).

Arboretum: A place in which trees and shrubs, especially rare ones, are grown for scientific or other purposes; a botanical tree garden.

Arboriculture: The cultivation of trees; the art of planting, training, pruning, and cultivating trees and shrubs for decorative purposes.

Arbuscle: A dwarf tree or tree-like shrub, in size between a tree and a shrub.

Archaea: Single-celled life forms adapted to existence in high pressure, anaerobic, environments such as at extreme ocean depths. These organisms are seen as a promising source of enzymes robust enough for a number of demanding industrial processes.

Archegonia: Reproductive structure that produces female gametes (egg).

Archegonium: The multicellular female gametangium of bryophytes and most vascular plants other than angiosperms.

Areolate: Divided into many angular or squarish spaces.

Areole: The cushion-like growing point (actually a modified leaf bud) on a cactus from which grows its spines, leaves, side shoots, offsets, or flowers. By identifying the areole on a plant, you can determine if it is a cactus, as only cactus have areoles. The areole generally has some wool or small hairs also growing from it.

Aril: An additional covering that forms on some seeds after fertilization, and developing from the stalk of the ovule.

Arillate: General term for an outgrowth from the funiculus, seed coat or chalaza; or a fleshy seed coat

Arista: An awn or bristle; hence aristate, bearing or tapering into an awn or bristle.

Aristate: More than 3:1 l/w, usually prolonged, straight and stiff.

Armature: Covering or occurrence of spines, hooks or prickles; hence armed.

ARMG: Abbreviation for antibiotic resistance marker gene.

Aromatic: With a resinous, spicy or distinctive smell.

Arthrodontous: Of moss sporophytes, having peristome teeth which are formed by walls growing between the rows of cells making up the mouth of the spore capsule.

Article: A segment of a jointed stem or of a fruit with constrictions between the seeds.

Articulate: Provided with joints or nodes, at which points separation takes place naturally. Jointed, consisting of segments united by joints. An example is Christmas Cactus (Schlumbergera bridgesii)

Artificial inembryonation: Non-surgical transfer of embryo(s) to a recipient female. As in vitro embryo technology develops, artificial inembryonation may replace artificial insemination.

Artificial insemination (AI): The deposition of semen, using a syringe, at the mouth of the uterus to make conception possible.

Artificial light: Light other than sunlight, often fluorescent tubes, used to grow plants.

Artificial seed: Encapsulated or coated somatic embryos that are planted and treated like seed.

Artificial selection: The practice of choosing individuals from a population for reproduction, usually because these individuals possess one or more desirable traits.

Ascending: Growing obliquely at first but finally upwards; rising or growing upwards.

Ascidium: Any tubular, horn-shaped, or pitcher-like formation of a plant, usually arising from the union of the margins of a leaf or other organ. The ascidium, commonly known as a pitcher, is usually covered with a lid and contains a fluid in which insects are drowned and dissolved. Examples are the pitcher plants (Nepenthes and Sarracenia).

Ascites: Abnormal accumulation of fluid in the peritoneal cavity, occurring naturally as a complication of cirrhosis of the liver, among other conditions. In the context of monoclonal antibody production, hybridoma cells are injected into mice to induce their proliferation in the resulting ascites. This method has been largely superseded by in vitro culture of hybridomas.

Ascospore: One of the spores contained in the ascus of certain fungi.

Ascus: One of often numerous, frequently fingerlike hollow structures in which the fusion of two haploid nuclei is followed by meiosis; a row of ascospores (usually eight) is ultimately produced in each ascus on or within the sexually initiated reproductive bodies of cup (sac) fungi.

Aseptic: Sterile, free of contaminating organisms (bacteria, fungi, algae but not generally including viruses, and particularly not internal symbionts).

Asexual: 1. Not-sexual; having no sex. 2. Produced by other than sexual processes, as asexual reproduction. Asexual reproduction is any process of propagation that isn't effected by means of sexual organs, as when propagation is carried out by buds, offshoots, bulbs, etc.

Asexual propagation: Vegetative, somatic, non-sexual reproduction of a plant without fertilization.

Asexual reproduction: Reproduction that does not involve the formation and union of gametes from the different sexes or mating types. It occurs mainly in lower animals, micro-organisms and plants. In plants, asexual reproduction is by vegetative propagation (e.g. bulbs, tubers, corms) and by formation of spores.

Asparagus-knife: A tool for prying and pulling out long-rooted plants. Also called dandelion weeder or fishtail weeder.

Aspera: Rough to the touch; hence asperites, asperate; rough or harsh (dimin. asperulous).

Aspergillus caesiellus: This species is only occasionally pathogenic.

Aspergillus candidus: Conidia dimensions 2.5-4 microns. Found in warm soils, grain and in the secondary decay of vegetation. Associated with respiratory complaints in a recent house investigation. (MAC) Can produce the toxin petulin which may be associated with disease in humans and other animals.

Aspergillus carneus: This species is only occasionally pathogenic.

Aspergillus clavatus: Conidia dimensions 3-4.5 x 2.5-4.5 microns. Found in soils and animal manure. Can produce the toxin petulin which may be associated with disease in humans and other animals. This species is only occasionally pathogenic.

Aspergillus deflectus: This species is only occasionally pathogenic).

Aspergillus flavus: Conidia dimensions 3-6 microns or 3-5 microns. It grows on moldy corn and peanuts. It can be found in warm soil, foods and dairy products. Some strains are capable of producing a group of mycotoxins - in the aflatoxin group. Aflatoxins are known animal carcinogen. There is limited evidence to suggest that this toxin is a human carcinogen. The toxin is a poisonous to humans by ingestion. It may also result in occupational disease via inhalation. Experiments have indicated that it is teratogenic and mutagenic. It is toxic to the liver. It is reported to be allergenic. Its presence is associated with reports of asthma. It can be found in water damaged carpets (NC). The production of the fungal toxin is dependent on the growth conditions and on the substrate used as a food source. This fungus is associated with aspergillosis of the lungs andor disseminated aspergillosis. This fungus is occasionally identified as the cause of corneal, otomycotic and nasoorbital infections.

Aspergillus fumigatus: Conidia dimensions 2-3.5 microns. Major cause of aspergillosis. Both invasive and allergic aspergillosis are caused by this organism. Aspergillosis affects individuals who are immune compromised. It is considered a human pathogen. It grows well at 35 degrees C. It is commonly found outdoors in compost piles with temperatures higher than 40 degrees C, in mild to warm soils and on cereals.

Aspergillus glaucus: Conidia dimensions 5-6.5 microns. Common outdoor fungus in the winter (NC). It is reported to be allergenic. This species is only occasionally pathogenic. It can grow on leather (NC). This fungus can grow at low moisture levels on grains, sugary food products, meat and wool.

Aspergillus niger: Conidia dimensions 3.5 - 5 microns or 4 to 5 microns. Less common cause of aspergillosis. It has a musty odor. It is commonly found in the environment on textiles, in soils, grains, fruits and vegetables. It has been reported to cause skin and pulmonary infections. It is a common cause of fungal related ear infections-otomycosis.

Aspergillus ochraceus: Conidia dimensions 2.5 - 3 microns. Found in grains, soil and salted food products. It is not usually associated with decaying vegetation. Can produce a kidney toxin ochratoxin A which may produce ochratoxicosis in humans. This is also known as Balkan nephropathy. The toxin is produced at optimum growth conditions at 25 degrees C and high moisture conditions. The ochratoxin may also be produced by other Aspergillus sp. and Penicillium sp. Other toxins which can be produced by this fungus include penicillic acid, xanthomegnin and viomellein. These are all reported to be kidney and liver toxins.

Aspergillus parasiticus: Some strains are capable of producing a group of mycotoxins - in the aflatoxin group. Aflatoxins are known animal carcinogen. There is limited evidence to suggest that this toxin is a human carcinogen. The toxin is a poisonous to humans by ingestion. Experiments have indicated that it is teratogenic and mutagenic. It is toxic to the liver. The production of the fungal toxin is dependent on the growth conditions and on the substrate used as a food source.

Aspergillus penicilloides: Conidia dimensions 3-3.5 x 4-5 microns. Can grow in areas with low water activity. It is found in house dust and food.

Aspergillus sydowi: This species is only occasionally pathogenic.

Aspergillus terreus: Aw 0.78. Conidia dimensions 1.8-2.4 microns or 2 - 2.5 microns. Aleurospores 6 - 7 microns in diameter are also produced. Found in warmer soil and in grains, straw. cotton and decomposing vegetation. Can produce the toxin patulin and citrinin which may be associated with disease in humans and other animals. This fungus is associated with aspergillosis of the lungs and or disseminated aspergillosis. Found as an isolate from otomycosis—ear infection and onychomycosis—infection of finger or toe nails.

Aspergillus ustus: This species is only occasionally pathogenic.

Aspergillus versicolor: Aw 0.78. Conidia dimensions 2-3.5 microns. It is commonly found in soil, hay. cotton and dairy products, It can produce a mycotoxin sterigmatocystin and cyclopiaxonic acid. These toxins can cause diarrhea and upset stomach. It is reported to be a kidney and liver carcinogen. This species is only occasionally pathogenic.

Aspergillus: Reported to be allergenic. Members of this genus are reported to cause ear infections. Many species produce mycotoxins which may be associated with disease in humans and other animals. Toxin production is dependent on the species or a strain within a species and on the food source for the fungus. Some of these toxins have been found to be carcinogenic in animal species. Several toxins are considered potential human carcinogens. Common cause of extrinsic asthma (immeadiate-type hypersensitivity: type I). Acute symptoms include edema and bronchiospasms, chronic cases may develop pulmonary emphysema.

Asperulate: Slightly rough to the touch.

Assay: 1. To test or evaluate. 2. The procedure for measuring the quantity of a given substance in a sample (chemically or by other means).

Assimilation: Cellular conversion of raw materials into protoplasm and cell walls.

Assortative mating: Mating in which the partners are chosen on the basis of phenotypic similarity.

Assurgent: Directed upward or forward

Astemonous or anandrous: No stamens or androecium

Astylocarpepodic: Without a style, with a stipe

Asymmetric hybrid: A hybrid formed, usually via protoplast fusion, between two donors, where the chromosome complement of one of the donors is incomplete. This chromosome loss can be induced by irradiation or chemical treatment, or can occur naturally.

Asynapsis: The failure or partial failure in the pairing of homologous chromosomes during the first meiotic prophase.

Atom: The smallest individual unit of an element that retains the properties of the element.

ATPase: An enzyme that brings about the hydrolysis of adenosine triphosphate, by the cleavage of either one phosphate groups with the formation of ADP and inorganic phosphate, or of two phosphate groups, with the formation of AMP and pyrophosphate.

Attar: A general term used for a perfume from flowers. In Europe, it denotes only the attar of roses, an essential oil. It takes 150 pounds of roses to provide less than an ounce of attar. The fragrance is too strong when it is concentrated and must be diluted to smell nice.

Attenuate: Elongate, tapering, usually applied to base.

Attenuated vaccine: A virulent organism that has been modified to produce a less virulent form, but nevertheless retains the ability to elicit antibodies against the virulent form.

Attenuation: A mechanism for controlling gene expression in prokaryotes that involves premature termination of transcription.

Attenuator: A nucleotide sequence in the 5' region of a prokaryotic gene (or in its RNA) that causes premature termination of transcription, possibly by forming a secondary structure.

Atypical: Having no distinct typical character; not typical; not conformable to the type.

Auger: A tool for boring a hole in the soil. Different-sized augers, powered by hand or electric drills, are used in planting or transplanting seeds, seedlings, or bulbs or in fertilizing shrubs, trees and ground covers.

Aureofacin: An antifungal antibiotic produced by a strain of Streptomyces aureofaciens. A possible candidate for the transgenic control of plant fungal disease.

Auricle: Ear-shaped projection or appendage. Ear-shaped lobes, often paired, as on the labellum or column of an Orchid.

Auriculate: Lobe rounded; sinus depth variable; outer margin concave, inner convex or straight.

Auriculiform: Usually obovate with two small rounded, basal lobes.

Authentic protein: A recombinant protein that has all the properties - including any post-translational modifications - of its naturally occurring counterpart.

Auto immune disease: Disorder in which the immune systems of affected individuals produce antibodies against molecules that are normally produced by those individuals (called self antigens).

Autocarpous: Consisting of ripened pericarp alone, having no adnate parts; applied to fruits that are free from the perianth.

Autochthonous: Of the inhabitants of a region, original; earliest known; (applied to an element of the australian flora rich in endemics and believed to have been evolving in australia for a long period of time).

Autoclave: An enclosed chamber in which materials can be heated under pressure to sterilize utensils, liquids, glassware, etc., using steam.

Autogamous: Self-fertilized; applied to flowers that are fertilized by their own pollen.

Autogamy: Self-fertilization, pollination of a flower by its own pollen.

Autogenous control: The action of a gene product to inhibit (negative autogenous control) or enhance (positive autogenous control) the expression of the gene that codes for it.

Auto-immunity: A disorder in the body's defence mechanism in which an immune response is elicited against its own (self) tissues.

Autologous cells: Cells taken from an individual, cultured (or stored), and, possibly, genetically manipulated before being transferred back into the original donor.

Autolysis: The process of self destruction of a cell, cell organelle, or tissue, through the action of lysosomic enzymes.

Autonomous: A term applied to any biological unit that can function on its own, i.e. without the help of another unit, such as a transposable element that encodes an enzyme for its own transposition.

Autonym: The name of a species automatically applied at the infraspecific level to the type when another infrospecific taxon is described in that species.

Autopolyploid: A polyploid whose constituent genomes are derived from the same or nearly the same progenitor. In an autotetraploid, each chromosome is present in four copies, so meiotic configurations may include many (or exclusively) quadrivalents (four paired chromosomes), and the inheritance of alleles will be quadruplex. Quadrivalents do not always segregate normaly at meiosis, resulting in lowered fertility, so some established autotetraploid species that reproduce sexually have restricted quadrivalent formation.

Autoradiograph: A technique for visualizing the presence, location and intensity of radioactivity in histological preparations, paper chromatograms or electrophoretic gel separations, obtained by overlaying the surface with X-ray film and allowing the radiation to form an image on the film.

Autosome: Any of the chromosomes except the sex chromosomes.

Autotroph: Organism capable of self-nourishment utilizing carbon dioxide or carbonates as the sole source of carbon and obtaining energy from radiant energy or from the oxidation of inorganic elements, or compounds such as iron, sulphur, hydrogen, ammonium and nitrites. Opposite: heterotroph.

Autotrophic: Independent of other organisms in respect of organic nutrition; able to fix carbon dioxide, by photosynthesis, to form carbohydrates.

Autotrophic nutrition: Synthesis of organic food molecules from inorganic compounds such as carbon dioxide

Auxiliary cell: A specialized cell in the gametophyte thallus of some red algae, e.g. Polysiphonia, situated adjacent to the carpogonium. Following fertilization of the carpogonium the zygote produces filaments that grow towards and fuse with the auxiliary cell. This process appears necessary for the production of carpospores.

Auxin cytokinin ratio: The relative proportion of auxin to cytokinin present in plant tissue culture media. Varying the relative amounts of these two hormones affects the proportional growth of shoots and roots.

Auxin: A group of plant growth regulators (natural or synthetic) which stimulate cell division, enlargement, apical dominance, root initiation, and flowering.

Auxotonic: Determined by growth. Applied to the movements of plants that are the result of growth, rather than outside stimulation.

Auxotroph: A type of biochemical mutant that can grow normally if provided with a supplement in its diet to replace the substance it has lost the ability to make. For example, certain mutants of the mould Neurospora crassa need the amino acid arginine in the culture medium to grow normally (the unmutated mould can synthesize all the amino acids it requires from ammonia). By supplying the auxotrophic mould with various precursors of arginine it can be established which of the enzymes in the pathway to arginine is missing.

Available nutrient: Nutrients found in the soil that can be taken in by plants at rates and amounts that are significant to the plants' growth.

Avena curvature test: A quantitative method used to correlate the degree of curvature obtained in a plant part, after the application of an external stimulus, with the amount of endogenous growth substance (auxin) required to bring it about. The tips of Avena (oat) coleoptiles are used as a standard. These are removed and placed on an agar block and auxin allowed to diffuse out for a predetermined time. The auxin-impregnated agar is then used to measure the curvature produced when pieces are placed acen-trally on decapitated coleoptiles. The response is plotted against the auxin concentration in the block. Over a certain range, increases in auxin concentration result in a regular increase in the degree of bending in the coleoptile, but the linear response is lost at higher levels. Only the straight line section of the graph is useful for assays. By noting the angle of curvature produced by a given stimulus under otherwise controlled standard conditions, one can find the quantity of auxin involved in producing the response.

Avidin: A glycoprotein present in egg white, which has a strong affinity to biotin. Can lead to biotin deficiency if given in large quantities. Used as a biological reagent in the same way as streptavidin.

Avirulence gene: Many plants contain R genes, which confer simply-inherited resistance to a specific pathogen race. The plants are able to recognize the presence of the pathogen by an interaction between their R gene and the matching pathogen's avirulence gene. Successful recognition triggers a cascade of further genes, often leading to a hypersensitive response.

Awl-shaped Leaf: Subulate; narrow, flat, stiff, sharp-pointed, usually less than 1/2 in. long; e.g., Juniperus.

Awl-shaped: Tapering from the base to a slender and stiff point.

Awn: A sharp point or bristle, commonly found on grass seed and flower heads; the bristle-shaped terminal appendage, such as the beard of barley, wheat and many grasses.

Axenic culture: A culture consisting of only one type of organism or cell. Axenic cultures are derived from pure parent cultures and grown under sterile conditions. Such uncontaminated cultures are necessary in investigating the properties of, a particular microorganism or cell type and in maintaining cultures of microorganisms over a long period of time.

Axil: The angle formed between a leaf's petiole and a stem where an axillary bud develops. The angle formed on an inflorescence, pedicel and rachis (of an Orchid).

Axile: With the placentae along the central axis in a compound ovary with septa.

Axillary bud proliferation: Propagation of plant tissue in vitro to promote axillary growth, to generate large numbers of plantlets in culture.

Axillary bud: A bud found at the axil of a leaf. Synonym: lateral bud.

Axillary or Lateral: In axils of leaves or leaf scars; axillary leaves - leaves borne in the axils of branches, as in heterosporous species of Selaginella Baccacetum or Etaerio An aggregation of berries, as in Actaea.

Axis: The main or central line or stem about which the lateral organs or parts are arranged.

Axoneme: The fibrillar component of flagella and cilia.

B chromosome: A supernumerary chromosome present in some individuals (both plant and animal). They are smaller than the normal chromosomes, behave abnormally in both mitosis and meiosis, can vary in number between somatic cells and are not thought to have any significant gene content.

BABS: Abbreviation for biosynthetic antibody binding sites.

BAC: Abbreviation for bacterial artificial chromosome.

Baccate: Shaped like a berry as, for example, the arils of yew (Taxus baccata).

Bacillus thuringiensis (Bt): A bacterium that produces a toxin against certain insects, particularly Coloeoptera and Lepidoptera; a major means of insecticide for organic farming. Some of the toxin genes are important for transgenic approaches to crop protection.

Bacillus: Any bacterium that is rod shaped and more or less straight.

Back mutation: A second mutation at the same site in a gene as the original mutation. The second mutation restores the wild-type protein sequence.

Backcross: Crossing a hybrid back to one of the original parents, called the recurrent parent. In agronomy, the recurrent parent is usually a single genotype, often a named variety. In forestry, the recurrent parent is usually a different genotype from the same species or population. (This is done to prevent inbreeding depression.) Example: collecting pollen from a pitch pine x loblolly pine F1 hybrid and pollinating a pure loblolly pine. The seed produced would be called first backcross and the loblolly pine the recurrent parent.

Backcrossing: A technique used in plant breeding to introduce a desirable gene into a cultivated variety. Unlike the pedigree method of plant breeding, the aim of a backcrossing programme is not to create entirely new varieties but to modify existing varieties. The cultivated variety (the recurrent parent) is crossed with the donor parent, which may be quite useless agriculturally except for its possession of one particularly valued gene (e.g. for disease resistance). The progeny from this cross, which contain 50% of the donor genetic material, are screened for the character and those possessing disease resistance are crossed back to the recurrent parent. The progeny of this cross - the first backcross generation (B1) - now contain 25% of the genetic material of the donor. The plants are again screened, the resistant plants again backcrossed to the recurrent parent, and this process is repeated until about the seventh or eighth backcross generation, by which time less than 0.25% of the donor genetic material remains. At this stage the B7 or B8 generation plants are selfed (crossed with each other) to produce plants homozygous for disease resistance; these may be identified by a test cross . The process described above assumes the allele for disease resistance is dominant. If it were recessive then it is necessary to alternate backcrossing with selfing of the backcross generations. Backcrossing is more efficient with self-pollinating species but the method is not necessarily limited to self pollinators.

Backfill: To fill in a planting hole around a plant's roots with a soil mix.

Backward selection: Selection of parent trees based on results from a progeny test.

Bacteria: A group containing all the prokaryotic organisms with the exception of the blue-green algae. These however are included with the bacteria as Cyanobacteria in many classifications. Bacteria are found in virtually all habitats and, in terms of distribution and number, are the most successful of life forms. Many live sapro-phytically in the soil and are important as decomposers in the carbon cycle. Others, the nitrifying and denitrifying bacteria, are important in the nitrogen cycle. Some are pathogenic, causing rots, cankers, blights, and galls in plants and numerous diseases in animals, e.g. anthrax, brucellosis, and syphilis. Bacteria are important in many industrial processes. Fermenting bacteria, e.g. Acetobacter, Acetomonas, and Lactobacillus are widely used in the food industry. Cheese making and the production of silage are dependent on bacterial activity. Bacteria were once placed with the fungi in the class Schizomycetes. They are now often classified as a separate division or kingdom, Bacteria or Prokaryota. The numerous different kinds of bacteria are classified on the basis of shape, size, growth form, staining and serological reactions, metabolic activity, and motility.

Bacterial artificial chromosome: A plasmid vector that can be used to clone large inserts of DNA (up to 500 kb).

Bacterial toxin: A toxin produced by a bacterium, such as Bt toxin of Bacillus thuringiensis.

Bactericide: An agent that kills bacteria; specifically, one that kills bacterial plant diseases.

Bacteriochlorophyll: Any of the forms of chlorophyll found in photosynthetic bacteria. Bacteriochlorophyll a, found in all bacteria, differs from the chlorophyll of plants in being a tetrahydroporphyrin rather than a dihydroporphyrin (i.e. it has more hydrogen atoms in pyrrole rings 2 and 4 of the chlorophyll molecule). It also differs in its absorption spectrum having three peaks, at 365, 605, and 770 nm. Some bacteria contain additional forms of bacteriochlorophyll (Bchl) designated Bchl b, Bchl c, and Bchl d.

Bacteriocin: A protein produced by bacteria of one strain and active against those of a closely related strain.

Bacteriophage: Any virus that infects bacteria. Bacteriophages are often named according to the bacteria they infect, e.g. actinophages, which infect bacteria of the order Actinomycetales, and coliphages, which infect various strains of Escherichia coli. All RNA phages bring about the death of the host cell by lysis. Some DNA phages (the temperate phages) become integrated in the host DNA and are replicated with it. Some temperate phages, e.g. the lambda virus, have been shown to transfer genes from one bacterium to another in a process termed transduction.

Bacteriostat: A substance that inhibits or slows down growth and reproduction of bacteria.

Baculovirus expression vector (BEV): A method for the in vitro production of complex recombinant eukaryotic proteins. A genetically engineered baculovirus (a virus that infects certain types of insects) is introduced into appropriate cultured insect cells, which then express the recombinant protein.

Baculovirus: A class of insect virus used to make DNA cloning vectors for gene expression in eukaryotic cells. Production of a target protein can be up to 50% of the cells' protein content, and several proteins can be made simultaneously, so that multi-sub-unit enzymes can be made by this system.

Baking soada: Sodium or potassium bicarbonate. Sometimes mixed with horticultural oils and applied to plants (usually roses) to prevent fungal diseases, such as black spot and powdery mildew.

Balanced lethal system: A system for maintaining a recessive lethal allele at each of two loci on the same pair of chromosomes. In a closed population with no crossing-over between the loci, only the double heterozygotes for the lethal mutations survive.

Balanced polymorphism: Two or more phenotypes maintained in the same breeding population.

Balausta: Many-seeded, many- loculed indehiscent fruit with a tough, leathery pericarp, as in Punica

Balm: An oily, aromatic resin or other substance exuding from trees; any aromatic substance secreted from plants.

Banded: Transverse stripes of one color crossing another.

Banding trees: To fasten a barrier around the trunk of a tree to mark the tree for some attention, such as pruning, or to discourage infestation by crawling insects.

Banding: 1. Placing fertilizer in continuous narrow bands and then covering it with soil. 2. Encircling part of a plant (usually the trunk) or a portion of a garden with some type of material that traps, kills, or keeps out pests. Examples include sticky materials, poisonous baits and copper stripping.

Banner: 1. The upper petal, usually broad and growing straight up, of some flowers. 2. One of the usually erect petals of the inner upright section of an iris. Also called the standard.

Barbate: Bearded, provided with tufts of long, weak hairs.

Barbed: Bearing sharp, spine-like hooks which are bent backwards (dimin. barbellate).

Barbellae: Short, straight, stiff hairs or barbs.

Barbellate: Provided, usually laterally, with fine, short points or barbs.

Barbulae: In scaevola, outgrowths on the margin of the wings or in the throat of the corolla; they may be simple or have apical hairs or papillae.

Bark ringing: This method is used to try to force fruit trees and some other woody plants to flower. A complete ring is cut around the trunk below the lowest branch and another ring is cut right below the first.

The bark between the rings is removed and the scar should be covered with grafting wax.

Bark: The dry, dead outer covering of woody branches, stems and roots of plants that is very distinct and separable from the wood itself. It includes all tissue outside the true cambium (growth layer between bark and wood).

Barnase: A bacterial ribonuclease, which, when transformed into plants and expressed in the anthers, generates a male sterile phenotype. Thus it is a technology applicable to F1 hybrid seed production, which relies on the ability to genetically sterilize genotypes to ensure that all seed borne on the plant are the result of outcrossing. The sterility phenotype is suppressed by the barstar protein, which can therefore be used to reverse the sterility where this is necessary.

Barr body: A condensed mass of chromatin found in the nuclei of female mammals. It is a late-replicating, inactive X-chromosome.

Barren: Sterile, incapable of reproducing.

Barstar protein: A polypeptide inhibitor of barnase.

Basal leaves: Leaves growing at the base or bottom of a plant.

Basal or Radical: 1. Located at the base of a plant or a plant organ. 2. A fundamental formulation of a tissue culture medium containing nutrients but no growth promoting agents.

Base analogue: A non-natural purine or pyrimidine base that differs slightly in structure from the normal bases, but can be incorporated into nucleic acids. They are often mutagenic.

Base: One of the components of nucleosides, nucleotides and nucleic acids. Four different bases are found in naturally occurring DNA - the purines A (adenine) and G (guanine); and the pyrimidines C (cytosine) and T (thymine, the common name for 5-methyluracil). In RNA, T is replaced by U (uracil).

Basicidal: Capsule one that dehisces through basal slits or fissures, as in some species of aristolochia

Basidiomycetes: Fungal spores which are from mushrooms. The specific mushroom species can not be identified on the culture plate. Many mushroom spores are reported to be allergenic.

Basidium: One of usually numerous, frequently club-shaped hollow structures in which the fusion of two haploid nuclei is followed by meiosis, the four resulting nuclei becoming e.g. (temally borne basidiospores: basidia are produced on or within sexually initiated reproductive bodies of the club fungi (e.g., mushrooms, puffballs).

Basifixed: Attached at or by the base, e.g. of anthers, by the base of the connective.

Basifugal: The growth of leaves that develop from the base upward.

Basin irrigation: The irrigation of level areas that are surrounded by ridges or levees to retain the water.

Basionym: The synonym or combination from which the specific epiphet was derived.

Basipetal: Developing, in sequence, from the apex towards the base.

Basipetiolar: At the base of the petiole.

Basiramous: Leaves on lower part of branch.

Basiscopic: Pointing towards the base (applied to the first lateral vein of a leaflet on the side nearer the leaf base).

Basophil: A type of leukocyte produced by stem cells in the red bone marrow.

Bast bundles (peripheral strands): Bundles of thick-walled cells parallel to the midrib, as in Isoetes.

Bast: A woody fiber obtained from the phloem, or inner bark used to make hemp, jute, ramie, etc.

Batch culture: A suspension culture in which cells grow in a finite volume of liquid nutrient medium and follow a sigmoid pattern of growth. All cells are harvested at the same time.

Bathyphyll: A lower leaf or frond, especially of high-climbing ferns.

Bay: A part of a sea or lake indenting the shore line; the word is often applied to very large tracts of water around which the land forms a curve, as Hudson's Bay.

Beak: A pointed projection, a prominent projection of an organ.

Beard: 1. A crest, tuft, or covering of spreading hairs. 2. The awn or bristle-like appendage upon the chaff of grain and other grasses.

Bearded or Barbate: With long trichomes usually in a tuft, line or zone.

Bed: An area within a garden or lawn in which plants are grown.

Bedding plant: An ornamental plant grown for its flowers or foliage that is suited by habit for growing in beds or masses.

Bench scale process: A small- or laboratory-scale process; commonly used in connection with fermentation.

Bendiocarb: A synthetic insecticide used to control a variety of house and garden pests including earwigs and ants.

Benomyl: A systemic fungicide used to control a variety of diseases of ornamentals, usually foliar. It is absorbed into the system of the plant to fight off infection. Common name is Benlate.

Bent: Foliate embryo with expanded and usually thick cotyledons in an axile position bent upon the hypocotyl in a jacknife position

Benthos: The organisms that live on a lake or sea bed. The plants (phytobenthos) that grow below low-tide mark include members of the flowering plant family Zosteraceae, such as eelgrasses (Zostera), and certain red algae, such as dulse (Rhodymenia palmata). A variety of plants grow rooted in the littoral zone of lakes and ponds, including water lilies (Nuphar, Nymphaea), pondweeds (Potamogeton), and water milfoils (Myriophyllwn).

Berry: A small, pulpy fruit, which usually contains several seeds (i.e. Huckleberry, mulberry, etc.); any simple fruit in which the inside is fleshy, except the outer skin (i.e. Tomato, banana, grape, etc.); the dry kernel of certain kinds of grain.

Best linear prediction (BLP): A statistical method which utilities matrix algebra to predict breeding values for any trait or selection index; in BLP fixed effects are assumed to be known. BLP is especially suited for analyses of messy or unbalanced data.

Best linear unbiased prediction (BLUP): A statistical method which predicts breeding values for any trait or selection index; unlike BLP, in BLUP the fixed effects are estimated. Like BLP, BLUP is well suited for analyses of messy or unbalanced data.

Beta DNA: The form of DNA generally found in nature. A right-handed helix.

Beta-glucuronidase (GUS): An enzyme produced by certain bacteria, which catalyses the cleavage of a whole range of beta-glucuronides. Because this activity is largely absent in plants, the encoding bacterial gene has been widely used as a reporter gene in plant transgenesis.

Beta-lactamase: An enzyme that detoxifies penicillin group antibiotics, such as ampicillin. The â-lactamase gene is commonly used as a marker for successful transformation, where only transformed cells are able to tolerate the presence of ampicillin.

Bibacca: A fused double berry, as in lonicera

Bicollateral bundle: Vascular bundles where primary phloem differentiates not only in the normal exarch position but on the inner edge of primary xylem as well.

Bicolorous: With white or clear walls and dark red or brown septae as in some hairs.

Biconvex: In section with both surfaces curved outwards away from the center.

Bicrenate or doubly-crenate: With smaller rounded teeth on larger rounded teeth

Biennial: A plant that needs two seasons of growth to produce flowers and fruit. It produces leaves the first year and blossoms, bears fruit, goes to seed and dies the next.

Bifacial: Of leaves, flat or channelled with distinct adaxial and abaxial surfaces.

Bifarious: Divided into two parts and pointing in two ways, or arranged in two opposite rows, as leaves that grow only on opposite sides of a branch.

Bifid: Divided into two equal lobes or parts by a space in the center; forked, like a snake's tongue; divided in two by a deep cleft.

Biflorous: Flowering in autumn as well as in spring.

Bifoliolate: Having two leaflets as in a compound leaf.

Bifollicular: Having two seed cases, or twin pods, especially in milkweed (Asclepias).

Biforate: Having two pores or perforations. Also biforous.

Bifurcate: Divided into two forks or branches.

Bigeminate, bijugate: With two orders of leaflets, each bifoliolate; doubly paired.

Bilabiate: Two-lipped, e.g. of a corolla in which fusion of an anterior group and a posterior group of petals extends beyond the top of the corolla tube.

Bilateral: Of, on, or with equal sides, eg bilaterally symmetric, bilaterally flattened or compressed etc.

Bilaterally symmetrical: Said of corolla or calyx (or flower) when divisible into equal halves in one plane only; zygomorphic.

Bilobate: Having or divided into two lobes, as a bilobate leaf.

Bimestrial: Periodicity: occurring every two months; duration: lasting two months.

Binary vector system: A two plasmid system in Agrobacterium tumefaciens designed to transfer T-DNA into plant cells, while avoiding the formation of crown gall tumours. One plasmid contains the virulence gene (responsible for transfer of the T-DNA), and the other the T-DNA borders, the selectable marker and the DNA to be transferred.

Binate: Being double or in couples; growing in pairs; having only two leaflets to a group.

Binding: The ability of molecules to bind each other non-covalently because of the exact shape and chemical nature of parts of their surfaces. A common biological phenomenon, as e.g. an enzyme to its substrate; an antibody to its antigen; a DNA strand to its complementary strand.

Bio: A prefix used in scientific words to associate the concept of "living organisms." Usually written with a hyphen before vowels, for emphasis or in neologisms.

Bio-accumulation: A problem that can arise when a stable chemical such as a heavy metal or DDT is introduced into a natural environment. Where there are no agents present able to biodegrade it, its concentration can increase as it passes up the food chain and higher organisms may suffer toxic effects. This phenomenon may be employed beneficially for the removal of toxic metals from wastewater, and for bioremediation.

Bio assay: 1. The assessment of a substance's activity on living cells or on organisms. Animals have been used extensively in drug research in bio-assays in the pharmaceutical and cosmetics industries. Current trends are to develop bio-assays using bacteria or animal or plant cells, as these are easier to handle than whole animals or plants, are cheaper to make and keep, and avoid the ethical problems associated with testing of animals. 2. An indirect method to detect sub-measurable amounts of a specific substance by observing a sample's influence on the growth of live material.

Bio augmentation: Increasing the activity of bacteria that decompose pollutants; a technique used in bioremediation.

Bio availability: The proportion of a nutrient or administered drug etc. that can be taken up by an organism in a biologically effective form. For example, some soils high in phosphorus have a low level of P availability because the pH of the soil renders much of the P insoluble.

Bio catalysis: The use of enzymes to improve the efficiency of chemical reactions.

Bio control: Pest control by biological means. Any process using deliberately introduced living organisms to restrain the growth and development of other organisms, such as the introduction of predatory insects to control an insect pest. Synonym: biological control.

Bio conversion: Conversion of one chemical into another by living organisms, as opposed to their conversion by isolated enzymes or fixed cells, or by chemical processes. Particularly useful for introducing chemical changes at specific points in large and complex molecules.

Bio degrade: The breakdown by micro-organisms of a compound to simpler chemicals. Materials that are easily biodegraded are colloquially termed biodegradable.

Bio desulphurization: The removal of organic and inorganic sulphur from coal by bacterial and soil micro-organisms. Certain bacteria can oxidize insoluble sulphur compounds into soluble sulphates, which can be washed away with the bacteria.

Bio diversity: The variety and variability (both in numbers and frequency) of the organisms and the genetic variability within each species. The term can be used to describe a particular site, a general habitat type, a small or large geographic region, or (less correctly), the genetic diversity of a particular species or population.

Bio dyanmic: Having to do with the dynamic relation between organisms and their environments.

Bio energetics: The study of the flow and the transformation of energy that occur in living organisms.

Bio engineering: The use of artificial tissues, organs and organ components to replace parts of the body that are damaged, lost or malfunctioning.

Bio ethics: The branch of ethics that deals with the life sciences and their potential impact on society.

Bio fuel: A gaseous, liquid or solid fuel derived from a biological source, e.g. ethanol, rapeseed oil or fish liver oil.

Bio gas: A mixture of methane and carbon dioxide resulting from the anaerobic decomposition of waste such as domestic, industrial and agricultural sewage.

Bio informatics: The use and organization of information of biological interest. In particular, concerned with organizing bio-molecular databases (particularly DNA sequences), utilizing computers for analysing this information, and integrating information from disparate biological sources.

Bio leaching: The recovery of metals from their ores, using the action of micro-organisms, rather than chemical or physical treatment. For example, Thiobacillus ferroxidans has been used to extract gold from refractory ores.

Bio mass concentration: The amount of biological material in a specific volume.

Bio mass: 1. The cell mass produced by a population of living organisms. 2. The organic matter that can be used either as a source of energy or for its chemical components. 3. All the organic matter that derives from the photosynthetic conversion of solar energy.

Biolistics: A technique to generate transgenic cells, in which DNA-coated small metal particles (tungsten or gold) are propelled by various means fast enough to puncture target cells. Provided that the cell is not irretrievably damaged, the DNA is frequently taken up by the cell. The technique has been successfully used to transform animal, plant and fungal cells, and even mitochondria inside cells. Synonym: microprojectile bombardment.

Biological containment: Restricting the movement of organisms from the laboratory. Can take two forms: making the organism unable to survive in the outside environment, or making the outside environment inhospitable to the organism. For micro-organisms, the favoured approach is to engineer organisms to require a supply of a specific nutrient that is usually available only in the laboratory. For higher organisms (plants and animals), it is more possible to ensure that the outside environment is unsuited to growth, spread and reproduction.

Biological oxygen demand (BOD): The dissolved oxygen required for the respiration of a population of aerobic organisms present in water.

Expressed in terms of the oxygen consumed in water at a temperature of 20°C per unit time. The BOD is used as an indication of the degree to which the sample of water is polluted, particularly by inorganic nutrients for plants.

Bioluminescence: The enzyme-catalyzed production of light by a number of diverse organisms (e.g. fireflies and many deep ocean marine organisms). Utilized as a reporter gene in plant transgenesis, and for the detection of food-borne pathogenic bacteria.

Biome: A major ecological community or complex of communities, extending over a large geographical area and characterized by a dominant type of vegetation.

Biometry: The application of statistical methods to the analysis of continuous variation in biological systems. Synonym: biometrics.

Biomimetic materials: Employed to describe synthetic analogues of natural materials with advantageous properties. For instance, some synthetic molecules act chemically like natural proteins, but are not as easily degraded by the digestive system. Other systems such as reverse micelles and/or liposomes exhibit certain properties that mimic certain aspects of living systems.

Biopesticide: A compound that kills organisms by virtue of specific biological effects rather than as a broader chemical poison. Differ from biocontrol agents in being passive agents, whereas biocontrol agents actively seek the pest. The rationale behind replacing conventional pesticides with biopesticides is that the latter are more likely to be selective and biodegradable.

Biopharming: The use of genetically transformed crop plants and livestock animals to produce valuable compounds, especially pharmaceuticals. Synonym: molecular pharming.

Biopiracy: The patenting of genetic stocks, and the subsequent privatization of genetic resources collections. The term implies a lack of consent on the part of the originator.

Biopolymer: Any large polymer (protein, nucleic acid, polysaccharide) produced by a living organism. Includes some materials (such as polyhydroxybutyrate) suitable for use as plastics. Synonym: biological polymer.

Bioprocess: Any process that uses complete living cells or their components (e.g. enzymes, chloroplasts) to effect desired physical or chemical changes.

Bioreactor: A tank in which cells, cell extracts or enzymes carry out a biological reaction. Often refers to a fermentation vessel for cells or micro-organisms.

Biorecovery: The use of micro-organisms for the recovery of valuable materials (metals or particular organic compounds) from complex mixtures.

Bioremediation: A process that uses living organisms to remove contaminants, pollutants or unwanted substances from soil or water.

Biosafety protocol: An inteRNAtionally agreed protocol set up to protect biological diversity from the potential risks posed by the release of genetically modified organisms. It establishes a procedure for ensuring that countries are provided with the information necessary to make informed decisions before agreeing to the import of such organisms into their territory. Synonym: Cartagena protocol.

Biosafety: Referring to the avoidance of risk to human health and safety, and to the conservation of the environment, as a result of the use for research and commerce of infectious or genetically modified organisms.

Biosensor: A device that uses an immobilized biologically-related agent (such as an enzyme, antibiotic, organelle or whole cell) to detect or measure a chemical compound. Reactions between the immobilized agent and the molecule being analysed are converted into an electric signal.

Biosorbents: Micro-organisms which, either by themselves or in conjunction with a substrate are able to extract and/or concentrate a desired molecule by means of its selective retention.

Biosphere: The part of the earth and its atmosphere that is inhabited by living organisms.

Biosynthesis: Synthesis of compounds by living cells, which is the essential feature of anabolism.

Biosynthetic pathway: A series of enzymatic reactions in which more complex molecules are built from simpler ones. Biosynthetic pathways are energy requiring, this energy usually being supplied either as phosphate bond energy by ATP or as reducing power by NADPH. Three stages of biosynthesis can be recognized. The first stage is concerned with the manufacture of simple organic molecules from inorganic molecules like carbon dioxide and water. These few simple molecules are then converted in the second stage to building blocks for the many biological macromolecules. Finally macromolecules are synthesized from their constituent subunits

Biosystematics: The study of variation and relationship in populations rather than individuals. The genetic and evolutionary nature of groups is assessed by the examination of cytology, comparative morphology, and ecology. Biosystematics is often described as the taxo-nomic application of genecology or, occasionally, as experimental taxonomy.

Biotic community: An association of plants, animals, and other organisms (e.g., woodland).

Biotic factor: Other living organisms that are a component of an organism's environment, and form the biotic environment, affecting the organism in many ways.

Biotic stress: Stress resulting from attack by pathogenic organisms.

Biotin: A vitamin of the B complex, it acts as a co-enzyme for various enzymes that catalyse the incorporation of carbon dioxide into various compounds, and is essential for the metabolism of fats. Adequate amounts are normally produced by the intestinal bacteria in animals. Significant as a molecular biology reagent due to its high affinity with avidin and streptavidin. Synonym: vitamin H.

Biotin labelling: The attachment of biotin to another molecule, especially DNA.

Biotinylated DNA: A DNA molecule labelled with biotin by incorporation of a biotinylated nucleotide (usually uracil) into a DNA molecule. The detection of the labelled DNA is achieved by complexing it with streptavidin to which is attached a colour-generating agent such as horseradish peroxidase that gives a fluorescent green colour upon reaction with various organic reagents.

Biotope: A small habitat in a large community.

Biotoxin: A naturally produced compound which shows pronounced biological activity, toxic to some or many organisms.

Biotransformation: The conversion of one chemical or material into another using a biological catalyst: a near synonym is biocatalysis, and hence the catalyst used is called a biocatalyst. Usually the catalyst is an enzyme, or a fixed whole, dead micro-organism that contains an enzyme or several enzymes.

Biotype: All the plants in a specific group, all of which resemble one another in some specific way.

Bipinnate: Describing a pinnate leaf in which the leaflets themselves are further subdivided in a pinnate fashion.

Biplicate: Doubly folded; twice folded together, transversely, as the first new leaves that sprout from a bean.

Bipolaris: A fungus with large spores which would be expected to be deposited in the upper respiratory tract. This fungus can produce the mycotoxin - sterigmatocystin which has been shown to produce liver and kidney damage when ingested by laboratory animals.

Biramous: Possessing two branches; dividing into two branches.

Bird netting: Nylon or plastic mesh used as a drape to keep birds out of fruit trees, berry patches, or vegetable gardens. Smaller mesh netting can be placed right over strawberries, raspberries, and corn; larger mesh netting may be draped over trees, bushes, grapes, or over a supporting structure.

Birimose: Opening by two slits, as the anthers of most plants.

Bisaccate: A pollen grain with two sacci. The two "sacs" or bladders are used to promote wind dispersal. Pollen of this type is known from as early as the Devonian.

Biserrate or Doubly-serrate: With sharply cut teeth on the margins of larger sharply cut teeth.

Bisexual: Having both female and male reproductive organs present and functional in the same flower; hermaphrodite; amphisporangiate; said of a plant having all bisexual flowers.

Bisporangiate: When a flower or cone produces both megaspores and microspores, it is said to be bisporangiate. Most flowers are bisporangiate.

Biternate: With two orders of leaflets, each ternately compound.

Bivalent: Two paired homologous chromosomes (one of maternal origin; the other of paternal origin) at prophase to anaphase of the first meiotic division. Because DNA is replicated in prophase, each duplicated chromosome comprises two chromatids, and thus a bivalent comprises four chromatids.

Bivalved: With two valves or flaps.

Black plastic: Sheet plastic that is placed around plants as a mulch to obstruct weeds, hold moisture, and absorb heat. Also called black polyethylene or black poly sheeting.

Blade: A plant's leaf, such as a blade of grass; the expanded part of a leaf, petal, sepal, etc. as distinguished from the petiole or leafstalk.

Blanch: To whiten or prevent from becoming green by excluding light. Blanching is applied to the stems or leaves of plants such as celery, lettuce, and endive. This is done by banking up the soil around the stems of the plants, tying the leaves together to keep the inner ones from light, or covering with pots, boxes, etc.

Blast cell: A large, rapidly dividing cell that develops from a B cell in response to an antigenic stimulus. The blast cell then becomes an antibody-producing plasma cell.

Blastema: The point of growth from which any organs or part of an organ is developed.

Blastocarpous: Germination of seeds while within the pericarp, as in Rhizophora

Blastocyst: A mammalian embryo (fertilized ovum) in the early stages of development, approximately up to the time of implantation. It consists of a hollow ball of cells.

Blastomere: Any one of the cells formed from the first few cleavages in animal embryology. The embryo usually divides into two, then four, then eight blastomeres, and so on.

Blastomyces: Human pathogen. The fungus is commonly found in soil. It is a dimorphic fungus which has filamentous fungus when grown at 25 degrees C and a yeast form at 37 degrees C.

Blastula: In animals, an early embryo form that follows the morula stage; typically, a single-layered sheet (blastoderm) or ball of cells (blastocyst).

Block: In a field study arranged in a randomized complete-block design, a block is a unit of land upon which at least one plot of all of the entries (families, clones provenances) are planted. (In this case a replication and a block are the same.)

Blot: As a verb, to transfer DNA, RNA or protein to an immobilizing matrix. As a noun, the immobilizing matrix carrying DNA, RNA or protein. The various types of blot are named according to the probe and/or the probed molecules: Southern blot (DNA/DNA), northern blot (DNA/mRNA), western blot (antibody/protein), southwestern blot (DNA/protein). Only "Southern" is written with an initial capital, as it is named after Ed Southern, the inventor of the technique.

Blotched: The color disposed in broad, irregular blotches.

Blowball: The downy heads of seeds produced after the flowers have died. (i.e. dandelion, salsify, etc.)

Blunt end ligation: The joining of two blunt-ended double-stranded DNA molecules.

Blunt end: The end of a double-stranded DNA molecule in which neither strand extends beyond the other. Synonym: flush end.

Bog garden: A garden devoted to moisture-loving plants. Low-lying, marshy sites are good for this.

Bog: A quagmire covered with grass or other plants; wet, spongy ground; a small marsh; plant community on wet, very acid peat.

Bole: The trunk of a tree, below the lowest branch.

Bond: A force that holds atoms together.

Bone meal: Ground bone, raw or steamed, that is used as a fertilizer to add phosphoric acid to the soil. It is especially beneficial in herb gardens.

Bonsai dish: A planter for holding a miniaturized tree or shrub.

Bonsai: Container-grown plants (usually trees) That have been dwarfed artificially through skillful pruning and manipulation of the growing medium.

Border fence: A short fence, usually only 12 to 18 inches high, of wood or metal, used to mark and separate flower beds from foot traffic and lawn mowers.

Border: A narrow strip of garden that encloses or separates a portion of lawn or other landform by a path, walk, driveway, street, or building. Usually planted with perennials or flowering shrubs for spring and summer bloom.

Boric acid: A salt that can be effectively used as a barrier against some crawling household pests such as ants. If kept dry, it can be used outdoors.

Boring platform: Sterile bottom half of a Petri dish used for preparing explants with a cork borer.

Boron: A trace element usually present in most soils but sometimes added by applying fertilizer.

Bosket: A grove; a thicket or small plantation in a garden, park, etc., formed of trees, shrubs, or tall plants.

Botanic: Pertaining to botany, or the scientific study of plants.

Botanical insecticide: Any natural insecticide derived from plants. They include pyrethrum, neem, rotenone, rynia, sabadilla, and nicotine sulfate. They break down quickly when exposed to sun and must be applied often. They are usually non-toxic, but not always.

Botany: The science of plants, their classification and study.

Botrytis: Conidia dimensions 7-14 x 5-9 microns. Reported to be allergenic. It is parasitic on plants and soft fruits. Found in soil and vegetables. Possibly associated with allergic symptoms (skin tests).

Bottomland: Lowlands along streams and rivers, usually on alluvial floodplains that are periodically flooded.

Botulism: Poisoning from consumption of food infected by botulism bacteria.

Bough: An arm or branch of a tree.

Bound water: Cellular water not released into the intercellular space upon freezing and thawing.

Bovine somatotrophin (BST): A natural protein in cattle. It has been cloned, using recombinant DNA technology, expressed in large amounts and marketed as an agricultural product to improve the growth rate and protein:fat ratios in farm cattle, and to improve milk yield. Its use is banned in some countries. Synonyms: bovine growth hormone.

Bovine spongiform enecelophalopathy (BSE): Cattle disease (colloquially called mad cow disease) caused by proteinaceous infectious particles.

Bow saw: A tool having a straight blade attached at both ends to a curved handle, in all making the shape of the letter D. It is used for cutting branches.

BP: Abbreviation for base pair.

Brackish: Of a mixture of salt and fresh waters.

Bract: A modified leaf at the base of a flower or flower cluster. It may resemble a normal leaf, be reduced and scale-like in appearance, or large and brilliantly colored.

Bracteal and Laminar: May be localized or found over entire structure

Bracteate: Having bracts.

Bracteole or Bractlet: A secondary or smaller bract

Branch: A stem growing from the trunk of a tree, shrub, or other plant (the smaller offshoots are called branchlets, twigs, or shoots); a bough.

Branchlet: A small usually terminal branch.

Breed at risk: An animal breed that is in danger of becoming extinct because its population has fallen below a critical number.

Breed: 1.A sub-specific group of domestic livestock with definable and identifiable external characteristics that enable it to be separated by visual appraisal from other similarly defined groups within the same species. 2. A group of domestic livestock for which geographical and/or cultural separation from phenotypically similar groups has led to acceptance of its separate identity.

Breeding: The process of sexual reproduction and production of offspring.

Breeding orchard (breeding seed orchard, breeding arboretum): A planting of selected trees, usually clonally propagated, designed to ease breeding work.

Breeding population: A group of individuals selected from a wild population for use in a breeding program. Usually phenotypically selected for desirable traits. In species with large natural ranges, there are usually several to many, more-or-less separate breeding populations, each designed to provide progeny suited to a particular geographic region.

Breeding value: A quantitative genetics term, describing that part of the deviation of an individual phenotype from the population mean that is due to the additive effects of alleles. Thus, if an individual is mated with a random sample of individuals from a population, its breeding value for a given trait is twice the average deviation of its offspring from the population mean for that trait.

Breeding zone: An area within which a single population of improved trees can be planted without fear of mis-adaptation.

Brewer's yeast: Strains of the yeast Saccharomyces cerevisiae that are used for the production of beer.

Bridge: A filter paper or other substrate used as a wick and support structure for a plant tissue in culture when a liquid medium is used.

Bristly: Beset with bristles.

Broad host range plasmid: A plasmid that can replicate in a number of different bacterial species.

Broad sense heritability: The proportion of the total phenotypic variation which results from genetic variation or interaction between the genotype and the environment.

Broad-base terrace: A low embankment that is constructed across a slope to reduce runoff and/or erosion.

Broadcast: Scattered upon the ground with the hand, as in sowing seed, instead of sowing in drills or rows.

Brochidodromous: With a single primary vein, the secondary veins not terminating at the margin but joined together in a series of prominent upward arches or marginal loops on each side of the primary vein.

Broodstock: The group of males and females from which fish are bred.

Broom-like: With many branches parallel or almost so and usually erect, as in spartium (spanish broom).

Brown podzolic soil: A mixed humus and mineral soil with a thin mat of decayed leaves; usually found under a deciduous (leafy) or mixed deciduous and coniferous forest.

Brown soil: A brown surface soil found under grasses and shrubs that gets lighter in color the deeper you dig.

Browning: Discolouration of freshly cut surfaces of plant tissue due to phenolic oxidation. In plant tissue culture, it may indicate a nutritional or pathogenic problem, generally leading to necrosis.

Bryokinin: A growth substance found in certain mosses, e.g. Funaria, that stimulates the formation of buds and subsequently leafy plants from the filamentous protonema.

Bryophyte: Plants in which the gametophyte generation is the larger, persistent phase; they generally lack conducting tissues. Bryophytes include the Hepaticophyta (liverworts), Anthocerotophyta (hornworts), and Bryophyta (mosses).

Bud: 1. A growing point enclosed by closely overlaid rudimentary leaves. Buds may contain foliage or flowers. Bulbs and bulbils are forms of leaf buds. Flower buds are unexpanded blossoms. 2. To graft a bud of 1 plant on the stem of another (i.e. to bud a garden rose on a brier).

Bud mutation: A bud variation resulting from local genetic alteration and producing a permanent modification that usually can be retained by grafting.

Bud sport: A somatic mutation arising in a bud, generating a genetically different shoot. Includes changes due to gene mutation, chromosomal mutation or polyploidy.

Bud variation: In the outgrowth of a bud, the deviation in any respect from the ordinary growth of the plant, producing what is commonly known as a sport. Many varieties arise this way, such as Red Delicious Apples, and these are perpetuated by bud propagation.

Budding strip: A rubber strip, typically 1/8th to 3/8th inches wide and up to 8 inches long, used to hold grafts.

Buffer strips: Strips of perennial grass or other erosion-resisting vegetation.

Buffer: A substance in the soil that will chemically act to resist changes in the soil's reaction or pH, usually clay or fine organic matter.

Bulb: A true bulb is a complete package containing next year's flower already forming inside. If you were to cut a tulip, daffodil, hyacinth, or amaryllis bulb in half, you would see a complete embryonic plant inside, with tiny flowers, stems, leaves, and roots. The contents of the bulb are often enclosed in protective, fleshy scales, which are held together by a small basal plate. The scales are modified leaves that contain enough nutrients to sustain the plant through dormancy and early growth. They may be loose and open like those of a lily, or tightly closed like those of a hyacinth. In many bulbs, a paper-thin tunic protects the scales (lilies don't have a tunic). Roots will grow from the bulb's basal plate. The foliage of bulbous plants shouldn't be cut off while green; it should be allowed to die naturally because it supplies the food for the next season's growth. There are several different ways in which bulbs reproduce. Some reproduce by a process called annual replacement. The old bulb, called the "mother" bulb, dies after flowering and is replaced by new "daughter" bulbs of various sizes. When the time is right, the largest of these will flower the following season, and the others will bloom in the years to come. Other bulbs reproduce by offsets. The mother bulb lives for two to three years, and the new bulbs (offsets) are produced alongside the mother bulb. Offsets can be removed and planted elsewhere in the garden.

Bulb planter: A sharp-edged, tapered cylinder used to remove a plug of soil or sod, in which a bulb is placed. The plug is then returned to the hole to cover the bulb.

Bulbel: A small bulb produced from the base of a larger bulb.

Bulbiferous: Bearing bulbs or bulbils for vegetative propogation.

Bulbil: A small deciduous bulb replacing flowers in an inflorescence, and functioning to propagate the plant vegetatively.

Bulblet: A little or secondary bulb; specifically, a small aerial bulb or bud with fleshy scales, growing in the axils of leaves, as in the tiger lily, or taking the place of flower buds, as in the common onion. Also called bulbil.

Bulbous: Bulb-shaped; swollen like an onion.

Bulked segregant analysis: A method to obtain markers linked to a target trait, in which DNA samples, prepared from a number of individuals of each of two contrasting phenotypes, are separately pooled and used to generate contrasting DNA fingerprints. DNA fragments unique to one pool become candidates for a marker linked to the gene controlling the trait.

Bullate: Bubble-like; puckered or blistered, describing a layer of tissure (part of a leaf, scales etc) strongly arched and raised between the margins.

Bundle scar: A small scar left by a vascular bundle within a leaf scar when the leaf separates from its stem through abscission

Bunt: A covered smut disease of wheat, sometimes called stinking smut because of the smell of rotten fish given off by the spore masses. The disease is caused by Tilletia caries. Dwarf bunt of wheat is caused by T. contraversa. Infected grains are transformed into balls of bunt spores. At threshing the spores are released and contaminate healthy seed as well as the combine harvester and grain-handling machinery. Contaminated seed in turn gives rise to more infected plants.

Buoyant density: The intrinsic density which a molecule, virus or sub-cellular particle has when suspended in an aqueous solution of a salt, such as CsCl, or a sugar, such as sucrose. DNA from different species has different characteristic buoyant densities, determined largely by the relative proportion of the base-pairs G+C, to A+T.

Bur: The rough, prickly covering of the seeds of certain plants, such as the chestnut or burdock. Also spelled burr.

Burl: A hard, woody growth on the trunks or branches of trees that is sometimes used for making bowls, veneer, and coffee tables, such as from the redwood.

Burlap: A loosely woven fabric made of jute or hemp used to protect newly seeded lawns from wind, water and birds.

Burn lime (CaO): A caustic solid used to neutralize acid soil or to raise the pH of the soil.

Burr: A rough or prickly propagule consisting of a seed or fruit and associated floral parts or bracts.

Bursiculate: Resembling a small pouch, or having a small, pouch-like cavity.

Butterfly garden: A garden planted for the purpose of attracting butterflies by using plants whose flowers produce nectar for them. (i.e. butterfly bush -Buddleia and butterfly flower - Asclepias).

Buttonbuah: Acommon name for Cephalanthus occidentalis, a North American shrub, on account of its globular flower heads.

Buttress root: A form of prop root that is asymmetrically thickened to give a planklike outgrowth on the upper side, providing extra support for the tree. Buttress roots are common in many tropical trees, e.g. certain figs (Ficus).

C: Abbreviation for cytosine.

C3 plant or C4 plant: Any plant that produces, as the first step in photosynthesis, phosphoglyceric acid, which contains three carbon atoms.

CAAT box: A conserved DNA sequence found within the promoter region of the protein-encoding genes of many eukaryotic organisms. So-called because of its consensus sequence GGCCAATCT, it occurs around 75 bases prior to the transcription initiation site; and is one of several sites for the recognition and binding of transcription factors. Synonym: CAT box.

Cactaceae: A large family of dicotyledonous xerophytic plants, the cacti. It includes over 2000 species in about 87 genera; some authorities however recognize many more, over 300 genera being listed in some classifications. The cacti are limited in distribution to the drier regions of South and Central America and central and southern North America. Some have become naturalized elsewhere, e.g. prickly pears (Opuntia) in Australia and the Mediterranean, and Rhipsalis, which is probably naturalized rather than native, in southern Africa. Cacti are succulents and, being leafless (the leaves are reduced to spines), are a particularly distinctive group of plants. It is this that has led to their popularity as unusual pot plants. Photosynthesis is carried out by the green expanded stems, which show various advanced characteristics in the arrangement of vascular tissues and many other features. The flowers however, which are borne singly directly on the stem, are comparatively primitive having large numbers of stamens, petals, sepals, and bracts arranged spirally. The fruit is a berry.

Cactus: This is the common name for plants in the group, Cactaceae. All cacti are succulent, although not all succulents are cacti. Cacti can be distinguished from other succulents by their areoles, or pad-like buds, from which shoots, flowers, and spines grow. Areoles aren't always easily seen.

Caespitose: Tufted or matted, growing in tufts or patches.

Calcareous Soil: Soil containing carbonate of lime or limestone; chalky or limy.

Calceolate: Slipper-shaped, as in the corolla of cypripedium.

Calcium: An element needed by plants. It can be added to the soil.

Calcium carbonate: A salt CaCo3 found in plant ashes, bones, shells, calcite and aragonite.

Calcium chloride: A deliquescent salt CaC12 used as a drying and dehumidifying agent.

Calcium cyanamide: A compound CaCN2 used as a fertilizer and weed killer.

Calcium phosphate: 1. A phosphate used as a fertilizer. 2. A naturally occurring phosphate of calcium occurring as the main constituent of phosphate rock.

Caliche: A term used to identify cemented deposits of calcium carbonate.

Callipyge: An inherited trait in livestock (e.g. sheep) that results in thicker, meatier hind-quarters, and hence a higher meat yield per animal.

Callosity: A thickened, raised area, which is usually hard; a callus.

Callus: 1. A protective tissue, consisting of parenchyma cells, that develops over a cut or damaged plant surface. 2. Mass of undifferentiated, thin-walled parenchyma cells induced by hormone treatment. 3. Actively dividing non-organized masses of undifferentiated and differentiated cells often developing from injury (wounding) or in tissue culture in the presence of growth regulators.

Callus culture: A technique of plant tissue culture, usually on solidified medium and initiated by inoculation of small explants. Used as the basis for organogenic (shoot or root forming) cultures, cell cultures or proliferation of embryoids. Callus cultures can be indefinitely maintained through regular sub-culturing.

Calybium: A hard one-loculed dry fruit derived from an inferior ovary, as in quercus.

Calyptra: In mosses, a derivative of the distal archegonium forms a hard, protective layer around the developing sporophyte called the epigonium. Later the epigonium breaks up, but the sporophyte retains a conical "dunce cap" over its distal end, and sometimes a ring around the base. The cap is the calyptra. The piece retained around the base is the vaginula.

Calyptrate: Furnished with a calyptra, as a capsule or a flower; resembling a calyptra, as a calyx that comes off like a lid.

Calyptrogen: The cell layer from which the root cap originates.

Calyx: The outer covering of a flower external to the corolla, which it encloses, and consisting of a whorl of leaves, or sepals, usually of a green color and less delicate in texture than the corolla.

Calyx tube: Tube formed by wholly or partially fused sepals. Not the floral tube of an epigynous or perigynous flower.

Cambial zone: Region in stems and roots consisting of the cambium and its recent derivatives.

Cambium: A layer of actively dividing cells (lateral meristem), found within stems and roots, that gives rise to secondary growth in perennial plants, causing an increase in girth. There are two main types of cambium vascular cambium, which gives rise to secondary xylem and phloem tissues, and cork cambium (or phellogen), which gives rise to secondary cortex and cork tissues, as in bark. The vascular cambium surrounds the roots, trunk, branches, and shoots, extending throughout a tree. Each year, the vascular cambium produces a new layer of phloem toward the outside of the tree and a new layer of xylem, or wood, toward the inside.

Campanulate: Bell-shaped; with flaring tube about as broad as long and a flaring limb.

Campylodromous: With several primary veins or their branches diverging at or close to a single point and running in strongly developed, basally recurved arches which converge toward the apex, reaching it or not.

Canaliculate: Longitudinally grooved, usually in relation to petioles or midribs.

Cancellate: Latticed, or resembling a latticed construction, usually said of a surface such as that of an achene or seed.

Candida: Part of the normal flora of mouth and other mucous membranes in the body. Thrush and other diseases caused by Candida albicans usually occur after prolonged treatment with antibiotics or steroids. The environment is not a likely source of exposure for this fungus. Cells from the organism are usually not airborne. Reported to be allergenic.

Candidate gene: A gene whose deduced function (on the basis of DNA sequence) suggests that it may be involved in the genetic control of an aspect of phenotype.

Candidate tree: A tree that has been tentatively selected for inclusion in a breeding program, but has not yet been measured or compared with surrounding trees.

Candidate-gene strategy: An experimental approach in which knowledge of the biochemistry and/or physiology of a trait is used to identify candidate genes. Synonym: functional gene cloning.

Canescent: Growing white or gray; applied to plants with grayish-white, short, downy leaf hairs.

Canker: A lesion or an oozing point of decay in the tissue of a plant, usually on the trunk or branches. Caused by wounds, disease, or insects.

Canola: A specific subgroup of oilseed rape cultivars; canola oil is the highly mono-unsaturated fatty acid and low in erucic acid product produced in the seed of these cultivars.

Canopy: The cover of foliage layer of a community especially forests.

Cantharophily: Pollinated by beetles.

Cap site: The site on a DNA template where transcription begins. It corresponds to the nucleotide at the 5' end of the RNA transcript which accepts the G cap.

Capacitation: The final stage, inside the female genital tract, in the maturation process of a spermatozoon, as it penetrates the ovum.

Capillary attraction: Water moving against gravity and moving up to the soil's surface.

Capillary bed: A bed, usually of gravel, for germinating punnets of seeds. Water is fed in continuously from the bottom and kept at a constant level. Heating may be provided. Replaces overhead watering which can lead to damping off (a fungal disease) or can disturb the surface of the seed mix.

Capillary electrophoresis: A form of electrophoresis used widely in current large-scale DNA sequencing facilities, where the sample is passed through a long, very-narrow-bore tube containing a re-usable matrix.

Capillary matting: An interwoven fabric that wicks water from a reservoir. Used in propagators, seed flats, pots, or English baskets to provide plants with a constant supply of moisture.

Capillary porosity: The volume of small pores in the soil that holds water.

Capillary water: Water held in the soil against the force of gravity; capillary water is available to plants.

Capillate: Hair-shapedcapitate head-like capitulum or head a determinate or indeterminate crowded group of sessile or subsessile flowers on a compound receptacle or torus.

Capitulum: An infloresence forming a head of sessile flowers or florets crowned together on a receptacle and usually surrounded by an involucre.

Capsid: The protein coat of a virus. The capsid often determines the shape of the virus. Synonym: coat protein.

Capsule: A case, pod, or fruit, containing seeds, spores, or carpels; it usually bursts when ripe.

Captan: A man-made fungicide used to control many disease such as leaf spots and damping-off.

Carbaryl: A man-made insecticide that kills insects (even beneficial ones) on contact. It is very poisonous to bees. Commonly called Sevin.

Carbohydrate: An organic compound containing carbon, hydrogen, and oxygen. With twice as many hydrogen as oxygen atoms per molecule.

Carbon: One of the most common chemical elements found in the soil and air that is needed by living plants.

Carbon dioxide (Co2): A colorless gas found in the air.

Carboniferous: The second period of the Upper Palaeozoic era from about 345 to 280 million years ago. During this period the climate was generally warm and humid and there were great forests and swamps, dominated by arborescent lycopsids and sphenopsids, from which the coal measures were formed. In the US the term Carboniferous is not widely used because rocks of this age in North America can be separated into two distinct types. American geologists refer to rocks of the Lower Carboniferous (345-310 million years ago) as Mississippian and of the Upper Carboniferous (310-280 million years ago) as Pennsylvanian. In North America only the Pennsylvanian rocks contain coal. Carboniferous fossil remains include mosses and liverworts, and herbaceous lycopsid fossils similar to present-day Lycopodium and Selaginella are abundant. Some of the arborescent lycopsids, as represented by Lepidodendron, appear to have had a rudimentary ovule. The sphenopsids are represented by the now extinct arborescent Calamitales (giant horsetails) and the extinct herbaceous Sphenophyllales. Equisetites hemingwayi in the Upper Carboniferous is one of the few herbaceous forms resembling the present-day Equisetum. The ferns were well represented as were the gymnosperms with fossils of the Pteridospermales, Cordaitales , and Coniferales all being found.

Carbon-nitrogen ratio: The ratio of weight of organic carbon to the weight of nitrogen found in the soil.

Carboxypeptidase: A class of enzymes which catalyse the cleavage of peptide bonds, requiring a free carboxyl group in the substrate. The peptide bond adjacent to this group is cleaved and a free amino acid is released. Used for deriving the amino acid sequence of peptides.

Carcinogen: A substance capable of inducing cancer in an organism.

Carcinoma: A malignant tumour derived from epithelial tissue, which forms the skin and the outer cell layers of internal organs.

Carinate: Shaped like the keel of a ship; having a longitudinal prominence on the back, like a keel; applied to a calyx, corolla or leaf.

Carnivorous plants: Those that are able to digest and absorb nutrient elements from the bodies of animals, mainly insects.

Carotene: A reddish-orange plastid pigment involved in photosynthesis. A carotenoid and precursor of vitamin A.

Carotenoid: A group of chemically similar red to yellow pigments responsible for the characteristic colour of many plant organs or fruits, such as tomatoes, carrots, etc. Oxygen-containing carotenoids are called xanthophylls. Carotenoids serve as light-harvesting molecules in photosynthetic assemblies and also play a role in protecting prokaryotes from the deleterious effects of light.

Carpel: An organ at the centre of a flower, bearing one or more ovules and having its margins fused together or with other carpels to enclose the ovule(s) in an ovary, and consisting also of a stigma and usually a style.

Carpogenic: Fruit-producing. Also carpogenous.

Carpophore: Generally the organ that supports the carpels; specifically, a very much elongated axis to which the carpels are attached.

Carpopodium: Short, thick, pistillate stalk

Carpotaxis: Arrangement of fruits, reproductive in function.

Carrier DNA: DNA of undefined sequence which is added to the transforming (plasmid) DNA used in physical DNA-transfer procedures. This additional DNA increases the efficiency of transformation in electroporation and chemically-mediated DNA delivery systems. The mechanism responsible is not known.

Carrier molecule: 1. A molecule that plays a role in moving electrons through the electron transport chain. They are usually proteins bound to non-protein groups and able to undergo oxidation and reduction relatively easily, thus allowing electrons to flow. 2. A lipid-soluble molecule that can bind to lipid-insoluble molecules and transport them across membranes. Carrier molecules have specific sites that interact with the molecules they transport. The efficiency of carrier molecules may be modified by changing the interacting sites through genetic engineering.

Carrier: A heterozygous individual bearing a recessive mutant allele for a defective condition that is "masked" by the presence of the dominant normal allele; the phenotype is normal, but the individual passes the defective (recessive) allele to half of its offspring.

Cartilaginous: Hard, tough, without chlrophyll and vasculature; like cartilage.

Caruncle: An outgrowth surrounding the scar on a seed.

Carunculate: With an excrescent outgrowth from integuments near the hilum, as in euphorbia; fibrous with stringy or cord-like seed coat, as mace in myristica.

Caryopsis or Grain: A small one-seeded, dry, indehiscent fruit, in which the seed adheres to the thin pericarp, so that the fruit and seed are incorporated into one body, as in wheat and other kinds of grain.

Casein hydrolysate: The mixture of amino acids and peptides produced by enzymatic or acid hydrolysis of casein.

Casein: A group of milk proteins.

Casparian strip: A band of suberin around the radial and transverse walls of an endodermal cell.

Castanea: A genus of trees typified by the common chestnut.

Castaneous: Relating to or having the color of a chestnut.

Catabolic pathway: A pathway by which an organic molecule is degraded in order to release energy for growth and other cellular processes.

Catabolite activator protein (CAP): A protein which combines with cyclic AMP. The cAMP-CAP complex binds to the promoter regions of E. coli and stimulates transcription of the relevant operon. Synonyms: catabolite regulator protein (CRP), cyclic AMP receptor protein.

Catabolite repression: Glucose-mediated reduction in the rates of transcription of genes that encode enzymes involved in catabolic pathways (e.g. the lac operon).

Catadromic, catadromous: With the first subbranch of a lateral branch produced on the basiscopic margin, mostly of venation in pinnate ferns.

Catalase: A metalloenzyme, present in both plants and animals, that catalyzes the decomposition of hydrogen peroxide to water and oxygen. This activity is important in the detoxification of reactive oxygen generated as part of the response to stress.

Catalyst: A substance that promotes a chemical reaction by lowering the activation energy of a chemical reaction, without itself undergoing any permanent chemical change.

Catalytic antibody: An antibody selected for its ability to catalyse a chemical reaction by binding to and stabilizing the transition-state intermediate. Synonym: abzyme.

Catalytic site: The part of the surface of an enzyme molecule (usually only a small portion of the total) necessary for the catalytic process.

Cataphyll: These are the rudimentary leaves that precede a stage of growth. (such as the cotyledons of an embryo, the scale-like leaf of a rhizome, bud, or at the base of a stem).

Cataphyllary leaves: Rudimentary or scale-like leaves which act as a covering of buds.

Catch crop: A method of increasing garden productivity by filling in the empty spaces created when slower-growing vegetables are harvested with fast-growing crops. (i.e. green onions or radishes are grown in the space created when a broccoli plant is cut.

Catena: The soil that is formed from similar parent materials but doesn't have like soil characteristics because of the differences in drainage or relief.

Cation exchange capacity: The measurement of the total amounts of exchangeable cations that can be held by the soil. Expressed as milliequivalents per 100 grams of soil.

Cation exchange: The exchange of cations, held by a soil absorbing complex, with other cations.

Catkin: A catkin is one of several types of inflorescences that can be described as a spike of unisexual flowers. The catkin can be either pendulous or erect depending upon the species. Catkins are also have the name, ament.

Caudate: Having a tail-like appendage; a "tail" or narrowed, apical extension of some sepals and petals.

Caudex: The swollen water-storage tissue, usually consisting of both the root and stem of a succulent or woody plant.

Caudiciform: Possessing a caudex; a plant with a swollen stem.

Caudicle: Extensions of tissue derived from the anther and connected to pollinia in many Orchids.

Caulescent: Having an obvious stem that grows above the soil's surface.

Cauliflower mosaic virus (CAMV): A DNA virus affecting cauliflower and many other dicot species. Its importance is due to the promoter of its 35S ribosomal DNA, which is constitutively active in most plant tissues, and has therefore been widely used as a promoter for the expression of transgenes.

Cauliflower mosaic virus 35S promoter (CAMV 35S): A promoter sequence isolated from the ribosomal gene of the cauliflower mosaic virus.

Cauline: May be all over (general) or along the ribs (costal), or in the grooves (canaliculate).

Caulocarpic: Plants having the stem living for many years, bearing flowers and fruits.

Caulocarpous: Bearing a fruit repeatedly on the same stem; applied to plants that have perennial stems.

Caulogenesis: Stem organogenesis; induction of shoot development from callus.

Cauloneme: A lateral process from the protoneme (initial, threadlike process) which develops into the gemetophore in mosses.

Caulous: With branches more or less evenly spaced along trunk

CBD: Abbreviation for Convention on Biological Diversity.

CCC DNA: Abbreviation for covalently-closed circle DNA.

CD molecules: Abbreviation for: cluster of differentiation molecules. Any group of surface antigens associated with a specific sub-population of T cells.

CDNA clone: A double-stranded cDNA molecule propagated in a vector, and used as a probe in RFLP analyses, as template for the production of EST sequences, and for gene expression studies.

CDNA library: An collection of cDNA clones.

CDR: Abbreviation for complementarity-determining regions.

Cell: The fundamental level of structural organization in complex organisms. Eukaryotic cells contain a nucleus (with chromosomes) and cytoplasm with the protein synthesis machinery, bounded by a membrane. Prokaryotic cells have no nucleus.

Cell biology: The biological discipline involving the study of cells and their functions. Cell culture The in vitro growth of cells isolated from multi-cellular organisms.

Cell cycle: The sequence of stages that a cell passes through between one division and the next. The cell cycle oscillates between mitosis (M) and the interphase, which is divided into the G1 phase (involving a high rate of biosynthesis and growth), the S phase (in which the DNA content is doubled as a consequence of chromosome replication), and the G2 phase (preparatory for cell division).

Cell differentiation: The transition of cells (by the programmed activation and de-activation of the necessary genes) from an tissue-unspecific type, in which daughter cells are similarly undifferentiated, to a committed type in which the cell line specializes to become a recognizable tissue or organ.

Cell division: Formation of two or more daughter cells from a single parent cell. The nucleus divides first, followed by the formation of a cell membrane between the daughter nuclei. Division of somatic cells is termed mitosis; egg and sperm precursors are formed following meiosis.

Cell fusion: Formation in vitro of a single hybrid cell from the coalescence of two cells of different species origin. In the hybrid cell, the donor nuclei may remain separate, or may fuse, but during subsequent cell divisions, a single spindle is formed so that each daughter cell has a single nucleus containing complete or partial sets of chromosomes from each parental line. Synonym: cell hybridization.

Cell generation time: The interval between the beginning of consecutive divisions of a cell, equivalent to the time that it takes for a population of single-celled organisms to double its cell number.

Cell line: 1. A cell lineage that can be maintained in vitro. Significant genetic changes can occur during lengthy periods in culture, so that the genotype of long-term cell lines may not be the same as that of the starter cell. 2. A cell lineage that can be recognized in vivo.

Cell plate: An opaque colloidal layer established by membrane-bound cavities in the equatorial region of the spindle at the telophase stage of mitosis. It separates the cytoplasm into two daughter protoplasts, each with a nucleus. Pectic substances within the vesicles contribute to the formation of a middle lamella between the newly formed cells.

Cell sap: Water and dissolved substances, sugar, amino acids, waste substances, etc., in the plant cell vacuole.

Cell selection: The process of selecting cells exhibiting specific traits within a group of genetically different cells. Selected cells are often sub-cultured onto fresh medium for continued selection and exposed to an increased level of the selection agent to eliminate false positives.

Cell strain: An in vitro culture initiated by asexual reproduction from a single cell. Such cell lines should represent a population of genetically homogenous cells. Strains are defined by specific properties or markers used for their selection. Synonym: single-cell line.

Cell suspension: Cells in culture in moving or shaking liquid medium, often used to describe suspension cultures of single cells and cell aggregates.

Cell wall: A rigid external structure which surrounds plant cells. It is formed outside the plasmalemma and consists primarily of cellulose.

Cellulase: Enzyme catalysing the breakdown of cellulose.

Cellulose: The chief substance composing the cell walls or woody part of plants; a carbohydrate of unknown molecular structure but having the composition represented by the empirical formula (C6H10O5)x.

Cellulosome: A multi-protein aggregate present in some micro-organisms which degrade cellulose. It contains multiple copies of the enzymes necessary for this process, and is often found on the outer surface of the micro-organism cell.

Centifugal: Tending outwards or developing from the centre outwards.

Centimorgan (cM): Unit of map distance. For small recombination fractions, cM and % recombination frequency are equivalent.

Central Canal: The large centrally located air space in the stem.

Central cell nuclei: Nuclei, frequently two in number, that unite with a sperm in an embryo sac, forming a primary endosperm nucleus.

Central dogma: The basic concept that, in nature, genetic information generally flows from DNA to RNA to protein. However, information contained in the RNA molecules of retroviruses can also flow back to DNA.

Central mother cell: A subsurface cell located in a plant apical meristem and characterized by a large vacuole.

Centre of origin: The geographic locations where a particular domesticated plant species originated. These areas are the likeliest source of natural genetic variation, and represent ideal targets for in situ conservation.

Centrifugation: Separating molecules by size or density using centrifugal forces generated by a spinning rotor. G-forces of several hundred thousand times gravity are generated in ultracentrifugation.

Centrifuge: A mechanical device which delivers the centrifugal forces necessary for centrifugation.

Centriole: An organelle in many animal cells that appears to be involved in the formation of the spindle during mitosis. During cell division, the two centrioles move to opposite sides of the nucleus to form the ends of the spindle.

Centripetal: Tending inwqrds or developing towards the centre from the outside.

Centromere: The eukaryotic chromosome structure, which appears as a constriction in karyotype analysis, to which the spindle fibres attach during mitotic and meiotic division. Composed of highly repetitive DNA.

Centroramous: At the center of the branch.

Centrosome: A specialized region of a living cell, situated next to the nucleus, where microtubules are assembled and broken down during cell division. The centrosome of most animal cells contains a pair of centrioles.

Cephalium: A densely spined crown, which produces flowers and fruit. It is produced only by species Discocactus and Melocactus.

Cephem type antibiotic: An antibiotic that shares the basic chemical structure of cephalosporin.

Ceraceous: Waxy; applied to bodies that have the texture and color of new wax, as the pollen masses of many orchids.

Cernuous: Drooping; pendulous; having the top curved or bent down.

Cespitose: Short, much-branched, plant forming a cushion.

Chaetomium: Large ascomycetous fungus producing perithecia. It is found on a variety of substrates containing cellulose including paper and plant compost. It has been found on paper in sheetrock(NC). It is reported to be allergenic. Can produce an Acremonium like state on fungal media.

Chaff: The glumes, husks, or other pieces of the leaves and stems of wheat, oats, or other grains and grasses, especially when separated from the seed by threshing and winnowing.

Chain terminator: 1 In the Sanger method of DNA sequencing, refers to the labelled di-deoxynucleotide triphosphates which are added to disrupt DNA polymerase extension.

Chakrabarty decision: A landmark legal case in the U.S.A., in which it was held that the inventor of a new micro-organism whose invention otherwise met the legal requirements for obtaining a patent, could not be denied a patent solely because the invention was alive. This has set the precedent for the patenting of life forms.

Chalaza: The part of the ovule where the seed stalk and the outer coverings attach to each other.

Chalazogamy: Pollen tube entrance through chalaza.

Channeled: Hollowed out; trough-like; applied to petioles, leaves, etc.

Chaperone: A family of proteins that ensure the correct assembly and conformation of other polypeptides in vivo as they emerge from the ribosome, but are not themselves components of the functional assembled structures. The prokaryotic equivalents are known as chaperonins.

Character (trait): A distinctive but not necessarily invariable feature exhibited by all individuals of a group and capable of being described or measured; e.g. color, size, performance. A character of a given individual will have a certain phenotype as determined by the individual's genotype and environment.

Characterization: Description of the essential properties of an organism or system.

Charcoal: The black porous residue of partly burnt wood, bones, etc; a form of carbon.

Chartaceous: Having the texture of thin but stiff paper.

Chasmantheric pollination: Pollen transferred from a normally dehisced anther by a pollinating agent with pollen grain germination on the stigma and subsequent growth of the pollen tube through stigma, style and the ovule into the embryo sac.

Chasmogamy: The opening of the perianth of a flower for the purpose of fertilization; contrast with cleistogamous.

Chelate: A cation bound to an organic molecule through electron pair donation from nitrogen and/or oxygen atoms in its structure. Ethylenediamine tetraacetic acid is a typical and frequently employed chelating agent. Soluble chelates can supply plants with micronutrients which would otherwise be unavailable because of precipitation.

Chemical gardening: A method of cultivating plants in which chemicals are used to control undesirable pests or weeds.

Chemical mutagen: A chemical capable of inducing mutations in living organisms.

Chemically-defined medium: When all of the chemical components of a culture medium are fully known and defined.

Chemiluminescence: The emission of light during the course of a chemical reaction.

Chemiosmosis: A theory that energy is provided for phosphorylation by protons being "pumped" across inner mitochondrial and thylakoid membranes.

Chemostat: A continuous and open culture in which growth rate and cell density arc maintained constant by a fixed rate of input of a growth-limiting nutrient.

Chemotaxis: The movement of a cell, or the whole or part of an organism, towards or away from an increasing concentration of a particular substance.

Chemotherapy: The treatment of disease, especially infections or cancer, by means of chemicals.

Chestnut soil: Dark brown surface soil.

Chiasma: The X-shaped configuration formed by two chromatids of homologous chromosomes as they remain attached to each other during prophase I of meiosis.

Chicken manure: Strong organic fertilizer derived from chicken droppings. Also called hen manure.

Chimera (or chimaera): 1. An organism whose cells are not all genotypically identical. This can occur as a result of: somatic mutation; grafting or because the individual is derived from two or more embryos or zygotes. 2. A recombinant DNA molecule that contains sequences from different organisms.

Chimeraplasty: A method designed to create defined alterations in DNA sequence at a target locus, with potential both for gene therapy and for investigating gene function. A synthetic nucleic acid that contains DNA interspersed with small amounts of RNA is introduced into the target cell, where it pairs with its target gene sequence and then triggers the cell's DNA repair machinery, resulting in the replacement of the native sequence by the synthetic one.

Chimeric gene: An engineered gene, where a coding sequence is fused to promoter and/or other sequences derived from a different gene. Most genes used in transformation are chimeric. Synonym: fusion gene.

Chimeric selectable marker gene: A gene that is constructed from parts of two or more different genes and allows the host cell to survive under conditions where it would otherwise die.

Chipper: A tool made of a chute, blades and an electric or gas motor; used for turning branches into wood chips.

Chitin: A polymer of repeating sugar molecules (a slightly modified glucose, poly-N-acetyl-D-glucosamine). Chitin is the material which makes up the exoskeleton of insects and, in more or less modified form, in almost all arthropods. In arthropods, chitin occurs in a cross-linked form, á-chitin. Significantly, it is also found in the radular "teeth" of mollusks, the setae (bristles) and jaws of annelid worms, and the cell walls of Fungi. So, this is exceedingly ancient stuff, possibly predating the split between bacteria and metazoans.

Chitinase: An enzyme which breaks down chitin.

Chitinozoan: marine microfossil of uncertain affinity generally shaped like a flask, occurring individually or in chains. Usually assumed to be animal remains.

Chloramphenicol: An antibiotic that interferes with protein synthesis.

Chlorenchyma: Plant tissue (leaf mesophyll and other parenchyma cells) containing chloroplasts.

Chlorophyll: One of the two pigments responsible for the green colour of most plants. It is an essential component of the machinery to absorb light energy for photosynthesis.

Chloroplast DNA: The DNA present in the chloroplast. Although the chloroplast has a small genome, the large number of chloroplasts per cell ensures that chloroplast DNA is a significant proportion of the total DNA in a plant cell.

Chloroplast transit peptide (CTP): A transit peptide that, when fused to a protein, acts to transport that protein into plant chloroplasts. Once inside the chloroplast, the transit peptide is cleaved off the protein. Used to target transgene expression to the chloroplast, where this is appropriate.

Chloroplast: Specialized plastid that contains chlorophyll. Lens-shaped and bounded by a double membrane, chloroplasts contain membranous structures (thylakoids) piled up into stacks, surrounded by a gel-like matrix (stroma). They are the site of solar energy transfer and some important reactions involved in starch or sugar synthesis. Chloroplasts have their own DNA; these genes are inherited only through the female parent, and are independent of nuclear genes.

Chlorosis: The appearance of yellow colour in plants, due to the failure of development or the breakdown of chlorophyll. This is generally a symptom of either nutritional disturbance or of pathogen infection.

Chlorothalonil: A multi-purpose fungicide used to treat a variety of plant diseases. Commonly known as Daconil.

Choripetalous: Polypetalous; having unconnected or separate petals.

Chromatid: Each of the two strands of chromatin comprising a duplicated chromosome. The term is applied only while the two chromatids are joined at the centromere. As soon as the centromere divides, setting the two chromatids adrift (during anaphase of mitosis; and during anaphase II of meiosis), they are called chromosomes.

Chromatin fibre: The standard structural conformation of chromatin in strands of 30 nm average diameter.

Chromatin: Substance of which eukaryotic chromosomes are composed. It consists of a complex of DNA, histone and non-histone chromosomal proteins (mainly histones), and a small amount of RNA.

Chromatography: A method for separating the components of mixtures of molecules by partitioning them between two phases, one stationary and the other mobile. Appropriate selection of partitioning mechanism can produce separation of very closely-related molecules.

Chromocentre: Body produced by fusion of the heterochromatic regions of the chromosomes in the polytene tissues (e.g. the salivary glands) of certain Diptera.

Chromogenic substrate: A compound or substance that contains a colour-forming group.

Chromomeres: Small dense bodies identified by their characteristic size and linear arrangement along a chromosome.

Chromonema (pl.: chromonemata): An optically single thread forming an axial structure within each chromosome.

Chromoplast: A plastid containing pigments other than chlorophyll; the pigments are usually yellow to orange.

Chromosomal aberration: An abnormal change in chromosome structure or number, including deficiency, duplication, inversion, translocation, aneuploidy, polyploidy, or any other change from the normal pattern. Although it can be a mechanism for enhancing genetic diversity, most alterations are fatal or debilitating, especially in animals.

Chromosomal integration site: A chromosomal location where foreign DNA can be integrated, often without impairing any essential function in the host organism.

Chromosomal polymorphism: The occurrence of one to several chromosomes in two or more alteRNAtive structural forms within a population; the structurally changed chromosomes are the result of chromosome mutations (i.e. any structural change involving the gain, loss or re-location of chromosome segments).

Chromosome banding: Differential staining of chromosomes in such a way that light and dark areas occur along the length of the chromosomes in repeatable patterns. Identical banding pattern implies chromosome homology.

Chromosome jumping: A technique that allows two segments of duplex DNA that are separated by thousands of base pairs (about 200 kb) to be cloned together. After sub-cloning, each segment can be used as a probe to identify cloned DNA sequences that, at the chromosome level, are roughly 200 kb apart.

Chromosome landing: An alteRNAtive to chromosome walking for positional cloning. Clones of genomic DNA are fragmented so as to include both the target gene and a closely linked marker and are screened to select ('land on') those clones that contain the target gene.

Chromosome mutation: A change in the gross structure of a chromosome, usually causing severely deleterious effects in the organism, but can be maintained in a population. They are often due to meiotic errors. The main types of chromosome mutation are translocation, duplication, s and inversion.

Chromosome number: The number of chromosomes found in a typical individual of a particular species. Typically the sex cells of a species have one-half the number of chromosomes found in the vegetative portion and are said to be haploid.

Chromosome theory of inheritance: The theory that chromosomes carry the genetic information and that their behaviour during meiosis provides the physical basis for segregation and independent assortment.

Chromosome walking: A strategy for mapping or sequencing a chromosome segment and for positional cloning. Large restriction fragments (or BAC clones) are generated and, after probing, a single starting point is identified. New probes are synthesized complementary to sequences of the same fragment (BAC clone) that are adjacent to the starting point, and these are then used to identify different restriction fragments (BAC clones) overlapping the one selected as the starting point. The procedure is used repetitively, working away from the starting point.

Chromosome: In eukaryotic cells, chromosomes are the nuclear bodies containing most of the genes largely responsible for the differentiation and activity of the cell. Chromosomes are most easily studied in their contracted state, which occurs around the metaphase of mitosis or meiosis; they contain most of the cell's DNA in the form of chromatin. Each eukaryotic species has a characteristic number of chromosomes. Bacterial and viral cells contain only one chromosome, which consists of a single or double strand of DNA or, in some viruses, RNA, without histones.

Chymosin: An enzyme that clots milk, used in the manufacture of cheese.

Cilia: In unicellular plants, gametes, spores etc., minute hair-like protoplasmic protrusions whose movement confers motility on the cell; in higher plants, hairs more or less confined to the margins of an organ. sing. Cilium.

Ciliolate: Marginally fringed with tiny hairs.

Cilium: A short hairlike structure usually found on the cells of unicellular aquatic organisms, normally in large numbers and arranged in rows; the most corrmlon tunction of cilia is propulsion of the cell.

Cincinnus: A form of definite flowering in which the successive axes arise alternately to the right and left of the preceding one, in distinction from the bostryx, in which the growth is all on one side; a scorpioid cyme.

Circadian rhythm: A mostly daily rhythm of growth and activity found in living organisms.

Circadian: Of physiological activity, etc.: recurring at approximately 24-hour intervals.

Circinate: Circular or ring-shaped. Applied to leaves that are rolled up on itself from the tip toward the bottom, like a shepherd's cane. (i.e. fern fronds and the leaves of the Sundew -Drosera)

Circularization: The self-ligation of a linear DNA fragment having complementary ends, generally generated by digestion with a restriction endonuclease. Successful ligation produces a molecule in the form of a covalently-closed circle. Plastid DNA and plasmids are examples of naturally circularized DNA.

Circumferential: At or near the circumference; surrounding a rounded structure.

Circumnutation: The continuous motion of some part of a plant, as the top of the stem or a tendril, in which it describes irregular ellipses or circles.

Circumsciss: Break open along a transverse line around the circumference.

Circumscissile: Opening or divided by a horizontal circular line; applied to pods or seed capsules that open with a lid, like a box. The fruit in such cases is called pyxidium.

Circumscissle capsule or pyxis: One that dehisces circumferentially, as in plantago.

Cirrhose: Tendril-like, with a slender, coiled or wavy tip.

Cirrhous: More than 10:1 l/w, coiled and flexuous.

Cirrose: 1. A leaf tipped with a tendril, or, in mosses, with a very narrow or hair-like sinuous point. 2. Resembling tendrils or coiling like them. Also cirrate, cirrous, cirrhous, cirrhose.

Cirrus: A tendril; a long thread-like part by which some plants climb. Also cirrhus.

Cis acting protein: A protein with the particular property of acting only on the molecule of DNA from which it was expressed.

Cis acting sequence: A nucleotide sequence that only affects the expression of genes located on the same chromosome.

Cis heterozygote: A double heterozygote that contains two mutations arranged in a cis configuration (e.g. a+ b+ / a b).

Citric acid cycle: A complex series of reactions following glycolysis in aerobic respiration that involves ATP, mitochondria, and enzymes and that results in the combining of free oxygen with protons and electrons from pyruvic acid to make water.

Cladocarpous: Having the fruit at the end of short side branches.

Cladode: The photosynthetic stem of a plant whose foliage leaves are absent or much reduced.

Cladodromous: With a single primary vein, the secondary veins not terminating at the margin and freely ramified toward it.

Cladophyll: A flattened, leaf-like photosynthetic stem not bearing leaves or scales.

Cladoptosis: The annual falling of leafy twigs instead of individual leaves. (An example of this process takes place in many trees of the Cypress family.)

Cladosporium (Hormodendrum sp.): Most commonly identified outdoor fungus. The outdoor numbers are reduced in the winter(NC).

The numbers are often high in the summer (NC). Often found indoors in numbers less than outdoor numbers. It is a common allergen. Indoor Cladosporium sp. may be different than the species identified outdoors. It is commonly found on the surface of fiberglass duct liner in the interior of supply ducts. A wide variety of plants are food sources for this fungus. It is found on dead plants, woody plants, food, straw, soil, paint and textiles. It can cause mycosis. Produces greater than 10 antigens. Antigens in commercial extracts are of variable quality and may degrade within weeks of preparation. Common cause of extrinsic asthma (immeadiate-type hypersensitivity: type I). Acute symptoms include edema and bronchiospasms, chronic cases may develop pulmonary emphysema.

Cladosporium fulvum (Fulvia fulva): Conidia dimensions 12-47 x 4-10 microns.It is found on the leaves of tomatoes.

Cladosporium macrocarpum: Conidia dimensions 9-29 x 5-13 microns. It is found on dead plants, woody plants, food, straw, soil, paint and textiles.

Clambering: Sprawling across objects, without climbing structures.

Clasping: Term used to describe a leaf with no petiole and partly surrounding the stem.

Classification of plants: Taxonomy; the systematic naming of plants devised by Carl von Linne.

Clathrate: In the form of a lattice; used to describe scales with a single layer of translucent cells with dark cross-like walls

Clavata: Club-shaped; having the form of a club; growing gradually thicker toward the top, as certain parts of a plant.

Claw: 1. The long and narrow base of a sepal or petal (including labellum), as in pinks, wallflowers, and Orchids. 2. A sharp tool usually having three tines, used to weed and cultivate.

Clay: 1. A type of soil. 2. Soil that contains 10% or more clay. 3. A soil particle less than 0.002 mm in diameter.

Clay mineral: A naturally occurring inorganic crystalline material with particles less than 0.002 mm in diameter.

Clay pan: 1. Soil rich in clay. 2. Soil hard when dry, stiff when wet and it will separate abruptly from overlying soil.

Clayey soil: Soil made up of fine particles that won't hold much air.

Cleave: To break phosphodiester bonds of double-stranded DNA, usually with a type II restriction endonuclease. Synonyms: cut; digest.

Cleaved amplified polymorphic sequence: A segment of DNA that can be amplified by polymerase chain reaction (PCR) and which contains a DNA sequence polymorphism. Following PCR amplification of a locus, the amplicon is treated with a restriction endonuclease. If the recognition site for this enzyme is present in the amplicon, two or more restriction fragments are generated. Thus sequence variation between individuals at the recognition site(s) can be detected by electrophoresis.

Cleft: Divided halfway down to the midrib or further, or generally, any deep lobe or cut.

Cleistantheric pollination: Pollen not transferred from a normally dehisced anther by a pollinating agent; pollen grain germinates within the anther with subsequent growth of the pollen tube through the anther wall and ovary wall into the ovule and embryo sac.

Cleistogamous: Of flowers, self-pollinating and setting fertile seed but never opening.

Cleistogamy: When a plant has regular, fully developed flowers as well as flowers in which development is checked in the bud, but are still fertile and produce a lot of seed. These undeveloped flowers are inconspicuous, non-opening, and lack petals, scent or nectar. They have small anthers that contain a few pollen grains and a dwarfed pistil. They are always fertile while the more perfect flowers of the same plant are usually nearly or completely sterile. Cleistogamy is known to happen in about 60 groups belonging to many different families, including Dicotyledonous. The violet is a good example.

Climate: The amount or variations of cold and heat, dryness and moisture, calm and wind, etc. in a region or country. The combined result of all the meteorological phenomena of any region, as affecting its vegetable production.

Climax vegetation: Vegetational association that perpetuates itself indefinitely at the culmination of ecological succession.

Climber: A plant that clambers upward by attaching itself to other plants or objects (such as a trellis). Climbing plants are distinguished as stem climbers, which wind upward around an erect support and, as tendril climbers, which cling to nearby objects by slender, coiling tendrils. Other plants climb and cling by means of spines or bristles, or by rootlets.

Climbing: Growing upward by means of tendrils, petioles, or adventitious roots.

Clinandrium: A cavity, at the apex of a column in orchids, in which the anthers rest.

Cline: An environmental gradient (temperature, rainfall, soil ph.) and a corresponding phenotypic gradient in a population of plants or animals. Where these have been evaluated by provenance tests, clines are often found to have a genetic basis.

Cloche: A bell-shaped cover used to protect a plant from frost or cold; an individual cold frame.

Clonal propagation: Asexual propagation of many new plants (ramets) from an individual (ortet); all have the same genotype.

Clonal selection: The production of a population of plasma cells all producing the same antibody in response to the interaction between a B lymphocyte producing that specific antibody and the antigen bound by that antibody.

Clonal test: A field planting of several to many vegetatively propagated plants. Such tests furnish estimates of the relative performance of different genotypes, but do not necessarily provide information on breeding behavior.

Clone: 1. To propagate a plant asexually usually by grafting, rooting cuttings, tissue culture, or apomictic seed. Except for an extremely low level of mutation, all plants from a clone are genetically identical. (This is the usage most common in agronomy, horticulture and forestry.) 2. To regenerate a whole plant from a single cell.(This usage is common in tissue culture research.) 3. To identify and isolate a gene controlling a specific trait from an organism. (This usage is common in molecular biology.) 4. A group of plants produced from cuttings, stump or root sprouts, tissue culture, or some other method that produces offspring genetically identical to the original plant. Most commonly used in forestry to establish grafted seed orchards, but becoming more common for commercial plantations.

Cloned strain or line: A strain or line descended directly from a clone.

Cloning vector: A small, self-replicating DNA molecule—usually a plasmid or viral DNA chromosome—into which foreign DNA is inserted in the process of cloning genes or other DNA sequences of interest. It can carry inserted DNA and be perpetuated in a host cell. Synonym: cloning vehicle.

Closed continuous culture: A culture system, in which the inflow of fresh medium is balanced by the outflow of corresponding volumes of spent medium. Cells are separated mechanically from outflowing medium and added back to the culture.

Clouded: Colors are unequally blended together

Club mosses: Within the plant kindgom, primitive vascular plants of the division lycophyta. These plants are not true mosses (which lack vascular tissue). In some species the spores are born in club-like structures.

Clustered, conglomerate, agglomerate, crowded, aggregate: Parts dense, usually irregularly overlapping each other.

Co cloning: The unintentional cloning of DNA fragments, along with the desired one, that can occur when the source of DNA being cloned is not sufficiently purified.

Co culture: The joint culture of two or more types of cells, such as a plant cell and a micro-organism, or two types of plant cells. Used in various dual-culture systems or in nurse culture.

Co dominance: Where both alleles are expressed in the heterozygous state, so that the phenotype reflects a contribution from both alleles. For example, roan coat colour in cattle results from a mixture of red hairs and white hairs, caused by heterozygosity for the red allele and the white allele.

Co enzyme: Synonym for co-factor.

Co evolution: The evolution of complementary adaptations in two species brought about by the selection pressure that each exerts on the other. Common in symbiotic associations, in insect-pollinated plants, etc.

Co factor: An organic molecule or inorganic ion necessary for the normal catalytic activity of an enzyme. Synonym: co-enzyme.

Co fermentation: The simultaneous growth of two micro-organisms in one bioreactor.

Co integrate vector system: A two plasmid system for plant transgenesis. One plasmid is engineered to carry a T-DNA segment incorporating the gene(s) to be introduced. After introduction into Agrobacterium tumefaciens, the plasmid undergoes homologous recombination with a resident disarmed Ti plasmid to form a single plasmid carrying the genetic information for transferring the genetically engineered T-DNA region to plant cells.

Co integrate: A chimeric DNA molecule formed by the incorporation at a single site of two different DNA molecules.

Co linearity: 1. A general relationship in which the units in one molecule occur in the same sequence as the units in another molecule which they specify; e.g. the nucleotides in a gene are co-linear with the amino acids in its encoded polypeptide. 2. The phenomenon whereby gene order is preserved between distinct species.

Co repressor: An effector molecule that forms a complex with a repressor and turns off the expression of a gene or set of genes.

Co segregation: The joint inheritance of two characters, usually the result of genetic linkage.

Co suppression: A natural gene silencing phenomenon, which probably evolved as part of plants' defence against viral attack, but which has become important in the context of plant transgenesis. Operates by inhibiting the expression of transgenes with homology to native DNA through the interaction of native and transgenic mRNA.

Co transfection: The procedure by which a baculovirus and a transfer vector are simultaneously introduced into insect cells in culture.

Co transformation: A protocol for producing transgenesis, in which host (plant or animal) cells are transformed simultaneously with two different plasmids, one of which carries a selectable marker, and the other the gene to be transferred. Relies on the observation that given a sufficiently high concentration of both plasmids, transformed cells will have incorporated both plasmids, possibly at different genomic loci. If the transgenes are separable through normal meiotic recombination, transgenic individuals without the selectable marker can be selected in subsequent generations.

Coalescent: With like or unlike parts or organs incompletely separated; partially fused in a more or less irregular fashion.

Coarse sand: A soil particle that measures between.50 to 1.0 millimeters.

Coccus: One of the (usually 1-seeded) lobes of a distinctly lobed fruit, becoming separate at maturity. pl. cocci.

Cochlear: Of the arrangement of corolla lobes in a bud, a variant of imbricate aestivation.

Coconut milk: Liquid endosperm of the coconut, often used to supply organic nutrients to in vitro cultures of plant cells and tissues.

Codex alimentarius commission: An international regulatory body (part of FAO) responsible for the definition of a set of international food standards. The Commission periodically determines, then publishes a list of food ingredients and maximum allowable levels (the Codex Alimentarius) deemed to be safe for human consumption.

Coding sequence: That portion of a gene which directly specifies the amino acid sequence of its product. Non-coding sequences of genes include introns and control regions, such as promoters, operators, and terminators.

Coding strand: The strand of a DNA double helix that contains the same base sequence (after substituting U for T) found in the mRNA molecule resulting from transcription of that segment of DNA. Sometimes called the sense strand. The mRNA molecule is transcribed from the other strand, known as the template or antisense strand.

Codon: One of the groups of three consecutive nucleotides in mRNA, which represent the unit of genetic coding by specifying a particular amino acid during the synthesis of polypeptides in a cell. Each codon is recognized by a tRNA carrying a specific amino acid, which is incorporated into a polypeptide chain during protein synthesis. In DNA, any informative triplet of bases, including both coding and control sequences.

Codon optimization: An experimental strategy in which codons within a cloned gene–ones not generally used by the host cell translation system–are changed by in vitro mutagenesis to the preferred codons, without changing the amino acids of the synthesized protein.

Coenocarpium (various structures): Multiple fruit derived from ovaries, floral parts, and receptacles of many coalesced flowers, as in ananas.

Coenocytic: Multinucleate, the nuclei not individually separated from one another by crosswalls, as in the hyphae of water molds.

Coenosorus: An extended sorus or series of sori that have united or coalesced

Coherent: With like parts or organs joined, but only superficially and without actual histological continuity.

Cohesion-tension theory: Theory that explains the rise of water in plants through a combination of cohesion of water molecules in vessels and tracheids and tension on the water columns brought about by transpiration.

Coincidence: The ratio of the observed to the expected frequency of double cross-overs, where the expected frequency is calculated by assuming that the two cross-over events occur independently of one another.

Colchicine: An alkaloid, obtained from the autumn crocus Colchicum autumnale, which inhibits spindle formation. When applied during mitosis, chromosomes are unable to separate during anaphase. This property is used to achieve a doubling of the chromosome number. A further use is to halt mitosis at metaphase, the stage at which karyotypes are best viewed.

Cold frame: A bottomless box consisting of a wooden or metal frame with a glass or polyethylene top. It is placed on the ground over plants to protect them from cold or frost.

Coleoptile: A protective sheath surrounding the emerging shoot of seedlings of the Grass Family (Poaceae) (e.g., corn, wheat).

Coleorhiza: A protective sheath surrounding the emerging radicle (immature root) of members of the Grass Family (Poaceae) (e.g., corn, wheat).

Collar: A ring placed loosely around the stem of a plant, especially tomatoes, to prevent cutworm damage.

Collateral: Situated side by side; adjacent and on the same radius of an axis.

Collenchyma: Living, supportive tissue with chloroplasts generally just beneath the surface consisting or more or less elongated cells usually thickened unevenly in a manner somewhat variable in different groups of plants.

Collet: External demarcation between hypocotyl and root.

Colleter: Mucinagious hairs that secrete gum.

Colliculate: Covered with small, rounded or hillock-like elevations (colliculae).

Colloid soil: Organic or inorganic tiny crystals that are small enough to be easily carried by air or water.

Colonial: Usually used to describe cloning by vegetative reproduction, the seemingly separate plants having arisen from rhizomes, stolons, or roots of a single or of neighboring "parent" plants.

Colony: 1. An group of genetically identical cells or individuals derived from a single progenitor. 2. A group of interdependent cells or organisms.

Colony hybridization: A technique that uses a nucleic acid probe to identify a recombinant bacterial colony carrying a particular inserted DNA.

Colporate: Of a pollen grain, having both an elongated and a rounded aperture.

Columella: This is another one of those anatomical terms of almost unbelievable generality. It refers to any small rod-like structure (and some that are not rod-like in the slightest), such as the ear ossicle of reptiles, the basal column of univalves in gastropods, the sterile support of the fruiting body in fungi, and, for our purposes, either (a) a structure closely analogous to the fungal columella in the sporophyte of basal plants; or (b) the central portion of the root cap in higher plants.

Column, gynostemium or gynandrium: With fused stamens and carpels (stigma and style) as in Orchis.

Column: An organ formed by the union of filaments with one another, as in Malvacea, or of stamens with the style and stigma, as in Orchids.

Columnar: Erect with a stout main stem or trunk

Column-foot: A basal extension of the column to which the labellum is attached, often flexibly.

Column-wings: Paired protuberances or wing-like flanges on the column.

Coma: The leafy head of a tree (such as Palms) or a tuft of leaves or bracts terminating a stem (such as the leafy top of a Pineapple). The silky hairs at the end of some seeds (such as fireweed - Epilobium).

Combination: Taxonomically the name of a genus combined with a specific epithet.

Combinatorial library: The many novel combinations (consisting of one heavy and one light immunoglobulin chain coding region) that are generated when a heavy-chain library is combined by random pairing with a light-chain library. These constructs are propagated in a vector, and their gene products screened for novel affinity properties.

Combining ability, general: Good general combining ability (GCA) is the ability of an individual to produce progeny with high genetic quality, when crossed to many other individuals in the population.

Commensalism: The interaction of two or more dissimilar organisms where the association is advantageous to one without affecting the other(s).

Commissure: A joint, seam, suture, or closure; the place where two bodies or parts of a body meet or unite. The face by which one carpel or mericarp attaches to another, as in Umbelliferae.

Community: A collective tern for all the living organisms sharing a common environment and interacting with one another.

Comose: With a tuft of trichomes, usually apical.

Compact: Pressing air out of the soil.

Companion cells: Companion cells always exist together with sieve-tube members. Sieve-tube members and companion cells are called sister cells because they originate from the same procambial cell or fusiform initial in the vascular cambium. The order of development is that the meristem cell begins to differentiate by dividing once to form two cells, then one of the two cells differentiates further into a companion cell and the other into a sieve-tube member.

Companion planting/cropping: A system of arranging plants in a way that a given species benefits from some characteristic of another. For example, it is thought that Tomatoes are protected from certain insects by the qdor of Marigolds.

Comparative mapping: The comparison of map locations of genes and markers between species. In comparisons between closely related species, this will usually uncover a high degree of conservation of synteny and co-linearity. In these cases, the likely location of many genes can be predicted from model system data. Comparisons across wider phylogenetic distances reveal increasing loss of synteny.

Comparative positional candidate gene: Relates to an indirect means of assigning function to a QTL. Where a QTL has been linked to a marker in one species, and that same marker is linked to a known gene in a model system, inferences may be drawn as to the nature of the QTL.

Complanate: Lying in one plane. Applied to leaves, especially of Mosses.

Complement proteins: Proteins that bind to antibody-antigen complexes and help degrade the complexes by proteolysis.

Complementarity determining regions (CDR): Regions of the light and heavy subunits of the immunoglobulin molecules that interact with the antigen. The primary amino acid sequences of these regions are highly variable between antibodies of the same class.

Complementary entity: 1. Synonym of base pair. 2. One of a pair of segments or strands of nucleic acid that will hybridize with one another.

Complementary genes: Two or more interdependent genes, such that (in the case of dominant complementarity) the dominant allele from either gene can only produce an effect on the phenotype of an organism if the dominant allele from the other gene is also present; in the case of recessive complementarity, only double homozygous recessive individuals show the effect.

Complementary homopolymeric tailing: The process of adding complementary nucleotide extensions to DNA molecules, (e.g. deoxyguanosine) to the 3' end of one DNA molecule and deoxycytidine to the 5' end of another DNA molecule) to facilitate the ligation of the two DNA molecules.

Complementary: Two DNA molecules are complementary to one another when each successive base position from the 5' end in the first molecule is matched by the corresponding residue in the second, starting at the 3' end, according to the normal base pair rules (i.e. A for T, C for G). In the appropriate conditions, two complementary single-stranded DNA molecules will renature to form a double-stranded molecule. Complementary nucleotides are members of the pairs adenine-thymine, adenine-uracil, and guanine-cytosine that have the ability to hydrogen bond to one another.

Complementation test: A genetic method to test whether or not independent mutations are allelic. In a cross between the two mutant individuals, the genotype will be m1m2 if the mutations are allelic and m1 +/+ m2 if non-allelic. The phenotype of the former will be mutant, but that of the latter will be wild type (normal).

Complete digest: The treatment of a DNA preparation with a restriction endonuclease for sufficient time for all of the potential target sites within that DNA to have been cleaved. Opposite: partial digest.

Complete: Leaf with blade, petiole, and stipules; flower with four types of floral parts.

Complex soil: 1. A pattern of soil. 2. A mixture of different kinds of soil whose areas are too small to be shown individually.

Complex tissue: Tissue that consists of more than one cell type, e.g. phloem.

Composite: A family of flowering plants (asteraceae or compositae) in which the distinctive feature is that relatively small flowers (florets) are crowded together in a dense "head". Florets come in two types: ray and disk flowers. Some species have ray flowers only, some have disk flowers only and some have both. Members of this family include daisy, sunflower, and dandelion.

Composite transposon: A transposon formed when two identical or nearly identical transposons insert on either side of a non-transposable segment of DNA.

Compost: A mixture of decomposed organic matter, particularly decomposed plant materials.

Compost activator: A substance, usually bacterial, that is used to speed the breakdown of organic waste into compost. Also called activator or compost inoculent.

Compost aerator: An elongated, flanged T-shaped device used to create passages for air and moisture in a compost pile. Also created compost turner.

Compost bin: A container to hold decomposing garden and yard wastes, fertilizer, peat, lime, and other substances during the composting process.

Compost inoculant: A substance that may contain bacteria, fungi, enzymes, and hormones that is used to speed the composting process and to improve the quality of the compost. Also called activator or compost activator.

Compost tea: A liquid fertilizer made of compost dissolved in water.

Compost thermometer: A thermometer having a long probe used to measure the temperature in the center of the compost pile.

Composter: A container utilizing air, moisture, and solar heat to turn grass clippings, garden waste, and kitchen scraps into compost. Composters may consist of stacked trays or other chambers arranged to facilitate periodic turning of the mixture.

Compound: Of a leaf, having the blade divided into two or more distinct leaflets; of an inflorescence, made up of an aggregate of smaller inflorescences.

Compound chromosome: A chromosome formed by the fusion of two separate chromosomes, as in attached-X chromosomes or attached-X-Y chromosomes.

Compound leaf: A compound leaf is a leaf that is divided into many separate parts (leaflets) along a midrib (the rachis). All the leaflets of a compound leaf are oriented in the same plane. When a compound leaf falls from the tree, it falls as a unit. A double compound leaf is one in which each leaflet of a compound leaf is also made up of secondary leaflets.

Compressed: Flattened in one plane, either dorsally (bringing the front and back closer together) or laterally (bringing the sides closer together).

Concatemer: A DNA segment made up of repeated sequences linked head to tail.

Conceptacle: An organ or a cavity that encloses reproductive bodies in some ferns, fungi, mosses, and algae.

Concolorous: Of uniform colour; of leaves, having both surfaces the same colour.

Concordance: Identity of matched pairs or groups for a given trait, such as sibs expressing the same trait.

Concrescence: The union of cell walls by means of a cementing substance formed in process of growth so that they are inseparably grown together. Also called cementation.

Concrete: A compact mass of sand, gravel, coarse pebbles, or stone chips cemented together to form a smooth surface for steps, patios, or walkways.

Concretions: Pellet-like grains from concentrations of compounds in soils that cement the soil grains together.

Conditional lethal mutation: A mutation that is lethal under one set of environmental conditions (the restrictive conditions, commonly associated with high temperature) but is viable under another set of environmental conditions (the permissive conditions).

Conditioner: A material added to a fertilizer that keeps it flowing free.

Conditioning: 1. The effects on phenotypic characters of external agents during critical developmental stages. 2. The undefined interaction between tissues and culture medium resulting in the growth of single cells or small aggregates. Conditioning may be accomplished by immersing cells or callus contained within a porous material (such as dialysis tubing) into fresh medium for a period dependent on cell density and a volume related to the amount of fresh medium.

Conductivity: The physical quantity that measures the readiness with which a medium transmits electricity. Expressed in micromhos per centimeter at 25° C.

Conduplicate: Longitudinally folded upward or downward along the central axis so that ventral and/or dorsal sides face each other.

Cone scale: A cone scale is one of the "leaves" of a cone. The cone scale starts out as a sporophyll with either spores or seed developing on its upper surface.

Cone: 1. A flower or cluster of flowers having a cone-like shape. 2. A dry, usually elongated, multiple fruit formed of compactly overlapped scales (such as those of Pines, Firs and Spruces), in which a pair of naked seeds is borne upon the upper side of each scale (technically called a strobilus or strobile).

Conelet: An immature cone (strobilus) in the conifers.

Conflorescence: A flower-bearing branch system in which the main axis does not end in a flower but the axes of the branches do.

Confluent: Blending or running together.

Conform: Of the same or similar shape, eg pinnate fronds with the apical pinnae similar to the lateral.

Conformation: The various three dimensional shapes that can be adopted by a given molecule. In particular, the different ways in which the primary sequence of a biological polymer may be folded. This is determined by intra-molecular forces, including hydrogen bonding and, in proteins, disulphide bridges. In proteins, conformation is often critical for biological activity, and the functions of some molecules are carried out by switching between two alternative stable conformations. The native conformation found in vivo may be changed to typically less ordered, uncharacterized, and usually biologically-inactive forms by denaturing.

Congeneric: Belonging to one and the same genus; hence congener.

Conical: Of a solid in the form of a cone, attached be the broad end.

Conidium: An asexually produced fungal spore formed outside of a sporangium.

Conifers: Vascular woody plants that bear their seeds in cones. They are usually evergreen and have needle-like leaves. Within the gymnosperms, this is the division coniferophyta.

Conjugation: 1. Union of gametes or unicellular organisms during fertilization. 2. The unidirectional transfer of plasmid DNA from one bacterium cell to another, involving cell-to-cell contact. The plasmid usually encodes the majority of the functions necessary for its own transfer. 3. Attachment of sugar and other polar molecules to less polar compounds, thus making them more water soluble.

Conjugative functions: Plasmid-based genes and their products that facilitate the transfer of a plasmid from one bacterium to another via conjugation.

Connate: With like parts or organs integrally fused to one another with histological continuity.

Connation: Fusion of like parts; e.g. sepal with sepal; contrasted with adnation.

Connective: The part of an anther that connects the lobes.

Connivent: Converging together, usually of organs with their bases separate and their appices approaching each other, not touching or fused.

Consanguinity: Related by descent from a common ancestor.

Conserved sequence: An identical or highly similar sequence of nucleotides or amino acids which occurs as part, or all of a number of different genes or proteins, in either the same or different species. This conservation can signify which part of the full sequence is responsible for the functionality.

Consolidate: To increase the density and reduce pore space in soil.

Conspecific: Belonging to one and the same species.

Constant domains: Regions of antibody chains that have the same amino acid sequence in different members of a particular class of antibody molecules.

Constitutive gene: A gene that is continually expressed in all cells of an organism.

Constitutive promoter: An unregulated promoter that allows for continual transcription of its associated gene.

Constitutive synthesis: Continual synthesis of a gene product by an organism.

Constitutive: The expression of a gene without any requirement for induction.

Construct: An engineered chimeric DNA designed to be transferred into a cell or tissue. Typically, the construct comprises the gene or genes of interest, a marker gene and appropriate control sequences as a single package. A repeatedly-used construct may be called a cassette.

Consumer: A consumer is a living thing that eats other living things to survive. It cannot make its own food (unlike most plants, which are producers). Primary consumers eat producers, secondary consumers eat primary consumers, and so on. There are always many more primary consumers than secondary consumers, etc.

Consumptive use: 1. The water used by plants. 2. Vapor loss. Expressed as equivalent depth of free water per unit of time.

Contaminant: 1. An undesired chemical present in a compound or mixture of compounds. 2. Any micro-organism accidentally introduced into a culture or culture medium. The contaminant may compete with the desired cells and consequently inhibit their growth, or totally replace them.

Contig: A set of overlapping cloned DNA fragments that can be assembled to represent a defined region of the chromosome or genome from which they were obtained. Contig definition is a necessary step for assembling whole genome sequences.

Contigous: Adjacent and touching but not united.

Continuous culture: A suspension culture continuously supplied with nutrients by the inflow of fresh medium. The culture volume is normally constant.

Continuous fermentation: A process in which cells or micro-organisms are maintained in culture in the exponential growth phase by the continuous addition of fresh medium that is exactly balanced by the removal of cell suspension from the bioreactor.

Continuous variation: Variation where individuals cannot be classified as belonging to one of a set of discrete classes. Characters showing continuous variation are referred to as quantitative.

Continuous: Not deviating from uniformity; the opposite of interrupted.

Contorted: Twisted around a central axis; twisted.

Contortuplicate: With weirdly folded corrugate cotyledons.

Contour basin: A basin made by a levee or border built on a contour.

Contour plowing: The plowman keeps to a level line at a right angle to the direction of the slope.

Contour terrace: Leveling soil out on a slope at a right angle to the direction of the slope.

Contour: An imaginary line connecting points of equal elevation on the soil's surface.

Contracted: Narrowed and/or shortened.

Contractile or Pull: Roots capable of shortening, usually drawing the plant or plant part deeper into the soil, usually with a wrinkled surface.

Control pollination: To purposely pollinate the female flowers of a tree with pollen from a known source, usually one specific tree. Usually the flowers are Protected from undesirable pollen by covering them with a pollen-tight cloth or paper bag before they are receptive and adding known-source pollen at receptivity. Full-sib families are produced.

Controlled environment: A closed environment in which parameters, such as light, temperature, relative humidity and sometimes the partial gas pressure (and possibly its composition), are fully controlled.

Controlling element: In eukaryotes, transposons which affect the activity of known genes. This can occur as a result of the integration within, or close to a gene, thereby disrupting its activity; or following its excision from such a site, thereby restoring activity.

Convention on biological diversity (CBD): The inteRNAtional treaty governing the conservation and use of biological resources around the world, that has also called for the establishment of rules to govern the international movement of non-indigenous living organisms and genetically modified organisms.

Convergent: Growing or lying towards one another.

Conversion: The development of a somatic embryo into a plant.

Convolute: Of the arrangement of corolla lobes in a bud, a form of imbricate aestivation in which each segment has one edge overlapping the adjacent segment, like a furled umbrella.

Coordinate repression: Correlated regulation of a structural gene within an operon by a molecule that interacts with the operator.

Copper: An element used in various forms, including copper sulfate and Bordeaux mixture, to control fungal and bacterial diseases of plants. Also used in strips around tree trunks to act as a barrier to snails.

Copy number: The number of a particular plasmid per bacterium cell, or gene per genome.

Cordate leaf: A cordate leaf has a heart shape, with the wide part towards the petiole.

Cordate: With a sinus and rounded lobes at the base, the overall outline usually ovate; often restricted to the base rather than to the outline of the entire organ; heart-shaped.

Cordiform: Shaped like a heart (in three dimensions).

Coriaceous: Of a thick leathery texture.

Cork cambium: A narrow cylindrical sheath of cells between the exterior of a woody root or stem and the central vascular tissue: it produces cork to its exterior and phelloderm to its interior: it is also called phellogen.

Cork: A plant tissue composed of cells whose walls are impregnated with suberin and are non-living at maturity; cork is produced by the cork cambium.

Corking: Gradual ripening of a stem from the base, to produce a bark-like texture.

Corm: A corm in a rounded, thick underground stem that is modified into a mass of storage tissue. The foliage and flowers grow from buds on the stem. Corms are usually round and slightly flattened, not pointed like a true bulb. If you cut one in half, you won't see scale rings. The tunics of corms are usually netted and fibrous. One or more growing points, or eyes, grow from the top of the corm. At the bottom, roots grow from a basal plate. As the plant grows, the old corm dies, and new corms, called cormels, form around it. If a new cormel is large, it may produce flowers the following year, but normally it takes two to three years. Crocuses, montbretia, and gladioluses are typical corms.

Cormel: A smaller, secondary corm produced by an old corm; a bulblet.

Cormophyta: In older classifications, a division comprising all plants that have a stem and root.

Corniculate: Bearing, or terminating in, one or more small horns.

Corolla: The usually conspicuous part of a flower, called the petals. They are contained within the calyx and immediately surround the stamens and pistil.

Corona: A crown-like appendage or series of united appendages on the inner side of a corolla. It often resembles an outgrowth of the perianth, as in the Daffodil, or of the staminal circle, as in the milkweed.

Coronate: Tubular or flaring perianth or staminal outgrowth; petaloid appendage.

Coroniform: Crown-shaped.

Coronule: A little crown of a seed; the downy tuft on seeds.

Corpus: A part of the apical meristem below the tunica. In the corpus, cells divide in all directions, and increase in volume.

Correlation: A statistical association between variables.

Corrugate: With lamina irregularly folded in all directions, wrinkled

Cortex: The cylinder of primary tissue, within the stem of a plant, which extends from the vascular tissue in the center out to the bark, or epidermis. It may function in photosynthesis, food storage, support, and growth of the plant.

Corymb: A racemose type of inflorescence in which the lower pedicels are successively elongated forming a more or less flat-topped inflorescence, the outer flowers opening before the inner.

Corymbose: Having flowers in corymbs.

Cos ends: The 12-base, single-strand, complementary extensions of bacteriophage lambda DNA.

Cosmid: A synthetic plasmid which incorporates the cos ends, and one or more selectable markers such as an antibiotic resistance gene. Cosmids were designed as vectors able to incorporate DNA fragments up to 40-50 kb in size.

Cosmopolitan: World-wide in distribution.

Costa: Rib, especially the midrib of a leaf or pinna; hence costate.

Costal: Pertaining to or near the costa (dimin. costular).

Costate: Coarsely ribbed

Costule: Midrib of higher order pinnule or lobe; hence costulate.

Cot curve: A method to estimate the heterogeneity of sequence of a DNA preparation, based on the observation that the more homogenous the DNA, the more easily (and therefore faster) the annealing of single-stranded DNA will occur. The Cot curve plots the extent of annealing from a fully single-stranded preparation over time. The cot (product of initial concentration and time) at which half the DNA has re-natured is the half-cot, a parameter indicating both the degree of heterogeneity in a complex mixture, and of the extent of complementarity in a mixture of two single-stranded DNA molecules.

Cotyledon: The embryo leaf or leaves of seed plants that absorbs nutrients packaged in the seed, until the seedling is able to produce its first true leaves and begin photosynthesis. "The number of cotyledons present in an embryo is an important character in the classification of flowering plants (angiosperms). Monocotyledons (such as grasses, palms, and lilies) have a single cotyledon, whereas dicotyledons (the majority of plant species) have two. In seeds that also contain endosperm (nutritive tissue), the cotyledons are thin, but where they are the primary food-storing tissue, as in peas and beans, they may be quite large. After germination the cotyledons either remain below ground (hypogeal) or, more commonly, spread out above soil level (epigeal) and become the first green leaves. In gymnosperms there may be up to a dozen cotyledons within each seed.

Cotylespermous: With food reserve in cotyledon, derived from zygote.

Coupling: The phase state in which either two dominant or two recessive alleles of two different genes occur on the same chromosome.

Covalent bond: A force provided by pairs of electrons that travel between two or more atomic nuclei: holding atoms together and keeping them at a stable distance from eachother.

Covalently closed circular DNA (ccc DNA): A DNA molecule in which the free ends have ligated to form a circle. The strands remain linked together even after denaturation. Plasmids exist in this form in their in vivo state. In its native form, ccc DNA will adopt a supercoiled configuration.

Cover crop: A crop of nitrogen fixing plants that is planted with, or in rotation with, edible crops to increase nitrogen, stabilize soil, attract beneficial insects, or to be used as green manure.

CP4 EPSPS: Abbreviation for CP4 5-enolpyruvyl-shikimate-3-phosphate synthase.

CPDNA: Abbreviation for chloroplast DNA.

Craspedodromous: Simple - with a single primary vein, all of the secondary veins and their branches terminating at the margin. Mixed with a single primary vein, some of the secondary veins terminating at the margin and an approximately equal number otherwise.

Crater: A bowl; hence craterous, crateriform.

Crateriform: Shallow cup-shaped as the involucre of some species of quercus.

Creek: A natural stream of water normally smaller than and often tributary to a river.

Creep soil: The downward, slow, irregular mass movement of sloping soil.

Creeper: A plant that grows along the surface of the soil or any other surface such as a wall or fence, by sending out rootlets from the stem. (i.e. Ivy -Hedera, Virginia Creeper - Parthenocissus quinquefolia, Trumpet Creeper - Campsis radicans).

Crenate: Toothed with shallow, rounded scallops, as the edges of a leaf. When the scallops have smaller ones upon them, the leaf is said to be doubly crenate.

Crenulate: Diminutive of crenate, teeth cut to 1/16 distance to midrib or midvein

Crest: Also called fasciation; a mutation that results when the growing point of a plant forms a long line, rather that a single point. In botanical terms, it is usually signified by cristate.

Crested: With an elevated ridge or line along the summit of an organ.

Crispate: Curled or rippled at the edge such as the leaves of Pittosporum eugenioides. Also crisped.

Crisped: With the margins finely wavy, curled or crumpled.

Crista: Of mitochondria, folds in the internal membrane of the mitochondrion which gives the organelle its characteristic appearance. This is the site of the electron transport chain in oxidative metabolism. The cristae, therefore, serve as the physical link between the tricarboxylic acid cycle and oxidative phosphorylation (ATP synthesis).

Crocks: Broken pieces of clay pot, used to cover drainage holes of pots in order to provide free drainage and air circulation to the root system and to prevent the medium (i.e. soil) from washing down the holes.

Cross: To collect pollen from one tree and pollinate a second tree. The progeny of a control pollination.

Cross breeding: Mating between members of different populations (lines, breeds, races or species).

Cross hybridization: The annealing of a single-stranded DNA sequence to a single-stranded target DNA to which it is only partially complementary. Often, this refers to the use of a DNA probe to detect homologous sequences in species other than the origin of the probe.

Cross pollination efficiency: The ease with which cross pollination can be achieved. Generally measured by the number of hybrid progeny generated per flower pollinated.

Cross pollination: Application of pollen from one plant to another to effect the latter's fertilization.

Cross-fertilization: The fertilization of the ovules of one flower by the pollen of another, either between plants of the same species or between individuals of different species, resulting in the production of a hybrid.

Crossing groups: Any group of individuals which comprises a unique set of parents. A diallel CG is one in which controlled crosses are made between each pair of parents in the group but crosses with parents outside the group are excluded. A factorial CG is one in which a limited number of parents are used as male testers in controlled crosses with an unlimited number of female parents. An open-pollinated CG is one in which all parents in a breeding population are included in a progeny test or series of tests and which may be used for reforestation with genetically improved material.

Crossing over: The process by which homologous chromosomes exchange material at meiosis through the breakage and reunion of non-sister chromatids.

Crown: That part of a stem at or just below the surface of the ground; an inner appendage of a petal or the throat of a corolla; an appendage or extrusion standing between the corolla and stamens, or on the corolla; an outgrowth of the staminal part or circle as in milkweeds.

Crown division: The asexual production of multiple plants by division of the base of a stem (crown).

Crown gall: A tumorous growth at the base of certain plants characteristic of infection by Agrobacterium tumefaciens. The gall is induced by the transformation of the plant cell by portions of the Ti plasmid.

Crozier: The spirally coiled "fiddlehead" of an immature fern leaf.

CRP: Abbreviation for catabolite regulator protein.

Cruciate: Having leaves or flowers in the shape of a cross with equal arms, as certain members of the Mustard family.

Crumb structures: The porous granular structure in soil.

Crust: A thin, dry, hard layer of soil that forms on the surface of many soils when they are exposed to excessive heat.

Crustaceous: Brittle; of marine algae, encrusted with calcium carbonate.

Cry proteins: A class of crystalline proteins produced by strains of Bacillus thuringiensis, and engineered into crop plants to give resistance against insect pests. These proteins are toxic to certain categories of insects (e.g. corn borers, corn rootworms, mosquitoes, black flies, armyworms, tobacco hornworms, some types of beetles, etc.), but are harmless to mammals and most beneficial insects.

Cryobiological preservation: The preservation of germplasm resources in a dormant state by storage at ultra-low temperatures, often in liquid nitrogen. Currently applied to storage of plant seeds and pollen, micro-organisms, animal sperm, and tissue culture cell lines.

Cryogenic: At very low temperature.

Cryoprotectant: Compound preventing cell damage during successive freezing and thawing processes. Cryoprotectants are agents with high water solubility and low toxicity. Two types commonly used: permeating (glycerol and DMSO) and non-permeating (sugars, dextran, ethylene glycol, polyvinylpyrrolidone and hydroxyethyl starch).

Cryptantherous: With stamens included.

Cryptic: Anything hidden. 1. Structurally heterozygous individuals that are not identifiable as they do not show abnormal meiotic chromosome pairing configurations ('cryptic structural hybrids'). 2. A form of polymorphism controlled by recessive genes ('cryptic polymorphism'). 3. Any mutation which is exposed by a sensitizing mutation and otherwise poorly detected (such mutations probably escape detection because of the plasticity of composition of the corresponding polypeptide). 4. Phenotypically very similar species (cryptic species) which do not hybridize under normal conditions. 5. Cryptic genetic variation refers to the existence of, for example, alleles conferring high performance for a trait, in a breed that has low performance for that trait.

Cryptocotylar or hypogeous: With the cotyledons remaining inside the seed; seed usually remaining below ground.

Cryptogam (literally): A plant whose sexual reproductive parts are not conspicuous; a plant that produces spores, not seeds, in its sexual reproductive cycle, e.g. ferns, mosses, algae.

Cryptostroma corticale: Conidia dimensions 4-6.5 x 3.5-4 microns. Found on the bark of maple and sycamore trees and on stored logs.

CTP: Abbreviation for 1. cytidine 5'-triphosphate, which is required for RNA synthesis since it is a direct precursor molecule; 2. Chloroplast transit peptide.

Cucullate: Hooded or hood-shaped.

Culm: The jointed and usually hollow stem of grasses. It is in most cases herbaceous but is woody in the bamboo and some other stout species. The term is also sometimes applied to the solid, jointless stems of sedges.

Cultigen: A cultivated plant or group of specific rank for which a wild ancestor isn't known.

Cultivar: A contraction of "cultivated variety"; a group (or one among such a group) of cultivated plants clearly distinguished by one or more characteristics and which retains these characteristics when propagated; a distinct variety or race of plants that originated under cultivation and persists under cultivation. A cultivar may or may not be referable to a botanical species. Cultivars are given a name, usually distinguished by the use of single quotation marks, as in Zinnia elegans 'Tom Thumb'. Named varieties of hybrid Tea Roses and of garden Apples are examples of cultivars.

Culture: A population of plant or animal cells or micro-organisms grown under controlled conditions.

Culture alteration: A term used to indicate a persistent change in the properties of a culture's behaviour (e.g. altered morphology, chromosome constitution, virus susceptibility, nutritional requirements, proliferative capacity, etc.). The term should always be qualified by a precise description of the change which has occurred in the culture.

Culture medium: Any nutrient system for the cultivation of cells, bacteria or other organisms; usually a complex mixture of organic and inorganic nutrients.

Culture room: A dedicated room for maintaining cultures, often in a controlled environment.

Cuneate: Narrowly triangular with the acute angle toward the base; wedge-shaped; tapering toward the point of attachment.

Cunninghamella sp.: Can cause disseminated and pulmonary infections in immune compromised hosts.

Cupule: Structures that surround one or more ovules or seeds, e.g., the "cap" of an acorn. The cupule lobes may be free or united.

Cupuliform: Nearly hemispherical, cupola-shaped.

Curing: The elimination of a plasmid from its host cell. Many agents which interfere with DNA replication, e.g. ethidium bromide, can cure plasmids from either bacterial or eukaryotic cells.

Curvative or arcuate: With lamina folded transversely into an arc

Curvularia sp.: Reported to be allergenic. It may cause corneal infections, mycetoma and infections in immune compromised hosts.

Cushion, floral: A swollen floral axis on which several small flowers are borne.

Cusp: A sharp, rigid point; hence cuspidate, with the apex abruptly narrowed into a point.

Cuspidate: Ending in a rigid point. An example is a leaf that is tipped with a sharp point or spine, such as the leaves of thistles.

Cut and come again: Any plant that is cut or sheared after flowering and blooms again (i.e. Petunia, Pansy). Said of plants that continue to bloom when flowers are removed or cut.

Cut back: To prune.

Cut flowers: Flowers that are cut off the plant and used as decoration, usually indoors in a vase of water along with other flowers.

Cuticle: The continuous layer of cutin secreted by the epidermis, it prevents plant desiccation by being impervious to water and gas exchange and covers the aerial parts of the plant body, broken only by stomata and lenticels.

Cutting: A section of a plant that is removed and used for propagation. A cutting may consist of a whole or part of a stem (leafy or nonleafy), leaf, bulb or root. A root cutting consists of root only; other cuttings have no roots at the time they are made and inserted. A propagation that consists of part of the crown of a plant or of its aboveground portion and roots is called a division.

Cyathium: A type of inflorescence characteristic of some members of Euphorbiaceae; consisting of a cuplike involucre bearing unisexual flowers; staminate on its inner face, pistillate from the base.

Cyathus: A small conical or cup-shaped organ or cavity of a plant.

Cybrid: A hybrid, originating from the fusion of a cytoplast (the cytoplasm without nucleus) with a whole cell derived from a different species.

Cyclic adenosine monophosphate (cyclic AMP, cAMP): A "messenger" molecule that regulates many intracellular reactions by transducing signals from extracellular growth factors to cellular metabolic pathways.

Cyclic: Of floral organs, several borne at the same level on the axis; whorled.

Cyclodextrin: Cyclic oligomer of glucose.

Cycloheximide: A molecule that inhibits protein synthesis in eukaryotes, but not in prokaryotes. It blocks peptide bond formation by binding to the large ribosomal subunits. Synonym: actidione.

Cyclosis: The flowing or streaming of cytoplasm within a cell.

Cyclospermous: Having the embryo coiled about the central albumen, as the seeds of Caryophyllaceae.

Cymbiform: Boat-shaped.

Cyme or dichasium: A determinate, dichotomous inflorescence with the pedicels of equal length. Scorpioid cyme or rhipidium - A zigzag determinate inflorescence with branches developed on opposite sides of the rachis alternately. Compound

Cymose: Bearing a cyme; resembling or pertaining to a cyme.

Cymule: A diminutive cyme, usually few-flowered.

Cypsela: A dry, indehiscent, one-seeded fruit formed from an inferior ovary.

Cystolith: A mass of calcium carbonate concretion, occasionally silica, formed on ingrowths of modified epidermal cell walls in some plants, esp. of the Acanthaceae family.

Cytidine: The (ribo)nucleoside resulting from the combination of the base cytosine (C) and the sugar D-ribose. The corresponding deoxyribonucleoside is called deoxycytidine.

Cytidylic acid: Synonym for cytidine monophosphate (CMP), a (ribo)nucleotide containing the nucleoside cytidine. The corresponding deoxyribonucleotide is called deoxycytidine 5'-monophosphate or deoxycytidylic acid.

Cytochrome p450: A highly diversified set (more than 1500 known sequences) of heme-containing proteins. Frequently called hydroxylases, although P450 proteins can perform a wide spectrum of other reactions. In bacteria they are soluble and approximately 400 amino acids long; eukaryotic P450s are larger - about 500 amino acids. In mammals they are critical for drug metabolism, haemostasis, cholesterol biosynthesis and steroidogenesis; in plants they are involved in plant hormone synthesis, phytoalexin synthesis, flower petal pigment biosynthesis and many unknown functions. In fungi they make ergosterol and they are involved in pathogenesis. Bacterial P450s are key elements in antibiotic synthesis.

Cytochrome: A class of pigments in plant and animal cells, usually in the mitochondria. They function as electron carriers in respiration.

Cytogenetics: The biology of chromosomes and their relation to the transmission and recombination of genes.

Cytokine: A generic name for a diverse group of soluble proteins and peptides which act as humoral regulators at extremely small concentrations and which, either under normal or pathological conditions, modulate the functional activities of individual cells and tissues.

Cytokinesis: Cytoplasmic division and other changes exclusive of nuclear division that are a part of mitosis or meiosis.

Cytokinin: Plant growth regulators characterized as substances that induce cell division and cell differentiation. In tissue culture, these substances are associated with enhanced callus and shoot development. The compounds are derivatives of adenine.

Cytoplasm: The living material of the cell, exclusive of the nucleus, consisting of a complex protein matrix or gel, and where essential membranes and cellular organelles (mitochondria, plastids, etc.) reside.

Cytoplasmic genes: Genes located on DNA outside the nucleus, i.e. on plastids.

Cytoplasmic inheritance: Hereditary transmission dependent on cytoplasmic genes.

Cytoplasmic male sterility: Genetic defect due to faulty functioning of mitochondria in pollen development, preventing the formation of viable pollen. Commonly found or inducible in many plant species and exploited for some F1 hybrid seed programmes.

Cytoplasmic organelles: Discrete sub-cellular structures located in the cytoplasm of cells - mitochondria, plastids and lysosomes.

Cytosine: A nitrogenous base, more correctly described as 4-amino-2-oxy-Pynmidine, derived from amino acids and sugars and found in all living organisms. Cytosine is found in one of the nucleotides present in DNA and RNA and pairs specifically with the Purine base guanine. Substantial amounts of cytosine in DNA and RNA are found in the modified forms of 5-methylcytosine and 5-hydroxymethyl-cytosine. The affinity of these substances for guanine is similar to that of cytosine but the significance of their occurrence is uncertain. Recent evidence suggests that the regions of DNA with a large number of methylated cytosines are inactive. Thus gene activation may be brought about, at least in part, by selective demethylation.

Cytoskeleton: A network of microtubules and microfilaments involved in movement within a cell.

Cytosol: The fluid portion of the cytoplasm, i.e. the cytoplasm minus its organelles.

Cytotaxonomy: The use of chromosome studies (i.e. number, structure, and behaviour) in taxonomic work. Chromosome number is probably the most frequently quoted feature of the karyotype used by taxonomists. Chromosome counts are usually made on sporophytic tissue at mitosis and are therefore the diploid number (2n). When dealing with a polyploid series, the base number (i.e. the number of chromosomes present in the original haploid genome) may be given. The position of the centromere is a reliable feature of chromosome structure and consequently makes a good taxonomic character. More detailed studies of meiotic behaviour can reveal, for example, the heterozygosity of some inversions. Such a feature may be consistent for a particular taxon, thus providing additional taxonomic evidence. Cytological data is sometimes thought to be of special significance, and may be ascribed more weight than other taxonomic evidence.

Cytotype: A maternally inherited cellular condition in Drosophila that regulates the activity of transposable P elements.

D

DAB (domain antibody): Antibodies with only one (instead of two) protein chain derived from only one of the two domains of the normal antibody structure. Exploits the finding that for some antibodies, half of the molecule binds to its target antigen almost as well as the whole molecule. The major advantage of dAbs over other antibodies is that they can be cloned and expressed into bacteria, so that large numbers of antibodies can be generated and screened in parallel.

Dalton (Da): A unit of atomic mass roughly equivalent to the mass of a hydrogen atom. Used as to express molecular weight, which for biological macromolecules is usually in the range kilo- (kDa) to megaDaltons (MDa).

Damping off: A common name for a soil disease caused by a number of different organisms. It causes seeds to rot or seedlings to collapse. The best ways to prevent this is by planting in sterile soil, treating seeds with a fungicide, or soaking the soil with a fungicide; also avoid over-watering and planting warm-season vegetables in cold soil.

Dark reactions: The sequence of light-independent reactions that utilize the energy (in the form of ATP) and reducing power (in the form of NADPH), produced during the light reactions of photosynthesis, to reduce carbon dioxide. In eukaryotes, this process usually occurs in the chloroplast stroma and it can take one of two forms, depending on whether the subject is a C3 or a C4 plant . The details of the fixation of carbon dioxide differ in the two types of plants but the end result in both cases is the production of carbohydrates via the Calvin cycle.

Darwinian cloning: Selection of a clone from a large number of essentially random starting points, rather than isolating a natural gene or making a carefully designed artificial one. Molecules which are more similar to those needed are selected, mutated to generate new variants, and re-selected. The cycle proceeds until the required molecule is found. The advantage of the system is that the selection is from a vast number of possibilities.

DATP: Abbreviation for deoxyadenosine 5'-triphosphate. dATP is required for DNA synthesis since it is a direct precursor molecule.

Day-neutral plant: A plant that is not dependent on specific day lengths for the initiation offlowering.

DCTP: Abbreviation for deoxycytidine 5'-triphosphate. DCTP is required for DNA synthesis since it is a direct precursor molecule.

DDNTP: Abbreviation for di-deoxynucleotide.

De differentiation: The process, in response to wounding and in tissue cultures, by which plant cells can become unspecialized and start to proliferate by cell division to form a mass of undifferentiated cells (or callus) which, in response to appropriate stimuli, may later differentiate again to form either the same cell type or a different one.

De ionized water: Water from which most salts have been removed - with varying degrees of efficiency - by ion exchange.

Deadheading: The removal of dead flowers or flower heads.

Dealkalization: The removal of exchangeable sodium from the soil by a process of leaching or chemically treating the soil.

Deamination: The removal of an amino group from a compound. Breakdown of amino acids is by oxidative deamination. Glutamate, which is formed from many amino acids by transamination, is deaminated by the enzyme glutamate dehydrogenase, yielding á-ketoglutarate, ammonium ions, and reduced NAD or NADP.

Death phase: The final growth phase of cell culture, during which nutrients have been depleted and cell number decreases.

Decayed organic matter: Decomposed plant or animal matter, used to improve the soil.

Deceleration phase: The phase of declining growth rate, following the linear phase and preceding the stationary phase in most batch-suspension cultures.

Deciduous: Losing its leaves annually at the end of the growing season· semi-deciduous plants lose only some leaves.

Declinate: Bent or curved downward or forward.

Decomposer: Organism e.g., bacterium, fungus that breaks down organic material to forms capable of being recycled.

Decompound: Divided into a number of compound divisions, such as a leaf divided into leaflets or a cluster of flowers divided into numerous branchlets.

Decumbent: Reclining with the tips ascending; a plant that has its base lying on the ground and a stem that grows upward.

Decurrent: Extending downward, applied usually to leaves in which the blade is apparently prolonged downward as two wings along the petiole or along the stem.

Decurved: Curved downwards.

Dedifferentiation: The loss of the specialized features and reversal to a meristematic state of a differentiated cell. Dedifferentiation often occurs immediately prior to further reorganizational changes as in the production of a secondary meristem. The process may also be brought about by wounding or stimulation by growth substances. It is thought to involve the removal of inhibitors that normally prevent the expression of the complete genetic complement.

Deep percolation: The downward movement of water into the soil beyond the reach of a plant's roots.

Deep soil: Soil that is deeper than 40 inches and continues until it becomes rock or another strongly contrasting material.

Defective virus: A virus that, by itself, is unable to reproduce when infecting its host cell, but that can grow in the presence of another virus. This other virus provides the necessary molecular machinery that the first virus lacks.

Deficiency: Lack of adequate supply of nutritional, enzymatic, or environmental requirements, so that development, growth or physiological functions are affected.

Defined: 1. Fixed conditions of medium, environment and protocol for growth. 2. Precisely known and stated elements of a tissue culture medium.

Definite: Of a constant number; of stamens, twice as many as the petals or sepals, or less; of an inflorescence, ending in a flower or an aborted floral bud.

Deflexed: Bent downwards towards the base of the stem.

Deflocculate: To break up the soil into individual particles.

Defluent: Running downward; decurrent.

Defluvium: A falling off, such as the bark of a tree, from disease.

Defoliate: To deprive of foliage; to cut or pick the leaves of a plant, especially too early.

Defoliation: The loss of leaves (for instance, from the attack of insects); specifically, the dropping of leaves in autumn.

Defoliator: That which defoliates or strips of growth; specifically, in entomology, any insect that destroys the foliage of trees.

Deforest: To deprive of forests; to cut down and clear away forests.

Deforestation: The act of cutting down and clearing away forests of a region or stretch of land.

Degeneracy: The specification of one amino acid by more than one codon. It arises from the inevitable redundancy resulting from the 64 possible codons encoding only 20 amino acids.

Degeneration: 1. Changes in cells, tissues or organs due to disease. 2. The reduction in size or complete loss of organs during evolution.

Degradation: The change of one kind of soil to a more highly leached soil.

Dehiscence: Any process used to expel spores, microgametes, or seeds into the environment. To be more precise, dehisence refers to the steps which the plant performs to expose the seeds, etc. to the environment. Dispersal is the mechanism by which they are actually distributed in the environment. So, for example, moss spores may dehisce by the opening of the operculum and retraction of the peristomal teeth. They are then dispersed by wind. However some plants, like Sphagnum moss, may explosively dehisce and so get involved in dispersal as well.

Dehydrogenase: An enzyme that catalyses the removal of hydrogen atoms in biological reactions.

Dehydrogenation: A chemical reaction in which hydrogen is removed from a compound.

Deletion: A mutation involving the removal of one or more base pairs in a DNA sequence. Large deletions are sometimes microscopically visible in karyotype analyses.

Deliberate release: In a biotechnology context, the intentional release of genetically modified organisms.

Deliquescent: Softening and wasting away.

Deltoid: Triangular and attached to the stem at the wide end, such as a deltoid leaf.

Deme: A group of organisms in the same taxon.

Demineralize: To remove the mineral content (salts, ions) from a substance, especially water. Removal methods include distillation, electrodialysis and ion exchange.

Denature: To disrupt the normal in vivo conformation of a nucleic acid or (more usually) a protein by physical or chemical means, usually accompanied by the loss of activity.

Denatured DNA: Double-stranded DNA that has been converted to single strands by breaking the hydrogen bonds linking complementary nucleotide pairs. Often reversible. Usually achieved by heating.

Denatured protein: Altering the in vivo conformation of a protein by heat or salt treatment, thereby destroying its biological activity. Unlike denatured DNA, denatured proteins are seldom able to be renatured.

Denaturing gradient gel electrophoresis (DGGE): An electrophoresis method for separating similar sized DNA fragments on the basis of their sequence, by applying across the gel a gradient of increasingly denaturing conditions (usually by increasing the concentration of a denaturing chemical, such as formamide or urea). As the double-stranded molecules denature into a partially and eventually a fully single-stranded state, their electrophoretic mobility changes.

Dendriform, dendroid: Tree-like, mainly of branching and form but not in size.

Dendrimer: A polymer that repeatedly branches until stopped by the physical constraint of having formed a complete, hollow sphere. These structures possess sites on their exterior surface to which DNA fragments can be attached, and are thus useful as carriers of DNA for transgenesis.

Dendrochronology: the science of dating events and variations in environment in former periods by comparative study of growth rings in trees and aged wood.

Dendroid: Tree-like; dendriform; arborescent; branching like a tree.

Denitrification: The process by which bacterial action reduces nitrates in the soil to ammonia or free nitrogen that can escape into the air.

Denshire: To improve land by burning piles of earth, turf, and stubble and then spreading the ashes over the ground as compost. Also densher.

Density gradient centrifugation: High-speed centrifugation in which molecules are separated on the basis of their different densities using a concentration gradient of caesium chloride or sucrose. The density gradient may either be formed before centrifugation by mixing two solutions of different density (as in sucrose density gradients) or it can be formed by the process of centrifugation itself (as in CsCl and Cs2SO4 density gradients).

Dentate: Margins with rounded or sharp, coarse teeth that point outwards at right angles to midrib or midvein, cut 1/16 to 1/8 distance to midrib or midvein.

Denticidal capsule: One that dehisces apically, leaving a ring of teeth, as in Cerastium

Denticle: A small tooth or toothlike projecting point.

Denticulate: Diminutive of dentate, cut to 1/16 distance to midrib or midvein

Deoxythymidine: Strictly correct but rarely used synonym for thymidine.

Depauperate: Reduced in size, as if starved; impoverished, poor in composition (eg. few species, forms etc).

Depressed: Pressed closely to axis downward with angle of divergence of 166-180°

Derepression: The process of "turning on" the expression of a gene or set of genes whose expression has been repressed (turned off), usually by the displacement of a repressor from a promoter, since, when attached to the DNA, the repressor prevents transcription.

Derivative: 1. Resulting from or derived from. 2. Term used to identify a variant during meristematic cell division.

Desalinization: The removal of salts from saline soil.

Descending: Directed downward with an angle of divergence of 136-165°

Desert soil: Light-colored surface soil that develops in warm- to cool-arid climates.

Desiccant: Any compound used to remove moisture or water.

Desilting area: An area used to remove sediment from flowing water.

Desorption: The removal of absorbed materials from surfaces.

Desoxyribonucleic acid: Obsolete spelling of deoxyribonucleic acid.

Detailed soil map: A map showing the different classifications of soil in a designated area.

Detergent: Substance which lowers the surface tension of a solution, improving its cleaning properties.

Determinate growth: Growth determined and limited in time, with a bud or flower terminating the growth of the main axis. Once established, it is usually irreversible. Opposite: indeterminate growth.

Determination: Process by which undifferentiated cells in an embryo become committed to develop into specific cell types, such as neurons, fibroblasts or muscle cells.

Development: The sum total of events that contribute to the progressive elaboration of an organism. The two major aspects of development are growth and differentiation.

Deviation: 1. An alteration from the typical form, function or behaviour. Mutation or stress are the common reasons behind deviation. 2. A statistical term describing the difference between an actual observation and the mean of all observations.

Dextrin: An intermediate polysaccharide compound resulting from the hydrolysis of starch to maltose by amylase enzymes.

Dextrorse: Twining spirally upward around an axis, as in the hop or morning glory.

DGTP: Abbreviation for deoxyguanosine 5'-triphosphate. dGTP is required for DNA synthesis since it is a direct precursor molecule.

Di deoxynucleotide (ddNTP,didN): A synthetic deoxynucleotide that lacks a 3'-hydroxyl group, and is thus unable to form the 3'-5' phosphodiester bond necessary for chain elongation. Used as strand terminators in the Sanger DNA sequencing reaction and in the treatment of some viral diseases.

Diadelphous: Having stamens united in two sets by their filaments. In pea and bean flowers, nine out of ten stamens are usually united while one is by itself.

Diageotropism: A turning of the roots, branches, or rhizomes in a direction at right angles to that of gravity.

Diagnostic procedure: A test or assay used to determine the presence of a specific substance, organism or nucleic acid sequence alteration, etc.

Diaheliotropic: The turning of the upper surfaces of a plant's leaves toward the sunlight; pertaining to diaheliotropism.

Diakinesis: A stage of meiosis at the end of prophase I, in which the contraction of the chromosomes is almost at a maximum, pairing configurations are well defined, the nucleolus normally disappears and the nuclear envelope is disrupted.

Diallel, complete or full: A mating design and subsequent progeny test resulting from the crossing of 'n' parents in all possible 'n2' combinations including selfs and reciprocals. (Because of severe inbreeding depression in the selfs, these are often skipped and the test still called a "full" diallel.)

Diallel, incomplete or partial: A partial sampling any individual family or type of family may be omitted. In either the complete or incomplete diallel, identities of both seed and pollen parents are maintained for each family.

Dialycarpous: Bearing fruit composed of separate carpels. Also apocarpous.

Dialypetalous: Plants that have the corolla of the flower divided into distinct petals; also polypetalous.

Dialyphyllous: Made of separate leaves. Applied to a calyx formed from several sepals or a corolla formed by several petals.

Dialysepalous: Having a calyx made of separate sepals; polysepalous.

Dialysis: A biochemical technique by which large molecules such as proteins in solution are separated from smaller species such as salts. The technique is based on the properties of certain membrane structures, which selectively only allow the passage of the smaller molecules. A frequently used method for the purification of proteins.

Diatomaceous earth: A material made from the skeletal remains of diatoms (single-celled algae). It is used as an insecticide. The sharp edges of the diatoms wound soft-bodied insects like ants and aphids. It is ordinarily used as a barrier but can be applied to leaves. It is most effective in hot, dry weather.

Diazinon: A man-made insecticide widely used against many soil pests, especially in lawns; however, it is very toxic to birds.

Diazotroph: An organism that can fix atmospheric nitrogen.

Dibble: A pointed tool used to make holes in the ground for seeds and seedlings.

Dicentric chromosome: A chromosome having two active centromeres.

Dichasial: Pertaining to or resembling a dichasium.

Dichasium: A cymose inflorescence with opposite branching below the flower which terminates each axis.

Dichlamydeous: With perianth composed of distinct calyx and corolla.

Dichogamous: With maturation of stamens or anther and carpels or stigma at different times

Dichogamy: The condition in which the male and the female reproductive organs of a flower (or certain hermaphroditic animals) mature at different times, thereby making self-fertilization improbable or impossible.

Dichotomous branching: A type of branching in which the tip divides into two more-or-less equal apices; by repetition of this type of branching in various planes distinctive shoot systems may be produced.

Dichotomous: Having or consisting of a pair or pairs; paired.

Dichotomy: A mode of branching by repeated forking, as is shown in some stems, the veining of some leaves, etc.

Diclesium (Calyx): Achene or nut surrounded by a persistent calyx, as in Mirabalis.

Diclinous: Plant with imperfect flowers; stamens and carpels in separate flowers either monoecious or dioecious.

Dicoccous: Formed of two one-seeded carpels.

Dicots: Flowering plants whose embryo has two cotyledons.

Dicotyledon (dicot): A plant with two cotyledons. One of the two major classes of flowering plants (along with the monocotyledons). Examples include many crop plants (potato, pea, beans), ornamentals (rose, ivy) and timber trees (oak, beech, lime).

Dicotyledon leaf: Defined by the presence of a vascular cambium (which may or may not be active), as well as usually reticulate venation.

Dicotyledoneae: One of two major classes of plants, the other being Monocotyledonae. Dicotyledons have two seed leaves; the mature leaves branching with net-like veins and the flowers have five, or sometimes, four parts. They include deciduous trees, broadleaf evergreens, flowering perennials, most vegetables, and weeds.

Dicotyledonous: With two cotyledons.

Dictyogen: A monocotyledon having net-veined leaves.

Dictyogenous: Having the character of a dictyogen; having the general character of an endogen, but with netted leaf-veins.

Dictyosome: An organelle consisting of disc-shaped, often branching hollow tubules that function in accumulating and packaging substances used In the synthesis of materials by the cell.

Dictyostele: A complex stele with large overlapping leaf-gaps, in section composed of many meristeles.

Didymous: Twinned, the two parts similar and attached by a short portion of their inner surface.

Didynamy: The condition of being in two unequal pairs, such as stamens.

Dieback: The death of tips or shoots due to damage or disease.

Differential centrifugation: A method for separating sub-cellular particles according to their sedimentation coefficients, which are roughly proportional to their size. Cell extracts are subjected to a succession of centrifuge runs at progressively faster rotation speeds. Large particles, such as nuclei or mitochondria, will be precipitated at relatively slow speeds; higher G forces will be required to sediment small particles, such as ribosomes.

Differential display: A method to identify mRNAs which are present at different levels in different tissues, or in response to specific treatments. The mRNAs are converted to cDNA, and a defined proportion of these are amplified by the polymerase chain reaction, and separated by electrophoresis.

Differentially permeable: Referring to a membrane, through which different substances diffuse at different rates. Some substances may be unable to diffuse through such a membrane, usually because they are too large to fit through the pores of the membrane.

Differentiation: A process as a result of which unspecialized cells develop structures and functions characteristic of a particular type of cell, typically during the process of development from one cell to many cells, accompanied by a modification of the new cells for the performance of particular functions. The process is generally irreversible in vivo in higher organisms. In tissue culture, the term is used to describe the formation of different cell types.

Diffusion: The random movement of molecules or particles from a region of higher concentration to a region of lower concentration, ultimately resulting in unifolm distribution.

Digestion: An enzymecontrolled conversion of complex. Usually insoluble substances to simpler, usually soluble substances.

Digestive Glands: Enzyme-secreting glands found mostly on leaves of carnivorous and insectivorous plants.

Digitate: Having deep radiating divisions, like fingers, arising from one point; especially applied to compound leaflets that grow from the top of the leaf stem.

Dihaploid: An individual which arises from a doubled haploid.

Dihybrid cross: A cross involving two different pairs of genes and heterozygous parents.

Dihybrid: An individual that is heterozygous for two pairs of alleles; the progeny of a cross between homozygous parents differing at two loci.

Dikaryotic: Having a pair of nuclei in each cell or a type of the mycelium in club fungi.

Dilated: Widened; expanded.

Dimer: 1. A molecule formed by the covalent combination of two monomers, generally accompanied by elimination of water. 2. The reversible association of two similar (or nearly similar) molecules. The active form of many enzymes is as a dimer between two non-active monomeric subunits.

Dimerous: Having two parts in each whorl of flowers.

Dimethyl sulphoxide (DMSO): A highly hygroscopic liquid and powerful solvent with little odour, colour or toxicity when pure. It is employed in small quantities to dissolve organic substances in tissue culture media preparation and has uses as a cryoprotectant and in promoting the passage of chemicals through skin.

Dimidiate: Having one part so much smaller than the other as to appear to be missing, or almost so.

Dimorphic: Having two different sizes and/or shapes within the same species.

Dimorphism: The existence of two distinctly different types of individuals within a species. An obvious example is sexual dimorphism in mammals.

Dimorphous: Existing in two forms of leaf or flower or other part on the same plant or on plants of the same species.

Dinoflagellate: Unicellular aquatic organisms, motile and heterotrophic, parasitic, or photosynthetic.

Dinucleotide: A nucleotide dimer.

Dioeciopolygamous: Polygamous with a tendency to dioeciousness, or to the prevalence of flowers of one sex on individual plants, such as a plant with mostly female flowers.

Dioecious: Having unisexual flowers or cones. With the male flowers or cones confined to certain plants and the female flowers or cones of the same species confined to other different plants.

Diphyllous: Having two leaves.

Diplecolobal: With incumbent cotyledons folded two or more times

Diplecolobous: Of cotyledons in a seed, twice folded transversely.

Diploid: A nucleus is diploid if it contains two copies of each non-redundant gene. In Fungi, it is necessary to distinguish between diploid nuclei and diploid cells. A hypha may contain several haploid nuclei (either identical or from different individuals). Technically, the cell is diploid or polyploid. However, there may be no diploid nuclei.

Diplolepidous: Of moss sporophytes, having an inner (endostome) and outer (exostome) row of plates forming the peristome teeth.

Diplonema: Stage in prophase I of meiosis following the pachytene stage, but preceding diakinesis, in which one pair of sister chromatids begin to separate from the other pair.

Diplostemonous: With stamens in two whorls, outer opposite the sepals, inner opposite petals

Diplotegia: A seed capsule that develops from the ovary in some plants such as the iris, in which the ovary in situated below the floral envelopes.

Dipterous: Having two wing-like appendages.

Direct embryogenesis: The formation in culture, on the surface of zygotic or somatic embryos or on explant tissues (leaf section, root tip, etc.), of embryoids without an intervening callus phase. Opposite: indirect embryogenesis.

Direct organogenesis: Formation of organs directly on the surface of cultured intact explants. The process does not involve callus formation. Opposite: indirect organogenesis.

Directed amplification of minisatellite DNA (DAMD): A polymerase chain reaction technique used for obtaining molecular markers in the region of minisatellites. To target these regions, one of the primers is directed to a VNTR core sequence.

Directed mutagenesis: The generation of changes in the nucleotide sequence of a cloned gene by one of several procedures. Undertaken to explore the relationship between nucleotide sequence and gene function, and to modify gene products. Synonym: in vitro mutagenesis.

Directional cloning: The technique by which a vector and a DNA insert are both digested with two different restriction endonucleases to create non-complementary sticky ends at either end of both molecules, so favouring the insert to be ligated into the vector in a specific orientation, while also preventing the vector from re-circularizing.

Disarm: The deletion from a plasmid or virus of genes that are pathogenic.

Disarticulate: To separate at a joint or articulation.

Disboscation: The act of disforesting; the act of converting woodland into farmland.

Disbud: To remove buds or shoots; to remove unnecessary buds of a tree, vine or flowering plant to encourage production of high-quality flowers or fruits. Also called pinching back or stopping.

Disc: An elevated region of the labellum (of an Orchid), normally in the midlobe, distinguished by color and/or accessory features such as calli, keels, or lamellae.

Disc flowers: The radially symmetrical flowers of the head in Compositae, as distinguished from the ligulate ray flowers.

Discoid: 1. Pertaining to the button-like center of flowers belonging to the Compositae family (i.e. daisy, sunflower, etc.). 2. Having only the central part and not the outer petal-like parts of the flower, as in Tansy.

Discoidal: A single large spot of color in the center of another

Discolorous: Of different coulour, eg. when two sides of the leaf are different colours, also variegated.

Discontinuous variation: Variation where individuals can be classified as belonging to one of a set of discrete, non-overlapping classes. Generated by simple genetic control of a trait (one or a small number of genes, each of large effect) and involving minimal non-genetic effect. Characters showing discontinuous variation are referred to as qualitative. Opposite: continuous variation.

Discontinuous: Basal and lateral, basal and terminal, or lateral and terminal; not continuous.

Discordant: Members of a pair showing different, rather than similar, characteristics.

Discrete: Clearly seperate from each other, not united.

Disease free: A plant or animal certified through specific tests as being free of specified pathogens. Should be interpreted to mean "free from any known disease" as "new" diseases may yet be discovered to be present.

Disease indexing: Disease-indexed organisms have been assayed for the presence of known diseases according to standard testing procedures.

Disease resistance: The genetically determined ability to prevent the reproduction of a pathogen, thereby remaining healthy. Some resistances operate by pathogen exclusion, some by preventing pathogen spread, and some by tolerating pathogen toxin.

Dish garden: A collection of plants, generally small ornamentals, grown together in one container.

Disinfection: Attempted elimination by chemical means of internal micro-organisms (particularly pathogens) from a culture or sample; rarely attained.

Disinfest: The removing of surface contaminants from a plant surface.

Disinfestation: The elimination or inhibition of the activity of surface-adhering micro-organisms and removal of insects.

Disjunction: Separation of homologous chromosomes during anaphase I of meiosis, or of sister chromatids during anaphase of mitosis and anaphase II of meiosis.

Disk flower: In the family Compositae, one of the miniature, tubular components of the central area of the flower head.

Disk: 1. Any flattened circular organ of a plant, such as the adhesive ends of the tendrils of the Virginia creeper. 2. The button-like center of the flowers of plants such as sunflowers and asters. 3. A fleshy enlargement of the receptacle in some flowers.

Disomy: The presence of a pair of a specific homologous chromosomes. This is the norm for diploids.

Dispense: The transfer of a measured volume of a solution.

Dispermous: Having two seeds.

Dispersal: To disperse to dispel or scatter; in plants dispersal refers to mechanism of dispersing reproductive propagules like seeds or pollen.

Dispersion of soil: The breaking up of soil into very fine particles and its suspension in water.

Disrupter gene: Used to enforce the sterility of seed saved from a genetically engineered crop.

Dissected: Deeply divided or cut into many segments.

Dissecting microscope: A microscope with a magnifying power of about 50x, used as an aid in the manipulation of small objects, e.g. excision of embryos from young zygotes.

Dissection: Separation of a tissue by cutting into components, for analysis or observation.

Dissepiment: A partition within an organ of a plant (i.e. the membrane that separates sections of the orange and other citrus fruits).

Dissilient: Bursting open with some force, as the pod or capsule of Impatiens.

Distal: Farthest away from the point of attachment or origin.

Distichous: Two-ranked; in the case of plants with alternate leaves, the arrangement is such that 1st is directly below the 3rd.

Distillation: The process of heating a mixture to separate the more volatile from the less volatile parts, and then condensing fractions of the resulting vapour so as to produce a more nearly pure or refined substance.

Distinct: With like parts or organs unjoined and separate from one another.

Disulphide bridge: A chemical bond between pairs of sulphur atoms that stabilizes the three-dimensional structure of proteins, and hence the protein's normal function. These form particularly readily between cysteine residues in the same or different peptide molecules. Synonym: disulphide bond.

Ditype: In fungi, a tetrad that contains two kinds of meiotic products (spores), e.g. 2AB and 2ab.

Diuretic: A substance tending to increase the flow of urine.

Diurnal: An event that occurs repetitively on a daily basis, generally during daylight hours.

Divaricate: Spreading at a very wide angle, extremely divergent.

Divarication: The act of branching off or diverging; separation into branches.

Divergent, patent, or divaricate: More or less horizontally spreading with angle of divergence of 15° or less up or down from the horizontal.

Diverticulate: Having short offshoots approximately at right angles to axis.

Divided: Referring to the blade of an appendage when it is cut into distinct divisions to, or almost to, the midvein.

Division: A method of propagation by which a plant clump is lifted and divided into separate pieces, which include roots and a growing point, during dormancy. The pieces are immediately replanted.

Dizygotic twins: Two-egg twins, i.e. a pair of individuals that shared the same uterus at the same time, but which arose from separate and independent fertilization of two ova.

DNA: Abbreviation for deoxyribonucleic acid, former spelling desoxyribonucleic acid. A long chain polymer of deoxyribonucleotides. DNA constitutes the genetic material of most known organisms and organelles, and usually is in the form of a double helix, although some viral genomes consist of a single strand of DNA, and others of a single- or a double-stranded RNA. DNA amplification Many-fold multiplication of a particular DNA sequence either in vivo in a plasmid, phage or other vector; or in vitro using, most commonly, the polymerase chain reaction.

DNA amplification fingerprinting (DAF): A arbitrarily primed polymerase chain reaction technique for obtaining molecular markers using very short (5-8 bp) primers.

DNA construct: A chimeric DNA molecule, carrying all the genetic information necessary for its transgenic expression in a host cell.

DNA delivery system: A generic term for any procedure that transports DNA into a recipient cell.

DNA diagnostics: The use of DNA polymorphisms to detect the presence of a specific sequence, which could indicate the presence of a contaminant, of a pathogen, or of a particular allele at a target gene. Most commonly utilises the polymerase chain reaction.

DNA fingerprinting: The derivation of unique patterns of DNA fragments obtained using a number of marker techniques; historically these were RFLPs, but latterly they are generally polymerase chain reaction based. Synonym: genetic fingerprinting.

DNA helicase: An enzyme that catalyses the unwinding of the complementary strands of a DNA double helix. Synonym: gyrase.

DNA hybridization: The annealing of two single-stranded DNA molecules, possibly of different origin, to form a partial or complete double helix. The degree of hybridization varies with the extent of complementarity between the two molecules, and this is exploited to test for the presence of a specific nucleotide sequence in a DNA sample.

DNA ligase: An enzyme that catalyses a reaction to link two separate DNA molecules via the formation of a phosphodiester bond between the 3'-hydroxyl end of one and the 5'-phosphate of the other. Its natural role lies in DNA repair and replication. An essential tool in recombinant DNA technology, as it enables the incorporation of foreign DNA into vectors.

DNA polymorphism: The existence of two or more alteRNAtive alleles at a DNA-based marker locus.

DNA primase: An enzyme that catalyses the synthesis of the short strands of RNA that initiate the synthesis of DNA strands.

DNA repair: A variety of mechanisms that repair errors (e.g. the incorporation of a non-complementary nucleotide) that occur naturally during DNA replication.

DNA replication: The process whereby DNA copies itself, under the action of and control of DNA polymerase.

DNA sequencing: Procedures for determining the nucleotide sequence of a DNA fragment. Two common methods available: 1. The Maxam Gilbert technique, which uses chemicals to cleave DNA into fragments at specific bases; or, most commonly. 2. the Sanger technique (also called the di-deoxy or chain-terminating method) which uses DNA polymerase to make new DNA chains, in the presence of di-deoxynucleotides (chain terminators) to stop the chain randomly as it grows. In both cases, the DNA fragments are separated according to length by polyacrylamide gel electrophoresis, enabling the sequence to be read directly from the gel. The procedure has become increasingly automated and large-scale in recent years.

DNA topo-isomerase: An enzyme that catalyses the introduction or removal of supercoils in DNA. Synonym: topo-isomerase.

DNA vaccine: A vaccine generated by the injection of specific DNA fragments to stimulate an immune response.

DNAse: Abbreviation for deoxyribonuclease. Any enzyme that catalyses the cleavage of DNA phosphodiester bonds. DNAse I is a digestive endonuclease secreted by the pancreas, that degrades DNA into shorter fragments. Many other endonucleases and exonucleases are involved in DNA repair and replication. Synonym: DNAase.

Dodecamerous: Having the whorls of the flower (petals, sepals, etc.) in twelves. Also written 12- merous.

Dolabriform: Having the form of an axhead.

Dolly: The first mammal (a sheep) to be created (via nuclear transfer) by the cloning of an adult cell (from the mammary tissue of a ewe). This showed that the process of differentiation into adult tissue is not, as previously thought, irreversible.

Dolomitic limestone: A fertilizer that contains magnesium.

Domain: A portion of a protein or DNA molecule that has a discrete function or conformation. At the protein level, can be as small as a few amino acid residues or as large as half of the entire protein.

Domatia: Small structures on the lower surface of a leaf in some woody dicotyledons, usually consisting of depressions, partly enclosed by leaf tissue or hairs, located in the axils of the primary veins. sing. domatium.

Dominance, partial: The incomplete masking of the action of one allele by another. If an individual with red flowers is crossed with an individual with white flowers and all progeny have pink flowers, then the allele for red pigment is partially dominant over the allele for white flowers.

Dominance: In classical Mendelian genetics, the masking of the action of one allele by another. If an individual with red flowers is crossed with an individual with white flowers and all progeny have red flowers, then the allele for red pigment is fully dominant over the allele for white flowers.

Dominant marker selection: Selection of cells via a gene encoding a product that enables only the cells that carry the gene to grow under particular conditions. For example, plant and animal cells that express the introduced neor gene are resistant to neomycin and analogous antibiotics, while cells that do not carry neor are killed.

Dominant selectable marker: A gene that allows the host cell to survive under conditions where it would otherwise die. Synonym: positive selectable marker.

Dominant: 1. Of alleles, one whose effect with respect to a particular trait is the same in heterozygotes as in homozygotes. The opposite is recessive. 2. Of an individual animal, one that is allowed priority in access to food, mates, etc., by others of its species because of its success in previous aggressive encounters. 3. Of an animal or plant species, the most conspicuously abundant and characteristic in a particular location or environment.

Dommatia: Pits or pockets, sometimes with tufts of hair in the axils of nerves on the lower surfaces of leaves.

Donor junction site: The junction between the 5' end of an exon and the 3' end of an intron.

Dormancy: A period in the life of an animal (hibernation and aestivation) or plant during which growth slows or completely ceases. Evolved to allow survival of adverse environmental conditions. Annual plants survive the winter as dormant seeds, while many perennial plants survive as dormant tubers, rhizomes, or bulbs. Premature breaking of seed dormancy post harvest can be a major problem for maintaining nutritional and/or functional quality, while difficulties in breaking dormancy will lead to poor germination of the crop.

Dormant spray: Any type of pesticide applied to dormant, usually leafless, plants to control a number of insects and disease.

Dorsal: Pertaining to the surface most distant from the axis; back of an outer face of organ; lower side of leaf; abaxial. Dorsal side - back or abaxial side, or the lower side of a perianth part.

Dorsifixed: Attached at the back of a plant or plant part, such as the anthers of lilies.

Dorsilaminar: On dorsal side of blade.

Dorsi-ventral: Of leaves where the mesophyll is differentiated into an upper and lower layer (palisade and spongy mesophyll), contrasting with iso-bilateral.

Dosage compensation: A regulatory mechanism for sex-linked genes, to allow equivalent levels of gene expression from (in mammals) XY or XX genotypes, even though the gene copy number in XX is double that in XY.

Dotted: The color disposed in very small round spots.

Double: This is used to describe flowers which have more than one row of petals; this may be because the stamens and sometimes the pistils are transformed into petals or sometimes the petals split to form several more. Semi-double flowers are those which have only partially changed. Completely double flowers have lost their reproductive organs and are therefore unable to produce seeds. These flowers usually stay fresh longer than single flowers when cut. Double flowers are seen in the wild once in a while, but are mostly developed varieties.

Double crossing-over: The formation of two chiasmata within a chromosome arm, leading to the generation of a double recombinant gamete with respect to genes located within the segment defined by the two genes concerned.

Double fertilization: A process, unique to flowering plants, in which two male nuclei, which have travelled down the pollen tube, separately fuse with different female nuclei in the embryo sac. The first male nucleus fuses with the egg cell to form the zygote; the second male nucleus fuses with the two polar nuclei to form a triploid nucleus that develops into the endosperm.

Double fusion: The more or less simultaneous union of one sperm and egg (forming a zygote) and union of another sperm and central cell nuclei (forming a primary endosperm nucleus) that occur in the megagametophyte of flowering plants.

Double helix: Describes the coiling of the two strands of the double-stranded DNA molecule, resembling a spiral staircase in which the base pairs form the steps and the sugar-phosphate backbones form the rails on each side. One strand runs 3'-5', while the complementary one runs 5'-3'

Double integument: The two outermost layers of an ovule in angiosperms, one of which will differentiate into the seed coat. Double recessive An organism homozygous for a recessive allele at each of two loci.

Doubly serrate: Alternating large and small teeth.

Down promoter mutation: A mutation that decreases the frequency of initiation of transcription. This leads to a fall in the level of mRNA compared to the wild type state.

Down-regulate: To induce genetically a reduction in the level of a gene's expression.

Downstream processing A general term for biotechnological processes which follow the biology, i.e. fermentation of a micro-organism or growth of a plant. Particularly relevant to fermentation processes, which produce a large quantity of a dilute mixture of substances, products and micro-organisms. These must be separated, and the product concentrated, purified and converted into a useful form.

Downstream: 1. With respect to DNA, the nucleotides that lie in the 3' direction from the point of reference, which is frequently the site at which transcription is initiated. This is generally designated +1, with downstream nucleotides numbered +2, +10 etc. 2. In chemical engineering, those phases of a manufacturing process that follow the biotransformation stage. Usually refers to the recovery and purification of the product of a fermentation process.

Drain: To remove water from the soil by artificial means, such as drainage ditches, buried perforated plastic pipes, or a gravel sump. Also to improve heavy clay soils with sand or organic matter.

Drainage: 1. The removal of excessive water from the ground. 2. Water moving down in the soil. 3. A system of conduits, channels or passages by means of which something is drained.

Drain-well: A pit sunk through an impenetrable layer of earth or stone to a porous layer, to draw off water.

Drepaniform: Sickle-shaped.

Dreschlera sp.: Conidia dimensions 40-120 x 17-28 microns. Found on grasses, grains and decaying food. It can occasionally cause a corneal infection of the eye.

Dried blood: An organic fertilizer that leaves an acid reaction.

Dried flowers: Blossoms that have been dehydrated but have retained a natural shape and color.

Drift: Soil material deposited by geological process in one place after having been removed from another place.

Drill: 1. A machine used for planting seeds, as of grasses, wheat, oats, corn, etc. by dropping them in rows and covering them with earth. 2. A row of seeds deposited in the earth; the trench or channel in which the seeds are deposited. 3. To sow seeds in rows (i.e. the field was drilled, not sown broadcast).

Drip irrigation: A system of watering by which moisture running through a pоrous hose is slowly released through tiny holes, or emitters, to the root zone of plants.

Drosophila melanogaster: The fruit fly, used for many years as a model for eukaryotic genetics. Of the nearly 300 disease-causing genes in the human genome, more than half have an analogous gene in the Drosophila genome.

Drought-tolerant plants: Plants that can survive periods of time with little or no water.

Drowning: A surplus of water that drowns plant roots by eliminating oxygen from the soil.

Drug delivery: Method by which a drug is delivered to its site of action. For traditional drugs this is another name for formulation. However, biotechnology has allowed the development of a range of new therapeutic-agent delivery systems, such as liposomes and other encapsulation techniques, and a range of mechanisms that target a therapeutic agent to a particular cell or tissue.

Drupaceous: Pertaining to or producing drupes.

Drupe: A succulent fruit formed from one carpel, having the seed(s) enclosed in an inner stony layer of the fruit wall.

Drupecetum: An aggregation of drupelets, as in rubus

Drupelet: A small drupe, especially as applied to the individual components of aggregate fruits such as raspberries and blackberries, which consist of numerous seeds, each surrounded by its own fleshy layer. Also drupel.

Druse compound: Calcium oxalate crystal of more or less spherical shape, in which the many component crystals protrude from the surface giving a star-shaped appearance.

Druxy: Pertaining to a tree or timber, having decayed spots or streaks in the heartwooa.

Dry sand: A sandy deposit with low water-holding capacity.

Dry weight: The weight of tissue obtained following sufficiently prolonged oven-drying at high temperature to remove all water. Freeze-drying may also be employed but generates a slightly different result because bound water is not removed.

Dual culture: A culture made of a plant tissue and one organism (such as a nematode) or an obligate parasite/micro-organism (such as a fungus). Dual culturc tcchniques are used for a variety of purposes, including assessing host-parasite interactions and the production of axenic cultures.

Duff: The partly decomposed organic surface layer of forested soil.

Dune: A mound of loose sand piled up by wind.

Duplication: Multiple occurrence of: 1. A DNA sequence within a defined length of DNA; or 2. A specific segment in the same chromosome or genome.

Dust mulch: A dry, loose surface layer of cultivated soil, which reduces water loss from the underlying soil.

Duster: A device consisting of a bin, a wand with a nozzle, and a crank mechanism; used for applying dust or powder to plants.

Dwarf: Very small. Dwarf shoots or spurs - shoots that develop from preformed buds which have very short internodal lengths or intervals.

Dwarf fruit trees: 1. A small fruit tree reaching a height at maturity of 4 or 5 feet and bearing early, but normal fruit.

Dwarf plants: Plants of genetically small size or those dwarfed by grafting (i.e. dwarf apple trees) or by pruning and restricted root growth (i.e. bonsai).

Dwarf shrubs: Shrubs that are selected or hybridized that are typically shorter and more compact than the species.

Dwarfism: Stunted growth, often due to a fault in genetic composition. The condition often involves the alteration of the proportions of thc various body parts. In plants, dwarfism is frequently caused by a gibberellin deficiency, as in the case of the pea. The application of exogenous gibberellin usually causes internode elongation and the production of a plant of normal size.

Dyeing flowers: Blossoms capable of producing dyes.

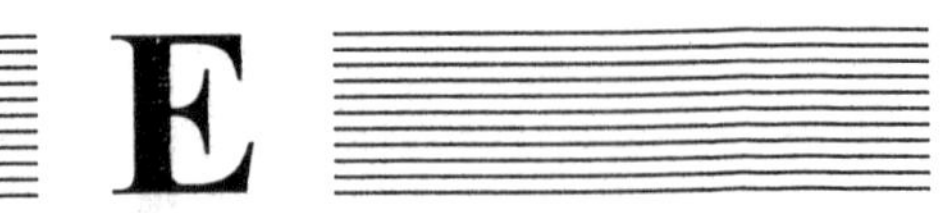

E

E: Prefix meaning 'lacking', e.g. Ebracteate.

Eared: Having ears or awns, such as in corn or wheat.

Ecalcarate: Having no spur.

Ecarinate: Without a carina or keel.

Ecaudate: Without a tail.

Eccentric: Off-center style

Ecdysone: A steroid hormone in insects stimulating the synthesis of proteins involved in moulting and metamorphosis.

Ecesis: The establishment of the first stage or sere in a succession.

Echinate: Set with prickles; prickly, like a hedgehog; having sharp points.

Eclosion: 1. Emergence of an adult insect from the pupal stage. 2. Initial phase of germination of fungal spores.

Ecocline: A cline that has been shown to be due to a specific environmental factor. For example, a gradual increase in heavy-metal tolerance can be correlated with increasing metal concentration in the soil.

Ecology: Branch of science concerned with the interrelationships of organisms and their environments esp. as manifested by natural cycles and rhythms, community development and structure, interaction between different kinds of organisms, geographic distributions and population alteration.

Economic trait locus (ETL): A locus influencing a trait that contributes to producer's income.

Ecostate: Lacking a costa or midrib.

Ecosystem: A unit comprising a community of living organisms and their environment. There is a continuous flow of energy and matter through the system. Ecosystems may be small or large, and simple or complex in structure. They range from small freshwater ponds or pools to the earth itself.

Ecotone: A transition zone or region separating two biomes. For example, in central Asia an area of wooded steppe, the grove belt, separates the coniferous forest from the temperate grassland.

Ecotype: A sub-population of a species that occurs in a particular well-defined environment, usually showing better adaptation to that environment than the species as a whole.

Ectophloic siphonostele: A cylindrical stele with a parenchymatous central strand and phloem around the outside only (medullated protostele).

Ectopic: Anomalous situation or relation, particularly with respect to pregnancy, where the foetus is implanted outside the uterus.

Edaphic factors: The physical, chemical, and biological properties of soil that influence the life of organisms. The main edaphic factors include water content, organic content, texture, and pH.

Eddish: Stubble; a stubble field. Also called earsh and ersh.

Edged: One color is surrounded by a very narrow rim of another.

Edging: 1. Any nonbiodegradable material, ordinarily plastic or metal, installed in the ground to separate flower beds from lawn or other landscape areas. 2. A border; a skirting; specifically, a row of plants set along the border of a flower bed.

Edible vaccine: Edible antigen-containing material, that activates the immune system via gut-associated lymphoid tissues. A preferred route for vaccine administration, particularly in areas where the technological infrastructure needed for maintenance of vaccines is absent. The vaccine is synthesized in vivo in the edible parts of transgenic plants (e.g. grains, tubers, fruits, etc.) or eggs.

Effector cells: Cells of the immune system that are responsible for the production of cell-mediated cytotoxicity.

Effector molecule: A molecule that influences the behaviour of a regulatory molecule, such as a repressor protein, thereby influencing gene expression.

Efflorescence: The time or state of flowering; anthesis.

Effuse: Spreading loosely.

Elaiosome: An appendage of a seed, usually rich in oil, not essential for the viability of the seed but attractive to fauna (especially ants) as a food for larvae etc. and hence an aid to dispersal by such fauna.

Elastin: A fibrous protein that is the major constituent of the yellow elastic fibres of animal connective tissue.

Elater: A straplike appendage (usually occurring in pairs) attached to a horsetail (Equisetum) spore; also, a somewhat spindle-shaped sterile cell occurring in large numbers in liverwort sporangia; both types of elaters facilitate spore dispersal.

Electric hotbed: A cold frame used for extending the growing season. They are usually heated by an electrical mat or heating element.

Electro-blotting: The electrophoretic transfer of DNA, RNA or protein from a gel, in which they have been separated, to a support matrix, such as nitrocellulose. A transfer technique employed in Southern and northern blotting.

Electrochemical sensor: Biosensors, such as an enzyme electrode, in which a biological process is harnessed to an electrical sensor system. Other types couple a biological event to an electrical one via a range of mechanisms, including the reduction of oxygen or pH change.

Electron: A negatively charged particle ofan atom.

Electron microscope (EM): A microscope that uses an electron beam focussed by magnetic 'lenses'.

Electrophoresis: A ubiquitous molecular biology technique, with many variants, used to resolve complex mixtures of macromolecules into their components. Its principle is to subject samples to an electric field applied across a porous matrix. Molecules will migrate under these conditions at a rate dependent on their net electric charge and/ or their molecular weight.

Electroporation: The induction of transient pores in bacterial cells or protoplasts by the application of a pulse of electricity. These pores allow the entry of exogenous DNA into the cell. Widely used for the transformation of bacteria.

Element: One of more than 100 types of matter, most existing naturally but some human-made, each of which is composed of one kind of atom.

Elisa: Abbreviation for enzyme-linked immunosorbent assay. An immunoassay, i.e. an antibody-based technique for the diagnosis of the presence and quantity of specific molecules in a mixed sample. It combines the specificity of an immunoglobulin with the detectability of an enzyme-generated coloured product. In one form, the primary antibody (specific to the test protein) is adsorbed onto a solid substrate, and a known amount of the sample is added; all the antigen in the sample is bound by the antibody. A second antibody (conjugated with an enzyme) specific for a second site on the test protein is added; and the enzyme generates a colour change in the presence of a substrate reagent.

Elite tree: A tree that has been shown by progeny testing to produce superior offspring.

Ellipsoid: Of a solid body with an elliptic section or outline.

Elliptic: An outline that is oval, narrowed to rounded at the ends and widest at about the middle (as the outline of a football); ellipsoid, a solid with an elliptical outline.

Elongation factors: Soluble proteins required for the elongation of polypeptide chains on ribosomes.

Eluviation: The movement of moisture and nutrients from one place to another in the soil.

Emarginate: Said of leaves, sepals, or petals, and other structures that are notched at the apex.

Emargination: A notching of the edge, such as along the edge of a leaf.

Embossed: With a small central nodule.

Embryo: An immature organism in the early stages of development. In mammals, develops in the first months in the uterus. In plants, it is the structure that develops in the megagametophyte, as result of the fertilization of an egg cell, or occasionally without fertilization. Somatic embryos can often be induced in in vitro plant cell cultures.

Embryo cloning: The creation of identical copies of an embryo by embryo splitting or by nuclear transfer from undifferentiated embryonic cells.

Embryo culture: The culture of embryos on nutrient media.

Embryo multiplication and transfer (EMT): The cloning of animal embryos and their subsequent transfer to recipients via artificial inembryonation. The cloned embryos can be derived from embryonic or adult tissue.

Embryo rescue: A sequence of tissue culture techniques utilized to enable a fertilized immature embryo resulting from an interspecific cross to continue growth and development, until it can be regenerated into an adult plant.

Embryo sac: The mature female gametophyte in angiosperms. Generally a seven-celled structure - two synergids, one egg cell, three antipodal cells (each with a single haploid nucleus) and one endosperm mother cell with two haploid nuclei.

Embryo sexing: The determination of the sex of an embryo prior to birth. Typically achieved by the polymerase chain reaction-mediated amplification of DNA extracted from a sample of embryonic tissue. Dependent on the availability of reliable markers for the differential sex chromosome.

Embryo splitting: The splitting of young embryos into several sections, each of which develops into an animal. A form of animal cloning, i.e. of producing animals that are genetically identical. In practice, the number of animals that can be produced from a single embryo is less than 10.

Embryo storage: Cryogenic preservation of animal embryos, allowing inembryonation or other manipulations long after embryo formation.

Embryo technology: Generic name for any modification of mammalian embryos. It encompasses embryo cloning, embryo splitting, embryo storage, and in vitro fertilization.

Embryogenesis: 1. (General) Development of an embryo. 2. (In plants) In vitro formation of plants from plant tissues, through a pathway closely resembling normal embryogeny from the zygote. Somatic cell embryogenesis is an alteRNAtive technique. The generation of embryos has two stages: initiation and maturation. Initiation needs a high level of the group of plant hormones called auxins; maturation needs a lower level.

Embryoid: Plant biotechnology term no longer commonly used. An embryo-like body developing in vitro, forming a complete, self-contained plantlet with no vascular connection with the callus.

Embryonic stem cells (ES cells): Cells of the early embryo that can give rise to all differentiated cells, including germ line cells.

Embryophyte: Synonym for the Plantae, as here defined. It includes all green photosynthetic organisms which begin the development of the sporophyte generation within the archegonium.

Embryotega: A small circular thickening near the seed scar on the seeds of some plants, such as members of the spiderwort family.

Emerge: To rise out of a fluid or other covering.

Emersed plants: Plants growing with their roots and a portion of the shoot below the water and the remainder of the shoot above the surface of the water.

Emersed: Standing out of or rising above a surface as an aquatic plant with flower stalk emersed.

Emersifolious: With emergent leaves.

Emission wavelength: The specific wavelength of light emitted by a fluorescent molecule, such as a labelled probe, upon absorption of light at the (higher) excitation wavelength.

Enantioblastic: Pertaining to a plant embryo, originating at the end directly opposite the hilum.

Enation: An abnormal growth of an organ or of an excresence upon any part of a plant.

Encapsidation: The process by which the nucleic acid of a virus is enclosed in a capsid.

Encapsulating agents: Anything which forms a shell around an enzyme or bacterium, common agents being polysaccharides such as alginate or agar. The agents are inert and allow nutrients and oxygen to diffuse readily into and out of the sphere, and are easy to convert from gel (solid) to sol (liquid) or solution form by altering the temperature or the concentration of ions.

Encapsulation: Any method packaging an enzyme or bacterium and maintaining its normal functions. Used to immobilize cells in a bioreactor.

Encode: The gene product specified by a particular nucleic acid sequence.

End product inhibition: The inhibition of an enzyme by a metabolite. Typically, the enzyme is the first enzyme in a biosynthetic pathway, and the metabolite the product of the last step in the pathway.

Endangered species: A plant or animal species in immediate danger of extinction because its population number has reached a critical level, or its habitat has been drastically reduced.

Endarch: Referring to cells differentiating towards the inside of the stem, contrasting with exarch.

Endemic: A plant that is native to a particular country or region; not introduced or naturalized.

Endocarp: The inter layer of the wall of a matured ovary; when its texture differs from the outer wall, it may be hard and stony, membranous, or fleshy.

Endocrine gland: Any gland in an animal that manufactures hormones and secretes them directly into the bloodstream to act at distant sites in the body, known as target organs or cells.

Endocrine interference: Interference with the normal balance of hormones.

Endocytosis: The process by which materials enter a cell without passing through the cell membrane. The membrane folds around material outside the cell, resulting in the formation of a sac-like vesicle inside which the material is entrapped. This vesicle is then pinched off from the cell surface so that it lies within the cell.

Endoderm: The internal layer of cells of the gastrula, which develops into the alimentary canal (gut) and digestive glands of the adult.

Endodermis: The layer of living cells, with various characteristically thickened walls and no intercellular spaces, which surrounds the vascular tissue of certain plants and occurs in nearly all roots and certain stems and leaves. It separates the cortical cells from cells of the pericycle.

Endogen: A plant that develops from or on the inside, as most monocots.

Endogenous: 1. Of or pertaining to endogens (endogenous plants). 2. Proceeding from within (endogenous growth).

Endomitosis: Duplication of chromosomes without division of the nucleus, resulting in a doubling (or more) in the chromosome number within a cell.

Endonuclease: An enzyme that cleaves a phosphodiester bond within a DNA strand, forming two smaller strands.

Endophyte: An organism that lives inside a plant.

Endoplasmic reticulum: A complex system of interlinked double-membrane channels subdividing the cytoplasm of a cell into compartments; parts of it are lined with ribosomes.

Endopolyploidy: The net result of endomitoses. The somatic chromosome number has doubled (or more), forming a polyploid cell line. If these differentiate into a germ line, then the gametic number will have also increased proportionately, giving rise to homogeneously polyploid individuals, termed endopolyploids.

Endoprotease: An enzyme that cleaves internal peptide bonds within a polypeptide molecule. Site of cleavage is usually specific to certain amino acid residues.

Endoreduplication: Chromosome reproduction during interphase. Four-chromatid chromosomes (diplochromosomes) are seen during this phase.

Endosperm mother cell: One of the seven cells of the mature plant embryo sac, containing the two polar nuclei and, which, following fertilization, gives rise to the primary endosperm cell from which the endosperm develops.

Endosperm: A food-storage tissue that develops through divisions of the primary endosperm nucleus; it is digested by the sporophyte after germination in some species (e.g., com) or before maturation of the seed in other species (e.g. Beans).

Endospory: A condition in which the gametophyte develops within the spore wall, rather than externally.

Endostome: Of moss sporophytes, the inner row of walls forming the peristome teeth.

Endosulfan: A broad spectrum, synthetic insecticide used to control many plant pests, including whiteflies and thrips. Common trade name is Thiodan.

Endosymbiont hypothesis: The theory that mitochondria and chloroplasts were free-living bacteria that became incorporated in cells.

Endothecium: The inner cell mass of the sporpphyte in basal plants. It usually produces both the central columella and the spores, which accumulate around the surface of the columella.

Endotoxin: A component of the cell wall of gram-negative bacteria that elicits, in mammals, an inflammatory response and fever.

Energy: The capacity to do work; some forms of energy are heat, light.

Enhancer: 1. A substance or object that increases a chemical activity or a physiological process. 2. A eukaryotic DNA sequence (also found in some eukaryotic viruses) which increases the transcription of a gene. Located up to several kbp, usually (but not exclusively) upstream of the gene in question. In some cases can activate transcription of a gene with no (known) promoter. 3. A major or modifier gene that increases the rate of a physiological process.

Enolpyruvyl shikimate 3 phosphate synthase (Abbreviation EPSP synthase or EPSPS): An enzyme produced by virtually all plants, which is essential for normal metabolism, and for the biosynthesis of aromatic amino acids. Glyphosate- and sulfosate-containing herbicides act by inhibiting EPSP synthase activity, but because strain CP4 of Agrobacterium sp. is unaffected by glyphosate, the introduction of the CP4 EPSPS gene into crop plants generates a tolerance of glyphosate-containing herbicides.

Ensiform: Having sharp edges and tapering to a slender point; having a shape suggesting a sword.

Enterotoxin: A bacterial protein that, following release into the intestine, causes cramps, diarrhoea and nausea.

Entire: Having a margin devoid of any indentations, teeth, or lobes.

Entire margin: In leaves, the condition in which the margin forms a smooth line or arc without noticeable serrations; note that lobed leaves can also have entire margins; compare to lobed margin and toothed margin.

Entomophilous: Applied to flowers whose structure ordinarily requires insects to pollinate them.

Entomophily: Pollinated by insects.

Entomophily: Seed plants which are pollinated by insects are said to be entomophilous.

Enucleated ovum: Egg cell from which the nucleus has been removed, usually as a preparatory step for nuclear transfer.

Enzyme: A protein which, even in very low concentration, catalyses specific chemical reactions but is not used up in the reaction. Enzymes are classified into six major groups (1-6), according to the type of reaction they catalyse: 1. oxidoreductases; 2. transferases; 3. hydrolases; 4. lyases; 5. isomerases; 6. ligases. Generally enzymes are named by the addition of the suffix -ase to the name of their substrate, and are classified by a standard numerical system: the Enzyme Commission (EC) number.

Enzyme bioreactor: A reactor in which a chemical conversion reaction is catalysed by an enzyme.

Enzyme commission number (EC number): Systematic label which identifies an enzyme in the technical literature. Consists of four numbers separated by dots: the first classifies the enzyme into one of the six broad enzyme groups; each group is subdivided into sub-groups, each sub-group into sub-sub-groups, and the last number is specific for the enzyme.

Enzyme electrode: A type of biosensor, in which an enzyme is immobilized onto the surface of an electrode. When the enzyme catalyses its reaction, electrons are transferred from the reactant to the electrode, and so a current is generated. There are two types of enzyme electrodes: 1. Ampometric (measuring current flow) where the electrode is kept as near zero voltage as possible. When the enzyme catalyses its reaction, electrons move into the electrode, and so a current flows; 2. Potentiometric (measuring changes in electrical potential) when the electrode is held at a voltage which counteracts the voltage determined by the enzyme's tendency to push electrons into it. Usually enzymes transfer their electrons inefficiently to the electrode, so a mediator compound is coated onto the electrode to help the transfer.

Enzyme immunoassay: A range of immunoassay techniques employing enzymes, which includes ELISA.

Enzyme kinetics: The quantitative characteristics of enzyme reactions.

Enzyme stabilization: Maintaining the active conformation of an enzyme. This can be achieved in vitro by providing the appropriate chemical environment and cofactors. In some cases the criticality of these factors can be reduced by binding an antibody to the enzyme, in such a way that the active site of the enzyme is left unblocked.

Eophyll: Term applied to first few leaves with green, expanded lamina developed by seedlings; transitional type leaves developed before formation of adult leaves.

Epappose: Having no tuft of bristles, a feature often found on seeds that are scattered by the wind, such as the seeds of a dandelion.

Epetiolate: Without petiole, leaf sessile.

Ephemeral: Referring to an organ living a very short time, usually a day or less; lasting a very short time.

Epicalyx: A calyx-like involucre of bracts below the true calyx, as in the mallow, or of sepals, as in the potentilla.

Epicarp: The outer layer of the wall of a fruit, i.e. the 'skin'.

Epichilium: The terminal part of the lip of some orchids. Also epichil or epichile.

Epicoccum sp.: Conidia dimensions 15-25 microns. A common allergen. It is found in plants, soil, grains, textiles and paper products.

Epicormic Shoots or Water Sprouts: Shoots that develop from dormant lateral buds on the trunk which have very long and frequently variable internodal lengths or intervals.

Epicormic: Of buds, shoots or flowers, borne on the old wood of trees (applied especially to shoots arising from dormant buds after injury or fire).

Epicortical: On top of the bark, i.e. outside the bark.

Epicotyl: The part of an embryo or seedling above the attachment point of the cotyledon(s).

Epicotyle: The part of a plant embryo or seedling above the cotyledons.

Epicotyledonary: Pertaining to the epicotyl; situated above the seed leaves (cotyledons).

Epidermis: 1. The outmost layer of cells of the body of an animal. In invertebrates the epidermis is normally only one cell thick and is covered by an impermeable cuticle. In vertebrates the epidermis is the thinner of the two layers of skin. 2. The outermost layer of cells covering a plant. It is overlaid by a cuticle and its functions are principally to protect the plant from injury and to reduce water loss. Some epidermal cells are modified to form guard cells or hairs of various types. In woody plants the functions of the shoot epidermis are taken over by the periderm tissues and in mature roots the epidermis is sloughed off and replaced by the hypodermis.

Epidermophyton sp.: Can cause infections of skin and nails.

Epigeal: 1. A plant that grows above the surface of the soil, as most plants in the garden do. 2. A cotyledon that is forced above the ground in the process of germination, as in beans, morning glories, and others. 3. Cotyledons that appear above ground. Also epigeous, epigean, epigaean, or epigeic.

Epigenesis: Describes the developmental process whereby each successive stage of normal development is built up on the foundations created by the preceding stages of development; an embryo is built up from a zygote, a seedling from an embryo, and so on.

Epigenetic variation: Non-hereditary and reversible variation; often the result of a change in gene expression due to methylation of DNA.

Epigonium: In mosses, a derivative of the archegonium which forms a hard, protective layer around the developing sporophyte. Later it breaks up, but the sporophyte retains a conical "dunce cap" or calyptra over its distal end. Strictly speaking, the term calyptra refers only to the "dunce cap," and the piece of the epigonium retained around the base (if any) is the vaginula.

Epigynous: Of floral parts (especially stamens), attached above the level of insertion of the ovary, and arising from tissue that is fused to the ovary wall.

Epigyny: The condition in which the sepals, petals, stamens are attached to the floral tube above the ovary with the ovary adnate to the tube or hypanthium.

Epihyperigyny: The condition in which the sepals, petals, stamens are attached to the floral tube or hypanthium surrounding the ovary; a combination perigyny and partly inferior ovary.

Epimatium: Fleshy covering of the seed and more or less fused with the integument; arising from the chalazal end of the ovule like an additional integument; e.g., Podocarpus.

Epinasty: A process by which the growth of branches or petioles is abnormally pointing downward. This phenomenon is caused by the more rapid growth of the upper side. Epinasty may result from either nutritional deficiencies or irregularities at the plant growth regulator level. Not to be confused with wilting, as epinastic tissues are turgid.

Epiperigyny: The condition in which the sepals, petals, stamens are attached to the floral or hypanthium cup above the ovary with the lower part of the hypanthium completely adnate to the ovary.

Epipetalous: Borne on the petals or the corolla of a flower; applied to stamens and to plants whose stamens are attached to the corolla.

Epipetiolar: With branches arising from buds on the petiole.

Epiphyllous: From a phylloclad or peculiar bract, as in Tilia.

Epiphyte: A plant that grows on another plant, or which uses a rock or host plant merely as a place of residence and obtains its moisture and nutrients directly from the air; an air plant. A type of growth form. No parasitism is involved. The epiphyte is rooted on the surface of the host. Vines rooted in the soil and climbing up on another plant are not epiphytes.

Epiphytic: Upon another plant.

Epirhizous: With roots upon another plant.

Episepalous: With stamens attached or inserted upon sepals or calyx.

Episome: A genetic extrachromosomal element (e.g. the F factor in Escherichia coli) which replicates within a cell independently of the chromosome and is able to integrate into the host chromosome. The step of integration may be governed by a variety of factors and so the term episome has lost favour and been superseded by the wider term plasmid.

Episperm: The hard external covering of a seed.

Epispore: The outer coat or membrane of a spore.

Epistasis: Interaction between genes at different loci, e.g. one gene suppresses the effect of another gene that is situated at a different locus. Dominance is associated with members of allelic pairs, whereas epistasis describes an interaction among products of non-alleles.

Epitope: Synonym for antigenic determinant.

Epitropous: Dorsal-ovule pendulous or hanging, micropyle above, raphe dorsal (away from ventral bundle). Ventral - ovule pendulous or hanging, micropyle above, raphe ventral (toward ventral bundle).

Epixylous: Growing on wood.

Epizootic: A disease simultaneously affecting a large number of animals.

Epruinose: Having no bloom or powdery coating upon the surface of the leaf, stem or other plant part; not pruinose.

EPSP synthase: Abbreviation for enolpyruvyl-shikimate 3-phosphate synthase.

Equational division: A chromosome division in which the two chromatids of each duplicated chromosome separate longitudinally, prior to being incorporated into two daughter nuclei. Seen at the mitotic-type second division of meiosis; also in somatic mitosis and the non-reductional division of meiosis. The number of chromosomes is the same at the end of the division as at the beginning.

Equilateral: Of stamens, with anthers regularly spaced around the style.

Equilibrium density gradient centrifugation: A procedure used to separate macromolecules based on their density (mass per unit volume).

Equinoctial: Having flowers which expand and close regularly at particular hours of the day

Equitant: Of leaves, folded in half along the midline so that the adaxial surface disappears, and overlapping the edges of a similarly folded leaf on the opposite side of the stem.

Eramous: With unbranched stems.

Erect: Upright.

Erecto-patent: Between spreading and erect.

Eremean: Pertaining to regions of low, irregular rainfall.

Ergotism: A disease resulting from consumption of goods made with flour containing ergot fungus.

Ericaceous: Applied to acid potting mix with a pH of 6.5 or less. It is usually used for plants that cannot tolerate lime.

Ericetal: Composed of or containing heaths.

Erlenmeyer flask: A conical flat-bottomed laboratory flask with a narrow neck, widely used for culturing micro-organisms.

Erodible: A term used to describe a soil that is vulnerable to erosion.

Erose: With an irregular, jagged margin, as if torn or bitten.

Erosion: The wearing away of the land through the action of moving water, wind, or other geological agents.

Erosive: Used to describe water that has enough force to cause erosion.

Erubescent: Inclined to be reddish.

Escape: A plant that has escaped from cultivation and naturalized more or less permanently (i.e. Queen Anne's lace is an escaped carrot).

Escent: Suffix meaning 'inclined to be' or 'becoming', e.g. accrescent, coalescent.

Escherichia coli: A commensal bacterium inhabiting the colon of many animal species, including human. E. coli is widely used as a model of cell biochemical function, and as a host for cloning DNA. In environmental studies, its presence is a key indicator of water pollution due to human sewage effluent. Some strains, notably E. coli 0157:H7, are significant pathogens.

Espalier: 1. A trelliswork of various forms on which the branches of fruit trees or fruit bushes are extended horizontally, in fan shape, etc., in a single plane. The object it to provide better air circulation and sun exposure for the plants. 2. A tree or plant trained on such a trellis or system. Trees trained to espaliers aren't as liable to suffer abrupt variations of temperature as are wall trees. 3. To train on or protect by an espalier, as a tree or trees.

Espathate: Lacking a spathe.

Esquamulose: Lacking minute scales; not squamulose.

Essential amino acid: An amino acid required for normal metabolism, but which cannot be synthesized by an organism. It therefore has to be supplied via feed or food.

Essential derivation of varieties: Genotypes very similar to an originating cultivar, obtained, for example, by the selection of a mutant or a variant individual from plants of the initial variety, or by backcrossing or transformation.

Essential element: Any of a number of elements required by living organisms to ensure normal growth, development and maintenance.

Essential flower parts: The stamen and pistil organs of the flower that are required for pollination.

Essential nutrient: Any substance required by living organisms to ensure normal growth, development and maintenance.

Essential organs: The androecium and gynoecium.

Essential requirement: In plant cell tissue culture, comprises inorganic salts, including all of the elements necessary for plant metabolism; organic factors (amino acids, vitamins); usually also endogenous plant growth regulators (auxins, cytokinins and often gibberellins); as well as a carbon source (sucrose or glucose).

Established culture: 1. An aseptic viable explant. 2. A suspension culture subjected to several passages with a constant cell number per unit time.

Estaurine: Pertaining to estuaries or river mouths, usually brackish conditions.

Estimated breeding value (EBV): Twice the expected progeny difference. The difference is doubled because breeding value is a reflection of all the genes of an individual, in contrast to progeny difference, which is a reflection of a sample half of an individual's genes. The predicted performance of the offspring of the mating between any two parents is the average of their EBVs (averaged because each parent makes an equal contribution to each offspring).

Estuary: An inlet or arm of the sea; especially the wide mouth of a river, where the tide meets the current. pl. estuaries.

ET: Abbreviation for embryo transfer.

Etagere: A series of open shelves for growing and displaying plants; a tiered plant stand.

Ethanol: Commonly used to disinfect plant tissues, glassware utensils and working surfaces in tissue culture manipulations; to precipitate aqueous solutions of nucleic acids; and to dissolve water-insoluble components of culture media. Synonym: ethyl alcohol.

Ethephon: A synthetic compound commonly used as a source of ethylene, a gaseous plant growth regulator.

Ethereal oil producing glands: Mostly aromatic compound producing glands found on various parts of the plant, without definitely known functions.

Ethidium bromide: A fluorescent dye which can intercalate between base pairs of double-stranded DNA, and hence is much used to stain DNA in gels. The dye fluoresces when exposed to UV light. It is a known to be a strong mutagen and is also possibly both a carcinogen and a teratogen.

Ethion: A synthetic insecticide effective against sucking and chewing insects, especially whiteflies and mites.

Ethylene: A gaseous plant growth regulator acting on various aspects of vegetative growth, fruit ripening and abscission of plant parts. Synonym: ethene.

Ethylenediamine tetraacetic acid (EDTA): A chelating compound. Used to keep nutrients, such as iron, bound in a soluble form that leaves them still available to the plant cells in vitro. Also a potent inhibitor of DNase activity and therefore used as an additive for long term storage of dissolved DNA.

Etiolate: To blanch or whiten a plant or part of a plant by excluding sunlight. This is often done with endive, celery, and cauliflower.

Etiolation: An abnormal increase in stem elongation, accompanied by poor (if any) leaf development. Physiological etiolation is caused by a lack of chlorophyll, and is typical of plants growing under low light intensity or in complete darkness. It can also be induced by some fungal pathogens.

Eucamptodromous: With a single primary vein, the secondary veins curved upward and gradually iminishing distally within the margin and interconnected by a series of cross-veins without forming conspicuous marginal loops.

Euchromatin: Chromosomal material that is stained less intensely by certain dyes. Thought to be the chromosomal domains which are gene-rich, since the DNA in these regions remains less contracted than those rich in repetitive DNA - the heterochromatin.

Eucyclic: Having a regular alternation of parts; applied to flowers in which the petals, stamens, etc. are equal in number in each whorl and alternate with one another.

Eugenics: The application of the principles of genetics to the 'improvement' of humankind. Wholly discredited as a scientific approach since the Nazi period.

Eukaryote: One of the two major evolutionary clades, characterized by having the nucleus enclosed by a membrane, and possessing chromosomes that undergo mitosis and meiosis. Eukaryotic organisms include animals, plants, fungi and some algae.

Eukaryotic: Pertaining to cells having distinct membrane-bound organelles, including a nucleus with chromosomes.

Euploid: An organism or cell having a chromosome number that is an exact multiple of the haploid number. Terms used to identify different levels in an euploid series are diploid (2x), triploid (3x), tetraploid (4x) etc.

Eusporanagiate: Of primative ferns with sporangial walls more than one cell thick originating from several cells.

Eusporangium: Sporangia that arise from a group of superficial cells; this is the primitive character state in vascular plants; compare to leptosporangium.

Eustele: When a plant's vascular tissue develops in discrete bundles, it is said to have a eustele.

Eutrophic: The gradual increase in nutrients in a body of water. Natural eutrophication is a gradual process, but human activities may greatly accelerate the process.

Eutrophication: The gradual enrichment of a body of water through the accumulation of nutrients. Resulting in a corresponding increase in algae and other organisms.

Evanescent: Passing away, disappearing early.

Evapotranspiration: 1. The loss of water from the soil by evaporation and plant transpiration. 2. Water on the surface taken away by water, wind, air, and elements.

Even-pinnate: Said of compound leaves having an even number of leaflets, this is usually easily determined because there is a pair terminally.

Everbloomer: A plant that blooms continuously throughout the growing season.

Evergreen: Opposite of deciduous, i.e. evergreen plants do not shed all their leaves annually, but shed and grow new leaves continually; most conifers are evergreen, but the evergreen habit is not restricted to conifers.

Everlastings: This describes plants whose flowers maintain their color, brightness and form long after being gathered.

Evident: Clearly visible macroscopically.

Evolution: The process by which the present diversity of plant and animal life has arisen, and which continues to drive changes in form and mode of existence of all living organisms.

Ex situ conservation: The conservation of components of biological diversity outside their natural habitats.

Ex situ management: The management of planted stands of trees to protect them and insure survival, growth and identity; the conservation or preservation of trees as seed, pollen, tissue culture, or excised plant parts.

Ex vitro: Organisms removed from tissue culture and transplanted; generally plants to soil or potting mixture.

Ex vivo gene therapy: The delivery of a gene or genes to the isolated cells of an individual, with the intention of alleviating a genetic disorder. After culturing, the transformed cells are re-introduced into the individual by transfusion, infusion or injection.

Exalate: Lacking wings or wing-like appendages; not alate.

Exalbuminous: Without endosperm; applied to seeds. Also endospermous, exendospermic.

Exanthem: 1. A blotch on the surface of a leaf, etc. 2. A copper-deficiency disease of plants, prevalent in citrus and olive, and characterized by dieback and blotches on leaves and fruit.

Exarch: Referring to cells differentiating towards the outside of the stem, contrasting with endarch.

Exchangeable sodium: Sodium that is attached to the surface of soil particles and that can be exchanged with other positively charged ions in the soil solution.

Exchangeable: A term used to describe ions in the absorbing complex of soil that can be exchanged with other ions.

Excinuclease: The endonuclease-containing protein complex that excises a segment of damaged DNA during excision repair.

Excision repair: DNA repair processes that involve the removal of a damaged or incorrect segment of one strand of double-stranded DNA and its replacement by the synthesis of a new segment using the complementary strand of DNA as template.

Excision: 1. The natural or in vitro enzymatic removal of a DNA segment from a chromosome or cloning vector. 2. The cutting out and preparation of a tissue, organ, etc., for culture. 3. The removal of adventitious shoots from callus tissue.

Excitation wavelength: The specific wavelength of light required to stimulate a fluorescent molecule, such as a labelled probe, to emit light at the (lower) emission wavelength.

Excrescence: A normal outgrowth; a disfiguring addition.

Excrete: To transport material out of a cell or organism.

Excurrent: Running or proceeding outwards, away from the axis or costa; or of a vein that proceeds beyond the margin.

Exfoliate: Peeling off in thin layers, shreds, or plates, as the bark of some trees.

Exindusiate: Lacking an indusium.

Exine: The outer of two layers forming the wall of certain spores (as pollen grains) called also exosporium.

Exit site (E site): The ribosome binding site that contains the free tRNA prior to its release.

Exocarp: The outer layer of the covering of a fruit when it consists of two dissimilar layers.

Exocrine gland: An animal gland that secretes through a duct.

Exogen: A plant in which the growth of the stem is in successive concentric layers, such as most trees.

Exogenous DNA: DNA that has been derived from one organism, and is to be introduced into a cell a different species. Also referred to as foreign DNA or heterologous DNA.

Exon: A segment of a eukaryotic gene that is transcribed as part of the primary transcript and is retained, after processing, with other exons to form a functional mRNA molecule. Many eukaryotic genes are composed of a mosaic of exons and introns.

Exon amplification: A procedure that is used to amplify exons.

Exonuclease: An enzyme that digests DNA or RNA, beginning at the end of a strand. It therefore requires a free end in order to begin the degradation. 5'-exonucleases require a free 5' end and degrade the molecule in the 5'-3' direction. 3'-exonucleases require a free 3' end and degrade in the opposite direction.

Exopolysaccharide: A polysaccharide that is secreted by a micro-organism into the surrounding environment.

Exostome: Of moss sporophytes, the outer wall of plates forming the peristome teeth.

Exotic: Of foreign origin or character; introduced from a foreign country or a different region. An exotic plant is one not native to the place where it is growing such as Japanese Honeysuckle, which has naturalized in the northeastern states, or Eucalyptus trees, which have been naturalized on the West Coast.

Exotoxin: A toxin released by a bacterium into the medium in which it grows.

Expected progeny difference (EPD): The predicted performance of the future offspring of an individual for a particular trait, calculated from measurement(s) of the individual's own performance and/or the performance of one or more of its relatives, for the trait in question and/or for one or more correlated traits. Typically, the prediction is expressed as a deviation from a well-defined base population, assuming the individual in question is mated to a sample of individuals whose average genetic merit equals that of the base population. The predicted performance of the offspring of the mating between any two individuals is the sum of their EPDs.

Explanate: Spread out flat.

Explant: A portion of a plant aseptically excised and prepared for culture in a nutrient medium.

Explant donor: The plant from which an explant has been taken.

Explantation: The removal of cells, tissues or organs of animals and plants for observation of their growth and development in appropriate culture media.

Explosion method: A technique for the genetic transformation of cells, in which the transgene is driven into the target (plant) cells by the sudden vaporization (effected by the application of a pulse of high voltage) of a water droplet containing the DNA and gold particles.

Export: The removal of a compound from a cell by active transport.

Express: To transcribe and translate a gene.

Expressed sequence tag (EST): Partially sequenced cDNA clone. Because the read length of a standard DNA sequencing reaction is shorter than the majority of cDNA clones, full length sequence can only be obtained by further manipulations. For the purposes of assigning putative function to a cDNA and designing PCR primers to extract the genomic DNA equivalent to the cDNA, full length sequence is usually unnecessary. By restricting sequencing to a single run, large numbers of cDNAs can be characterized at the EST level.

Expression library: A cDNA library that has been inserted into a bacterial host cell engineered to express transgenes.

Expression system: Combination of host and vector which provides a genetic context for making a cloned gene functional, i.e. produce peptide, in the host cell.

Expression vector: A cloning vector that has been constructed in such a way that, after insertion of a DNA molecule, its coding sequence is properly transcribed and the mRNA is translated. The cloned gene is put under the control of a promoter sequence for the initiation of transcription, and often also has a transcription termination sequence at its end.

Expressivity: Degree of expression of a trait controlled by a particular gene. The gene may show different degrees of expression in different individuals.

Exsert: To put forth; to thrust out; to protrude.

Exsuccous: Dry, without juice, sap, or moisture; withered.

Extension: The short single-stranded stretch of nucleotides remaining on a double-stranded DNA molecule, following treatment with a restriction endonuclease which makes a staggered cut. The presence of these unpaired regions make the molecule more easily ligatable, and are thus important in gene cloning. Synonyms: protruding end; sticky end; overhang; cohesive end.

Extracellular: Taking place or located outside the cell.

Extrachromosomal: In eukaryotes, non-nuclear DNA, present in cytoplasm organelles such as mitochondria and chloroplasts. In prokaryotes, non-chromosomal DNA, i.e. plasmids.

Extrafloral: Of a plant part that doesn't form part of a flower.

Extranuclear DNA: DNA found outside the nucleus, typically in plastids and mitochondria.

Extranuclear genes: Genes residing elsewhere than in the nucleus (e.g. in mitochondria, chloroplasts or plastids).

Extravaginal: Of a shoot, arising from an axillary bud which breaks through the sheath of the subtending leaf.

Extrorse: Describing anthers that release their pollen to the outside of the flower so promoting cross pollination.

Extrorse: Facing away from the direction of the growth (in reference to the anther of a flower).

Exudate: A liquid, resinous or gelatinous substance secreted by organs or parts of the plant, or yielded when the plant is damaged.

Eyespot: Often reddish structure within a motile unicellular organism; it appears to be sensitive to light.

F

F1, F2, Fn: Subsequent hybrid generations, counting from the F1. Thus, for example, F4 describes the progeny of the F3, which is the progeny of the F2 generation, where all progeny are derived from intercrossing or self-fertilization.

Factor: (Mendelian factor) The inherited component that is responsible for the determination of a characteristic. In modern terminology, chromosomal gene or cistron may be used instead.

Factorial experiment: An experiment in which the material is divided into a number of groups, such that each combination of treatments can be tried separately on at least one group and there are enough groups for every combination to be applied.

Factorial mating: A mating scheme in which each male parent is mated with each female parent. Made possible in animals by means of in vitro embryo production. Such a mating scheme substantially reduces the rate of inbreeding in a selection programme.

Facultative anaerobe: An organism that will grow under either aerobic or anaerobic conditions.

Facultative: Occasional; not essential; incidental.

FAD: (Flavin Adenine Dinucleotide) A riboflavin-derived coenzyme that acts as a prosthetic group to several dehydrogenase enzymes, accepting electrons from the substrate and thus being reduced to FADH2. The most important FAD-linked enzymes are succinate dehydrogenase, which oxidizes succinate to fumarate, and dihydrolipoyl dehydrogenase, a component of the pyruvate dehydrogenase complex, which oxidizes pyruvate to acetyl CoA.

Fagaceae: A family of hardwood trees containing about 1000 species but only eight genera. However these include Quercus (oaks), Fagus (beeches), Castanea (chestnuts), and Nothofagus (southern beeches), which together make up a large proportion of the broad-leaved forests of the world. It is probable that, in terms of biomass, this is the most abundant family of flowering plants. Representatives are not, however, found in the equatorial rain forests of Africa and South America. The flowers are unisexual and usually borne in catkins or spikes. The fruit is a nut, which is partly or completely enclosed within a cupule. Certain species of chestnut, especially sweet chestnut (C. sativa), are grown for their fruits. However timber, obviously, is the most economically important product of this family and, on a far smaller scale, certain species of oak yield cork (Q. suber) and tannins. Many species are grown as ornamentals.

Falcate: Hooked; curved like a scythe or sickle; falciform.

Fallow: Plowed and left unseeded; left for a considerable time unworked or unseeded after tillage; untilled; uncultivated.

Falls: The drooping or horizontal petals of irises.

False indusium: A covering of the sorus formed from the reflexed margin of the lamina.

False veins: Zones of epidermal cells of similar appearance to veins but not associated with vascular tissue, eg. in some Davallia and Hymenophyllaceae.

Family: This consists of genera that resemble one another in certain broad characteristics. The family usually consists of numerous genera, though some only consist of one. The family name usually ends with -aceae or -ae. For example, Compositae, which is the largest family of plants, consists of 950 genera and 20,000 species. Asters, Sunflowers, Mums, and Dahlias are all well-known members of that family and these genera contain numerous species.

Family selection: The selection of progeny families on their mean performance. In addition, the best individuals are usually selected in the best families.

Fan training: A method of training a tree or vine on a trellis or wall in a way that causes the branches radiate from the trunk at regular intervals and at continually smaller angles, the lower branch on each side being horizontal.

Farina: A mealy or flour-like covering; hence farinose, farinaceous.

Farinaceous: Containing starch grains; mealy; resembling flour.

Farinose: Covered with mealy powder.

Farm animal genetic resources: Those animal species that are used, or may be used, for the production of food and agriculture, and the populations within each of them. Within each species, these populations can be classified as wild and feral populations, landraces and primary populations, standardized breeds, selected lines, and any conserved genetic material.

Farmers' rights: Rights first recognized by Resolution 5 of the 1989 FAO Conference as "rights arising from the past, present and future contributions of farmers in the conservation, improvement and the making available of plant genetic resources"; this item became an attachment to the 'International Undertaking on Plant Genetic Resources'. The binding 'International Treaty of Plant Genetic Resources for Food and Agriculture' that resulted from the renegotiations of the Undertaking makes provision for the Farmers' Rights in Article 9.

Fasciated: Unnaturally and often monstrously connate or adnate, the coalesced parts often unnaturally proliferated in size and/ or number; e.g., inflorescence of Celosia

Fasciation: A malformation in plants, in which a stem or branch becomes expanded into a flat, ribbon-like shape, as if several stems were joined together lengthwise.

Fascicle Sheath: Closely imbricated bud scales at the base of the fascicle of needles; e.g., pinus.

Fascicle: A close cluster or bundle, as of leaves, stems, or flowers. Sometimes limited in use to a compacted cyme.

Fasciculate: Leaves or other structures in a cluster from a common point.

Fastigiate trees: Trees grown for their narrow, columnar shape.

Fastigiate: Branches close to stem and erect.

Fat: An organic compound containing carbon. Hydrogen. And oxygen but with proportionately much less oxygen than is present in a carbohydrate molecule.

Faveolate: Honeycombed; alveolate. In botany, also favose.

Favulariate: Of a surface, finely ribbed, the ribs separated by zig-zag furrows.

Fc: A product of hydrolysis of an IgG antibody, consisting of parts of the constant regions of two heavy chains held together by a disulphide bridge, but excluding the antigen-binding regions, and also excluding the light chains.

Fed batch fermentation: Culture of cells or micro-organisms where nutrients are added periodically to the bioreactor.

Feedback inhibition: The process by which the accumulated end product of a biochemical pathway stops synthesis of that product. The effect is that a late metabolite of a synthetic pathway regulates the synthesis of an earlier step of the pathway.

Female: A plant that produces fruit; the plant that bears the pistil and receives the pollen or fertilizing element of the male plant, or the analagous organ in cryptogams. Pertaining to the kind of plants that produce fruit; pistil bearing; pistillate; producing pistillate flowers.

Fen: Low land covered wholly or partially with water but producing sedge, coarse grasses, or other aquatic plants; boggy land; a moor or marsh; plant community on alkaline, neutral, or slightly acid peat.

Fenestrated: A type of leaf anatomy with small perforation or transparent spots. Confined to a few tropical monocotyledons which grow on the island of Madagascar.

Fermentation substrates: Materials used as food for growing micro-organisms. The fermentation substrates and the trace materials needed, together with chemicals added to make the fermentation easier, form the culture medium.

Fermentation: The anaerobic breakdown of complex organic substances, especially carbohydrates, by micro-organisms, yielding energy. Often misused to describe large-scale aerobic cell culture in specialized vessels (fermenters, bioreactors) for secondary product synthesis.

Fern: Ferns are in the division Pterophyta and consist of four different orders: Ophioglossales, Pteridales, Salvineales, and Marsilcalcs. The ferns that most people grow in their homes or in their gardens is in the order Pteridales. These ferns are characterized by a rhizome with adventitious roots and leaf branches off of the nodes. Spores are borne on the lower surface of the leaf.

Fernery: A place where ferns are growing, often in a greenhouse; a plantation of ferns.

Ferns: Plants of the division Pterophyta, with leaves (fronds) often consisting of many leaflets.

Ferric iron: An oxidized or high-volence form of iron.

Ferruginous: Rust-covered.

Fertile: 1. Producing abundantly; capable of sustaining abundant growth, as fertile soil. 2. Capable of producing fruit; having a functional pistil, bearing functional pollen, etc. 3. Capable of fertilizing, as an anther with well-developed pollen.

Fertilisation: The union of male and female gametes.

Fertility: The quality of soil that enables it to provide compounds in adequate amounts and in proper balance for the growth of specified plants.

Fertilization: The union of two gametes from opposite sexes to form a zygote. Typically, each gamete contains a haploid set of chromosomes. Hence the zygotic nucleus contains a diploid set of chromosomes. Several categories can be distinguished: 1. Self-fertilization (selfing): fusion of male and female gametes from the same individual. 2. Cross-fertilization (crossing): fusion of male and female gametes from different individuals. 3. Double fertilization; restricted to flowering plants, in which the fusion of one male gamete with the ovum occurs at about the same time as the second male gamete nucleus fuses with the female polar nuclei (or secondary nucleus) to form the endosperm.

Fertilizer: Any substance that is added to soil in order to increase its productivity. Fertilizers can be of biological origin (e.g. composts), or they can be synthetic (artificial fertilizer).

Fertilizer grade: An expression that indicates the percentage of plant nutrients in a fertilizer.

Fertilizer injector: A device connected to the faucet end of a garden hose; it contains about a pint of liquid or water soluble fertilizer and mixes it at a predetermined rate with water flowing through the hose.

Fetid: Having an unpleasant, rotten odor.

Feulgen staining: A histochemical stain by which the distribution of DNA in the chromosomes of dividing cell nuclei can be observed.

FIA: Abbreviation for fluorescence immuno-assay.

Fiber: Elongated and thickened cell found in xylem tissue. It strengthens and supports the surrounding cells.

Fiber cell: A long-walled plant cell which is often dead at maturity; fibers impart elasticity, flexibility and tensile strength to plant structure.

Fibonacci phyllotaxis: A fundamental type of leaf arrangement expressed as a fraction in which each succeeding fraction is the sum of the two previous numerators and the sum of the two previous denominators, i.e., 1/2, 1/3, 2/5, 3/8, 5/13, 8/ 21, etc. The numerator represents the number of turns or spirals around a stem before one leaf is directly above another and the denominator represents the number of leaves in the turns or spirals before one is directly above the other. 2/5 phyllotaxy would mean two twists and five leaves before one leaf is directly above the other or an angle of divergence of 144 between succeeding leaves in the stem (2/5 of 360).According to Leppik anthotaxis and semataxis do not necessarily follow the same pattern, with anthotaxis in Michelia cited as being in 2/7, 3/7, 3/8, and 4/10 systems of arrangement.

Fibre: A relatively long sclerenchyma cell, usually occurring in bundles or strands.

Fibril: A microscopic to sub-microscopic cellulose thread that is part of the cellulose matrix of plant cell walls.

Fibrillose: Finely fibrous furnished with thread-like structures.

Fibroblasts: Irregularly shaped, branching cells distributed throughout vertebrate connective tissue. A cell type which is readily cultured in vitro.

Fibrous root: Root system in which both primary and lateral roots have approximately equal diameters. Opposite: tap root.

Fibrous: With fine, threadlike or slender roots or fibers.

Fid: Suffix meaning 'dividend or lobed =/- half way', eg. bifid, trifid, 6-fid, pinnatifid etc.

Field capacity: The highest amount of moisture remaining in a soil after free water has been allowed to drain away. Expressed as a percentage of oven-dry weight of soil or other convenient unit.

Field moisture: The water that soil contains under field conditions.

Filament: The stalk of a stamen; a thread one or more cells thick; in blue-green Algae, a trichome enclosed in a mucilaginous sheath.

Filantherous or typical: Stamen with distinct anther and filament with or without thecal appendages, as in rhexia or vaccinium.

Filiciform: In the shape of a fern or fern frond.

Filiferous filamentose or filiferous: With coarse marginal fibers or threads.

Filiform: Thread-like, long and very slender.

Filter bioreactor: A cell culture system, in which cells are grown on a fine mesh of an inert material, which allows the culture medium to flow past it but retains the cells. This is similar in idea to membrane and hollow fibre reactors, but can be much easier to set up, being similar to conventional tower bioreactors, but with the mesh replacing the central reactor space. Synonym: mesh bioreactor.

Filter sterilization: Process of removing microbial contaminants from a liquid by passing through a filter with pores too small to allow the passage of micro-organisms and spores.

Filtration: 1. Separation of solids from liquids by using a porous material that only allows passage of the liquid or of solids smaller than the pore size of the filter. The material passing the filter forms the filtrate. 2. Removal of cell aggregates to obtain a filtrate of single cells that can be utilized as plating inocula.

Fimble: The male hemp plant or the fiber made from it. Also called fimble hemp.

Fimbria: A fringe-like border; the peristome of a moss.

Fimbriate: Fringed; bordered with hairs or with slender processes, as a fimbriate petal. Also fimbriated.

Fine sand: Soil particles measuring from.10 to.25 millimeter.

Fine-textured soil: A clayey soil containing 35% or more clay.

Firming: A term used to indicate light-packing of soil around roots.

First bottom: The normal flood plain of a stream.

Fish meal: An organic fertilizer made of fish.

Fission: Asexual reproduction involving the division of a single-celled individual into two daughter single-celled individuals of approximately equal size.

Fissurcs: Linear splits or cracks. Term commonly refers to bark or stems.

Fistular: Hollow throughout its length.

Fistulous: Having the form or nature of a fistula.

Fitness: The survival value and the reproductive capability of an individual, compared to that of competitor individuals of the same or other species within a population or an environment.

Fitness, adaptive: The ability of a population to survive, reproduce, and adapt genetically to a changing environment for at least a modest number (usually fewer than 50) generations.

Fixation: The situation in which only one allele for a given gene/locus is present in a population. This can occur as a result of direct selection where the allele delivers a greater level of fitness; because of indirect selection, where the locus is linked to a gene that is subject to direct selection; or because of genetic drift.

Flabellate: Fan-shaped, with a wedge-shaped outline and sometimes conspicuously plaited or nerved. eg. the leaf of Gingko.

Flabelliform: Fan-shaped.

Flaccid: Weak, limp, soft, or flabby; leaves that do not have enough water and are about to wilt or are wilting.

Flagellate: Bearing flagella, whip-like strands or organs.

Flagellum: A eukaryotic flagellum is a bundle of nine fused pairs of microtubules called "doublets" surrounding two central single microtubules (the so-called 9+1 structure of paired microtubules; also called the "axoneme"). At the base of a eukaryotic flagellum is a microtubule organizing center about 500 nm long, called the basal body or kinetosome. The flagellum is encased within the cell's plasma membrane, so that the interior of the flagellum is accessible to the cell's cytoplasm. This is necessary because the flagellum's flexing is driven by the protein dynein bridging the microtubules all along its length and forcing them to slide relative to each other, and ATP must be transported to them for them to function. This extension of the cytoplasm is called the axosome. The eukaryotic flagellum is completely different from the prokaryote flagellum in structure and in evolutionary origin. The only thing that the bacterial, archaean, and eukaryotic flagella have in common is that they stick outside of the cell and wiggle to produce propulsion.

Flaming: A technique for sterilizing instruments, to remove live micro-organism contaminants. The instrument is dipped in alcohol, and the alcohol remaining on the instrument is ignited, thereby heat-sterilizing the surface.

Flanking region: The DNA sequences extending either side of a specific sequence.

Flash tape: A breeze-activated, metalized plastic tape that produces bursts of light in response to breezes; suspended over crops to scare away birds.

Flat: A container for holding packs of plant starter cells. Also called seed flat.

Flavin adenine dinucleotide (FAD): A co-enzyme important in various biochemical reactions. It comprises a phosphorylated vitamin B2 (riboflavin) molecule linked to AMP, and functions as a hydrogen acceptor in dehydrogenation reactions. The reduced form is oxidized back to FAD by the electron transport chain, generating two molecules of ATP per molecule of reduced FADH.

Fleshy: Succulent roots.

Flexible: Casily bent but recovering the original form.

Flexuous: With a series of long or open vertical curves at right angles to the central axis.

Floating row cover: This is a lightweight fiber sheet, water and air penetrable, that is placed over a row of plants for protection from heat, cold or insects.

Floating: Upon the surface of the water.

Floccose a. (L. floccus, a lock of wool): Said of pubescence which gives the impression of irregular tufts of cotton or wool.

Flocculant: A chemical agent that causes small particles to aggregate (flocculate).

Flocculate: To clump together individual tiny soil particles.

Floccule: A micro-organism aggregate or colloidal particle floating in or on a liquid. The cloudy appearance of micro-organism contaminated liquid media illustrates the flocculation phenomenon.

Floccus: A small tuft of woolly hairs.

Floetid: With a stinking odour; smelling offensively.

Flood irrigation: A shallow flood of water over level soil.

Flora: Plant life in general, often in contrast to fauna. The plants native to or adapted to a particular region, habitat, etc. or belonging to a particular period.

Floral envelope: The perianth of a flower.

Floral: Containing, belonging to, or relating to a flower; pertaining to flowers in general; made of flowers.

Florescence: Blooming; the unfolding of a flower; the state of being in bloom.

Florescent: Being at the point or stage of florescence.

Floret: One of the small individual flowers of a crowded inflorescence such as capitulum; flower with lemma and palea, of grasses; alt. floscule.

Floricane: The stem at flowering and fruiting stage (of a bramble, Rubus).

Floriculture: The cultivation of flowers or of flowering plants, usually commercially.

Floriculturist: A person who specializes in growing flowers.

Floriferous: Flower-bearing, usually used to indicate profuse flowering.

Florigen: One or more hormones once thought from circumstantial evidence to initiate ftowering but which have never been isolated or proved to exist.

Floriparous: This pertains to plants that normally bear fruit but instead produce secondary flowers.

Florist: One who sells flowers and ornamentals.

Florist's flower vase: A tapered metal bucket, slightly flared at the top, is used to hold cut flowers.

Floscular: Same as discoid, as applied to disk flowers in the family Compositae; composed of florets. Also flosculous, flosculose.

Floscule: A small flower; a floret.

Flotophyllous: With floating leaves.

Flow cytometry: Automated measurements on large numbers of individual cells or other small biological materials, made as the cells flow one by one in a fluid stream past optical and/or electronic sensors. A similar approach may be used for sorting cells.

Flower: 1. The part of the plant that ordinarily contains the reproductive organs, which are usually surrounded by colorful petals and sepals. A flower containing only stamens, is male, or staminate; a flower containing only pistils, is female, or pistillate. When a flower contains both pistils and stamens it is called a bisexual, or perfect, flower; if it also has a corolla and calyx, it is called a complete flower. 2. Flower is also generally used to describe any blossom or inflorescence or any plant of which the blossom is the essential feature; a plant grown for its floral beauty.

Flower arrangement: A combination of individual cut flowers to create an attractive decoration.

Flower heads: A mass of small flowers or florets that together appear to form a single flower (e.g. Daisy); a form of inflorescence giving the effect of a single flower, consisting of a compact cluster of florets sessile upon the shortened summit of the axis.

Flower press: A contraption in which flowers may be dried and preserved. A flower press consists of layers of cardboard and blotting paper sandwiched between two wooden boards, which are held together in the corners by adjustable screws.

Flower ring: A wire loop supported by stakes to prop and contain a cluster of weak-stemmed flowers such as bachelor buttons or campanulas.

Flower stalk: A peduncle or pedicel; the ordinarily leafless part of a stem or branch that bears a flower cluster or a single flower.

Flower support: A stake, usually made of plastic coated wire, to prop or brace a single weak-stemmed plant such as lily or gladiolus. Also called loop stake.

Floweret: A floret; sometimes refers to one of the segments of a cauliflower head.

Fluorescence activated cell sorting (FACS): A flow cytometry method in which targets (cells, individual chromosomes etc.) are labelled with a fluorescent dye, which is excited by a laser beam. Differences in the fluorescence signal emitted are used as a criterion for sorting the material. A specific application is in sperm sexing.

Fluorescence immunoassay (FIA): An immunoassay based on the use of fluorescence-labelled antibody.

Fluorescence in situ hybridization (FISH): Hybridization of cloned, fluorescently labelled DNA or RNA, to intact biological materials, notably chromosome spreads and thin tissue sections. The technique allows the visualization of the physical location of nucleic acid sequences homologous to the probe, and is used for the placement of genes on chromosomes and for the spatial and temporal pattern of gene expression of specific mRNA molecules.

Fluorescent probe: A probe which is labelled with a fluorescent dye, so that the signal emitted can be captured by photometric methods.

Fluorescent tube: A type of light bulb that emits ultraviolet light. Fluorescent lamps are used to start and maintain plants indoors.

Fluorescent-light gardening: The process of growing plants under artificial lights.

Flush: A period of rapid vegetative growth, often involving the expansion of non-green or pale green leaves at the soot extremeties.

Flushing shoots: Shoots that develop from mature terminal buds several times during a season. Terminal bud will develop shoot with new terminal bud which will develop more shoots and a terminal bud which will develop etc.—several times in a season with several flushes of growth.

Fly trap: Hinged, insectivorous leaf, as in dionaea.

Foetus: Pre-natal stage of a viviparous animal, between the embryonic stage and birth. AlteRNAtive spelling: fetus.

Fog: Fine particles of liquid suspended in the air, such as of water in a fog chamber used for acclimatizing recent ex vitro transplants.

Fold back: The structure of a double-stranded DNA molecule formed when a molecule containing an inverted repeat sequence is denatured and then allowed to re-anneal at low DNA concentrations. Under these conditions, the repeated sequence self-anneals to form a double-stranded region within each of the separated strands of the original molecule.

Folded genome: The condensed state of the chromosomal DNA of a bacterium. The DNA is segregated into domains, and each domain is independently negatively supercoiled.

Folded: Foliate embryo with cotyledons usually thin and extensively expanded and folded in various ways

Foliaceous: Being or resembling a leaf. In botany, having the texture or form of a leaf, as a foliaceous sepal or bract.

Foliage plant: A plant grown for its attractive foliage rather than for its flowers, as the various kinds of Coleus and Philodendron.

Foliage: The mass of growing plant leaves in their natural form and condition, or a cluster of the same; leafage.

Foliar: Consisting of or pertaining to leaves.

Foliar feeding: Feeding plants by spraying plant food on their leaves.

Foliate: Leaved, clothed in leaves; also as a suffix, eg. Bifoliate.

Foliation: The leafing of plants; the disposition of the beginning leaves within the bud.

Foliicolous: Growing upon leaves; parasitic on leaves, as many fungi.

Foliolate: Pertaining to, consisting of, or having leaflets. Used in combination, as bifoliolate, having two leaflets.

Foliole: A leaflet; a small part resembling a leaf.

Foliose: Bearing numerous crowded leaves.

Follicetum: An aggregation of follicles, as in caltha

Follicle stimulating hormone (FSH): A hormone, secreted by the anterior pituitary gland in mammals, that stimulates the ripening of the specialized structures in the ovary (Graafian follicles) that produce ova in female mammals; and in males, the formation of sperm in the testis. FSH is a major constituent of fertility drugs.

Follicle: An enclosing cluster of cells that protects and nourishes a cell or structure within. Thus a follicle in the ovary contains a developing egg cell, while a hair follicle envelops the root of hair.

Food chain: A natural chain of organisms of a community wherein each member of the chain feeds on members below it and is consumed by members above it, with autotrophic organisms (producers) being at the bottom; interconnected food chains are referred to as food webs.

Food processing enzyme: Enzyme used to control food texture, flavour, appearance, or nutritional value. Amylases break down complex polysaccharides to simpler sugars; proteases tenderize meat proteins. A prominent target of food biotechnology is to develop novel food enzymes which can improve the quality of processed foods.

Footstalk: The stalk, or petiole, of a leaf or the peduncle of a flower.

Forb: A small, upright soft-stemmed or non-woody plant with broadleaves; the growth form of many common wildflowers.

Forced cloning: The insertion of foreign DNA into a cloning vector in a predetermined orientation.

Forcing house: A hothouse used for forcing plants.

Forcing pit: A pit of wood or masonry, sunk in the earth, for containing fermenting materials to produce bottom heat in forcing plants.

Forcing: The practice of bringing a plant into growth or flower (usually by artificial heat or controlling daylight) at a season earlier than its natural one.

Foreign DNA Exogenous: DNA that is incorporated into a host genome.

Forest: A community dominated by trees with long trunks.

Forest genetics: The study of heredity in forest trees.

Forest tree improvement: The application of genetic principles to the improvement and management of forest trees.

Form: A botanical category ranking below a variety and differing only trivially from other related forms, such as in flower color.

Fornicate: Overarched fornices, as the throat of the corolla of the forget-me-not. Also forniciform.

Fornix: A small, arching scale or appendage in the throat of the corolla of some plants, such as in forget-me-nots.

Forskolin: A medicinal, diterpenoid, compound exclusive to plant roots and used in the preparation of drugs for the treatment of cardiomyopathy, glaucoma and certain cancers.

Fortify: To add strengthening components or beneficial ingredients to a nutrient medium.

Forward mutation: A mutation from the wild type to the mutant type. Opposite: reverse mutation.

Forward selection: Choosing the best individuals out of a progeny test for use in seed orchards and/or subsequent generations of breeding.

Fossil: The remains or impressions of any natura] object that has been preserved in the earth's crust.

Fouling: The coating or plugging (by materials or micro-organisms) of equipment, thus preventing it from functioning properly.

Founder animal: An organism that carries a transgene in its germ line and can be used in matings to establish a pure-breeding transgenic line, or one that acts as a breeding stock for transgenic animals.

Founder principle: The possibility that a new, isolated population, initiated by a small number of individuals taken from a parent population, may be genetically different from the parent population, because the founding individuals might not be typical of the parent population.

Four base cutter: A type II restriction endonuclease with a four-nucleotide recognition site. Because any particular sequence of four bases occurs more frequently by chance than one of six bases, four-base cutters cleave more frequently than six-base cutters, and therefore generate, on average, smaller restriction fragments. Synonyms: four-base-pair-cutter, four-cutter.

Fovea: Pit or depression containing the sporangium in the leaf base of Isoetes

Fractionation: The separation in components of a complex mixture of molecules.

Fragipans: The hard and brittle layers in soil that roots and water can't penetrate because it is so dense and compact.

Frame: A garden frame is a bottomless box with a transparent top that is used to provide favorable conditions for the plant's growth and to cover them during harsh weather. The top is made of plastic or glass set in a wooden or metal frame. To allow for proper ventilation, the top is formed with one or two moveable sections called sash; the sashes are moved by sliding them up and down or, if they are hinged, by raising their fronts. Their are unheated and heated frames and they are both good for raising seedlings ahead of the outdoor season and for growing early crops of Lettuce, Cauliflower, Radishes, Corn, Snapdragons, and other vegetables and flowers.

Frameshift mutation: A mutation that changes the reading frame of a DNA, either by the insertion or the deletion of nucleotides. Because of the triplet nature of codons, this occurs if the number of nucleotides involved is not a multiple of three.

Free: Used to describe the condition of a substance within a mixture when it isn't chemically combined with other components of the mixture.

Free living conditions: Natural or greenhouse conditions experienced by plantlets upon transfer from in vitro conditions to soil. Prior to transfer, nutrients were supplied by the culture medium, but following transfer, plantlets must take up nutrients from soil and synthesize their own food supply.

Free water: The cellular water released into the intercellular spaces when tissue is frozen and thawed. Opposite: bound water.

Free-adnate: Hypanthium fused with ovary and having a free limb around or above ovary

Free-central: A placentation in which the ovules are borne on a free-standing central placenta within the ovary.

Freeze dry: The removal of water as vapour from frozen material under vacuum. Used to measure water content and to preserve samples, particularly spores. Unlike oven-drying, bound water remains associated with the specimen. Synonym: lyophilize.

Fresh weight: Same as wet weight. Generally not a useful measurement for aquatic plants.

Friable: Rich, loamy soil that is easily worked and loose; soil of a crumbly texture, able to be worked easily. Friable soil crumbles easily when worked with a spade, fork, rake, etc. The opposite is a tenacious, clayey soil. The particles of this soil cling together forming clods that are difficult to pulverize. Nonfriable soil can be enhanced by the following methods: Mixing in organic matter such as manure, leaf mold, peat moss and compost; turning under cover crops or green manures such as Winter Rye, Ryegrass and Buckwheat and adding sand or gritty coal cinders; liming; and the use of synthetic soil conditioners.

Fringe: The modified margin of a petal, sepal, tepal or lip.

Frond: A leaf especially of a fern, cycad or palm; a leaf-like portion of a non-vascular plant (e.g. a foliose alga).

Frondescence: The period or state of coming into leaf; leafage; foliage.

Frondiferous: Producing fronds or leaves.

Frondose: Bearing or resembling fronds.

Fronds: The leaves of ferns. Fern fronds maybe uncut (undivided), once-cut (divided into subdivisions), twice-cut (divided into subdivisions twice-the subdivisions are themselves subdivided), or thrice-cut (divided into subdivisions three times-the subdivisions of the subdivisions are also subdivided!). Thrice-cut ferns are also called lacy ferns.

Frost: 1. That state or temperature of the air that occasions freezing of water. 2. The state or condition of being frozen; said of the surface of the ground when frost extends to a depth of 10 inches.

Frost control: The act of minimizing frost damage to plants by covering them, watering them lightly, or placing them in a protected area.

Fructiferous: Bearing or producing fruit.

Fructification: 1. The production of fruit by a plant; fruiting. 2. The ripened ovary and its appendages; the fruit of a plant.

Fructify: To bear or produce fruit; to make fruitful.

Fruit: 1. Any product of vegetable growth useful to humans or animals (i.e. grapes, figs, corn, cotton, flax, and all cultivated plants). There are many kinds of fruit and they differ greatly in character and degree of complexity. 2. The reproductive product of a plant; the seed of plants, or the part that contains the seeds. 3. An edible, juicy product of a plant, usually covering the seeds (i.e. apple, orange, a berry, a melon, etc.). 4. The matured ovary of a plant, consisting of the seeds and their pericarp (coating) and including whatever may be incorporated with it; also, the spores of cryptogams and the organs accessory to them. (verb) 1. To produce fruit; to come into bearing.

Fruit dot: The sorus of ferns.

Fruit trees, dwarf: Describes genetic dwarf trees and trees grafted onto dwarf roots. For example, peaches that are genetic dwarfs produce full size fruit on trees that hardly ever grow more than 3 feet high. Fruit trees grafted onto dwarf rootstock, such as citrus or apples, produce normal fruit on trees that only grow up to 8 feet high. Many grafted fruit trees are also sold as semi-dwarf, growing to about 10 feet high. Dwarf fruit trees are great for growing in suburban yards, containers, and in areas with little space.

Fruit, compound: A fruit that is made of several ovaries.

Fruiting body: A specialized organ for producing spores, as in mosses and mushrooms.

Fruitlet: 1. A small fruit. 2. A unit of a collective fruit.

Frumentaceous: Having the character of or resembling wheat or other cereal.

Frutescent: Having the appearance or habit of a shrub; shrubby, as a frutescent stem.

Fruticose: Resembling a shrub; shrubby, as a fruticose stem.

Fucoxanthin: A brownish pigment occulting in brown and other algae.

Fugacious: Ephemeral, usually applied to plant parts

Fulvous: Yellow, tawny, dull yellow with a mixture of grey or brown.

Fumigant: A volatile chemical used to kill pathogens in the soil or in glasshouses. Fumigants are usually applied to the soil by injection. Chemicals used as fumigants include methyl bromide, chloropicrin, formaldehyde, metham, ethylene, dibromide, and carbon disulphide.

Functional food: A foodstuff that provides a health benefit beyond basic nutrition, demonstrating specific health or medical benefits, including the prevention and treatment of disease.

Functional genomics: The field of research, that aims to determine patterns of gene expression and interaction in the genome, based on the knowledge of extensive or complete genomic sequence of an organism.

Fungal: Pertaining to, characteristic of, or consisting of a fungus or fungi. Also fungous.

Fungi: A division of diverse plants that lack chlorophyll and do not photosynthesize. Included are mushrooms, molds, rusts, smuts, and yeasts. Some are edible, such as Boletus; many are plant diseases, such as powdery mildew.

Fungicide: A chemical that kills fungi. Fungicides are used to prevent or control fungal diseases. They are applied to seeds as a dust or slurry and to standing crops usually as a spray. For control of postharvest diseases fruits may be dipped or sprayed, or packed in fungicide-impregnated materials. Fungicides can also be applied to the soil for control of damping-off and root diseases. Fungicides, like other pesticides, usually have three names - the chemical name of the active ingredient, the approved common name, and the trade name. For example, methyl N-[1-(butylcarbamoyl)-2-benzimidazole] carbamate is the chemical name of benomyl, which has the trade name Benlate. Fungicides fall into two major categories: the inorganic fungicides including copper fungicides and sulphur dust; and the organic fungicides, a group comprising the more modern fungicides, including systemic fungicides.

Funicular: With a persistent elongate funiculus attached to seed coat, as in Magnolia.

Funiculus: (funicle) The stalk attaching the ovule, and later the seed, to the placenta or ovary wall in angiosperms. It serves as an anchor and provides a vascular supply to the ovule and seed.

Funnel form: Having the shape of a funnel; applied to the corolla of a flower in which the tube enlarges gradually from below, as the morning glory; infundibuliform.

Furcated: Forked, also as bifurcate, trifurcate etc.

Furfuraceous: Coated with bran-like, flaky particles; scurfy.

Furrow: 1. A trench in the earth, especially one make by a plow. 2. To cut a furrow in; make furrows in; plow.

Furrowed: Having longitudinal channels, ridges, or grooves, as a furrowed stem.

Fusarium sp.: A common soil fungus (17,5). It is found on a wide range of plants. It is often found in humidifiers. Several species in this genus can produce potent trichothecene toxins. The trichothecene (scirpene) toxin targets, the following systems: circulatory, alimentary, skin and nervous. Produces vomitoxin on grains during unusually damp growing conditions. Symptoms may occur either through ingestion of contaminated grains or possibly inhalation of spores. The genera can produce hemorrhagic syndrome in humans (alimentary toxic aleukia). This is characterized by nausea, vomiting, diarrhea, dermatitis, and extensive internal bleeding. Reported to be allergenic. Frequently involved in eye, skin and nail infections.

Fuscous: Dusky, blackish, of a brownish or greyish brown colour.

Fusiform initials: More or less elongate initials in the vascular cambium that give rise to the components of the axial (longitudinal) system of the secondary xylem and secondary phloem (e.g. vessel elements, tracheids, and sieve tube elements). They also give rise to the ray initials.

Fusiform: A spindle- or cigar-shaped, a solid swollen in the middle and tapering at both ends.

Fusion biopharmaceuticals: Fusion proteins with pharmaceutical properties. Their advantages are: 1. Synergistic activities in one molecule, i.e. when the molecule binds to its target, it can perform more than one function simultaneously; 2. An adverse effect or poor stability of one part of the molecule may be offset by the properties of the other; and 3. One part of the molecule can act as a targeting mechanism for the active protein.

Fusion protein: A polypeptide translated from a chimeric gene. The different genes are joined so that their coding sequences are in the same reading frame, and the resulting construct is transcribed and translated as a single gene, producing a single protein. These are used for a number of purposes, including: 1. To add an affinity tag to a protein; 2. To produce a protein with the combined characteristics of two natural proteins; 3. To produce a protein where two different activities are physically linked.

Fusion toxin: A fusion protein that consists of a toxic protein domain plus a cell receptor binding domain. The latter delivers the toxin directly to the target cell, thus sparing other healthy tissues from the effect of the toxin.

G: Abbreviation for guanine.

G protein: Proteins found on the inner surface of the plasma membrane, which bind to the guanine nucleotides, GTP and GDP. They transmit signals from outside the membrane, via trans-membrane (G-protein-coupled) receptors, to adenylate cyclase, which catalyses the formation of the second messenger, cyclic AMP, inside the cell.

Galactan: A polysaccharide in which the major monosaccharide subunit is galactose, though other sugars, notably arabinose, are often also present. Galactans are structural polysaccharides, often found among the pectic substances of cell walls.

Galactomannan: A gum in which the structural chain is made up of D-mannose units with 1-4 linkages. The ratio of galactose to mannose is 1:2.

Galactose: An aldohexose sugar commonly found in plants. It normally does not exist in the free state but as polymers. It is also a constituent of the oligosaccharides raffinose and stachyose. Oxidation of galactose yields galacturonic acid, which on polymerization forms pectic acid.

Galbulus: A spherical cone formed of thick scales with a narrow base, as in the Cypress, or berry-like with fleshy scales, as in the Juniper.

Galea: A helmet-shaped part of a calyx or corolla, as the upper lip of a ringent or labiate corolla. The "helmet" formed by the dorsal sepal or fusion of dorsal sepal and petals in some Orchids.

Galeate: Having a galea; helmet-shaped (i.e. the helmet-shaped upper sepal of Monkshood).

Gall: An abnormal plant growth on leaves, branches, or roots that is caused by irritation from an insect, a fungus or a virus.

Gametangium: Any cell or structure in which gametes are produced.

Gamete and embryo storage: Storage of ova, sperm or fertilized embryos outside their original source. Almost invariably this means cryopreservation.

Gamete: A mature reproductive cell which is capable of fusing with a cell of similar origin but of opposite sex to form a zygote from which a new organism can develop. Gametes normally have a haploid chromosome content. In animals, a gamete is a sperm or egg; in plants, it is pollen, spermatic nucleus, or ovum.

Gametic (phase) equilibrium: In relation to any two loci, the occurrence of haplotypes (gametes) at a frequency equal to the product of the frequency of the two relevant alleles. For example, A and B are in gametic equilibrium if the frequency of AiBi gametes equals the product of the frequencies of alleles Ai and Bi. Opposite: gametic (phase) disequilibrium.

Gametoclone: A plant regenerated from a tissue culture originating from gametic tissue.

Gametogenesis: The process of the formation of gametes.

Gametophore: The structure on the gametophyte which actually produces the gamete. Note that this distinction between gemetophyte and gametophore is usually only necessary in the liverworts and mosses, in which the gametophyte generation is dominant and the gametophyte includes all the basic structures for vegetative growth.

Gametophyte: The generation or stage of a plant producing gametes, existing only as a rudimentary structure in seed plants and as distinguished from the sporophyte, or asexual form.

Gametophytic incompatibility: A phenomenon in plants, in which a pollen grain is genetically incapable of fertilizing a particular egg, because both gametes carry the identical allele at an incompatibility locus (usually denoted S). This is a mechanism for forcing crossfertilization.

Gamopetalous: (sympetalous) Having petals that are fused along their margins to the base, forming a corolla tube. Most plants possessing such flowers are grouped together in the Sympetalae.

Garden compost: An organic matter such as well-decayed leaves, grass-clippings, and vegetable waste, added to the soil as an amendment to improve its texture and drainage and to enrich it with nutrients.

Gas transfer: The rate at which gases are transferred from gas into solution, an important parameter in fermentation systems because it controls the rate at which the organism can metabolize. Efficient gas transfer can be achieved in several ways, including the use of small bubbles, from which gas dissolves faster than from larger ones, due to their larger surface area per unit of volume; or spreading the liquid out, for example in a thin sheet, or in a thin permeable tube, as in hollow fibre bioreactor.

Gas vacuole: A structure made up of numerous gas-filled vesicles, many of which may be found in the cells of certain aquatic bacteria and blue-green algae. The density of the cell depends on how much gas is contained within the vesicles. The position of the organism in a column of water can thus be regulated by these structures. The vesicles are unusual in being bound by a protein rather than phosphoglyceride membrane.

Gastrula: An early animal embryo consisting of two layers of cells; an embryological stage following the blastula.

Gazebo: An ornamental garden structure, resembling a free-standing porch, which may contain benches or statuary.

GC island: A segment of double-stranded DNA that is rich in GC base pairs. This type of sequence is characteristic of eukaryotic genomic regions with a high gene content.

GDP: Abbreviation for guanosine 5'-diphosphate.

Geitonogamy: The pollination of a pistil by pollen from another flower of the same plant.

Gel filtration: A method of protein or DNA purification, where differences in size are used to separate the components of a complex mixture.

Gel: A jelly-like solid, used widely as a matrix for the electrophoresis of macromolecules, for encapsulation, and to solidify media for cell cultures.

Gelatin: A glutinous, proteinaceous gelling and solidifying agent. Gelatin is produced by the partial hydrolysis (via boiling) of collagen, found in the connective tissues of many farm animals. Used to gel or solidify nutrient solutions for tissue culture, and as a food additive.

Gelatinization: The swelling of starch when added to hot water. Hydrolysis causes the molecule to lose structure, and technically gelatinization is not complete until there is no structure left at all.

Gelatinous: Of a slimy, clear sticky nature, water soluble, like gelatine.

Gelrite: The brand name of a Pseudomonas-derived refined polysaccharide used as a gelling agent and agar substitute.

GEM: Abbreviation for genetically engineered micro-organism.

Geminate: Twinned, arranged in pairs.

Geminiflorous: Having flowers in pairs.

Gemma: A small outgrowth of tissue that becomes detached from the parent body and is capable of developing into a complete new plant or other organism; gemmae are produced in cuplike structures on liverwort thalli and are also produced by certain fungi.

Gemmates: Buds or outgrowths of a plant which develop into a new individual.

Gemmation: The act of budding; asexual reproduction in which a new organism originates locally within the body or on the surface of the parent. Also gemmulation.

Gemmoid: Having the nature or form of a gemma.

Gene: The unit of heredity transmitted from generation to generation during sexual or asexual reproduction. More generally, the term is used in relation to the transmission and inheritance of particular identifiable traits. The simplest gene consists a segment of nucleic acid that encodes an individual protein or RNA.

Gene addition: The addition of a functional copy of a gene to the genome of an organism.

Gene amplification: The selective production of multiple copies of one gene without a proportional increase in others.

Gene bank: 1. The physical location where collections of genetic material in the form of seeds, tissues or reproductive cells of plants or animals are stored. 2. Field gene bank: A facility established for the ex situ storage and maintenance, using horticultural techniques, of individual plants. Used for species whose seeds are recalcitrant, or for clonally propagated species of agricultural importance, e.g. apple varieties. 3. A collection of cloned DNA fragments from a single genome. Ideally the bank should contain cloned representatives of all the DNA sequences in the genome.

Gene cloning: The synthesis of multiple copies of a chosen DNA sequence using a bacterial cell or another organism as a host. The gene of interest is inserted into a vector, and the resulting recombinant DNA molecule is amplified in an appropriate host cell.

Gene conversion: A process, often associated with recombination, during which one allele is replicated at the expense of another, leading to non-Mendelian segregation ratios.

Gene expression: The process by which a gene produces mRNA and protein, and hence exerts its effect on the phenotype of an organism.

Gene flow: The spread of genes from one breeding population to another (usually) related population by migration, thereby generating changes in allele frequency.

Gene imprinting: The differential expression of a single gene according to its parental origin.

Gene insertion: The incorporation of one or more copies of a gene into a chromosome.

Gene interaction: The modification of the action of one gene by another, non-allelic gene.

Gene modification: Chemical change to a gene's DNA sequence.

Gene pool, primary: The sum total of all the genetic variation in the breeding population of a species and closely related species that commonly interbreed with, or can be routinely crossed with, the species.

Gene pool, secondary: The sum total of all the genetic variation in the breeding populations of related species that can be crossed with the species using mentor pollen, embryo rescue or other unusual measures.

Gene pool, tertiary: The sum total of all the genetic variation in other organisms that cannot be crossed with the species. (With the development of genetic engineering, it is theoretically possible to transfer genes isolated from any organism (plant, animals, virus, or bacterium) into a plant. This makes the line between the secondary and tertiary gene pools somewhat fuzzy.)

Gene pool: 1. The sum of all genetic information in a breeding population at a given time. 2. In plant genetic resources, use is made of the terms 'primary', 'secondary' and 'tertiary' gene pools. In general, members of the primary gene pool are inter-fertile; those of the secondary can be crossed with those in the primary gene pool under special circumstances; but to introgress variation from the tertiary gene pool, special techniques are required to achieve crossing.

Gene regulation: The process of controlling the synthesis or suppression of gene products in specific cells or tissues.

Gene replacement: The incorporation of a transgene into a chromosome at its normal location by homologous recombination, thus replacing the copy of the gene originally present at the locus.

Gene synthesizer: A machine that creates specific DNA sequences.

Gene therapy: The proposed treatment of an inherited disease by the transformation of an affected individual with a wild-type copy of the defective gene causing the disorder. In germ-line (or heritable) gene therapy, reproductive cells are transformed; in somatic-cell (or non-inheritable) gene therapy, cells other than reproductive ones are modified.

Gene tracking: Following the inheritance of a particular gene from generation to generation.

Gene translocation: The movement of a gene from one chromosomal location to another.

Generally regarded as safe (GRAS): Designation given to foods, drugs, and other materials with a long-term history of not causing illness to humans, even though formal toxicity testing may not been conducted. Certain host organisms for recombinant DNA experimentation have recently been given this status.

Generative cell: The cell of the male gametophyte of angiosperms that divides, producing two sperms; also, the cell of the male gametophyte of gymnosperms that divides, producing a sterile cell and a spermatogenous cell.

Generative nucleus: In many flowering plants, shed pollen is two-celled (in others it is three-celled or has a variable number). Before pollen is shed, the male gametophyte divides mitotically to give a generative and a vegetative nucleus. The former is the progenitor of the sperm cells.

Generic: 1. Pertaining to a genus, or a kind or group of similar things; comprehending a number of like things, without specifying them. 2. Having the taxonomic rank or classificatory value of a genus (i.e. a generic name or description, generic characters or differences, generic identity). In the botanic classification of Genipa Americana, Genipa is the generic name of over 75 trees with similar characteristics, differing from other genera or groups of plants. 3. Distinctly characteristic; so marked as to constitute or denote a distinct kind.

Generic agreement/identity: The agreement of objects that belong to the same genus.

Generic area: The region to which the members of a genus (group) are limited in distribution. (The place in a generic area where the genus is most represented by species or individuals is known as its metropolis.)

Generic description/diagnosis: A description or characterization of a genus in botany.

Generic diversity: The differences between individuals of different genera.

Generic name: The denomination that comprehends all the species, as of a group of animals, plants or fossils, which have generic characteristics in common.

Genet: The individual(s) descended vegetatively from a single sexually produced zygote, including all entities derived from it. All these individuals are genetically identical to one another (barring mutation).

Genetic assimilation: Eventual extinction of a natural species as massive gene flow occurs from a related species.

Genetic code: The correspondence between the set of 64 possible nucleotide triplets and the amino acids and stop codons that they specify.

Genetic complementation: When two DNA molecules that are in the same cell together produce a function that neither DNA molecule can supply on its own.

Genetic disease: A disease caused by an abnormality in the genetic material, which could be at the level of DNA sequence at a locus, or at the level of karyotype. Usually refers to inherited diseases, although somatic mutations can also cause disease without being inherited.

Genetic distance: A measure of the genetic similarity between any pair of populations. This is measured on the basis of variation in a combination of phenotypic traits, allele frequencies or DNA sequences. For example, the genetic distance between two populations having the same allele frequencies at a particular locus, and based solely on that locus, is zero.

Genetic diversity: The amount of genotypic variability in a population. Quantitative definition: the number of different alleles per loci and the proportion of loci with more than one allele in a species or population.

Genetic drift: Change in allele frequency from one generation to another within a population, due to the sampling of finite numbers of genes that is inevitable in all finite-sized populations. The smaller the population, the greater is the genetic drift, with the result that some alleles are lost, and genetic diversity is reduced. Thus minimization of genetic drift is an important consideration for conservation of genetic resources.

Genetic engineering: The introduction, by artificial means. Of genes from one form of DNA into another form of DNA.

Genetic equilibrium: The maintenance of a steady state with respect to allele frequencies in a group of interbreeding organisms.

Genetic erosion: The loss over time of allelic diversity, particularly in farmed organisms, caused by either natural or man-made processes.

Genetic gain: The change achieved by artificial selection in a specific trait. Gain is usually expressed as the change per generation or the change per year. Gain is influenced by selection intensity, parental variation, and heritability.

Genetic heterogeneity: Occurs where the genetic determination of a given phenotype differs between individuals.

Genetic immunization: Delivery to a host organism of a cloned gene that encodes an antigen. After the cloned gene is expressed, it elicits an antibody response that protects the organism from infection by the relevant pathogen.

Genetic information: Information contained in a nucleotide base sequence in chromosomal DNA or RNA.

Genetic map: The linear array of genes on a chromosome, based on recombination frequencies (linkage map) or physical location (physical or chromosomal map).

Genetic marker: A DNA sequence used to identify a particular location (locus) on a particular chromosome.

Genetic pollution: Uncontrolled spread of genetic information (frequently referring to transgenes) into the genomes of organisms in which such genes are not present in nature.

Genetic relatedness: A quantitative estimate of the proportion of genes, →, shared between the genomes of any two individuals, groups or populations, e.g. r = 0.5 for full siblings and parent offspring pairs.

Genetic resources: Genetic material of actual or potential value.

Genetic selection: The process of selecting genes, cells, clones, etc., within populations or between populations or species. Genetic selection usually results in differential survival rates of the various genotypes, reflecting many variables, including the selection pressure and genetic variability present in populations.

Genetic use restriction technology (GURT): A proposed technology applying transgenesis to genetically compromise the fertility or the performance of saved seed of a cultivar or of second generation animals. The intention is to protect the market for the seed producer or to prevent undesired escape of genes. Two types of GURTs have been patented: variety-level GURT (V-GURT), which produces sterile progeny, and trait-specific GURT (T-GURT), in which only the added value transgenic trait is genetically protected.

Genetic variation: Differences between individuals attributable to differences in genotype.

Genetically engineered organism (GEO): Occasional alternative term for genetically modified organism.

Genetically modified organism (GMO): An organism that has been transformed by the insertion of one or more transgenes.

Genetics: Genetics is the basic science dealing with causes of resemblances and differences among organisms related by descent. It takes into account the effects of genes and the environment.

Geniculate: Bent like a knee; bent abruptly at the nodes.

Genome: 1. The entire complement of genetic material (genes plus non-coding sequences) present in each cell of an organism, virus or organelle. 2. The complete set of chromosomes (hence of genes) inherited as a unit from one parent.

Genomic library: A clone library specifically constructed from restriction fragments of the genomic DNA of an organism.

Genomics: The research strategy that uses molecular characterization and cloning of whole genomes to understand the structure, function and evolution of genes and to answer fundamental biological questions.

Genotype-environment interaction: Changes in rank or levels of performance among individuals when tested in different environments.

Genus: A category in plant classification, consisting of one or more related species. Thus, all Roses are grouped in the genus Rosa, all

Willows in the genus Salix and all Oaks in the genus Quercus. Each genus, or group, includes a number of species. For example, Quercus contains the Pin Oak (Q. palustris), the Red Oak (Q. coccinea), the Black Oak (Q. velutina), and many others. Some genera, such as Ginkgo and Sanguinaria, consist of only a single species. The genera name is also known as the botanical name. Just as there are species assigned to a single genus, there a number of genera assigned to a family.

Geocarpous: Fruits below ground, as in Amphicarpum.

Geoflorous: With subterranean flower.

Geographic variation: The phenotypic differences among native trees growing in different portions of a species' range. If the differences are largely genetic rather than environmental, the variation is usually specified as racial, ecotypic, or clinal.

Geophyte: Plants with an underground dormant part such as a tuber, bulb, rhizome, etc. to help the plant survive adverse conditions.

Geotrichum sp.: Conidia dimensions 6-12 x 3-6 microns. Aw 0.90 A common contaminant of grains, fruits, dairy products, paper, textiles, soil and water, and often present as part of the normal human flora. The species Geotrichum candidum can cause a secondary infection (geotrichosis) in association with tuberculosis. This rare disease can cause lesions of the skin, bronchi mouth, lung and intestine.

Geotropic: Pertaining to, or exhibiting, geotropism.

Geotropism: 1. Tropism in which gravity is the orienting factor, up or down. 2. Tropism in which growth is toward the earth. Also geotropy.

Germ: 1.The botanical term for a plant embryo. 2. Colloquial: a disease-causing micro-organism.

Germ cell gene therapy: The repair or replacement of a defective gene within the gamete-forming tissues, resulting in a heritable change in an organism's genetic constitution.

Germ cell: A member of a cell lineage (the germ line) leading to the production of gametes. In mammals, germ cells are found in the germinal epithelium of the ovaries and testes. Synonym: germ line cell.

Germ layer: The layers of cells in an animal embryo at the gastrula stage, from which the various organs of the animal's body will be derived.

Germ line gene therapy: The delivery of a gene or genes to a fertilized egg or an early embryonic cell. The transferred gene(s) is present in all or some of the nuclei of the cells of the mature individual, including possibly the reproductive cells, and alters the phenotype of the individual that develops.

Germ line: A lineage of cells which, during the development of an organism, are set aside as potential gamete-forming tissues. The location, nature and time of formation of potential gamete-forming tissues are species specific, and may vary greatly from one species to another.

Germ plasm: The sum total of all the genes of a species or group of organisms.

Germ tube: A tubular, thread-like growth first formed by most spores in germination.

Germicide: Any chemical agent used to control or kill any pathogenic and non-pathogenic micro-organisms.

Germinal epithelium: 1. A layer of epithelial cells on the surface of the ovary that are continuous with the mesothelium. 2. The layer of epithelial cells lining the seminiferous tubules of the testis, which gives rise to spermatogonia.

Germinate: To cause to grow or sprout; to begin growing.

Germination: 1. The act, process, or result of germinating; the development of a seed. The development of a seed into a plant. Oxygen, warmth and moisture are necessary for germination to occur. The moisture softens the seed, relaxes tissues in the embryo and dissolves nutrients. Oxygen is necessary for the chemical changes needed for growth. The temperature needed varies between the species. Some seeds, such as wheat seeds, will germinate on melting ice; others need temperatures higher than 60° F. When germination takes place, a root is produced that grows down into the soil; at the same time, a stem and leaves are growing upward. 2. The similar development of a plant from a spore in cryptogams, such as ferns. 3. The early period of growth in a bud, as a bulb or a rhizome. 4. The protrusion and growth of the pollen tube from the pollen grain.

Germinative: Pertaining to germination; capable of germination.

Germ-line mutation: A mutation in a cell from which gametes are derived; the mutation can be passed on to offspring.

Germplasm: 1. An individual, group of individuals or a clone representing a genotype, variety, species or culture, held in an in situ or ex situ collection. 2. Original meaning, now no longer in use: the genetic material that forms the physical basis of inheritance and which is transmitted from one generation to the next by means of the germ cells.

Gestation: The period between conception (fertilization of the egg) to parturition (birth) spent in utero by the foetus of viviparous animals.

Gibberellins: A class of plant growth regulators which are active in the elongation, enhancement of flower, fruit and leaf size, germination, vernalization and other physiological processes.

Gibbous: A distended, rounded swelling on one side, as on a calyx or corolla tube or segment.

Gill: One of the flattened plates of compact mycelium that radiate out from the stalk on the underside of the caps of most mushrooms.

Girdling (gurd'ling): The removal of a band of tissues extending inward to the vascular cambium on the stem of a woody plant.

Glabrate: Becoming glabrous with age.

Glabrescent: Becoming naked or devoid of covering at maturity.

Glabrous: With a smooth, even surface; without hairs.

Glade: Open space surrounded by woods or a forest; a marshy and usually low-lying area; a periodically inundated grassy marsh often running between adjacent slopes; a marshy area bounding or forming the headwaters of a stream.

Gladiate: Sword-shaped; ensiform.

Gland: A specialized group of cells or a single cell in animals or plants that secretes a specific substance. The two types of animal glands are: endocrine, which secrete directly into the blood vessels; and exocrine, which secrete through a duct or network of ducts into a body cavity or onto the body surface.

Glandular: 1. Resembling or pertaining to a gland. 2. Bearing glands. 3. Derived from glands. Also glandulous.

Glandular-pubescent: Hairs or trichomes capitate and secretory.

Glans (involucre): Nut subtended by a cupulate, dry involucre, as in quercus.

Glaucescent: Slightly glaucous or becoming so.

Glaucous: 1. Blue-green, blue-gray, gray, or pale yellow-green color. 2. Having a waxy or powdery, bluish-white or bluish-gray bloom that can be rubbed off (i.e. glaucous plums or grapes).

Gley soil: A layer of soil that has turned gray because of lack of oxygen and excessive water.

Gliocladium sp.: A fungus which is structurally similar to Penicillium sp. It is reported to be allergenic.

Globose: Rounded; almost spherical; globular.

Globulins: Common class of proteins in blood, eggs and milk, and seeds. Characterized by their slight solubility in water but are freely soluble in dilute salt solutions. Gamma- globulins are defined further by their electrophoretic behaviour, and include the immunoglobulins.

Glochid: A barbed hair or bristle.

Glochidiate: With barbed trichomes, glochids, usually in tufts.

Glochidium: A very dense cluster; hence glomerulate.

Glochids: Barbed bristly hairs or spines, often very fine and easily detached, on an Opuntia cactus.

Glomerate: To gather or wind into a ball; growing, collected or arranged in a rounded mass, as glands, flowers, etc.; clustered.

Glomerulate: Arranged in small, compact clusters. Also glomerulose.

Glomerule: A compact flower cluster that forms a head, as in the flowering Dogwood, Cornus florida.

GLP: Abbreviation for good laboratory practice.

Glucocorticoid: A steroid hormone that regulates gene expression in higher animals.

Glucose isomerase: An enzyme that catalyses the interconversion of the two sugars, glucose and fructose. As fructose is a lower energy compound compared with glucose, a mixture of glucose and fructose with the enzyme will end up almost entirely as fructose.

Glucosinolates: A class of molecules produced in the seeds and green tissue of a range of plants, in particular brassicas. Their natural role is thought to be involved in plant-insect interactions. Their importance in plant breeding is largely because of their negative influence on taste and their positive effect on the prevention of cancers of the alimentary tract.

Glumaceous: Glume-like; having glumes; chaffy.

Glume: A chaffy bract as in the Gramineae (grass family) and related plants; especially an empty bract at the base of a grass spikelet.

Glumiferous: Having glumes.

Gluten: A mixture of two seed storage protein classes, gliadin and glutenin, found in the endosperm of cereal (particularly wheat) grain. High levels of gluten impart elasticity to dough, and thus the composition of wheat glutens largely determines whether a specific flour is suitable for biscuit or bread making. Sensitivity of the lining of the intestine to gluten in some humans results in coeliac disease, a condition that requires a gluten-free diet.

Glutinous: Having a sticky, moist surface; a gluey or sticky exudation.

Glycoalkaloids: A group of modified alkaloids, including solanine and tomatine, having a range of toxic effects in humans and other species. They are of particular significance in food plants from the Solanaceae.

Glycoform: One of several structures possible for a given glycoprotein, determined by the type and position of attachment of the component oligosaccharide(s). Certain glycoforms may exhibit different biological activities from one another because the oligosaccharide units mediate interactions with other cell components.

Glycolysis: The initial phase of all types of respiration in which glucose is converted to pyruvic acid without involving free oxygen.

Glycoprotein: A protein molecule modified by the addition of one or several oligosaccharide groups.

Glycoprotein remodelling: The use of restriction endoglycosidases to enzymatically remove oligosaccharide branches from glycoprotein molecules. Removal of one or more oligosaccharide branches can lessen or abolish the antigenicity of the glycoprotein, so allowing its injection for pharmaceutical purposes without incurring an unwanted immune response.

Glycosylation: The covalent addition of sugar or sugar-related molecules to other classes of molecule, including proteins or nucleic acids.

Glyphosate: An active ingredient in some herbicides, killing plants by inhibiting the activity of plant enolpyruvyl-shikimate 3-phosphate synthase.

Glyphosate oxidase: An enzyme which catalyses the break-down of glyphosate, discovered in a strain of Pseudomonas bacteria which were found to produce unusually large amounts of the enzyme. The gene responsible has been incorporated into a variety of crop plants to enable them to tolerate applications of glyphosate-containing herbicides. It has also been used in conjunction with the CP4 EPSPS gene.

GM food: Abbreviation for genetically modified food. Food that contains above a certain legal minimum content of raw material obtained from genetically modified organisms.

GMO: Abbreviation for genetically modified organism.

GMP: Abbreviation for 1. guanosine 5'-monophosphate. Synonym: guanylic acid. 2. good manufacturing practice.

Golden rice: A biotechnology-derived rice, which contains large amounts of beta carotene (a precursor of vitamin A) in its seeds. Achieved by inserting two genes from daffodil and one from the bacterium Erwinia uredovora.

Golgi apparatus: An assembly of vesicles and folded membranes within the cytoplasm of plant and animal cells that stores and transports secretory products (such as enzymes and hormones) and plays a role in formation of a cell wall (when this is present).

Gonad: One of the (usually paired) animal organs that produce reproductive cells (gametes). The most important gonads are the male testis, which produces spermatozoa, and the female ovary, which produces ova (egg cells). The gonads also produce hormones that control secondary sexual characteristics.

Good laboratory practice (GLP): Written codes of practice designed to reduce to a minimum the chance of procedural or instrument problems which could adversely affect a research project or other laboratory work.

Good manufacturing practice (GMP): Codes of practice designed to reduce to a minimum the chance of procedural or instrument/ manufacturing plant problems which could adversely affect a manufactured product.

Gradate: Graded, or stepped, of a sorus with the youngest sporangia at the apex and the older ones lower down.

Graft chimera: A plant which is a mosaic of two sorts of tissue differing in genetic constitution and assumed to have arisen as the result of a nuclear fusion following grafting.

Graft hybrid: A hybrid produced by grafting a branch of one species (scion) onto another (rootstock), in which the two grow together to form a single plant or tree.

Graft inoculation test: A test based on the use of a suspected viral carrier which is grafted to an indicator plant. If symptoms appear in the indicator plant, the viral assay is positive.

Graft union: The point at which a scion from one plant is joined to a rootstock from another plant.

Graft: 1. Method of propagation by which an artificial union is made between different parts of individual plants. The stem or shoot that is inserted into a rooted plant is called the scion; the plant or part of a plant into which the scion is inserted is called the stock or understock. There are many different methods of grafting including flat grafting, split grafting, and side grafting, among others. 2. The point where a scion is inserted in the stock.

Grafting: The process of making a graft.

Grafting tape Tape backed with biodegradable cloth; used in budding and grafting operations and in banding tree wounds. Also called nurseryman's tape.

Grafting thread: Fine waxed string used in budding and grafting operations.

Grafting wax: A waxy substance used to hold and seal tree or rose grafts.

Graft-versus-host disease: The rejection of transplanted organs by the recipient's immune system, due to attack of the recipient's T lymphocytes on the transplanted organ caused by differences in major histocompatibility complex proteins

Grain: 1. The unhusked or threshed seed of one of the cereal plants: wheat, oats, rye, barley, maize, or millet; a corn. 2. Corn in general; the gathered seeds of cereal plants in mass.

Gram staining: A technique to distinguish between two major bacterial groups, based on whether or not their cell wall retains the Gram stain. Gram-positive bacteria are stained dark purple, while Gram-negative bacteria are only faintly coloured. Stain retention is determined by the structure of the cell wall.

Gramineous: Grass-like; belonging to the family Gramineāe. Also graminaceous, gramineal.

Graniform: Having the form of a seed or grain.

Granular fertilizer: A fertilizer made up to particles 0.1 inch in diameter.

Granular: Containing, bearing, resembling, or composed of grains or granules. Covered with small grains or granules. Also granulose, granulous.

Granulate: 1. To form into granules; make rough on the surface. 2. To become formed into grains; become granular; consisting of or resembling grains or granules. Also granulated.

Granulation: 1. The process of granulating. 2. One of the little elevations in a granulated surface.

Granule: A little grain; a fine particle.

Granum: Structure within the chloroplasts, appear as green granules with the light microscope and as a series of parallel lamellae with the electron microscope. They contain the chlorophyll and carotenoid pigments directly involved in photo-synthesis.

GRAS: Abbreviation for generally regarded as safe.

Grass leaves: Grass leaves have a considerably different morphology than do leaves of most all other plants. Grass leaves are composed of a sheath, blade, auricle and ligule. The sheath is the blade-like portion that acts like the petiole of the leaf, only it is flat and blade-like and surrounds the stem, connecting to the node below. The blade extends at a right angle to the sheath. The ligule is a small tongue-like flat of tissue that extends out from the sheath and parallel to it above the blade and perpendicular to the blade. The auricles are two small flaps of tissue that extend out from the blade and perpendicular to the sheath, partially surrounding the stem.

Grassland: A community dominated by grass species.

Gratuitous inducer: A substance that can induce transcription of a gene or genes, but is not a substrate for the induced enzyme(s).

Gravitational water: Water that drains out of the pore spaces of a soil after a rain.

Gravitropism: Growth response to gravity.

Greasy or Unctuous: Slick, oily, slippery to touch

Great soil group: Any one of several broad groups of soil with fundamental characteristics in common.

Green fluorescent protein (GFP): A protein derived from a species of jelly fish, that fluoresces when exposed to ultra violet light. Its encoding gene has been isolated and is replacing GUS as a reporter gene in plant transgenesis, since it can be assayed non-destructively in real time.

Green manure: An organic crop material, turned under the soil, to be used as a fertilizer to add nitrogen to the soil. The green plants decay in the soil and provide humus and make stiff soil more porous and friable. A quick-growing crop is sown and dug into the ground before it reaches maturity (when it will provide the greatest bulk without being to tall to turn under).

Green revolution: Name given to the dramatic increase in crop productivity during the third quarter of the 20th century, as a result of integrated advances in genetics and plant breeding, agronomy, and pest and disease control.

Greenhouse effect: The greenhouse effect is an increase in the temperature of a planet as heat energy from sunlight is trapped in the atmosphere. Excess carbon dioxide and water vapor increase this effect. The greenhouse effect is strong on Earth, maintaining (and possible exacerbating) warm temperatures.

Greenhouse: A building of glass or plastic that is used to grow and protect tender plants.

Gro luxa: A wide-spectrum fluorescent lamp suitable for artificial light for plant growth.

Ground cover: Refers to low-growing or trailing plants that are used to carpet the ground, as underneath trees or as an overplanting for bulbs.

Ground meristem: Meristem that produces all the primary tissues other than the epidermis and stele (e.g., cortex, pith).

Ground water: 1. Water that fills all unblocked pores of underlying material below the water table. 2. The upper limit of saturation.

Grow light: A broad-spectrum florescent light used to grow plants indoors.

Growing point: The tip of a shoot from which new growth emerges.

Growing tray: A tray having compartments like an ice-cube tray, used for starting seeds. Also called a cell tray.

Growth: Progressive increase in size and volume through natural development.

Growth cabinet: An enclosed space in which environmental conditions can be controlled. The degree of control over temperature, light and humidity is a function of the quality of the cabinet.

Growth form: The overall morphology of a plant species, including its stature, leaf type, and habit. The general description of the type of growth exhibited by a plant, such as herbaceous, shrubby (bush-like) and arborescent (tree-like). The most basic grow forms are trees, shrubs, forbs, and graminoids; but there are many more specialized growth forms such as epiphytes, lianas, and stem succulents.

Growth hormone (GH): A group of hormones, secreted by the mammalian pituitary gland, that stimulates protein synthesis and growth of the long bones in the legs and arms. They also promote the breakdown and use of fats as an energy source, rather than glucose.

Growth inhibitor: Any substance inhibiting the growth of an organism. The inhibitory effect can range from mild inhibition (growth retardation) to severe inhibition or death (toxic reaction). The concentration of the inhibitor, the length of exposure to it, and the relative susceptibility of the organisms exposed to the inhibitor, are all important factors which determine the extent of the inhibitory effect.

Growth phase: Each of the characteristic periods in the growth curve of a bacterial culture, as indicated by the shape of a graph of viable cell number versus time, namely: lag phase; logarithmic phase; stationary phase; death phase.

Growth rate: Change in an organism's mass per unit of time.

Growth regulator: A synthetic or natural compound that at low concentrations elicits and controls growth responses in a manner similar to hormones.

Growth retardant: A chemical that selectively interferes with normal hormonal promotion of growth and other physiological processes, but without appreciable toxic effects.

Growth ring: Rings visible in a cross-section of a woody stem, such as a tree trunk. Each ring represents the xylem formed in one year as a result of fluctuating activity of the vascular cambium.

Growth substance: Any organic substance, other than a nutrient, that is synthesized by plants and regulates growth and development. They are usually made in a particular region, such as the shoot tip, and transported to other regions, where they take effect.

Grumrose: Made of clustered, coarse grains or granules. Also grumous.

Guanine (G): One of the bases found in DNA and RNA.

Guano: A strong, organic fertilizer composed of bird droppings.

Guanosine: The (ribo)nucleoside resulting from the combination of the base guanine (G) and a D-ribose sugar. The corresponding deoxyribonucleoside is called deoxy-guanosine.

Guanylic acid: Synonym for guanosine monophosphate (GMP), a (ribo)nucleotide containing the nucleoside guanosine. The corresponding deoxyribonucleotide is called deoxy-guanylic acid.

Guard cell: Each stoma has two crescent-shaped guard cells that control the size of the opening of the stoma using turgor pressure. This changes the amount of water vapor and other gases that can enter and leave the plant.

Guide sequence: An RNA molecule (or a part of it) which hybridizes with eukaryotic mRNA and aids in the splicing of intron sequences. Guide sequences may be either external (EGS) or internal (IGS) to the RNA being processed and may hybridize with either intron or exon sequences close to the splice junction.

Gumbo soil: 1. Adobe soil. 2. An alkaline soil found in the West and Southwest of the U.S. that has enough nutrients to grow plants but is too compact for most gardening purposes.

GUS: Abbreviation for beta-glucuronidase.

Gus gene: An E. coli gene that encodes for production of beta-glucuronidase (GUS). Because this activity is absent in plants, the gene is commonly utilized as a reporter gene to detect the occurrence of transformation events.

Guttate: Spotted, as by drops. Also guttated.

Guttation: Formation of drops of water on plants from moisture in air; the process of water being exuded from hydathodes at the enlarged terminations of veins around the margins of the leaves.

Guttiferous: Producing gum or resinous substances.

Gymnocarpous: Having a naked fruit, especially in lichens.

Gymnosperm: A class of plant (e.g. conifers) whose ovules and the seeds into which they develop are borne unprotected, rather than enclosed in ovaries, as are those of the flowering plants, the (angiosperms).

Gymnospermae: An important division of the plant kingdom, being woody plants with alternation of generations, having the gametophyte retained on the sporophyte and seeds produced on the surface of the sporophylls and not enclosed in an ovary.

Gymnospore: A naked spore.

Gymnosporous: Having naked spores.

Gynaecium: The female organs of the flower, consisting of one or more carpels forming one or several ovaries with their stigmas and styles.

Gynagamous: Inflorescence with pistillate flowers inside or above and neuter flowers outside or below (gynagamocephalous)

Gynandrial or gynostemial: With fused stamens and carpels (stigma and style) as in the Orchidaceae

Gynandromorph: An individual in which one part of the body is female and another part is male; a sex mosaic.

Gynandrous: Describing stamens that are inserted on the gynoecium.

Gynecandrous: Inflorescence with pistillate flowers inside or above and staminate outside or below, as in spikes of some species of Carex

Gynehermaphroditic: Inflorescence with pistillate flowers inside or above and hermaphroditic outside or below (gynehermaphrodicephalous)

Gynobase: A prolongation or enlargement of the flower receptacle that bears the gynoecium.

Gynodioecious: Describing plants that bear female and hermaphrodite flowers on separate individuals, as in thymes (Thymus) and oregano (Origanum vulgare).

Gynoecium: (gynaecium) The female component of the angiosperm flower, which may be made up of one or more carpels. The gynoecium usually occupies the most central part of the floral axis, although in more advanced forms it may not be symmetrically placed. If the gynoecium contains only one carpel it is termed monocarpellary, unicarpellous, or stylodious. If there are two or more separate carpels it is apocarpous and if the carpels are fused syncarpous. The gynoecium is represented by the letter G in the floral formula.

Gynogenesis: Female parthenogenesis: after fertilization of the ovum, the male nucleus is eliminated and the haploid (gynogenetic) individual possesses the maternal genome only.

Gynomonoecious: Having both perfect and female flowers upon the same plant.

Gynophore: An elongation of the receptacle of a flower, bearing the gynoecium at its apex, as in some Capparidaceae.

Gynostegium: A protective covering for a gynaecium, especially as formed by the union of stamens and style.

H: Prefix used to designate the human form of an enzyme. For example, hGH is human growth hormone.

Habituation: The process of becoming accustomed to a new environment. The term is applied specifically to the ability of certain long-established callus cultures to synthesize auxin and hence become independent of exogenous supplies. Such habituated cultures are also called anergized cultures.

HAC: Abbreviation for human artificial chromosome.

Haemoglobin: Protein containing iron, located in erythrocytes of vertebrates; important for the transportation of oxygen to the cells of the body.

Haemolymph: The mixture of blood and other fluids in the body cavity of an invertebrate.

Haemophilia: A sex-linked hereditary bleeding disorder in which it takes a long time for the blood to clot and abnormal bleeding occurs. This disease affects mostly males.

Hairpin loop: A region in one strand of a polynucleotide which, due to an inverted repeat in the sequence, may under appropriate conditions fold back on itself and form a limited segment of double-stranded DNA with a loop at one end.

Hairy root culture: A culture consisting of highly branched roots of a plant. A plant tissue is treated with the bacterium Agrobacterium rhizogenes containing the Ri plasmid, which causes the explant to grow highly branched roots from the sites of infection. Transgenes engineered into the plasmid can be expressed in these cultures.

Hairy root disease: A disease of broad-leaved plants, where a proliferation of root-like tissue is formed from the stem. Hairy root disease is a tumorous state similar to crown gall, and is induced by the bacterium Agrobacterium rhizogenes, when containing an Ri plasmid.

Half-inferior: Other floral organs attached around ovary with hypanthium adnate to lower half of ovary.

Half-life: The amount of time it takes for a radioactive element to lose half of its radioactivity.

Half-terete: Flat on one side, terete on other; semicircular in cross section.

Halophilous: Preferring or habitually growing in salty soil as maritime plants.

Halophyte: A plant species adapted to soils containing a concentration of salt that is toxic to most plant species.

Halosere: A pioneer plant community that develops in a low-lying region of land originally beneath the sea and subsequently silted up with mud, silt, and shingle. The plants must be adapted to survive inundation by the tide twice a day. A major pioneer plant is glasswort (Salicornia europaea), which gradually gives way to salt-marsh grasses (Puccinellia) or sea aster (Aster tripolium). when the salinity decreases other species, such as thrift (Armeria maritima) and seablites (Suaeda), grow. The region becomes stabilized to form mudflats and salt marshes.

Handpicking: A method of controlling pests by literally removing the pest from the plant by hand. This is effective with larger pests, such as tomato hornworms and snails.

Hanging basket: A container hung from a brace, tree, etc., with a rope or cord, which is used to grow ornamental plants.

Hanging plant rotator: A device that rotates a hanging plant a certain amount (usually 90°) to ensure even lighting.

Haploid: A nucleus is haploid if it contains only one copy of each non-redundant gene. The great majority of animals, and higher plants, are diploid. That is, the form we usually observe has two copies of each gene, one from each parent. In lower plants there are numerous exceptions to the rule. Further-more, the gametophyte generation is always haploid.

Haplomorphic: Flowers with parts spirally arranged at a simple level in a semispheric or hemispheric form; petals or tepals colored; parts numerous; e.g., Nymphaea, Magnolia.

Haplophyte: Having the number of chromosomes characteristic of the gametes for the organism.

Haplotype: A specimen where doubt exists if the author actually handled the specimen mention in the description.

Hapten: A small molecule, which by itself is not an antigen, but which as a part of a larger structure when linked to a carrier protein, can serve as an antigenic determinant.

Hapteron: Holdfast, specialized root-like projections that function to anchor a plant.

Haptoglobin: A serum protein that interacts with haemoglobin during recycling of the iron molecule of haemoglobin. Synonym: alpha globulin.

Hardening off: The gradual process of acclimating plants started indoors to outside conditions. Setting them in a sheltered location outdoors for increasing lengths of time over a period of days is said to be hardening off the plants. If the plants are just set outside without getting used to the different atmospheres, they will most likely suffer.

Hardiness zones: Areas classified by climate and temperature range for the purpose of determining which plants can be grown where. The U.S. is divided into eleven zones. One is the coldest and eleven is the warmest. Plants living in zones one through four are considered vary hardy; those in zones 5 - 7 are hardy; those in zones 8 - 9 are fairly hardy; those in zone 10 are said to be very tender, which means most will not survive freezing; zone 11 is frost-free since it consists of subtropical or tropical regions. The zones are classified by their average low temperature. Zone 1 has an average low temperature of -50° F. Zone 2 = -50° to -40°; zone 3 = -40° to -30°; zone 4 = -30° to -20°; zone 5 -20° to -10°; zone 6 = -10° to 0°; zone 7 = 0° to 10°; zone 8 = 10° to 20°; zone 9 = 20° to 30°; zone 10 = 30° to 40°; zone 11 = no lower that 40°.

Hardpan: A hard or cement-like soil or soil layer.

Hardwood: The wood from trees with encapsulated seeds (i.e. nuts or fruits), as distinguished from a conifer or cone-bearing tree, which has naked seeds. Oaks, Walnuts and Maples are all hardwoods. Pines and firs are softwoods.

Hardy: Used to describe a plant that is able to survive the cold temperatures of a given location without protection. When a range is given, hardiness also describes a plant's ability to tolerate the hottest temperatures normally experienced. (For example, a Palm tree isn't hardy in Alaska, because it is a tropical plant requiring a warm, humid atmosphere.)

Hardy weinberg equilibrium: The frequencies of genotypes at a locus resulting from random mating at that locus; for two alleles, A1 and A2, with respective frequencies in a population of p and q, the Hardy-Weinberg equilibrium frequencies are p2 A1A1; 2pq A1A2; q2 A2A2. Departure from these frequencies is an indication that random mating is not occurring.

Harrow: 1. A rake-like tool that is drug over plowed soil to prepare it for planting. 2. To draw a harrow over soil; to break or tear with a harrow, as to harrow ground.

Harvesting: 1. The process involved in gathering ripened crops. 2. The collection of cells from cell cultures or of organs from donors for the purpose of transplantation.

Hastate: Spear-shaped; of a leaf blade, narrow and pointed but with two basal lobes spreading approximately at right angles.

Hastiform: Triangular with two flaring basal lobes.

Haustaurium: Absorbing organ through which a parasitic plant absorbs nourishment from its host.

Haustorial: Absorbing roots, within host of some parasitic species

Head: 1. The top of a plant consisting of a compact mass of leaves, such as a head of lettuce. 2. A short, dense bunch of flowers. 3. To form a head. 4. To cut back the shoots of plants in order to induce lateral growth.

Heartwood: The older, harder wood in the middle of a tree trunk that can no longer transport water up to the leaves. This wood is often saturated with decay-protecting chemicals that also make it a different color from the outer wood.

Heat mat: A low-voltage heater used to warm soil during seed germination, seedling development, and root growth of cuttings.

Heat shock protein (HSP): A class of protein chaperones which are typically over-expressed as a response to heat stress. Two such proteins - HSP 90 and HSP 70 - have a role in ensuring that crucial proteins are folded into the correct conformation.

Heating cable: An electric device used to heat soil in a greenhouse or cold frame.

Heating system: A unit consisting of an adjustable temperature controller and a heat mat; used to maintain soil temperature during germination and seedling development or during root growth of cuttings.

Heaving: The pushing of plants out of the soil because of alternate freezing and thawing action.

Heavy soil: Fine-textured, clay soil.

Hedge binding: Something that is used to bind together the bushes composing a hedge.

Hedge: 1. A barrier or fence formed by bushes or small trees growing together; a closely planted row of shrubbery. 2. To enclose or fence with a hedge; to separate by a hedge.

Heel: When a cutting it taken with a "heel" of wood, it means a piece of the old branch or shoot is detached from the old branch or shoot along with the cutting.

Heirloom variety: A previously popular plant variety that is c1,1rrently being maintained because of certain desirable qualities.

Helicoid cyme or bostryx: A determinate inflorescence in which the branches develop on one side only, appearing simple.

Heliophilous: Fond of the sun; attracted by or becoming most active in sunshine.

Heliotropic: Turning toward the sun, as leaves or flowers.

Heliotropism: The tendency of plant parts, such as foliage, stems, or flowers, to position themselves according to the direction in which the sun hits them.

Helix: A structure with a spiral shape. The normal state of double-stranded DNA is in the form of a double helix.

Helminth: A class of parasitic worms, especially those which are internal parasites of man and animals.

Helminthosporium sp.: Reported to be allergenic.

Helobious: Living in swamps or marshes.

Helophytes: Marsh plants.

Helper cell: T cells that assist in stimulating B and T lymphocytes to develop into antibody-producing plasma cells and killer T cells, respectively.

Helper plasmid: A plasmid that provides a function or functions to another plasmid in the same cell.

Helper virus: A virus that provides a function or functions to another virus in the same cell.

Hemianatropous or hemitropous: With body half-inverted so that funiculus is attached near middle with micropyle terminal and at right angles

Hemicellulase: An enzyme that catalyses the degradation of hemicellulose.

Hemicellulose: Any cellulose-like carbohydrate, but excluding cellulose itself. Together with pectin and lignin, hemicelluloses form the cell wall matrix.

Hemicryptophyte: A perennial plant having its overwintering buds located at the soil surface.

Hemiparasite: A parasitic plant capable of limited photosynthetic production of sugars etc.

Hemizygous: The condition in which genes are present only once in the genotype and not in pairs. Occurs for all genes in haploids, for all genes located in the differential segments of the sex chromosomes in diploids, and in various aneuploids and deletion mutant heterozygotes. Synonym: haplozygous.

Henequen: A strong fiber, similar to sisal, which is produced from the leaves of a Central American Agave and used mainly for making twine. Also spelled heniquen.

HEPA filter: Abbreviation for high efficiency particulate air filter. A filter capable of excluding particles larger than 0.3ìm. HEPA filters are used in laminar air flow cabinets to ensure that the air is pathogen-free.

Herb: 1. A plant grown for its medicinal or flavoring properties or for its scented foliage. 2. Also refers to plants without persistent, woody stems. This botanical use of the word "herb" is used to distinguish between trees and shrubs.

Herbaceous: A non-woody plant in which the upper parts die back to the rootstock at the end of the growing season. An example is the Peony.

Herbage: Herbs collectively; the green foliage and juicy stems of herbs.

Herbal: Pertaining to or consisting of herbs.

Herbalism: The knowledge of herbs.

Herbalist: 1. Someone who is skilled in the knowledge of plants or makes collections of them. 2. A dealer in medicinal plants; a person who treats diseases with botanical remedies only.

Herbarium: A collection of dried pressed specimens, usually mounted on paper and provided with a label that gives collection information and an identification.

Herbicide resistance: The ability of a plant to remain unaffected by the application of a herbicide.

Herbicide: A substance that is toxic to plants; the active ingredient in agrochemicals intended to kill specific unwanted plants, especially weeds.

Herborist: An herbalist.

Herborization: An excursion for studying or collecting plants.

Hercogamous: Incapable of self-pollination.

Hercogamy: A condition in which structural obstacles within a flower make self-pollination impossible.

Heredity: Resemblance among individuals related by descent; transmission of traits from parents to offspring.

Heritability, broad sense: The proportion of the total phenotypic variability for which genetic differences are responsible.

Hermaphrodagamous: Inflorescence with hermaphroditic flowers inside or above and neuter outside or below (hermaphro-dagamocephalous)

Hermaphrodite: 1. An animal that has both male and female reproductive organs, or a mixture of male and female attributes. 2. A plant whose flowers contain both stamen and carpels. Synonym: intersex.

Hesperidium: A thick-skinned septate berry with the bulk of the fruit derived from glandular hairs, as in citrus

Heteranthous: Having different states in two different sets of flowers, only one state present in each set

Heterauxesis: The irregular growth of a plant due to unequal rates of growth in its parts.

Heteroblastic: Having the adult parts of the plant (especially the leaves) distinctly different in form from the juvenile parts.

Heteroblasty: With juvenile foliage distinctly different from adult foliage in size or shape

Heterocephalous, heterocymous, heterospicous: Heads, cymes, spikes with flowers of different sexual conditions.

Heterochromatin: Regions of chromosomes that remain contracted during interphase and therefore stain more intensely in cytological preparations. These regions have a high content of repetitive DNA, and a low content of genes; thus they are for the most part genetically inactive. Opposite: euchromatin.

Heterocladous: With stems of different sizes and/or shapes

Heterocyst: A transparent, thick-walled, slightly enlarged cell occurring in the filaments of certain cyanobacteria.

Heterodromous: Having the genetic spiral of the branches different from that of the main stem, affecting the way in which leaves are arranged around a stem.

Heterodromy: A difference in direction of the genetic spiral in the branch and the main stem.

Heteroduplex analysis: The use of the electrophoretic mobility of heteroduplex DNA to estimate the degree of non-homology between the sequences of the two strands. Gel mobility tends to be reduced as the amount of sequence divergence increases, because the effective size of a fully complementary pair of strands is smaller than that of a partially complementary structure.

Heteroduplex: A double-stranded DNA molecule or DNA-RNA hybrid, where each strand is of a different origin. Where the two DNAs differ significantly in sequence, single-stranded regions will be revealed when the heteroduplex is observed under the electron microscope. A map of homologous and non-homologous regions of the two molecules may thereby be constructed (heteroduplex mapping). Synonym: hybrid DNA (DNA/RNA).

Heterogametes: Male and female gametes that are morphologically distinguishable.

Heterogametic: Producing unlike gametes with regard to the sex chromosomes. In mammals, the XY male is heterogametic, and the XX female is homogametic.

Heterogamous: Producing flowers of two or more kinds with respect to their fertile organs, e.g. male and female or bisexual and female.

Heterogamy: The condition of being heterogamous.

Heterogeneous nuclear RNA (hnRNA): Large RNA molecules, which are found in the nucleus of a eukaryotic cell and the precursors of mRNA and other RNA molecules.

Heterokaryon: A cell with two or more different nuclei as a result of cell fusion.

Heterologous: From a different source.

Heterologous probe: A DNA probe that is derived from one species and used to screen for a similar DNA sequence from another species.

Heteromerous: In reference to flowers, having the parts of adjoining whorls different in number.

Heteromorphic, heteromorphous: Existing in two or more easily recognisable forms.

Heteromorphism: The condition of being heteromorphic.

Heterophyllous: The presence on a single individual of two or more distinct leaf shapes. These leaves may differ markedly in shape, yet have similar gross anatomical organization.

Heterophylly: The presence of more than one type of leaf on the same plant, such as floating or aerial leaves and submersed leaves on the same aquatic plant.

Heterophytous: Having different states in two different sets of plants, only one state present in each set.

Heteroplasmy: A condition in which two genetically different organelles are present in the same cell. The equivalent to heterozygous in the context of nuclear genes. Opposite: homoplasmy.

Heteroploid: Cells with nuclei containing chromosome numbers other than diploid.

Heteropyknosis: The property of certain chromosomes, or of their parts, to remain more dense during the cell cycle and to stain more intensely than other chromosomes or parts.

Heterosepalous: With sepals of different sizes and/or shapes

Heterosexual: Inflorescences or flowers within the plant with different sexual conditions

Heterosis: Hybrid vigor; superior qualities of heterozygous off spring as compared with those of their homozygous parents.

Heterosporangiate: Producing two different kinds of sporangia, specifically micro-sporangia and megasporangia. Compare with heterosporous.

Heterosporous: Producing two different sizes or kinds of spores. These may come from the same or different sporangia, and may produce similar or different gametophytes. Contrast with homosporous, and compare with heterosporangiate.

Heterospory: A condition in which an organism produces two different types and sizes of spores, viz. microspores and megaspores. As a reproductive strategy, heterospory involves the following steps The mature diploid plant (sporophyte) produces "male" and "female" spores. Typically, the plant produces numerous small "male" spores (microspores) and fewer, but larger "female" spores (megaspores). The megaspores are usually retained on the sporophyte, where a haploid female gametophyte develops inside the spore. The microspores may or may not be retained on the sporophyte. They develop into sperm-producing, haploid gametophytes. The sperm are released into the environment, and dispersed between plants. The sperm fertilize female gametophytes grown from megaspores, producing a diploid zygote (fertilized cell). The zygote develops into an embryo and finally a new diploid sporophyte. Heterospory evolved a number of times among different ancient plants. Lycopsids, ferns, sphenopsids and progymnosperms all developed heterospory. Many of these plants also evolved into large trees. The obvious advantage for heterosporous trees is that their great height would enhance the dispersal of windborne microspores. Competition for light in the shady Archaeopteris forests, may have also have encouraged heterospory, since the macrospores, like seeds, included food reserves to assist early plant growth. Heterospory is generally regarded as the precursor to the evolution of seeds. Microspore dispersal and macrospore viability in pteridosperms thus become pollen dispersal and ovule viability in seed-bearing plants. The change in sexual reproduction from moisture-bound gametophytes to seeds-bearing sporophytes enable vascular plants to colonize drier habitats and upland environments, and also provided the embryo with a protective case against hungry invertebrate herbivores.

Heterostyled: Having the styles of the flower of two or more different forms.

Heterostylous: Species in which flowers are similar except that the stigmas and anthers are held at different levels relative to each other, because style length differs between plants.

Heterotactic: Characterized by heterotaxis.

Heterotaxis: Abnormal arrangement of parts or organs as compared to a normal type.

Heterotrichous: A growth pattern of algae with prostrate filaments for attachment and erect, spreading filaments for photosynthesis.

Heterotroph: Organism non capable of self-nourishment utilizing carbon dioxide or carbonates as the sole source of carbon and obtaining energy from radiant energy or from the oxidation of inorganic elements, or compounds such as iron, sulphur, hydrogen, ammonium and nitrites. Opposite: autotroph.

Heterotrophic: Incapable of synthesizing food and therefore dependent on other organisms for it.

Heterozygote: An individual with non-identical alleles for a particular gene or genes. The condition is termed "heterozygous". Opposite: homozygote.

Heterozygous: Having two different alleles at a locus. When used to refer to the whole genotype, indicates that the individual has different alleles at most loci. When used to refer to a species as having low or high heterozygosity relative to other species, indicates that the species has a relatively high number of variable loci.

Hexapetaloid: Of a flower, having six petals. Also hexapetalous.

Hibernaculum: A plant organ such as a bud, rhizome, turion, etc. which allows a plant to live through adverse conditions.

Hibernal or hiemal: Appearing in the winter

High throughput screening: Automated systems designed to process large numbers of assays, especially in the context of genotyping.

Hilar: Belonging to the hilum, or scar, on a seed produced by the attachment to the pod, as with beans.

Hill: 1. A small raised mound or raised row with a cluster of cultivated plants, such as potatoes. 2. A group of vining plants or others planted in a cluster instead of a row, such as a hill of squash or pumpkin, even if the soil isn't mounded above the level of the garden.

Hilum: The scar on a seed marking the place where it was attached to the seed stalk.

Hip or cynarrhodion (receptacle and hypanthium): An aggregation of achenes surrounded by an urceolate receptacle and hypanthium, as in rosa.

Hippocrepiform: Horseshoe-shaped.

Hirsute: Covered with long, rather stiff trichomes.

Hirsutullous or hirtellous: Minutely hirsute.

Hispid: having stiff hairs, spines, or bristles.

Hispidity: The state of being hispid.

Hispidulous: Approaching hispid, minutely hispid.

Histocompatibility: The degree to which tissue from one organism is tolerated by the immune system of another organism.

Histoglobulin: The peptides present on the surface of nucleate cells, responsible for the differences between genetically non-identical individuals that cause rejection of tissue grafts between such individuals. Products of the major histocompatibility complex genes.

Histology: Science that deals with the microscopic structure of animal and plant tissues.

Histone: Group of water-soluble proteins rich in basic amino acids, closely associated with DNA in plant and animal chromatin. Histones are involved in the coiling of DNA in chromosomes and in the regulation of gene activity.

Histoplasma sp.: A fungus which has filamentous growth at 25 degrees C and yeast growth at 37 degrees C. It is reported to be a human pathogen. It may be associated with birds.

Hoary: Covered with hairs so fine as to not be readily visible to the naked eye, giving the surface a pale greyish hue.

Hogness box: Synonym for TATA box.

Hold fast: Attachment organ or cell at the base of the thallus or filament of certain algae.

Hollow fibre: A tube of porous material, with an internal diameter of a fraction of a millimetre, making its ratio of surface area to internal volume very large. Employed as filters or in bioreactors as a method of retaining cells while allowing the easy removal of spent medium and/or products.

Holometabolous: An insect that undergoes complete metamorphosis to the adult from a morphologically distinct larval stage.

Holophyte: A plant maintained entirely by its own organs.

Holotype: A single specimen designated by the author of a plant (or animal) name, at the time of original publication, as that to which the name shall apply; the 'voucher specimen' of a name.

Homandrous: With stamens of same size and shape.

Homanthous: Having more than one state within each individual flower, all flowers the same.

Homeobox: A highly conserved 180 bp DNA sequence that controls body part-, organ- or tissue-specific gene expression, most particularly involved in segmentation in animals (e.g. development of antennae or legs of Drosophila melanogaster), but also in a variety of other eukaryotes. It encodes a DNA-binding region, the homeodomain, which acts as a transcription factor.

Homeotic genes: Genes that act in concert to determine fundamental patterns of development.

Homeotic mutation: A mutation that causes a body part to develop in an inappropriate position in an organism, such as the mutation in Drosophila melanogaster that causes legs to develop on the head in place of antennae.

Homo: Prefix meaning 'even' or similar'.

Homoallele: One of a number of otherwise identical alleles which differ at the same site in their sequence. Homoalleles are inherited as strict alteRNAtives; but heteroalleles, in principle, could through recombination create a genotype which contains a 'double' variant.

Homocarpous: With carpels of same size and shape.

Homocephalous: Homocymous, homospicous heads, cymes, spikes with flowers sexually uniform

Homochlamydeous: With perianth composed of similar parts, each part a tepal.

Homodimer: A protein comprising two identical polypeptide chains, or a dimer of identical residues.

Homoduplex DNA: A double-stranded fully complementary DNA molecule.

Homoeologous: Referring to chromosomes which are descended from a common progenitor, but which have evolved to be no longer fully homologous. Homoeologous chromosomes have similar gene content to one another, but are structurally altered in subtle ways to inhibit, and sometimes completely prevent their pairing with one another at meiosis.

Homogametic: Producing similar gametes with regard to the sex chromosomes. In mammals, the female is homogametic (XX), and the male is heterogametic (XY).

Homogamous: 1. Of a plant, having all the flowers alike. 2. Of a flower, having the stamens and pistils maturing at the same period.

Homogenotization: An allele replacement technique, in which a bacterial cell is transformed with a plasmid containing an altered copy of the target sequence, and a double recombination event effects the substitution of the wild type allele by the altered one. An antibiotic resistance gene is usually fused to the altered copy in the plasmid, so that double recombinants can be selected.

Homogony: The state of being homogonous.

Homokaryon: A cell with two or more identical nuclei as a result of fusion. Opposite: heterokaryon.

Homologous recombination: The exchange of DNA fragments between the two non-sister chromatids of the same chromosome in the course of meiosis.

Homologous: 1. General definition: from the same source, or having the same evolutionary function or structure. 2. Of chromosomes: identical with respect to gene content and linear ordering. Homologous chromosomes pair and recombine with one another at meiosis. 3. Of DNA/proteins: identical, or nearly identical nucleotide/amino acid sequence.

Homology: 1. The degree of identity between individuals, or characters. 2. The degree of identity of sequence (nucleotide or amino acid) between a number of DNA or polypeptide molecules.

Homomallous: Referring to the leaves of mosses, curving to one side.

Homonym: The same name; a combination where the genus-species pair is exactly the same as an already existing combination, based on a different type.

Homophytous: Having more than one state within each individual plant, all plants the same.

Homoplasmy: The condition in which all copies of an organelle in a cell are genetically identical. Opposite: heteroplasmy.

Homopolymer: A polymer (nucleic acid, polypeptide, etc.) which contains only one kind of residue (e.g. the polynucleotide GGGGGGGG.).

Homosexual: Inflorescences or flowers sexually uniform.

Homosporous: producing only one kind of spore in the sexual reproductive cycle, and hence one gametophyte which produces both male and female gametes.

Homospory: A condition in which an organism produces only one type and size of spores, (microspores).

Homostyled: Having all styles one length.

Homostylous: Species in which the flowers have stigmas and anthers held at the same level relative to each other on all plants.

Homozygote: An individual that has two copies of the same allele for a given gene on its two homologous chromosomes. The condition is termed "homozygous". Opposite: heterozygote.

Homozygous: Having two identical alleles at the same locus on a pair of homologous chromosomes.

Honeydew: 1. A sweet substance found on the leaves of trees and other plants in small drops, like dew. It is the sugary substance secreted from the leaves of plants, occurring most often in hot weather. It usually is seen as small, glistening drops, but it may drip abundantly from the leaves, when it has been called manna. This especially happens with Fraxinus Ornus (the Manna Ash) and Carduus arctiodes. 2. A sweetish secretion exuded by many insects, such as aphids, mealybugs, scale and whiteflies. The secretion attracts ants, which harvest the honeydew and protect the pests from natural predators. It also develops a blackish mold, known as sooty mold. Plants that are heavily infested, especially trees, drip honeydew, staining anything underneath, such as vehicles. The best control is to eliminate ants (banding with sticky materials is effective) from the plant and then control the source pest. Insecticidal soaps will help clean the foliage.

Hood: A cover-shaped perianth part, usually with a turned down margin

Hook climber: A plant that climbs by the aid of hooks or prickles, such as certain types of roses.

Horizon soil: A layer of soil approximately parallel to the soil surface.

Hormone: A substance which can be transported through an organism and can affect growth, reproduction or metabolism (rate at which food is converted into part of the living thing). Certain synthetic hormones can be applied to cuttings to encourage quick root formation. They are particularly useful for slow rooting species. Hormones must be used with great care.

Horn: A curved, pointed and hollow protuberance from the perianth

Horticultural oil: A refined oil sprayed on plants to control a variety of pests. It kills by smothering the pests and their eggs or by disrupting membrane functions. It may also prevent some fungal diseases. Highly refined types are called summer, superior, or verdant oils and can be used during the growing season as long as temperatures are below 90° F. Heavier types are called dormant oils and are used on dormant, deciduous plants.

Horticulture: The cultivation of a garden, an orchard, or a nursery; the art and science of cultivating flowers, fruits, vegetables, and ornamental plants.

Horticulturist: A person who specializes in horticulture.

Hortus siccus: A collection of specimens of plants carefully dried and preserved for botanical purposes; and herbarium.

Hose in hose: A flower that appears to have a double corolla, one within another, as in certain Azaleas.

Host: The plant on which a parasite lives and from which it derives its nourishment; also the plants on which epiphytes grow.

Host-specific toxin: A metabolite, produced by a pathogen, and which is responsible for the adverse effects of the pathogen. The toxin has a host specificity equivalent to that of the pathogen. Utilized for in vitro selection experiments to screen for tolerance or resistance to the pathogen.

Hotbed: A bed of soil heated by fermenting substances and covered with glass to keep out cold air; intended for raising early plants or for protecting tender exotics.

Hotcap: An individual, conical plant cover used to protect against frost, sun, birds, and insects.

Hothouse: A structure kept heated for the growth of tender, exotic plants or subtropical plants, or for the production of native fruits, flowers, etc., out of season. The temperature of the hothouse is kept between the temperatures of the greenhouse and the stove-house, or orchid-house.

Houseplant: Any plant that is suitable for growing in the conditions of a house.

Hull: 1. The outer covering of a seed, nut, or fruit. 2. To remove the hull of.

Human artificial chromosome (HAC): Analogous to yeast artificial chromosome, a construct comprising a human centromere and telomeres, which would allow for the cloning of very large fragments of DNA, and their transfer into human cells for the purpose of gene therapy. Not yet established as a working technology, although some partial success has been reported.

Humicuola sp.: Grow on products with a high cellulose content. These fungi are also found in soil and on plant debris.

Humid acids: 1. The term sometimes interchangeable for humus. 2. The alkali-soluble end products of the decomposition or organic matter in mineral soils.

Humidity meter: An instrument used to measure the amount of moisture in house or greenhouse air.

Humming line: A ribbon suspended over crops that emits am ultrasonic sound to discourage birds.

Humus: The organic residue of decayed vegetable matter in soil. Also often used to describe partly decayed matter such as leafmold or compost. Humus retains moisture and keeps the ground from drying out quickly in hot weather; it is the main indirect food supply for plants. Soil which lacks humus soon becomes impoverished. Humus is supplied mainly by adding animal manure, leaf mold, decayed garden refuse (compost), peat moss, sedge peat and by turning under crops grown as cover crops or green manures.

Hyalescent: Becoming translucent.

Hyaline Mycelia: Sterile mycelia which is white or transparent. No fruiting structures are produced by the mycelia. Visual identification of these organism is not possible. Often associated with allergic symptoms.

Hybrid: The offspring of genetically different parents, often produced accidentally or artificially in cultivation, but occasionally arising in the wild.

Hybrid arrested translation: A method used to identify what protein(s) are encoded by a particular cloned DNA sequence. A total mRNA preparation, which contains many different mRNAs, is hybridized with cloned DNA, so that those mRNA molecules homologous to the cloned DNA will anneal to give DNA/RNA heteroduplexes. The non-annealed mRNA molecules can be translated in vitro and this is then compared to translation products from the untreated mRNAs.

Hybrid dysgenesis: Infertility and an increased incidence of chromosome mutations thought to be caused by the activation of transposons.

Hybrid released translation: A method used to identify the gene product of a cloned gene. The cloned DNA is immobilized and hybridized with a mixed mRNA sample, so that only mRNA sequences homologous to the cloned DNA will be retained. These mRNA molecules are subsequently removed and translated in vitro.

Hybrid seed: 1. Seed produced by crossing genetically dissimilar parents. 2. In plant breeding, used colloquially for seed produced by specific crosses of selected pure lines, such that the F1 crop is genetically uniform and displays hybrid vigour. As the F1 plants are heterozygous with respect to many genes, the crop does not breed true and so new seed must be purchased each season.

Hybrid selection: The process of choosing individuals possessing desired characteristics from among a hybrid population.

Hybrid swarm: A population of hybrids and plants derived from backcrossing the hybrids with the parent species.

Hybrid vigour: The extent to which a hybrid individual outperforms both its parents with respect to one or many traits. The genetic basis of hybrid vigour is not well understood, but the phenomenon is widespread, particularly in inbreeding plant species. Synonym: heterosis.

Hybridizable: Capable of producing hybrid offspring by crossing with another variety, species, or genus.

Hybridization: 1. The process of forming a hybrid by cross pollination of plants or by mating animals of different types. 2. The production of offspring of genetically different parents, normally from sexual reproduction, but also asexually by the fusion of protoplasts or by transformation. 3. The pairing of two DNA strands, often from different sources, by hydrogen bonding between complementary nucleotides.

Hybridize: To produce or cause to produce a hybrid.

Hybridoma: A synthetic hybrid cell, derived by fusing a B lymphocyte with a tumour cell. The former secretes a single antibody, while the latter confers the property of growing indefinitely in tissue culture. The underlying technology behind the monoclonal antibody.

Hydathode: Water-secreting gland on the surface of margin or leaf, at the ends of veins, often indicated by a white deposit of salts.

Hydathodes: An epidermal structure specialized for secretion, or for exudation, of water.

Hydric: Characterized by an abundant supply of water.

Hydrogen: An element, found in the soil, that plants need in order to grow.

Hydrogen-uptake positive (Hup+): A term describing a micro-organism that is capable of assimilating (or taking up) hydrogen gas.

Hydroid: The water storage or water vascular cells of Bryophyta. Analogous to xylem in tracheophytes.

Hydrolysis: A chemical reaction in which water is added across a covalent bond, often cleaving the molecule into two. Occurs for example when polynucleotides, poly-peptides, and polysaccharides are broken into their component monomers. Thus sucrose can be hydrolysed to glucose and fructose; and proteins to individual amino acids.

Hydrophily: The flowers are produced under the surface of the water and that is where the transfer of pollen takes place. Fairly rare occurrence.

Hydrophobic interaction: An interaction between a hydrophobic ('water-hating') part of a molecule and an aqueous environment. Particularly significant in establishing the conformation of molecules in solution, and thus their biological activity. Many enzymes have a structure where the polypeptide chain is folded to form a hydrophobic core and a hydrophilic ('water-loving') surface.

Hydrophytes: Plants normally living with the vegetative parts submerged or floating in water, or only partially emergent.

Hydroponics: The growing of plants without soil. Plants are fed with an aerated solution of nutrients, and the roots are either supported within an inert matrix, or are freely floating in the nutrient solution.

Hydropote: A cell or cell group found on the lower epidermis of some species such as Nymphaea. These cells are thought to function in the uptake of ions from the water.

Hydrosere: A primary succession that is initiated in a wet habitat.

Hydroxyapatite: A member of the apatite groups or mineral rich in the hydroxyl groups.

Hydrphyte: A plant growing submerged, or almost so, in water.

Hygromycin: An antibiotic used as selective agent in bacterial and transgenic plant cell cultures.

Hygroscopic water: Water that is chemically bound to soil particles and therefore unavailable to plants.

Hygroscopic: Absorbing water and undergoing movements or changes brought about by changes in water content.

Hymenopterophily: Pollinated by bees.

Hypanepigyny: The condition in which the sepals, petals, stamens are attached to the elongate floral tube or hypanthium above the inferior ovary, as in Oenothera.

Hypanthial: Pertaining to or resembling a hypanthium.

Hypanthium: An expansion of the receptacle of a flower that forms a saucer-shaped, cup-shaped, or tubular structure (often simulating a calyx tube) bearing the perianth and stamens at or near its rim; it may be free from or united to the ovary.

Hypanthodium: An inflorescence with flowers on wall of a concave capitulum, as in Ficus

Hyperploid: The situation in which a particular chromosome or chromosome segment is present in more than the normal number. Opposite: hypoploid.

Hypersensitive response: 1. A specific reaction of a plant to attack by a pathogen. The plant cells surrounding the point of infection rapidly die and dry out, so that pathogen spread within the plant is prevented. Often associated with the interaction of race-specific R genes with a matching pathogen avirulence. 2. The abnormal response of an animal to the presence of a particular antigen.

Hypersensitive site: Regions in the DNA that are highly susceptible to digestion with restriction endonucleases.

Hypertonic: A solution with an osmotic potential greater than that of living cells. Treatment with such solutions leads to the plasmolysis of cells. Opposite: hypotonic.

Hypertrophy: Excessive growth or overdevelopement of the organs of plants.

Hypervariable region: The parts of both the heavy and light chains of an antibody molecule that enable it to bind to a specific site on an antigen.

Hypervariable segment: A region of a protein that varies considerably between strains or individuals.

Hyphodromous: With a single primary vein and all other venation absent, rudimentaryj or concealed within a coriaceous or fleshy blade

Hypochile: The basal part of the labellum (of an Orchid) in some groups, such as Stanhopea.

Hypocotyl: The portion of an embryo or seedling below the cotyledons. A transitional area between stem and root.

Hypocotyledonary: Located below the seed leaves.

Hypocotylespermous or macropodial: With food reserve stored in hypocotyl, derived from zygote.

Hypodermis: A layer of cells immediately beneath the epidermis and distinct from the parenchyma cells of the cortex in certain plants.

Hypogeal: Of germination, having the cotyledon(s) remaining within the seed coat (testa).

Hypogenous: Growing on the under surface, especially pertaining to a fungus on the underside of a leaf.

Hypogynium: Perianth-like structure of bony scales subtending the ovary, as in Scleria and other members of the cyperaceae.

Hypogynous: Arising below the level of insertion of the ovary (often applied, loosely, to a flower in which the sepals, petals and stamens are inserted below the ovary).

Hypogyny: The most commonly seen arrangement of floral parts in which the stamens, sepals, and petals are inserted below the ovary, giving a superior ovary.

Hypomorph: A mutation that reduces, but does not completely abolish gene expression.

Hyponasty: A nastic movement in which the plant responds by more rapid growth on the lower side of an organ, resulting in a curving upwards of that part.

Hypophyllous: With small leaves, as bracts, scales, cataphylls.

Hypoplastic: Defective and reduced growth or development (e.g. dwarfing and stunting in plants) resulting from an abnormal condition, for example disease or nutritional stress.

Hypoploid: The situation in which a particular chromosome or chromosome segment is present in less than the normal number. Opposite: hyperploid.

Hypostasis: The situation in which the expression of one gene (the hypostatic gene) is dependent on a second gene (the epistatic gene). The genes need not be on the same chromosome.

Hypothalamic peptides: Peptides generated in the vertebrate forebrain and concerned with regulating the body's physiological state.

Hypotonic: Osmotic potential less than that of living cells. Cells placed in a hypotonic solution will absorb water and display swelling and turgidity. Opposite: hypertonic.

Hypotropous: Dorsal–ovule erect, micropyle below, raphe dorsal (away from ventral bundle). Ventral–ovule erect, micropyle below, raphe ventral (toward ventral bundle).

Hypsophyll: A leaf located underneath spore-bearing leaves.

I/E region: Abbreviation for integration-excision region.

Ideotype: The ideal type or perfect specimen. A description or illustration of what the final goal of genetic improvement for a species would look like. The ideotype is developed without regard to heritabilities for the individual traits involved. It is not intended to be a practical field guide for selecting "+" trees, but as a starting point for developing a field-selection guide.

Idioblast: Any cell markedly differing from the cells of the surrounding tissue. The brachysclereids of pear fruits are an example.

Idiotype: An identifying property or characteristic of an item or system. 1.A plant form expected on physiological grounds to represent an optimal type for the environment in which the plant is to be grown. 2. A classification of antibody molecules according to the antigenicity of the variable regions. Each idiotype is unique to a particular immunoglobulin raised to a particular antigen.

Igneous rock: A rock produced through the cooling of melted mineral matter.

IGS: Abbreviation for 1. internal guide sequence. 2. intergenic spacer.

Illuvial horizon: An accumulation of material in the B horizon (subsoil) that moved into it from the A horizon (topsoil).

Imaginal disc: A mass of cells in the larvae of Drosophila melanogaster and other holometabolous insects that gives rise to particular adult organs, such as antennae, eyes or wings.

Imbibition: 1. The absorption of liquids or vapours into the ultramicroscopic spaces or pores found in materials. 2. The initial water uptake by seeds prior to germination.

Imbricate: Having parts overlapping each other like roof tiles.

Imino acid: A molecule containing a carboxylic acid group and an imino (NH) group. Proline and hydroxyproline, often described as amino acids, are in fact imino acids. Other imino acids are probably formed during the degradation of amino acids.

Immarginate: Having no margin.

Immature soil: A soil that lacks clear individual horizons.

Immediate early gene: A viral gene that is expressed promptly after infection.

Immobilized cells: Cells entrapped in matrices such as alginate, polyacrylamide and agarose, for use in membrane and filter bioreactors.

Immortalization: The genetic transformation of a cell type into a cell line which can proliferate indefinitely.

Immortalizing oncogene: A gene that, upon transfection, enables a primary cell to grow indefinitely in culture.

Immortelle: Any one of the flowers called everlasting. These flowers feel papery and keep their natural color and appearance after drying, therefore they are widely used for wreaths and other floral arrangements.

Immune response: The processes, including the synthesis of antibodies, that are used by vertebrates to respond to the presence of a foreign antigen.

Immunity: The lack of susceptibility of an animal or plant to infection by a particular pathogen, or to the harmful effects of their toxins.

Immunization: The production of immunity in an individual by artificial means. Active immunization involves the introduction, either orally or by infection, of specially treated bacteria, viruses or their toxins so as to stimulate the production of antibodies.

Immunoaffinity chromatography: A purification technique in which an antibody is bound to a matrix and is used to isolate a protein from a complex mixture.

Immunoassay: An detection system for a particular molecule, which exploits the specific binding of an antibody raised against it. For measurement, the antibody can incorporate a radioactive or fluorescent label, or be linked to an enzyme which catalyses an easily monitored reaction such as a change in colour.

Immunogenicity: The ability to elicit an immune response.

Immunoprophylaxis: The process of active or passive immunization. Active immunization with vaccines leads to long-term protection through mobilizing the organism's own immune system. Passive immunization is achieved by injection of antibody against a specific pathogen obtained either by fractionation of blood from an individual previously infected with the pathogen, or by monoclonal antibody technology.

Immunosensor: A biosensor having an antibody as the biological element.

Immunosuppression: The suppression of the immune response. Necessary following organ transplants from a genetically different donor in order to prevent the host rejecting the grafted organ.

Immunotherapy: The use of an antibody or a fusion protein containing the antigen binding site of an antibody to cure a disease or enhance the well-being of a patient. Synonym: immunochemical control.

Immunotoxin: Protein drugs consisting of an antibody joined to a toxin molecule. Made by either chemically linking the molecules, or by fusing the genes for the toxin and the antibody, and expressing a fusion protein. The antibody portion of the molecule targets the toxin.

Imparipinnate: Pinnate with a conform terminal leaflet. Imparipinnately compound—odd-pinnately compound, with a terminal leaflet

Impeller: An agitator that is used for mixing the contents of a bioreactor.

Imperfect: Diclinous; having the pistils and stamens in separate flowers. Flowers having only male or female parts.

Imperfect flower: A flower containing stamen and pistil organs required for pollination but lacking sepals or petals or both of these organs.

Imperfect or unisexual: With stamens or carpels absent in the flower

Impervious soil: A soil through which water, air, or roots penetrate very slowly or not at all.

Implicate: With both lamina margins folded sharply inward

Impressed: Sunk or immersed below the level of the surface.

In silico: In a computer file. In the present context, the use of data bases of DNA and protein sequence to help answer biological questions. This is growing area of biology as the amount of genomics and proteomics data continues to grow.

In situ: In the natural place or in the original place. 1. Experimental treatments performed on cells or tissue rather than on extracts from them. 2. Assays or manipulations performed with intact tissues.

In situ colony hybridization: A procedure for screening bacterial colonies or plaques growing on plates or membranes for the presence of specific DNA sequences by the hybridization of nucleic acid probes to the DNA molecules present in these colonies or plaques. Synonym: in situ plaque hybridization.

In situ conservation: The conservation of ecosystems and natural habitats and the maintenance and recovery of viable populations of species in their natural surroundings and, in the case of domesticated or cultivated species, in the surroundings where they have developed their distinctive properties.

In situ hybridization: The visualization of in vivo location of macromolecules (particularly polynucleotides and polypeptides) by the histological staining of tissue sections or cytological preparations via labelled probes/antibodies.

In vitro: Outside the organism, or in an artificial environment. Applied for example to cells, tissues or organs cultured in glass or plastic containers.

In vitro embryo production (IVEP): The combination of ovum pickup, in vitro maturation of ova, and in vitro fertilization. A potential means of overcoming the variability between donors in number of ova collected in embryo-transfer programmes.

In vitro fertilization (IVF): A widely used technique in human and animal science, whereby the egg is fertilized with sperm outside the body before re-implanting into the uterus.

In vitro maturation (IVM): Culture of immature ova in the laboratory, usually until they are ready for in vitro fertilization.

In vitro translation: The synthesis of proteins from isolated mRNA molecules in the test-tube. Synonym: cell-free translation.

In vivo: The natural conditions in which organisms reside. Refers to biological processes that take place within a living organism or cell under normal conditions.

In vivo gene therapy: The delivery of a gene or genes to a tissue or organ of a complete living individual to alleviate a genetic disorder.

In: Prefix meaning 'not' or 'inwards'.

Inactivated agent: A virus, bacterium or other organism that has been treated to prevent it from causing a disease.

Inarable: Not arable; not capable of being plowed or tilled.

Inarch: To graft by uniting a scion to the stock, without separating the scion from its parent tree.

Inarching: This is a method of grafting new plant growth onto a stronger root system by establishing young plants (usually, one that is in a pot) near an existing tree and at the point where they meet, removing matching areas of bark. The two cut surfaces are then fitted together and bound with soft tying material until they grow together and can be gradually separated with the new branches attached to the older rootstock.

Inbred line: The product of inbreeding, i.e. the intercrossing of individuals that have ancestors in common. In plants and laboratory animals, it refers to populations resulting from at least 6 generations of selfing or 20 generations of brother-sister mating, so that they have become, for all practical purposes, completely homozygous. In farm animals, the term is sometimes used to describe populations that have resulted from several generations of the mating of close relatives, without having reached complete homozygosity.

Inbreeding depression: The reduction in vigor often observed in progeny from matings between close relatives. Inbreeding depression is due to the expression of recessive deleterious alleles and is usually severe in open-pollinated outcrossing species (most forest trees) that occur in fairly high population densities.

Inbreeding: Deliberate self-pollination of a plant by transferring pollen from one of its flowers to the stigma of the same flower or to another flower of the same plant. Repeating this process for several generations ensures that the line will breed true.

Incertae sedis: Of uncertain position, used taxonomically.

Incised: Cut deeply, sharply and often irregularly (an intermediate condition between toothed and lobed).

Inclinate: With lamina folded or curved transversely near the apex.

Included veinlets: Veins ending inside areoles

Included: Not sticking out or projecting, as when pistils are included in the corolla.

Inclusion body: A protein that is overproduced in a recombinant bacterium and forms a crystalline structure inside the bacterial cell.

Incompatibility: The failure of gametes from genetically similar material to fuse due to physiological or morphological mechanisms. In some fungi, e.g. Mucor, sexual fusion cannot occur between similar races or strains. In seed plants complex mechanisms have developed involving the interactions of pollen and stigmatic tissue.

Incompatibility group: Plasmids must belong to different incompatibility groups to co-exist within the same cell. A plasmid cloning vector should always belong to an incompatibility group different from that of the host bacterium's endogenous plasmids.

Incomplete dominance: A condition in which the heterozygous phenotype is intermediate to the two homozygous phenotypes as a result of one allele only partly masking another allele.

Incomplete penetrance: Where the phenotype does not allow perfect prediction of the genotype as a result of interference in gene expression by the environment.

Inconspicuous: Not easily seen.

Incrassate: Thickened; of a pollen grain, with thickened margins around the apertures.

Incubation: 1. The hatching of eggs by means of heat, either natural or artificial. 2. Period between infection and appearance of symptoms induced by a pathogen. 3. The culture of cells and organisms.

Incubator: An apparatus in which environ-mental conditions (light, photo-period, temperature, humidity, etc.) are fully controlled; used for hatching eggs, multi-plying micro-organisms, culturing plants, etc.

Incubous: Overlapping, like shingles.

Incumbent: Of the orientation of an embryo, with the cotyledons lying face to face and folded downwards beside the radicle; of anthers, lying against the inner face of the filament.

Incumbent or notorhizal: Reclinate with sides of cotyledons against hypocotyl.

Incurved: Applied to petals and florets that curve inward to form a compact, rounded shaped.

Indeciduous: Not deciduous; not losing its leaves annually; evergreen, as trees.

Indefinite: Variable in number; numerous; of stamens, more than twice as many as the petals or sepals; of an inflorescence, not terminating in a flower (i.e. having a continuing, terminal growing point).

Indehiscent capsule: One that does not dehisce at maturity, as in peplis.

Indehiscent: Fruits which do not open to release seeds, but whole fruit is shed from the plant; not opening to release spores.

Independent assortment: The random distribution during meiosis of alleles (at different genes) to the gametes that is the case when the genes in question are located on different chromosomes or are unlinked on the same chromosome.

Indeterminate growth: The condition in which the terminal bud persists and produces successive lateral branches over an indefinite period. Opposite: determinate growth.

Indeterminate: A plant part that continues to grow while flowering, such as indeterminate tomatoes, which continue to grow until they die, or a flower spike that continues to grow longer while it's lower blossoms open.

Indigenous: Native; originating or occurring naturally in the place specified.

Indirect embryogenesis: Plant embryo formation on callus tissues derived from explants, including zygotic or somatic embryos and seedlings. Opposite: direct embryogenesis.

Indole-acetic acid (IAA): A natural growth hormone found in plants.

Indoor gardening: The art of growing plants indoors using natural and/ or artificial light.

Inducer: A low-molecular-weight compound or a physical agent that associates with a repressor protein to produce a complex that can no longer bind to the operator. Thus, the presence of the inducer turns on the expression of the gene(s) controlled by the operator.

Inducible: A gene or gene product whose transcription or synthesis is increased by exposure of the cells to an inducer or to a condition, e.g. heat. Opposite: constitutive.

Inducible enzyme: An enzyme that is synthesized only in the presence of the substrate that acts as an inducer.

Inducible gene: A gene that is expressed only in the presence of a specific metabolite, the inducer.

Inducible promoter: The activation of a promoter in response to either the presence of a particular compound, i.e. the inducer, or to a defined external condition, e.g. elevated temperature.

Induction: The act or process of causing some specific effect to occur; for example the transcription of a specific gene or operon, or the production of a protein by an organism after it is exposed to a specific stimulus.

Induction media: 1. Media used to induce the formation of organs or other structures. 2. Media causing variation or mutation in the tissues exposed to it.

Indumentum: The epidermal appendages, e.g. hairs or scales, collectively.

Induplicate: The margins bent inwards, and the external faces of these edges applied to each other, without twisting.

Indurated: Hardened and toughened.

Indusium: A small flap covering the sori, or fruit dots, in ferns; a collection of hairs united so as to form a sort of cup and enclosing the stigma of a flower.

Inequilateral: With unequal sides.

Inermous: Unarmed, without prickles or spines

Infection: The successful colonization of any living organism by a pathogen.

Infectious agent: Synonym of pathogen.

Inferior ovary: An ovary to which parts of the calyx, corolla, and stamens have become more or less united so they appear to be attached at the top of it.

Infertile: Poor in plant nutrients.

Infiltrate: The entry of liquid into pores or other spaces.

Infiltration rate: The rate of water controlled by surface conditions that enters the soil.

Inflated: Enlarged or swelled out, as an inflated perianth.

Inflexed: Bent abruptly inward or upward.

Inflorescence: A flower or putting forth blossoms; the mode of development and arrangement of flowers on an axis; a flowering branch.

Infrafoliar: On the stem below the leaves, as in the arecaceae.

Infrapetiolar or subpetiolar: Axillary bud surrounded by base of petiole.

Infrared mulch: A plastic sheet that is placed around plants to warm the soil by infrared radiation and to inhibit weed growth by blocking most visible radiation.

Infraspecific: Of taxonomic divisions of a lower rank than species; similarly infrageneric, infrafamilial etc.

Infructescence: The grouping or arrangement in which fruits are borne on a plant.

Infundibular: Funnel-shaped.

Infundibuliform: Having the form of a funnel.

Ingraft: To insert, as a scion of one tree or plant into another, for propagation. Also spelled engraft.

Inheritance: The transmission of genes and phenotypes from generation to generation.

Inhibitor: 1. Any substance or object that retards a chemical reaction. 2. A metabolite or modifier gene that interferes with a reaction or with the expression of another gene.

Initiation factor: Soluble protein required for the initiation of translation.

Initiation: Causing something to start. 1. Early steps or stages of a tissue culture process. 2. Early stages of biosynthesis.

Innovation: A new vigorous shoot, carrying on the continued growth of the plant.

Inoculate: Deliberately introduce, in contrast to contamination. 1. In bacteriology, tissue culture, etc., placing an inoculum into (or onto) medium to initiate a culture. 2. In immunology, to carry out immunization. 3. In plant pathology, application of pathogen spores etc. on to plants under conditions where infection should result in the absence of resistance.

Inoculation cabinet: Small room or cabinet for inoculation (of tissue or micro-organism cultures) operations, often with a current of sterile air to carry contaminants away from the work area.

Inoculum: 1. A small piece of tissue cut from callus, or an explant from a tissue or organ, or a small amount of cell material from a suspension culture, transferred into fresh medium for continued growth of the culture. 2. Microbial spores or parts (such as mycelium). 3. Vaccine.

Inorganic: 1. Not natural; artificial. 2. Composed of other than animal or plant matter; mineral.

Inorganic compound: Historically, chemicals that could not be derived from living processes. In modern usage, chemicals that do not contain carbon, although carbonates and a few other simple carbon compounds are generally regarded as inorganic.

Inorganic fertilizer: A chemical fertilizer that quickly releases nitrogen into the soil.

Inorganic nitrogen: The element nitrogen in combination with other mineral elements.

Inositol :A cyclic acid (hexahydroxycy-clohexane) that is a constituent of certain cell phosphoglycerides. It is a nutrient frequently referred to as a "vitamin" in plant tissue culture. Also acts as a growth factor in some animals and micro-organisms.

Inositol lipid: A membrane-anchored phospholipid that transduces hormonal signals by stimulating the release of any of several chemical messengers.

Insecticidal soap: A low-toxicity pesticide made from the salts of fatty acids. It kills soft-bodied insects, like aphids, spider mites, thrips, and whiteflies, by disrupting cell membranes. It may burn foliage in hot weather. It is sometimes combined with other materials, such as citrus oil or sulfur, to increase efficiency. Complete coverage of the plant is necessary for it to work.

Insecticide: An agent that kills insects; specifically, that which kills insect pests of plants and humans.

Insectivorous (plants): Plants that are specially adapted for catching insects. Most, but not all, are grown for interest rather than beauty. Once their prey is captured, the plants secrete a fluid, which breaks down the insect's bodies so that they may be absorbed as plant food. The following are few examples of insectivorous plants: Dionaea (Venus's Flytrap), Nepenthes, Sarracenia (Pitcher Plant), Darlingtonia (California Pitcher Plant) and Utricularia (Bladderwort).

Inserted: Attached to or growing upon; hence insertion, the place or modeof attachment.

Insertion element: Generic term for DNA sequences found in bacteria capable of genome insertion. Postulated to be responsible for site-specific phage and plasmid integration. Synonym: insertion sequence.

Insertion mutation: Changes in the base sequence of a DNA molecule resulting from the random integration of DNA from another source.

Insertion site: 1. A unique restriction site in a vector DNA molecule into which foreign DNA can readily be inserted. This is achieved by treating both the vector and the insert with the relevant restriction endonuclease and then ligating the two different molecules, both having the same sticky ends. Synonym: cloning site. 2. The position of integration of a transposon.

Insertion: The place or manner of attachment, as the insertion of petals.

Instability: A lack of consistent phenotype, usually as a result of uncontrolled genetic changes. These may be due to transposon activity, or in cell lines, to changes in karyotype.

Insulin: A peptide hormone secreted by the Langerhans islets of the pancreas, and that regulates the level of sugar in the blood.

Intake rate: The rate at which rain or water enters the soil. Expressed in inches per hour.

Integrating vector: A vector that is designed to integrate cloned DNA into the host's chromosomal DNA.

Integration: The recombination process which inserts a small DNA molecule (usually by homologous recombination) into a larger one. If the molecules are circular, integration involves only a single crossing-over; if linear, then two crossings-over are required.

Integration-excision region (I/E): The portion of bacteriophage lambda DNA that enables ë-DNA to be inserted into a specific site in the E. coli bacteriophage lambda chromosome or excised from this site.

Integument: The outermost layer of an ovule; usually develops into a seed coat; a gymnosperm ovule usually has a single integument, and an angiosperm ovule usually has two integuments.

Intellectual property rights (IPR): The legal framework, which includes patenting and plant variety protection, by which inventors control the commercial application of their work.

Intensifying screen: A plastic sheet impregnated with a rare-earth compound, such as calcium tungstate, which reacts to radiation by emitting light. When placed on one side of a piece of X-ray film with a radioactive sample on the other side, the intensifying screen will capture some of the radioactive energy which has passed through the film, exposing the X-ray film and so enhancing the sensitivity of the detection. Often used in Southern and northern blotting procedures.

Interaxillary: Situated between or within the axils of leaves.

Intercalary: 1. Meristematic tissue or growth not restricted to the apex of an organ, i.e. growth at nodes. 2. Referring to internal segments of a chromosomes (i.e. not at the ends).

Intercalary growth: A pattern of stem elongation typical of grasses. Elongation proceeds from the lower internodes to the upper internodes through the differentiation of meristematic tissue at the base of each internode.

Intercalary meristem: Intercalary meristem is meristem at the base of the internode in monocot stems (particularly grass stems). Only the apical meristem is active. If the tip of the stem is removed, the uppermost intact intercalary meristem becomes the apical meristem and starts intercalary growth.

Intercalating agent: A chemical capable of inserting between adjacent base pairs in a double-stranded nucleic acid. A prominent example is ethidium bromide.

Intercellular: Lying between cells, as intercellular space in plant tissue.

Intercellular space: The pore space between cells, especially typical of leaf tissues.

Interfascicular cambium: Cambium that arises between vascular bundles.

Interference: The effect of one crossing over event in altering the probability of another crossing over event occurring at a nearby location. This probability can be either increased (positive interference) or decreased (negative interference), but the latter is the more usual.

Interferon: One of a group of small proteins synthesized by certain T cells of vertebrates, which inhibit virus replication. There are three types of interferon in humans.

Interfoliaceous: Situated between the leaves, especially opposite leaves. Also interfoliar.

Interfoliar: On the stem between the leaves, as in the Arecaceae

Intergeneric cross: A hybrid made between parents belonging to two different genera.

Intergenic regions: Non-coding DNA located between genes; this comprises a variable but considerable proportion of all eukaryotic genomic DNA, and its function is largely unknown.

Intergenic spacer (IGS): Non-coding DNA separating tandemly arranged copies of a repeated gene sequence (typically ribosomal DNA). Of particular interest because, unlike the coding sequence itself, the spacers show high levels of interspecific sequence polymorphism, and are thus useful as assays for species identification.

Interleukin: A group of proteins that transmit signals between immune cells and are necessary for mounting normal immune responses.

Intermediate-day plant: A plant that has two critical photoperiods; it will not flower if the days are either too short or too long.

Intermittent: A renewal and cessation of meristematic activity which produces clusters of stems and/or leaves along an axis

Internal transcribed spacer (ITS): Non-coding regions separating the individual components of the ribosomal DNA units. These regions show much more sequence polymorphism than the genic regions themselves, and therefore, like the intergenic spacers, are useful a source of genetic markers for the ribosomal DNA locus.

International treaty on plant genetic resources for food and agriculture: The international treaty resulting from the revision of the International Undertaking on Plant Genetic Resources was adopted by the 2001 FAO Conference as a binding international instrument to enter into force after ratification by 40 states. Its objectives are the conservation and sustainable use of plant genetic resources for food and agriculture and equitable sharing of the benefits of this use.

International undertaking on plant genetic resources: The first comprehensive voluntary, international agreement (adopted in 1983) dealing with plant genetic resources for food and agriculture. Designed as an instrument to promote international harmony in matters regarding access to plant genetic resources for food and agriculture. Following extensive negotiations to revise the Undertaking in harmony with the Convention on Biological Diversity, the binding International Treaty on Plant Genetic Resources for Food and Agriculture was adopted by the 2001 FAO Conference.

Internode: the Portion of a stem between the level of insertion of two successive leaves or leaf pairs (or branches of an inflorescence).

Interpetiolar: Of stipules, between the petioles of two opposite leaves.

Interphase: The stage in the cell cycle when the cell is not dividing and during part of which DNA replication occurs; it follows telophase of one mitotic division and extends to the beginning of prophase in the next division.

Interrupted: Of an inflorescence, having the flowers unevenly distributed along the axis, with conspicuous gaps.

Interrupted or discontinuous: Symmetry of arrangement broken, with uneven lengths of internodes.

Intersex: Synonym of hermaphrodite.

Inter-simple sequence repeat (ISSR): A PCR-based molecular marker assay of genomic sequence lying between adjacent microsatellites. Primers carrying, at their 3'-end, sequence complementary to the repeat unit of the microsatellite will amplify this genomic DNA.

Interspecific competition: Competition between species for nutrients, space, light, etc.

Interspecific cross: A hybrid made between parents belonging to two different species.

Interstitial: Growth all-over in an organ, no localized meristems, as in some fruits

Intine: the innermost wall of a spore or pollen grain.

Intra: A combining form meaning within, inside of, as intracellular.

Intracellular: Being or occurring within a body cell or within the body cells.

Intracytoplasmic sperm injection (ICSI): The micro-injection of a single sperm into the cytoplasm of a mature oocyte.

Intrageneric: Within a genus, such as an intrageneric cross, or intrageneric variation.

Intrageneric cross: A hybrid made between parents belonging to two species in the same genus.

Intragenic complementation: Occurs when wild type phenotype is restored in an F1 individual made by crossing two independent mutants, carrying different heteroalleles.

Intramarginal: Situated inside but close to the margin, e.g. of a vein in a leaf.

Intrapetiolar: Between a petiole and the subtending stem.

Intraspecific competition: A type of competition whereby an individual plant competes with one or more members of the same species for nutrients, space, light, etc.

Intraspecific: Within a species, such as an intraspecific cross, or intraspecific variation.

Intrazonal: A term used to describe a soil group with characteristics determined by local factors, such as parent material.

Introduced: Not indigenous, not native to the area in which it now occurs, brought in by accident or design.

Introgression: The movement of genes from one population into another through hybridi-zation followed by backcrossing. Usually refers to movement of genes from one species to another or among sub-species that have been geographically isolated then brought back together by changes in the species ranges or planting of exotic populations.

Intron: A segment of the primary transcript of a eukaryotic gene, removed (before the mature mRNA is translated) in a process known as intron splicing. Some eukaryotic genes contain a large number of introns, which make up the bulk of the DNA sequence of the gene. Introns are also found in genes whose RNA transcripts are not translated, namely eukaryotic rRNA and tRNA genes. In these cases the intron sequence does not appear in the functional RNA molecule. Synonym: intervening sequence.

Introrse: Turned or facing inward, such as an introrse anther facing toward the center of the flower.

Invasiveness: The ability of a plant, particularly a weed, to spread beyond its presently established site, and become established in new locations.

Inversion: A chromosome re-arrangement, which involves the re-orientation of a segment so that the order of a linear array of genes within it is reversed.

Inverted: Upside down.

Inverted repeat: Two sequences of nucleotides occurring in one strand, where, relative to the first sequence, the second has comple-mentary bases but in the inverted order. Under appropriate conditions this allows formation of a hairpin loop in the single strand.

Investing: Axial embryo usually erect with thick cotyledons overlapping and encasing the somewhat dwarfed hypocotyl; endosperm wanting or limited

Involucel: A secondary involucre, as the bracts subtending the secondary umbels in the Umbelliferae.

Involucrate: Having an involucre.

Involucre: A group of bracts enveloping a condensed inflorescence; a layer of tissue enveloping particular structures, e.g. an archegonium in Bryophyta, sporangia in Hymenophyllaceae.

Involucriform: Resembling an involucre.

Involute: Leaves having the edges rolled inwards at each side, toward the adaxial side.

Ion: A molecule or atom that has become electrically charged through the loss or gain of one or more electrons.

Ion channel: A protein integral to a cell membrane, through which selective ion transport occurs.

IPTG: Abbreviation for isopropyl-3-D-thiogalactopyranoside. A synthetic inducer of beta-galactosidase activity in many bacteria. Used in combination with the synthetic chromogenic substrate Xgal to differentiate recombinant from non-recombinant bacterial colonies in cloning strategies using plasmid vectors containing the lacZ gene: blue coloured colonies are produced when galactosidase activity is not disrupted by an insert; but when it is disrupted, the colonies are white. Hence white colonies are indicative of recombinant plasmids, and blue colonies of non-recombinant ones.

Iron: Plants need this soil nutrient to manufacture chlorophyll. In alkaline soil, plants may not be able to absorb iron from the soil, which causes the leaves to turn yellow with green veins. Products, containing iron chelates can be added to the soil or sprayed on the plant's leaves to make iron available to the roots and foliage.

Iron chelate: A form of iron that is readily available to plants when iron in the soil isn't available to the roots. Products that contain iron chelates can be added to the soil or sprayed on the foliage.

Irradiation: Illumination with electromagnetic radiation, typically of sufficiently high energy (low-wavelength UV or gamma, etc.) to disrupt biological macromolecules and hence induce mutations.

Irregular: Not having all the members of the same part alike; asymmetrical; lacking uniformity (often refers to flowers).

Irrigate: To pass a liquid over or through; specifically, to water by causing a stream or streams to flow over land.

Irrigation: The act of watering or moistening; the covering of anything with water or other liquid for the purpose of making or keeping it moist, such as the distribution of water over land to promote the growth of plants.

IS element: Abbreviation for insertion sequence element. A short (800-1400 nucleotide pairs) DNA sequence found in bacteria that is capable of transposing to a new genomic location; DNA sequences contained within an IS element can be transposed along with the IS itself.

Isadelphous: Having the separate bundles of stamens equal in number, as in the flowers of beans.

Iso electric focusing gel (IEF gel): A variant of gel electrophoresis, in which macromolecules (usually proteins) are separated on the basis of differing iso-electric point, rather than on the basis of size.

Isoallele: Multiple similar copies of a gene, usually located at independent positions in the genome, which encode similar gene products and produce the same, or a very similar phenotype.

Isochromosome: A chromosome produced following an error in meiosis, in which the two arms are mirror images of each other. The presence of an isochromosome results in the duplication of all genes present on the originating chromosome arm.

Isocotylous: With cotyledons of same size and shape.

Isodiametric: Of a shape (eg. a cell) with all diameters +/- equal.

Isoform: 1. A tissue-specific form of a protein. 2. Synonym of isoenzyme.

Isogamy: Sexual reproduction in certain algae and fungi having gametes that are alike in size.

Isogenic stock: Strains of organisms that are genetically nearly identical, except with respect to identified genes. Generally produced by repeated backcrossing, or by transformation.

Isogenic: A group of individuals that possesses the same genotype, irrespective of their being homozygous or heterozygous.

Isogynous: Having the pistils, or the carpels of which the single pistil is composed, equal in number to the sepals.

Isolateral: Having structurally similar upper and lower surfaces.

Isolating mechanism: The properties of an organism that prevent interbreeding (and therefore exchange of genetic material) between members of different species that inhabit the same geographical area.

Isolation medium: An optimum plant tissue culture medium suitable for explant survival, growth and development.

Isomer: 1. Structural isomers have the same chemical formula but different structures; e.g. leucine and isoleucine. 2. Stereoisomers are different topological forms of an otherwise single chemical structure, due to changes in bond configurations about some axis or plane of symmetry; eg, D- and L-glucose or cis- and trans-cinnamic acid.

Isomerase: Any of a class of enzymes that catalyse the re-arrangement of the atoms within a molecule, thereby converting one isomer into another.

Isomerous: Composed each of an equal number of parts, as the members of the several circles of a flower; exhibiting isomerism.

Isomorphic: Of the same form or appearance.

Isopetalous: With petals of same size and shape

Isostemonous: Having the stamens equal in number to the sepals or petals.

Isostemony: The state of being isostemonous.

Isostichous: With equal rows.

Isotonic: Solutions with the same osmotic potential, as a result of being of the same molar concentration. For protoplasts to avoid losing or gaining water, the medium they are suspended in must be isotonic with them.

Isotype: A specimen collected at the same time and from the same plant or localized population of plants as the holotype. These duplicate specimens are often separated and deposited in several institutions.

Isozyme: A genetic variant of an enzyme. Isozymes for a given enzyme share the same function, but may differ in level of activity, as a result of minor differences in their amino acid sequence.

J

Jacob-Moncd model: (operon model) A theory to explain how gene activity is regulated, proposed by F. Jacob and J. Monod in 1960. The theory is well substantiated for prokaryotes but there is little evidence that it is directly applicable to eukaryotic cells. The operon model shows how messenger RNA synthesis, and thus the quantity of enzymes present, may be regulated. By controlling the latter, the system as a whole provides a method of coordinating and regulating cell metabolism at the level of transcription. A parallel model, taking into account the very different organization of chromosomal DNA, has since been proposed for eukaryotes.

Jiffy pots: Pots made from wood pulp and peat, commonly used for transplanting tissue culture-derived plants into soil medium.

Joining segment (J): A small DNA segment that links genes in order to yield a functional gene encoding an immunoglobulin.

Jointed: With stems that can be pulled apart easily at the nodes, as in equisetum.

Jugate: Yoked together in a pair, mostly of pairs, of pinnae in a pinnate leaf; also as a suffix, bijugate, 4-jugate etc.

Juvenile: Of leaves, formed on a young plant and different in form from the adult leaves.

Juvenile hormone: A hormone secreted by insects from a pair of endocrine glands close to the brain. Its function is to inhibit metamorphosis so maintaining the larval features.

Juvenile in vitro embryo technology (JIVT or JIVET): A technology involving collection of immature eggs from young animals, their in vitro maturation and fertilization, and the transfer of the resultant embryos into recipient females. The method is designed to achieve rapid generation turnover.

Juvenile leaves: The first-formed leaves, especially when they differ from the mature leaves.

Juvenility: The condition expressed in immature organisms, which are generally smaller in size than the adults and lack reproductive capability. The seedling represents the juvenile stage of many plants. The term is particularly used when the young plant form is very different from that of the adult. For example in gorse (Ulex), the juvenile leaves are flat and trifoliate but the adult plant has spines. In many conifers the seedlings bear needle-like juvenile leaves, and specialized leaves, such as the scalelike leaves of cypress (Cupressus) and the dwarf shoots of pine (Pinus), are formed later. The change is not always from a simple to more complex form. For example, in ivy (Hedera helix) the juvenile leaves are lobed while the mature leaves are entire. The submerged leaves of many aquatic plants are similar to the juvenile leaves of terrestrial forms of the same species. In some varieties of ornamental plants the juvenile foliage persists in the adult plant. Juvenile plants may also differ in various physiological ways from mature plants.

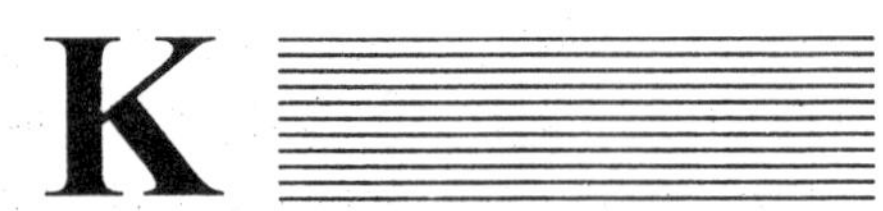

Kainite: A natural salt contained in a fertilizer that is used as a source of potash (14% k).

Kanamycin: An antibiotic of the aminoglycoside family that inhibits translation by binding to the ribosomes. Important as a substrate for selection of plant transformants.

Kaolin minerals: A group of nonswelling clay minerals in which one layer of silicon and oxygen alternates with a layer made up of aluminum, oxygen, and hydrogen.

Karyoevolution: Evolutionary change in the chromosome set, expressed as changes in number and gross structure of the chromosomes; (more broadly), evolutionary relationships between taxa as indicated by karyotype differences.

Karyogamy: The fusion of two nuclei during sexual reproduction. Fusion normally occurs between haploid nuclei and follows immediately after plasmogamy, resulting in the formation of a diploid zygote. In the higher fungi, especially the basidiomycetes, karyogamy may be delayed and occur separately from plasmogamy, resulting in a dikaryotic mycelium.

Karyogram: A diagrammatic representation of the full chromosome set of a species, highlighting characteristic physical features of individual chromosomes.

Karyokinesis: The division of a cell nucleus.

Karyotype: The chromosome constitution of a cell, an individual, or of a related group of individuals, as defined both by the number and the morphology of the chromosomes, usually in mitotic metaphase; chromosomes arranged in order of length and according to position of centromere; also, the abbreviated formula for the chromosome constitution, such as 47, + 21 for human trisomy-21 (Down's syndrome).

KB: Abbreviation for kilobase (of single-stranded nucleic acid).

KBP: Abbreviation for kilobase pairs (of double-stranded DNA).

Keel: 1. The two lower fused petals of a 'pea' flower, which form a boatlike structure around the stamens and styles. 2. Any ridgelike structure.

Keeled: Of leaves or bracts, folded and ridged along the midrib.

Keiki: A vegetative offshoot (plantlet) formed at a node, as on an inflorescence (of an Orchid).

Kernel: 1. The inner portion of a seed, usually refers to an edible seed or the central part of a nut or fruit seed. 2. The whole seed of a cereal such as corn or wheat. 3. To form kernels.

Killer T cell: T cells that kill cells displaying recognized antigens.

Kilobase (kb): A length of single-stranded nucleic acid composed of 1000 bases. One kilobase of single-stranded DNA has a mass of about 330 kiloDalton (exact mass depends on base composition).

Kilobase pairs (kbp): A length of double-stranded DNA composed of 1000 base pairs.

Kinase: An enzyme that catalyses the transfer of a phosphate group from a high energy state (as in ATP) to another molecule.

Kinetics: Dynamic processes involving motion. Often used as a suffix to indicate studies involving movement or rates of reactions.

Kinetochore: Structure at the centromere of eukaryotic chromosomes. The kinetochore consists of inner and outer electron dense plates and a central zone containing repetitive DNA elements. Kinetochores are involved in the control of chromosome movement in cell division.

Kinetosome: Granular cytoplasmic structure which forms the base of a cilium or flagellum. Synonym: basal body.

Kingdom: The highest category of classification (e.g., Plant Kingdom, Animal Kingdom).

Kinin: A substance promoting cell division. In plant systems, the prefix cyto- has been added (cytokinin) to distinguish it from kinin in animal systems.

Klenow fragment: A truncated form of DNA polymerase I from E. coli, used extensively for the production of synthetic DNA molecules as it retains polymerase and 3'-exonuclease activities, but not 5'-exonuclease activity.

Kleptotype: A fragment removed from or stolen from the type; a highly illegal and immoral procedure.

Km: A dissociation constant that characterizes the binding of an enzyme to a substrate. The smaller the value of Km, the tighter the binding of the enzyme to the substrate. Also called the Michaelis constant.

Knee: 1. A sharp bend in a tree branch. 2. A protruding enlargement of the roots at the base of certain swamp-growing trees.

Kneeler: A device to help gardeners lower themselves down or push themselves up from a kneeling position. It usually has handholds several feet high attached to a cushioned platform. It may be reversed and used as a garden bench.

Kneeling pads: A usually rectangular and waterproof mat that is used for cushioning the knees while gardening.

kneepads: Cushions that are strapped behind the knees to protect the kneecaps while kneeling or crawling.

Knockout: A mutant individual, in which a single functional gene has been replaced by a non-functional form of the gene. Used to understand gene function via the comparison of the phenotypes of wild type and knockouts.

Knot: A lump or swelling in or on a part of a plant, such as the node of grass, or the thick part of the wood of a tree where a branch grows out of the trunk.

Knurl: A thick, deformed knot in wood.

Kranz anatomy: Of leaves of C4 plants, where the vascular bundle sheath comprises large cells that often radiate out from the bundle sheath like spokes and contain a greater abundance of often larger chloroplasts than usual cells.

Kymograph: A slowly revolving drum, often covered with graph paper or smoked paper, on which a tracer records measurements of such activities as plant growth movements.

L

Labeling: The tagging of a compound with an isotopic tracer so that its fate within an organism can be followed.

Labellum: A lip; in orchidaceae, the distinctive median petal that serves as an alighting platform for pollinating insects.

Labium: The lower lip of a flower with two lips.

Lacerate: Appearing torn as the edge of a sepal or petal; irregularly cut or cleft.

Lacinia: A long slash or incision in a leaf, petal, or similar organ; one of the narrow lobes resulting from such cuts.

Laciniate: Irregularly cut into narrow-pointed lobes; fringed; refers to petals, bracts, leaves, etc. Also laciniated, laciniose.

Lacinula: A small, narrow lobe or fringe.

Lacinulate: Having small, finely cut leaves or petals.

Lactose: A disaccharide sugar produced in milk, composed of one unit each of glucose and galactose.

Lacuna: A gap, a space enclosed by but free from veins; hence lacunose, lacunate.

Lacunate: With air spaces or chambers in the midst of tissue.

Lacunulose: Having tiny holes.

Lacustrine deposit: Material deposited from lake waters.

Lag phase: 1. The state of apparent inactivity preceding a response to a treatment; also called a latent phase. 2. The initial growth phase, during which cell number remains relatively constant, prior to the onset of rapid cell division.

Lagging strand: The strand of DNA that is synthesized discontinuously during replication (because DNA synthesis can proceed only in the 5'-3' direction).

Lagoon: A shallow lake or pond, especially one connected with a larger body of water; an area of shallow salt water separated from the sea by sand dunes; the area of water surrounded by an atoll, or circular coral reef.

Lake: An inland body of water, usually fresh water, formed by glaciers, river drainage, etc., larger than a pool or pond.

Lambda chain: One of two classes of antibody light chains. The other is a kappa chain.

Lambda phage: A bacteriophage that infects E. coli, commonly used as a cloning vector.

Lamella: A thin plate, or an organ or part resembling one. Raised, membranous outgrowths on the labellum, as in the group, Coelogyne. Also lamel.

Lamellate: Composed of or having lamellae. Also lamellar.

Lamina: A thin, flat organ or part, especially the expanded blade of a leaf; hence laminate (dimin. lamella, lamellate).

Laminar: Leaf-like stamen without a distinct anther and filament but with embedded or superficial microsporangia, as in degeneria

Laminar air-flow cabinet: Cabinet designed for cell or tissue culture manipulations requiring a sterile environment. Achieved by a continuous, non-turbulent flow of filter-sterilized air over the working area. Synonym: laminar air-flow hood.

Laminarin: A storage polysaccharide of the brown algae.

Laminate: With the placenta over the inner surface of the ovary wall.

Lammas shoots: Abnormal late season shoots that develop from the terminal bud, not a recurring phenomenon as in flushing shoots

Lampbrush chromosome: Large diplotene chromosomes present in oocyte nuclei, and particularly conspicuous in amphibians. These chromosomes have extended regions called loops, which are active sites of transcription.

Lanate: Woolly; covered with long, fine, curly hairs.

Lance linear: Long, thin, and pointed. (i.e. a lance-linear leaf)

Lanceolate: Lance-shaped, of a plane several times longer than wide, widest in the basal third, tapering gradually towards the tip, more rapidly towards the base.

Lanciform: Lance-shaped; long, narrow and pointed, sometimes broader at the base than at the tip.

Land: 1. Refers to the solid surface of the earth. 2. A broad term that refers to soil, surface soil, mineral deposits, and water supplies in a certain area.

Land capability classification: Soil that is grouped into special units, subclasses, and/or classes according to their capability for intense use and treatments that are required for sustained use.

Land race: A population of trees of a non-native species that has undergone one or more generations of natural selection in a new environment, i.e., Norway spruce in New York State.

Landform: A geomorphological term used to express earthly surface formations.

Landscape: A view or prospect of rural scenery, more or less extensive, such as seen from a single point of view.

Landscape architect: A person who designs and often supervises the placement of elements (plants, footpaths, etc.) in an outdoor setting.

Landscape fabric: Any of various porous organic or inorganic cloths or mats used to discourage weeds from growing. Also called weed mat.

Landscape-gardening: The art of laying out grounds and arranging trees, shrubs, flowers, paths, fountains, etc. to produce an attractive surrounding.

Lanuginose: Cottony, similar to lanate but trichomes shorter

Lanugo: Soft, thick downy growth.

Larva: The first stage of an insect after hatching from the egg. (i.e. A caterpillar is a larva of a butterfly or moth.) The larvae are often more serious pests than the adults.

Latent agent: A pathogen, usually a virus, present in a host organism without producing any symptoms.

Latent bud: An inactive bud not held back by rest or dormant period, but which may start growth if stimulated.

Lateral lobes: The two lobes to either side of the midlobe of a three-lobed labellum.

Lateral meristem: A meristem giving rise to secondary plant tissues, such as the vascular and cork cambia.

Lateral or axillary: On the side of a structure or at the nodes of the axis. Lateral embryo-basal or baso-lateral embryo, discoid or lenticular, usually surrounded by copious endosperm. Lateral Leaf - Leaf on the side of the stem, as in heterophyllous species of selaginella.

Latex: A milky, usually white or yellowish fluid produced by plants, such as Asclepias and Euphorbia.

Lath house: A framework of widely spaced narrow boards used to protect plants from the sun by providing partial shade.

Laticifer: Specialized cells or ducts resembling vessels; they form branched networks of latex-secreting cells in the phloem and other parts of plants.

Laticiferous: Bearing, containing, or secreting latex.

Latiseptate: With broad partitions.

Latrorse: Directed laterally or sideways.

Lawn: A uniform and uninterrupted layer of bacterial growth, typically on agar medium, in which individual colonies cannot be observed.

Lax: Loosely or widely spaced, as a lax cluster of flowers.

Layering: A method of propagation in which a shoot of a living stem is bent and pegged down to the soil. The shoot develops roots while still attached to the parent plant; once established, it is cut from the mother plant to form a separate plant, which can then be potted up. The illustration shows a shoot bent down and forming roots below the soil's surface. A stake supports the end of the shoot.

LCR: Abbreviation for ligase chain reaction.

Leach: To wash or drain by trickling water through; to treat by downward drainage, as rain washing away nutrients from the soil.

Lead compound: A chemical that has demonstrated promising biological activity in preliminary assays.

Leader: The main or terminal shoot of a plant, such as the topmost point of a fir or larch tree or the strongest shoot of a young fruit tree.

Leader sequence: A variable length sequence of nucleotides at the 5' end of an mRNA molecule that precedes the AUG initiation codon where translation begins and is not itself translated into protein.

Leading strand: The strand of DNA that is synthesized continuously during replication.

Leaf: These grow along the sides of branches or stems or at the bases of the plants. Most are green and contain chlorophyll, though they vary in their shapes and sizes. They are the part of the plant that ordinarily performs photosynthesis, the process that converts sunlight and carbon dioxide into energy. It is common for leaves to grow, fall off, and be replaced. Plants entering dormancy may lose all their leaves. Maples, for example, drop their leaves in autumn and replace them in the spring and summer.

Leaf blade: The usually flattened portion of the leaf.

Leaf bud cutting: A cutting that includes a short section of stem with attached leaf.

Leaf gap: A parenchyma-filled interruption in a stem's cylinder of vascular tissue immediately above the point at which a branch of vascular tissue (leaf trace) leading to a leaf occurs.

Leaf margin: The outer edge of a leaf.

Leaf mold: This is a compost of decayed leaves. It is made by piling leaves of deciduous trees and shrubs together and allowing them to rot. The pile should be trodden firm and the leaves should be wet. Every 6 months or so, the pile should be turned over so the outer section of the pile is in the center. It takes a year and a half to two years for the leaves to decompose enough to use for leaf mold.

Leaf plant: A plant grown for its decorative foliage.

Leaf primordium: A lateral outgrowth from the apical meristem, which will become a leaf when fully developed and expanded.

Leaf roll: A symptom of some virus diseases, characterized by curling of the leaves. Can also occur as a response to water stress.

Leaf scar: A mark left on the stem where a leaf has been lost or removed. It can easily be seen on Palms where old leaves have been shed.

Leaf scorch: This may be caused by dryness, high temperatures, disease, or lack of certain elements in the soil. The foliage looks as if its been dried by heat.

Leaf trace: The strand of vascular tissue which connects the leaf veins to the central vascular system of the stem.

Leafbud: A bud producing a stem and leaf, unlike a flowerbud, which contains a blossom.

Leaflet: The basic element of a compound leaf.

Leaf-opposed: On stem opposite the base of the leaf, as in alchemilla.

Leafstalk: The stalk that attaches a leaf to the stem or branch; the petiole.

Leaf-trace: The vascular bundle from the stele entering the petiole.

Leaky mutant: A mutant in which the gene product still retains some biological activity.

Lectin: A group of plant proteins that can bind to specific oligosaccharides on the surface of cells, causing the cells to clump together.

Lectotype: A specimen or similar element selected from the original material to serve as the nomenclatural type when a holotype was not originally designated, or as long as it is missing.

Legume: A fruit characteristic of the families mimosaceae, caesalpiniaceae and fabaceae, formed from one carpel and either dehiscent along both sides, or indehiscent; in particular, an edible crop species in the family fabaceae.

Lemma: The lower (abaxial), and larger, of two membranous bracts enclosing the flower in grass.

Lenticel: A lens-shaped body of cells, formed on the outside of a woody plant stem, which serves in the exchange of gases between the stem and the outer air.

Lenticellate: Pertaining to or having lenticels.

Lenticular: Resembling a lentil or a double-convex lens, as some seeds.

Lentiginous: Covered with minute dots; freckled; speckled.

Lepidote or squamulose: Covered with minute scales.

Leprose: Having scaly or dry scales.

Lepto: Prefix meaning ‘thin’, ‘slender’ or ‘narrow’.

Leptocaul: Twiggy, with abundant, relatively slender branches.

Leptoid: Cells involved in solute storage and transport in Bryophyta. Analogous, possibly homologous, to the phloem of tracheo-phytes.

Leptonema: Stage in meiosis immediately preceding synapsis and post DNA replication, in which the chromosomes appear as single, fine, threadlike structures.

Leptophyllous: With leaves to 25 sq. mm in size.

Leptosporangiate: Having leptosporangia. This is a derived character state in the fern clade; compare to eusporangium.

Leptosporangium: Sporangium developed from a single superficial cell.

Lethal allele: A mutant form of a gene that, in the homozygous state, is fatal.

Leucoplast: A colorless plastid commonly associated with starch accumulation.

Leukocyte: White blood cell, up to 0.02 mm in diameter, of which there are normally 4-11 million per millilitre of human blood. There are several kinds, all involved in the body's defence mechanisms. Granulocytes have granules in their cytoplasm; monocytes ingest and feed on bacteria and other micro-organisms that cause infection; lymphocytes include the B cells that are involved with the production of antibodies.

Level: To prepare soil for planting by raking gently.

Level terrace: An embankment, constructed on a contour, which cuts horizontally across the slope. A means of creating a level area on hillsides or slopes.

Liana: A climbing and twining, usually woody, plant found mostly in tropical rainforests, which may climb to the level of the tree canopy. Also liane.

Library: A collection of cells, usually bacteria or yeast, that have been transformed with recombinant vectors carrying DNA derived from an unrelated organism.

Lid: The cap of a box-like seed capsule.

Life cycle: The sequence of events from a given developmental stage in one generation to the same stage in the following generation. In sexually reproduced organisms, the starting point is the fusion of gametes to form the zygote.

Ligand: A small molecule (e.g. activators, substrates and inhibitors of enzyme activity) bound to a protein by non-covalent forces; an ion or a molecule that binds to another chemical entity to form a larger complex.

Ligase chain reaction (LCR): A technique for the detection and amplification of target DNA sequences. Two oligonucleotides are synthesized which between them are complementary to the entire target sequence, one to the 5'-side and one to the 3'-side. If the target sequence is present in the DNA sample under examination, the oligonucleotides will bind to it with their ends abutting in the centre, and a heat-stable ligase will join them into a complete polynucleotide. No ligation occurs if the target sequence is absent or if the match between synthetic oligonucleotides and target sequence is imperfect in the region where they abut. At a high temperature, the new polynucleotide dissociates from the original DNA template, and upon cooling, it and the original DNA serve as templates for a second cycle of hybridization, ligation and thermal dissociation. At each cycle there is a doubling of the number of new complete polynucleotides.

Ligate, ligation: The joining of two linear double-stranded DNA fragments by the formation of phosphodiester bonds.

Light soil: A term used to indicate a sandy or coarse-textured soil that drains rapidly. It also may lack important plant nutrients.

Light-dependent reactions: A series of chemical and physical reactions through which light energy is converted to chemical energy with the aid of chlorophyll molecules; in the process, water molecules are split, with hydrogen ions and electrons being produced and oxygen gas being released: ATP and NADPH also are created.

Ligneous: Consisting of or resembling wood; woody, as distinguished from herbaceous.

Lignescent: Tending to be or become ligneous or woody; somewhat woody.

Lignification: The thickening and strengthening of a plant cell wall with lignin.

Lignify: To convert into wood or woody tissue; to become wood or woody by chemical and physical changes in the cell walls that convert some or all of the constituents into lignin or lignocellulose.

Lignin wood: Lignin is formed by the removal of hydroxyl groups from sugars, creating phenolic compounds and short-chain alcohol ligands. Lignin polymers are heavily cross-linked. There is great variation in lignin, even within the same plant. Undoubtedly, it has evolved to have a somewhat random structure to foil enzymatic attack. Lignin is, in fact, extremely difficult to dissociate — so much so that even as late as 1980 almost nothing was known of the detailed chemistry of lignin, the second most common biopolymer on the planet (next to cellulose). Fortunately, considerable progress has been made since then. The basic monomer of lignin can be thought of as 4-alkylcatechol. The alkyl ligand is a 1 to 3 carbon chain which may be substituted with hydroxy or keto ligands at any or all positions. Both phenol groups and the alkyl substitutions may cross-link to other monomers or their side chains, yielding a fairly light, but strongly cross-linked and randomly ordered mass, i.e., wood. What is more, the chemical structure virtually guarantees that any intermediate degradation product will be a highly toxic phenolic compound. Lignin was a rather early product of plant evolution. The necessary implication is that, contrary to most current thought on the subject, land plants were subject to biological attack (although not necessarily attack by herbivorous animals) by at least the Middle Devonian, and probably even earlier.

Ligniperdous: Destructive of wood.

Lignocellulose: The combination of lignin, hemicellulose and cellulose that forms the structural framework of plant cell walls.

Lignotuber: A woody swelling below or just above the ground, containing adventitious buds.from which new shoots develop if the top of the plant is cut or burnt (common in the shrubby eucalypts and in many other fire-tolerant Australian shrubs).

Lignule: Lignules (which means tongue) are the two small flaps at the base of a monocot's leaf that wrap around the stem.

Lignum: Woody tissue, as contrasted with soft tissue or with bark.

Ligulate: 1. Strap-shaped, such as a corolla, leaf, or petal. 2. Furnished with ligule, as a ligulate grass.

Ligule: An outgrowth or projection from the top of the sheath, as in the poaceae; the strap-shaped portion of a ray or ligulate corolla; a small membranous outgrowth or projection at the base of the leaf, appearing above the sporangium in fertile leaves, as in selaginella and Isoetes

Liguliflorous: Having heads composed exclusively of strap-shaped florets.

Liguliform: Tongue- or strap-shaped.

Limb: The spreading part of a synsepalous calyx or sympetalous corolla, usually referring only to the calyx or corolla lobes, sometimes to their lips.

Limbate: Bordered (i.e. a flower in which one color is edged with another color).

Lime: Compounds of calcium (ground limestone-calcium carbonate, hydrate limestone-calcium hydroxide, or burnt lime-calcium oxide/ CaO). The amount of lime in the soil determines whether it is acid, neutral or alkaline. Limestone that is worked into the soil raises the pH from an acid pH to one that is alkaline. When lime is dug into stiff or clayey soil, it tends to make it friable and more easily worked. On the other hand, loose, sandy soil that dries up quickly is made more compact and retentive of moisture by the addition of lime. Many diseases, such as club root and Clover sickness, come from the soil and attack certain crops; lime prevents some of these diseases. Furthermore, lime is distasteful, if not actually harmful, to some soil pests, such as slugs, wireworms and leatherjackets.

Lime requirement: The amount of standard ground limestone required to bring a layer of an acre of acid soil (6.6 pH) to some specific lesser degree of acidity. Expressed in tons per acre of nearly pure limestone.

Lime sulfur: A caustic pesticide made from calcium polysulfide. Usually used as a dormant spray to control various diseases, such as leaf spot, peach leaf curl, and powdery mildew. Also effective in controlling mites, scale, and some other insects.

Limnology: The scientific study of physical, chemical, meteorological, and biological conditions in fresh waters.

Line: Abbreviation for long interspersed nuclear element.

Lineage: A group of individuals, related by common descent, e.g. an in vitro cell line derived from a single cell.

Linear: Long and very narrow with parallel sides, such as a linear leaf. Can also be used in combination, as a linear-lanceolate leaf, which is a leaf that is long, narrow and pointed.

Linear phase: The growth phase during cell culture when cell number increases arithmetically. The linear phase follows a period of exponential growth.

Linearized vector: A covalently closed circular DNA vector (typically a plasmid) which has been opened by restriction digestion to convert it to a linear molecule. In molecular cloning, DNA to be cloned is mixed with the linearized vector, and treated with ligase to join and recircularize the resulting hybrid molecule.

Lineate: Marked with lines. Also lineated, lined.

Lingulate: Tongue-shaped, plano-convex in cross section.

Linkage map: A linear or circular diagram that shows the relative positions of genes on a chromosome as determined by recombi-nation fraction.

Linkage: The tendency of a set of genes to be inherited together more often than would be expected if they were assorting inde-pendently. exists between two genes when they are located sufficiently close to one another on the same chromosome that a proportion of gametes is produced without crossing-over occurring between them.

Linked gene, linked marker: A gene or marker that is linked to another gene or marker.

Linker: A synthetic double-stranded oligonucleotide that carries the recognition sequence for one or more restriction endonucleases. The ligation of a linker to each end of a DNA fragment facilitates the preparation of the fragment for cloning into a vector.

Lip or labellum: Either of two variously shaped parts into which a corolla or calyx is divided, usually into an upper and lower lip, as in the lamiaceae and orchidaceae. Lip cells - the line of cells between which the sporangium dehisces.

Lipase: A class of enzymes which break down lipids into their component fatty acids and glycerol. Lipases used in biotechnology are generally digestive, with a role in the break-down of fats in food into their components, so that these can be used to make other materials.

Lipid: A general term for fats, fatty substances, and oils.

Lipofection: Delivery into eukaryotic cells of DNA, RNA or other compounds that have been encapsulated in liposomes.

Lipopolysaccharide (LPS): A compound containing lipid bound to a polysaccharide; often a component of microbial cells walls.

Liposome: A synthetic microscopic spherical structure consisting of a phospholipid bilayer membrane containing a user-defined aqueous solution. Liposomes can be used to transport relatively toxic drugs into diseased cells, where they can exert their maximum effect. DNA molecules may be entrapped in, or bound to the surface of, the vesicles, and subsequent fusion of the liposome with the cell membrane will deliver the DNA into the cell. Liposomes have been used to develop an efficient transfection procedure for Streptomyces bacteria.

Liquefaction: Enzymatic digestion (often by alpha-amylase) of gelatinized starch to form lower molecular weight polysaccharides.

Liquid medium: Culture solution, without a solidifying agent, for in vitro cell growth.

Liquid membrane: Thin films made up of liquids (as opposed to solids) which are stable in another liquid (usually water). Thus the liquid must not dissolve in the water, but nevertheless must be prevented from collapsing into small droplets.

Liquid nitrogen: Nitrogen gas condensed to a liquid with a boiling point of about -196 °C. Commonly used as a medium for long-term storage of biological materials.

Lithophyte: A plant that grows on the surface of rocks, getting its nourishment from the air, as some orchids.

Lithosol: A shallow soil consisting of imperfectly weathered rock fragments or nearly all barren rock.

Litmus paper: A pH indicator paper. It turns red in acidic and blue in alkaline solutions.

Littoral: Pertaining to a shore, especially of the sea; growing on or near the shore.

Lituate: Forked, with the points turned outward.

Live recombinant vaccine: A vaccine created by the expression of a pathogen antigen in a non-pathogenic organism.

Live vaccine: A living, non-virulent form of a pathogenic micro-organism or virus used to elicit an antibody response for the protection against infection by a virulent form of the same pathogen.

Living modified organism (LMO): "Living organism that possess a novel combination of genetic material obtained through the use of modern biotechnology" (Convention on Biological Diversity). Synonym of GMO, but restricted to organisms that can endanger biological diversity.

Loam: Soil composed of sand, clay and organic matter.

Lobate: Lobe rounded; sinus depth variable; outer and inner margins concave.

Lobe: Partial portion of a leaf or other organ, especially when rounded; hence lobed, lobate.

Lobed: Divided into lobes (rounded segments) separated from adjacent segments by sinuses which reach halfway or less to the middle of the organ.

Lobed margin: (leaves) Margin indented one quarter or more of the distance from the margin to the mid-vein or (where this is lacking) to the long axis of the leaf; compare entire margin and toothed margin leaves.

Lobulate: Having small or indistinct lobes.

Loculicidal: Of the dehiscence of a fruit, along lines coinciding with the centres of loculi.

Loculus: A chamber, compartment or other limited volume which is used to accumulate or store either gametes or spores. Typically, the locule contains only gametes or spores. Thus a sporangium is a spore-producing organ, but a locule within the sporangium is where the spores are accumulated before release.

Lod score: The logarithm of the odds of linkage between two loci. Used to measure the statistical support for linkage.

Lodicule: One of a pair of tiny scales in a grass floret, between the lemma and the fertile parts of the flower, which may be reduced perianth segments.

Log phase: Abbreviation for logarithmic phase.

Logarithmic phase: The growth phase in cell culture, during which cell number doubles every 20-30 minutes. Synonym: exponential phase.

Lomentum: A legume having distinct constrictions or lines of abscission between the seeds and breaking into one-seeded segments when mature.

Long day plant: Plants requiring a period of short nights before the switch from vegetative to reproductive growth can be initiated.

Long interspersed nuclear element (LINE): Families of common DNA elements, of average length 6.5 kb, which are dispersed at numerous locations within the genome. The human genome contains over 500,000 LINEs (representing ca. 16% of the genome). They appear to represent degenerate copies of transposable elements.

Long shoot: Elongated internodes, rapid annual growth. Long bud shoots - abnormal buds or shoots which elongate, then have arrested growth without the development of leaves and lateral branches.

Long template: A DNA strand, synthesized during PCR, which has a primer sequence at one end but is extended beyond the site that is complementary to the second primer at the other end.

Long terminal repeat (LTR): A characteristic sequence of nucleotides that occurs at each end of a retrovirus element that has become integrated into the host genome. Involved in the integration process.

Long-day plant: (long-day plant) A plant in which flowering is not initialed unless exposure to more than a critical day length occurs.

Longitudinal: Dehiscing along long axis of theca

Loop bioreactor: Fermenters in which material is cycled between a bulk tank and a smaller tank or loop of pipes. The circulation helps to mix the materials and to ensure that gas injected into the fermenter is well distributed in the liquid. Particularly useful for photosynthetic fermentations, where the photosynthesizing organisms are passed through a system of many small transparent pipes, which allow the access of light.

Loose, distant, or scattered: Parts widely separated from one another, usually irregularly.

Lorate: With elongate vertical waves in the margins or sides at right angles to the longitudinal axis.

Lucid: With a shining surface.

Lunate: Crescent-shaped, with acute ends.

Luteinizing hormone: A pituitary hormone which causes growth of the yellow body of the ovary and also stimulates activity of the interstitial cells of the testis.

Luxury consumption: Nutrient absorption by an organism in excess of that required for optimum growth and productivity.

Lyase: Any of a class of enzymes that catalyse either the cleavage of a double bond and the addition of new groups to a substrate, or the formation of a double bond.

Lymphocyte: White blood cells that are important components of the immune system of vertebrates.

Lymphokine: Generic name for proteins that are released by lymphocytes to act on other cells involved in the immune response. The term includes interleukins and interferons. A sub-class of cytokines.

Lymphoma: Cancer originating in the lymph nodes, spleen and other lympho-reticular sites.

Lyrate: Resembling a lyre; for example, a lyrate leaf is one that is divided into several lobes, which increase in size toward one large terminal lobe.

Lysogen: A bacterial cell whose chromosome contains integrated bacteriophage DNA.

Lysogenic bacterium: Bacterium harbouring temperate (non-virulent, lysogenic) bacteriophages.

Lysogenic: Bacteria or bacteriophages undergoing lysogeny.

Lysogeny: The lysis of a bacterial cell following infection with a bacteriophage. All RNA phages and some DNA phages induce lysogeny. The lytic cycle involves: adsorption of the phage to a specific site on the bacterial cell wall; penetration of the cell by the phage; transcription and translation of the phage genetic material by the bacterium so that many new phages are formed; and lysis of the cell to release the newly synthesized particles.

Lysosome: An organelle, bounded by a single membrane, that contains hydrolytic enzymes (e.g. acid phosphatase, ribonuclease, â-galactosidase, protease) capable of degrading cellular components. Phagolysosomes are formed in association with vacuoles containing ingested material. Autolysis occurs when components of the cell, e.g. mitochondria or fragments of endoplasmic reticulum, are degraded by the activity of lysosomal enzymes. This process is important in the recycling of valuable nutrients from ageing plant tissue. Vesicles from the golgi apparatus are also involved in the intracellular translocation of lysosomal enzymes.

Lytic: A phase of the virus life cycle during which the virus replicates within the host cell, releasing a new generation of viruses when the infected cell undergoes lysis.

Lytic cycle: The steps in viral production that lead to cell lysis.

M

MAAP: Abbreviation for multiple arbitrary amplicon profiling.

Macerate: To disintegrate tissue to disrupt cells. Commonly achieved via mechanical shearing, plasmolysis or enzymatic cell wall degradation.

Maceration: In microscopical preparation, the chemical dissolution, often by the application of strong acids, of the matrix binding parts of a specimen. The isolated pieces of the specimen may then be examined or subjected to further preparation.

Macrofibrils: Fibrils within the cell wall that are large enough in some cases to be visible under the light microscope. They are formed from microfibrils lying parallel to each other.

Macrogametophyte: Megagametophtye.

Macromolecule: Any high molecular weight molecule. Often used as a synonym for polymers.

Macronutrient: A major chemical element essential for normal growth and development. In tissue culture media, macronutrients are those required in concentrations above 0.5 millimole/litre.

Macrophage: Large white blood cells that ingest foreign substances and display on their surfaces antigens which are recognized by other cells of the immune system.

Macrophyte: A member of the macroscopic plant life especially of a body of water; large aquatic plant; the term 'aquatic macrophyte' has no taxonomic significance.

Macropodous: Having a long stalk or stem; (of a plant embryo) having a large or long hypocotyl.

Macropore: A large, non-capillary pore found in soil through which water drains by gravity.

Macropropagation: Production of plant clones from growing parts.

Macroscopic: Items large enough to be observed by the naked eye.

Macrosporangium: Megasporangium.

Mad cow disease: Colloquial term for bovine spongiform encephalopathy.

MADS box: A highly conserved DNA sequence motif found in a large family of transcription factors, most of which play important roles in developmental processes. Most prominently, the MADS box genes known in flowering plants are intimately involved in the control of flower morphogenesis.

Magenta: A type of plastic container frequently used for plant micropropagation and tissue culture.

Magnesium: An element found in combination in minerals; in plants, located either in the seeds or in the chlorophyll.

Magnoliid: Any member of the basal assemblage of flowering plants.

Major histocompatibility antigen: A cell-surface protein or glycoprotein that allows the immune system to distinguish foreign or "non-self" from "self". A better term is histoglobulin. These are the antigens that must be matched between donors and recipients during organ and tissue transplants to prevent rejection.

Major histocompatibility complex (MHC): The large cluster of genes that encode the major histocompatibility antigens in mammals.

Malacophily: Pollinated by snails or slugs.

Malathion: A man-made insecticide that is effective in destroying a wide range of garden pests, such as aphids, scale and mites.

Male: Having flowers that do not produce fruit or seed and only contain stamens.

Male or staminate: Plant with staminate flowers only.

Mallee: A growth habit in which several woody stems arise separately from a lignotuber (usually applied to shrubby eucalypts); a plant having the above growth habit.

Malt extract: A mixture of organic compounds prepared from malt, used as a culture medium additive.

Malting: Enzymatic reduction of starch to sugars in germinating grain, used in brewing.

Mammary gland: The milk-producing organ of female mammals.

Management of farm animal genetic resources: The sum total of technical, policy and logistical operations involved in understanding (characterization), using and developing (utilization), maintaining (conservation), accessing, and sharing the benefits of animal genetic resources.

Mangroves: Trees that grow on the shores of river deltas, estuaries and coastlines in subtropical to tropical climates.

Mannitol: A sugar alcohol widely distributed in plants. Commonly used as a nutrient and osmoticum in suspension media for plant protoplasts.

Mannose: A hexose component of many polysaccharides, occasionally used as a carbohydrate source in plant tissue culture media.

Mannoxylic: Wood in which there is a great deal of parenchyma tissue among the xylem is called mannoxylic. Cycads and pteridosperms have mannoxylic wood. Contrast with pycnoxylic.

Map: 1. to determine the relative positions of loci (genes or DNA sequences) on a chromosome. Linkage maps are obtained from the frequency of recombination between loci. Physical maps are obtained commonly by the use of in situ hybridization of cloned DNA fragments to metaphase chromosomes, or by somatic-cell hybrids or radiation hybrids. 2. a diagram showing the relative position of, and distances between, loci on a chromosome.

Map unit: A unit of measure equivalent to 1% recombination.

Mapping: The construction of a localized (around a gene), or broad-based (whole genome) genetic map. More generally, determining the location of a locus (gene or genetic marker) on a chromosome.

Mapping function: A mathematical expression relating observed recombination fraction to map distance.

Marcescent: Usually ephemeral with persistent remains; withering persistent

Marginal: Attached or occurring at or along the margin or edge.

Marginal farmland: 1. Surface soil that is only a few inches deep. 2. Land repeatedly farmed without benefit of humus or chemical replacements.

Marine: Pertaining to the sea or salt water.

Maritime: Pertaining to the sea; coastal.

Marker: An identifiable DNA sequence that is inherited in Mendelian fashion, and which facilitates the study of inheritance of a trait or a linked gene.

Marker-assisted introgression: The use of DNA markers to increase the speed and efficiency of introgression of a new allele(s) or gene(s) into a breeding population. The markers will be closely linked to the gene(s) in question.

Marker-assisted selection (MAS): The use of DNA markers to improve response to selection in a population. The markers will be closely linked to one or more target loci, which may often be quantitative trait loci.

Marker gene: A gene of known function or known location, used for marker-assisted selection or genetic studies.

Marker peptide: A portion of fusion protein that facilitates its identification or purification.

Marl: An earthy deposit consisting mainly of calcium carbonate; used for liming acid soil.

Marsh: A tract of wet land principally inhabitated by emergent herbaceous vegetation.

Mass selection: As practised in plant and animal breeding, the selection ofa number of individuals, on the basis of their individual phenotypes, to interbreed to form the next generation.

Massula: Rounded mass of hardened cytoplasmic foam containing one or more spores in the Salvineales.

Maternal effect: An effect attributable to a genetic contribution of the female parent of the individual being evaluated.

Matric potential: A water potential component, always of negative value, resulting from the presence of solid (often finely divided) surfaces; primarily responsible for water uptake by a dry seed prior to germination.

Maturation: The formation of gametes or spores.

Matutinal: With flowers opening in the morning

MCS: Abbreviation for multiple cloning site.

MDA: Abbreviation for multiple drop array.

Meadow: 1. A piece of low-lying, moist land that is often used for growing hay or as pastureland. 2. An upland area covered with grass and usually surrounded by woods.

Mealy: Covered with a coarse flour-like powder.

Mean: In statistics, the arithmetic average; the sum of all measurements or values in a sample divided by the sample size.

Mechanical analysis: The physical analysis of soil material to determine its grain-size fraction.

Mechanical stability: The resistance of soil broken down by mechanical forces like tillage or abrasion.

Medial: Attached near or at the middle, especiallly midway between costa and margin.

Median: In a set of measurements, the central value above and below which there are an equal number of measurements.

Median leaf: Leaf on top of stem, as in heterophyllous species of Selaginella.

Medicinal plants: Plants that are or have been used medicinally.

Medifixed: Attached by or at the middle, e.g. of anthers, attached to the filament at the middle of the connective.

Medium: 1. In plant tissue culture, a term for the liquid or solid formulation upon which plant cells, tissues or organs develop. 2. In general terms, a substrate for plant growth, such as nutrient solution, soil, sand, etc., e.g. potting medium.

Medium formulation: In tissue culture, the particular constituents for the culture medium, commonly comprising macro- and micro-elements, vitamins, plant hormones, and a carbohydrate source. Some formulations are very specific to the kind of explant or plant species that can be maintained; some are very general.

Medium sand: Soil particles measuring between 0.25 to 0.50 millimeters.

Medulla: Parenchymatous tissue within the vascular cylinder.

Medullated protostele: A cylindrical stele with a nonvascular, parenchymatous centre, with the phloem around the outside only, also known as an ectphloic siphonostele.

Mega yeast artificial chromosome: A yeast artificial chromosome (YAC) which can carry particularly large inserts (up to 1Mbp)—standard YACs typically carry inserts of up to 500kbp.

Megabase (Mb): A length of DNA consisting of 106 bases.

Megabase cloning: The cloning of large DNA fragments of the order of 1Mb.

MegaDalton (MDa): One megaDalton is equal to 106 Dalton.

Megagamete: The "female" gamete, analogous to an egg and sometimes referred to as an ova (Latin for egg).

Megagametophyte: The female gametophyte of angiosperms, which, in approximately 70% of the species investigaled, 'contains eight nuclei.

Megaphyll: A leaf with branched veins and a flat area for receiving sunlight.

Megasporangium (also macrosporangium): The sporangium in heterosporous plants where the megaspores develop.

Megaspore: In plants which are heterosporous, the larger kind of spore is called a megaspore; it usually germinates into a female (egg-producing) gametophyte. Contrast with microspore.

Megasporocyte: A diploid cell that produces megaspores upon undergoing meiosis.

Megasporophyll (also macrosporophyll): Specialised leaf bearing or subtending one or more megasporangia.

Meiosis: A process common to almost sexual reproduction in eukaryotic cells. The homologous chromosomes of a diploid nucleus first exchange homologous genes (alleles) on a roughly random basis, so that the resulting chromosomes carry a mixture of genes from each parent. The nucleus then divides normally (by mitosis) to yield two diploid daughter nuclei. Finally, the nuclei divide again, but now without DNA replication, to yield four haploid cells.

Meiotic analysis: The use of patterns of chromosome pairing at meiotic prophase and metaphase to detect relationships between chromosomes, from which can be deduced the relationship between the parents of the organism studied.

Meiotic drive: Any mechanism that causes a particular allele or chromosome to be over-represented in a population of gametes.

Melanin: Dark pigment, produced by specialized epidermal cells called melanocytes.

Melittophily: Pollinated by bees.

Melting temperature (Tm): The temperature at which a double-stranded DNA molecule denatures into separate single strands. Tm is determined by the length of the molecule and its base composition. DNAs rich in G:C base pairs have higher Tm than A:T rich DNA, because since three hydrogen bonds are formed between G and C, but only two between A and T.

Membrane: A thin, soft, flexible, +/- translucent piece of tissue; hence membranous.

Membrane bioreactor: A vessel in which cells are cultured on or behind a permeable membrane, which allows the diffusion of nutrients to the cells, but retains the cells themselves. A variation is the hollow-fibre reactor.

Membranous: Having a thin, soft, pliable texture.

Memory cell: Long-lived B cells and T cells that mediate rapid secondary immune responses to a previously encountered antigen.

Mendel's laws: Two laws summarizing Gregor Mendel's theory of inheritance. The Law of Segregation states that each hereditary characteristic is controlled by two 'factors' (now called alleles), which segregate and pass into separate germ cells. The Law of Independent Assortment states that pairs of 'factors' segregate independently of each other when germ cells are formed.

Mendelian population: A natural, interbreeding unit of sexually reproducing plants or animals sharing a common gene pool.

Mendelian segregation: Occurs when alleles are inherited according to Mendel's Laws.

Meniscoid: Venation in which the veins are arranged pinnately from a main vein and anastomose with the neighbouring group to form a single excurent vein.

Mentum: A "chin" on some Orchid flowers, formed by the fusion of the lateral sepals and the column-foot.

Mericarp: One segment of a fruit that breaks at maturity into units derived from the individual carpels.

Mericlinal: Refers to a chimera with tissue of one genotype partly surrounded by that of another genotype.

Mericloning: A propagation method using shoot tips in culture to proliferate multiple buds, which can then be separated, rooted and planted out.

Meristele: The individual vascular bundle of a complex stele such as a dictyostele.

Meristem: A plant tissue containing cells that are actively dividing (or have the potential to do so). Meristem found in the tip of roots and stems, the apical meristem, is responsible for the growth in length (primary growth) of these organs. The cambium is a lateral meristem that is responsible for increase in girth (secondary growth) in perennial plants. Some plants also have intercalary meristem, as in the stems of grasses, for example. These are responsible for their continued growth after cutting or grazing has removed the apical meristem of the shoots.

Meristem culture: A tissue culture containing meristematic dome tissue without adjacent leaf primordia or stem tissue. The term may also imply the culture of meristemoidal regions of plants, or meristematic growth in culture.

Meristem tip: An explant comprising the meristem (meristematic dome) and usually one pair of leaf primordia. Also refers to explants originating from apical meristem tip or lateral or axillary meristem tip.

Meristem tip culture: Cultures derived from meristem tip explants. Used widely to achieve virus elimination and axillary shoot proliferation, less commonly for callus production.

Meristemoid: A localized group of callus cells, characterized by their accumulation of starch, RNA and protein, and giving rise to adventitious shoots or roots.

Mermaphrodigynous: Inflorescence with hermaphroditic flowers inside or above and pistillate outside or below (hermaphrodi-gynecephalous).

Merophytes: Group of cells which have all been produced from the same initial cell. Leaves and stems in particular are often built from specific patterns of merophytes.

Merozygote: Partial zygote produced by a process of partial genetic exchange, such as transformation in bacteria.

Mesic: Conditioned by temperate moist climate; neither xerix nor hydric; pertaining to conditions of medium moisture supply.

Mesocarp: The fleshy portion of the wall of a succulent fruit inside the skin and outside the stony layer, if any, surrounding the seed(s).

Mesochile: The middle part of the lip in certain orchids that have this organ divided into three parts.

Mesoderm: The middle germ layer that forms in the early animal embryo and gives rise to parts such as bone and connective tissue.

Mesophile: A micro-organism able to grow in the temperature range 20-50 °C; optimal growth often occurs at about 37 °C.

Mesophyll: Photosynthetic tissue of a green plant; of vegetation, characteristic of moist habitats and with soft, fairly large leaves predominating; a leaf whose area is within the approximate range 20<180 square cm.

Messenger RNA: mRNA.

Mestome sheath: The inner of 2 rings of cells (the bundle sheath) around the vascular bundle of monocots.

Metabolism: The biochemical processes whereby nutritive material is converted to living matter, or aids in building living matter, or by which complex substances and food are broken down into simple substances.

Metabolite: A low-molecular-weight biological compound that is usually synthesized enzymically.

Metabolomics: The large-scale study of the full complement of secondary metabolites produced by a given species in all its tissues and growth stages.

Metal affinity chromatography: A chromatographic technique, in which a compound interacting with a specific metal ion can be captured by immobilizing the relevant ion on the column's solid matrix.

Metalloenzyme: An enzyme which requires the presence of a metal in order to be catalytically active.

Metallothionein: A protective protein that binds heavy metals such as cadmium and lead.

Metaphase: Stage of mitosis or meiosis (following prophase and preceding anaphase) during which the chromosomes, or at least the kinetochores, lie in the central plane of the spindle. The stage of maximum chromosome condensation, at which karyotypes are generally described. In the first division of meiosis, metaphase represents the stage at which meiotic analysis is generally performed.

Metastasis: The spread of cancer cells to previously unaffected organs.

Metaxylem: The latter formed primary xylem, consisting of scalariform, reticulate and pitted vessels.

Methylation: The addition of a methyl group (-CH3) to a molecule, most commonly in the context of DNA where cytosine and, less often, adenine residues can be modified in this way, sometimes resulting in a change in transcription.

MHC: Abbreviation for major histocompatibility complex.

Micro: Axial embryo in minute seeds, less than 0.2 mm long; minute and undifferentiated to almost total size of seed.

Micro array: A large set of cloned DNA molecules immobilized as a compact and orderly pattern of sub-microlitre spots onto a solid matrix (typically a glass slide). Used to analyse patterns of gene expression, presence of markers, or nucleotide sequence. The major advantage of micro-arrays is the extent to which the process of genotyping can be automated, thereby enabling large numbers of individuals to be simultaneously genotyped at many loci. A similar approach may be used with other immobilized components for other purposes. Synonym: chip or DNA chip.

Micro carrier: Small particles used as a support material for (particularly mammalian) cells, which are too fragile to be pumped and stirred as bacterial cells are in a large-scale culture.

Micro element: A nutritional element required in very small quantities.

Micro encapsulation: A process of enclosing a substance in very small sealed capsules from which material is released by heat, solution or other means.

Micro environment: A small-scale environment in which the conditions (temperature, humidity, pH etc.) are distinct; typically used in connection with the surroundings of a living object.

Micro injection: The introduction of small amounts of (usually) liquid material (DNA, RNA, enzymes, cytotoxic agents) into a defined tissue or single cell with a fine, microscopic needle.

Micro isolating system: Mechanical separation of single cells or protoplasts thus allowing them to proliferate individually.

Micro nutrients: Very small amounts of nutrients needed by plants.

Microalgal culture: Culture in bioreactors of microalgae (including seaweeds).

Microbial mat: Layered microbial populations, usually growing on the surface of a solid medium or on a membrane.

Microbody: A frequently spherical cellular organelle, bound by a single membrane, 20-60 nm in diameter, and containing a variety of enzymes.

Microclimate: A small, local climate within a larger climate area, such as a greenhouse or a protected area of a garden.

Microdroplet array (MDA): A technique used to simultaneously evaluate large numbers of media modifications, employing small quantities of medium into which are placed small numbers of cells or protoplasts. These form a monolayer at the droplet meniscus and can easily be examined. Synonyms: multiple drop array, hanging droplet technique.

Microfibril: Microscopic fibres visible only at the high magnification of the electron microscope.

Microfilament: A protein filament involved with cytoplasmic streaming and with contraction and movement in eukaryotic cells.

Microgamete: The "male" gamete, analogous to sperm.

Microgametophyte: A plant body or cell lineage, formed by vegetative growth of the microspore, that produces the male gametes of a heterosporous plant.

Micronucleus: A nucleus, distinct from and smaller than the main nucleus, but lying within the same cell. They usually arise following abnormal meiotic or mitotic telophases, where individual chromosomes or chromosome fragments do not reach the pole.

Micronutrient: An essential element normally required in cell culture at concentrations under 0.5 millimole/litre.

Micro-organism: Organism visible only under magnification.

Microphyll: A kind of leaf, specifically one which has a single, unbranched vein in it. Microphylls are only found in the lycophytes.

Microphyllidious: Small, leaf-shaped.

Microphyllous: 1. Having small leaves. 2. Having leaves with only one unbranched vein.

Microplast: Vesicle produced by subdivision and fragmentation of protoplasts or thin-walled cells.

Micropropagation: Miniaturized in vitro multiplication and/or regeneration of plant material under aseptic and controlled environmental conditions.

Micropyle: 1. A small opening in the surface of a plant ovule through which the pollen tube passes prior to fertilization. 2. A small pore in some animal cells or tissues.

Microsatellite: A segment of DNA characterized by a variable number of copies(typically 5-50) of a sequence of around 5 or fewer bases (called a repeat unit). At any one locus (genomic site), there are usually several different "alleles" in a population, each allele identifiable according to the number of repeat units. This existence of multiple alleles (high level of polymorphism) has enabled microsatellites to be developed as powerful markers in many different species. They are detected by the polymerase chain reaction.

Microshoot: One of several to many shoots produced by a plant growing in vitro.

Microsporangium: In plants that produce two types of spores, the receptacle that contains only the smaller type; comparable to the pollen sac of the anther in a seed plant.

Microspore: In plants which are heterosporous, the smaller kind of spore is called a microspore; it usually germinates into a male (sperm-producing) gametophyte. Contrast with megaspore.

Microsporocyte: A diploid cell that produces microspores upon undergoing meiosis.

Microsporophyll: A leaf, usually reduced in size, on or within which microspores are produced.

Microsporum sp.: Causes ringworm in humans.

Microstylous: A flower that has short styles.

Microtuber: Miniature tuber, produced in tissue culture, which is readily regenerable into a normal tuberous plant.

Microtubule: Self-assembling components of the cytoskeleton. Microtubules are cylindrical protein polymers, interconnected by cross-bridging proteins, which structurally and dynamically organize functional activities in living cells. They form the spindle during mitosis.

Mid parent value: The average of the phenotypic measure, with respect to a given trait, of the two parents used to generate the population being analysed.

Middle lamella: A thin exclusively plant membrane separating two adjacent protoplasts and remaining as a distinct cementing layer between adjacent cell walls.

Midlobe: The middle lobe of a three-lobed labellum, usually brightly colored and furnished with calli (callus), keels, and/or lamelle.

Midrib: The central (main) vein of a pinnately veined leaf or leaflet.

Midvein: The central conducting and supporting structure of the blade of a leaflet.

Mildew: 1. A growth (usually whitish colored) produced on living plants by fungus. 2. A fungus that causes such growth.

Mineral soil: A general term for soil composed mainly of mineral matter.

Mineral: 1. An inorganic substance. 2. The solid homogeneous crystalline chemical element that results from the inorganic process of nature.

Mineralization: The conversion of organic compounds into inorganic (mineral) ones. For example, the conversion of ethanol into carbon dioxide and water.

Mini prep: A small-scale preparation of plasmid or phage DNA. Used to purify cloned DNA from the DNA of the vector.

Minimum effective cell density: The cell density below which reproducible cell growth fails. The minimum density is determined by both the source function of the tissue (species, explant, cell line) and by the culture phase of the initial inoculum.

Minimum inoculum size: The critical volume of inoculum required to initiate culture growth, due to the diffusive loss of cell materials into the medium. The subsequent culture growth cycle is dependent on the inoculum size, which is determined by the volume of medium and size of the culture vessel.

Minisatellite: A form of variable number tandem repeats in which the repeat unit size ranges from 10-100 bp. Used for DNA fingerprinting following Southern hybridization. Generally concentrated at the ends of chromosomes and in regions with a high frequency of recombination.

Minituber: Small tubers (5-15 mm in diameter) formed on shoot cultures or cuttings of tuber-forming crops, such as potato.

Minor: Smaller in size.

Minute: So small as to be difficult to see with the naked eye.

Mire: Synonymous with any peat-accumu-lating wetland.

Mismatch repair: A DNA repair process that corrects mismatched base pairs.

Mismatch: The occurrence of a non-complementary pairs of bases in a double helix of DNA, e.g. A:C, G:T.

Missense mutation: A mutation that changes a codon for one amino acid into a codon specifying another amino acid.

Mist propagation: Application of fine droplets of water to maintain humidity around plantlets or cuttings, which have not yet developed effective roots.

Mitochondrion: Organelle possessing its own DNA which appear in all eukaryotic cells (and never in prokaryotic cells) and produce adenosine triphosphate as an energy source for the cell via oxidative phosphorylation. Mitochondria contain many enzymes of the respiratory cycle, although most of these proteins are nuclear encoded.

Mitogen: A substance that can cause cells to initiate mitosis.

Mitosis: Splitting of replicated chromosomes, and the division of the cytoplasm to produce two genetically identical daughter cells. On the basis of the appearance of the chromosomes, it is separated into five stages: interphase, prophase, metaphase, anaphase and telophase.

Mitriform: Having a hollow conical shape, resembling a bishop's miter.

Mixed: Contains flower, leaf, and stem primordia; will give rise to branch with leaves and flower(s).

Mixed bud: A bud containing both rudimentary leaves and flowers.

Mixed sporangia: Sporangia of all ages borne at all levels in sorus.

Mixoploid: Groups of cells with variable (a mix of euploid, aneuploid, polyploid) chromosome numbers.

Mobilization: 1. The transfer between bacteria of a non-conjugative plasmid by a conjugative plasmid. 2. The transfer between bacteria of chromosomal genes by a conjugative plasmid.

Mobilizing function: The genes on a plasmid that give it the ability to facilitate the transfer of either a non-conjugative or a conjugative plasmid from one bacterium to another.

Modern biotechnology: The application of: a. In vitro nucleic acid techniques, including recombinant deoxyribonucleic acid (DNA) and direct injection of nucleic acid into cells or organelles, or b. Fusion of cells beyond the taxonomic family, that overcome natural physiological reproductive or recombination barriers and that are not techniques used in traditional breeding and selection (Convention on Biological Diversity).

Modification: Enzymatic attachment of one or more chemical groups to a macromolecule, affecting its biological activity or properties.

Modified stems: Modified stems are plant organs that contain nodes and internodes just like stems except they don't look like stems. A number of modified stems exist: rhizomes, tubers, thorns, bulbs, corms, stolon, cladophylls, etc.

Modifying gene: A gene that affects the expression of some other gene.

MOET: Abbreviation for multiple ovulation and embryo transfer.

Moisture tension: The force at which water is held by soil. Expressed as the equivalent of a unit column of water in centimeters.

Molecular biology: The study of living processes at the molecular level.

Molecular cloning: The biological amplification of a DNA sequence via the mitotic division of a host cell into which it has been transformed or transfected.

Molecular genetics: The study of the expression, regulation and inheritance of genes at the level of DNA and its transcription products.

Molecular marker: A genetic marker which is assayed at the DNA level.

Molecule: The smallest unit of an element or compound retaining its own identity; consists of two or more atoms.

Molybdenum: A trace element present in most soils and plants.

Monad: Pollen grains occurring singly.

Monadelphous: Having the stamens of a flower, united into one group, as can be seen in Hibiscus.

Monander: A plant that has only one stamen, such as certain orchids.

Monandrous: Having a single stamen.

Monilia sp.: Reported to be allergenic. This fungus produces soft rot of tree fruits. Other members produce a red bread mold. It is infrequently involved in corneal eye infections.

Moniliform: Of hairs, constricted between the cells like a string of beads; of fruits, constricted between the seeds.

Mono unsaturates: Oils containing mono-unsaturated fatty acids (i.e. where one -CH2-CH2- group in the hydrocarbon chain is replaced by -CH=CH-).

Mono: Prefix meaning 'one' or 'solitary' generally bean-shaped; also referred as 'bilateral'.

Monocarp: A plant that bears fruit once and then dies.

Monocarpellary: A flower consisting of only one carpel.

Monocarpic, hapaxanthic: Perennial or annual, flowering and fruiting once, then dying; fruiting once.

Monocarpous: A flower that has a single ovary, whether simple or compound.

Monocephalous: One-headed, as in composites

Monochasium: A cymose inflorescence with the branches arising singly.

Monochlamydeous: Of a flower, having only one whorl of perianth parts.

Monoclinous: A flower that has both the stamens and pistils.

Monocots: Flowering plants whose embryo has only one cotyledon.

Monocotyledon leaf: Lacks a vascular cambium and usually has parallel venation and the xylem arranged in a U or V shaped pattern in the vascular bundle.

Monoculture: The agricultural practice of cultivating a single crop over a whole farm or area.

Monoecious: A plant having unisexual male and female flowers on the same individual; said of a plant having unisexual flowers.

Monogastric animal: A non-ruminant animal with a simple stomach.

Monogenic: Trait controlled by a single gene. Opposite: multigenic, polygenic.

Monogynoecial: Formed from a single pistil of a flower, as in certain fruits.

Monohybrid cross: A cross between parents differing in only one trait or in which only one trait is being considered.

Monohybrid heterozygous: with respect to one gene.

Monokaryotic: Having a single nucleus in each cell or unit of the mycelium in club fungi.

Monokine: Generic name for proteins that are released by monocytes to act on other cells involved in the immune response. A sub-class of cytokines.

Monolayer: A single layer of cells growing on a surface.

Monolete spore: Bean-shaped, with a single scar line.

Monolignols: The building blocks of lignin that undergo polymerization.

Monomer: A small molecule (in the biological sciences typically individual amino acids, nucleotides or monosaccharides) that can combine with identical or similar others to form a larger, more complex molecule called a polymer.

Monomerous: 1. Having only one member in each whorl (pistil, stamen, sepal, or petal), said of a flower. 2. Monocarpellary.

Monomorphic: Absence of variation for a marker, gene, chromosome, or genetically determined trait in a population.

Monopetalous: 1. Having only one petal. 2. Having the petals united into one piece by their edges or at the base.

Monophyletic: A group descended from a single common ancestor within the group being studied. The term is also used in a slightly different sense. A "monophyletic group" usually refers to a clade, i.e. an organism and all of its descendants. Thus Sinraptor and Allosaurus are (very likely) monophyletic within Allosauroidea. However they are not, by themselves, a clade, because they do not include all descendants of their last common ancestor.

Monophyllous: One-leaved.

Monopodial: Of branching patterns, Monopodial branching is a pattern of branching in which there is one main shoot with lateral branches emerging from it. Many firs and spruces exhibit monopodial branching patterns, therefore the Christmas tree image is a good example of monopodial branching. Branching in which there is a clear central branch with lateral branches that develop some distance behind the end of the central branch.

Monopodium: An axis in which the growth is continued from year to year by the same growing point; hence monopodial.

Monosaccate: A pollen grain with one saccus or buoyant bladder. Compare bisaccate.

Monosaccharide: A simple sugar (e.g. glucose, fructose).

Monosepalous: 1. Having the sepals united. 2. Having only one sepal.

Monosomic: A form of aneuploidy in which a diploid organism lacks one member of a homologous chromosome pair.

Monosperm: A plant that produces only one seed.

Monospermous: Having only one seed.

Monostelic: With a single stele.

Monostichous: Arranged in a single row along a stem, as certain flowers.

Monostylous: Having only one style.

Monosymmetrical: Capable of being bisected into similar halves with reference to a single plane; bilaterally symmetrical, as in flower of the sweet pea.

Monotocous: Producing fruit only once, as annuals.

Monotypic: Containing only one taxon of the next lower rank (e.g. applied to a family containing only one genus).

Monovalent cations: Ions having a positive charge.

Monozygotic twin: One of a pair of twins derived from a single fertilized egg. Synonym: identical twin.

Monstrose: This mutation appears as randomly occurring growth from multiple growing points and usually results in a misshapen, club-like plant.

Montane: Pertaining to, occurring in mountains.

Morphic: Suffix pertaining to 'form', e.g. Dimorphic, polymorphic etc.

Morphogen: A substance that stimulates the development of form or structure in an organism.

Morphogenesis: The development, through growth and differentiation, of form and structure in an organism.

Morphogenic response: The effect on the developmental history of a plant or its parts exposed to a given set of growth conditions or to a change in the environment.

Morphology: A branch of biology that deals with the form and structure of animals and plants, a study of the forms, relationships, metamorphoses, and phylogenetic development of organs apart from their functions.

Mosaic: Unusual mottling, veining, or streaking, in the leaves of a plant, that is usually very colorful. It is usually caused by a virus.

Motif: A conserved sequence of nucleotides or amino acids that can be associated with some function of, respectively, a length of DNA or a protein.

Motile: Actively moving, self-propelled.

Mottled leaf: 1. A disease caused by a zinc deficiency that reduces the size of leaves and fruits in citrus plants. 2. A disease that causes the leaves of cherry trees to pucker and crinkle.

Mow: 1. A pile of hay or sheaves of grain, placed in a barn. 2. To cut down with a sharp tool (i.e. to mow grass with a lawn mower).

MRNA: Abbreviation for messenger RNA. The RNA molecule resulting from transcription of a protein-encoding gene, following any splicing. The information encoded in the mRNA molecule is translated into a gene product by the ribosomes.

MTDNA: Abbreviation for mitochondrial DNA.

Mucilage: A vegetable gelatine of slimy consistency, water-soluble; hence mucilaginous.

Mucilaginous: Gummy or gelatinous.

Mucor sp.: Often found in soil, dead plant material, horse dung, fruits and fruit juice. It is also found in leather, meat, dairy products, animal hair and jute. A Zygomycetes fungus which may be allergenic (skin and bronchial tests). This organism and other Zygomycetes will grow rapidly on most fungal media. May cause mucorosis in immune compromised individuals. The sites of infection are the lung, nasal sinus, brain, eye and skin. Infection may have multiple sites.

Mucro: A short, sharp tip, such as a prolong midrib; hence mucronate.

Mucronate: Produced into a short, sharp tip, or mucro.

Mucronulate: 1:1 l/w or broader than long; straight.

Mulch: Any substance, usually a layer of organic material, applied to the soil over or around a plant to conserve moisture, protect the roots from frost, reduce the growth of weeds, and enrich the soil (i.e. bark chips, rotted manure, garden compost, gravel, black plastic).

Mulching paper: A biodegradable sheet made of peat that is used to reduce water evaporation and keep weeds down.

Mule: A plant hybrid that is self-sterile and usually cross-sterile due to infertile pollen or undeveloped pistils.

Mull: A humus-rich layer of forested soils consisting of mixed organic and mineral matter.

Multi: Prefix meaning 'many'.

Multi copy: Describing plasmids which replicate to produce many copies per host bacterial cell.

Multi locus probe: A DNA sequence that hybridizes to a number of different genomic sites.

Multicarpellate: Having a compound pistil or ovary formed by the joining of several carpels.

Multicellular: Many-celled.

Multicipital: With many axes or stems from one rootstock or caudex.

Multicostal: Many-ribbed.

Multifarious: Many-ranked, in many rows.

Multifid: Divided into many parts.

Multigene family: A set of genes (not necessarily mapping to the same genomic location) that are related in nucleotide sequence and/or that produce polypeptides with similar amino acid sequences. Sequence similarity does not always result in functional similarity.

Multigenic: Trait controlled by several genes, as opposed to monogenic. Synonym: polygenic.

Multimer: A protein made up of more than one polypeptide chain.

Multinodal shoot: Spring shoot developing from the terminal winter bud and producing 2 or more whorls of branches; the cones are partly lateral in the middle of the shoot; e.g., Pinus echinata.

Multiple alleles: The existence of more than two alleles at a locus in a population.

Multiple arbitrary amplicon profiling: A collective term for a number of related polymerase chain reaction techniques, all of which use arbitrary primers, and which generate a number of distinct amplification products.

Multiple fruit: A fruit derived from several to many individual flowers in a single inflorescence.

Multiple ovulation and embryo transfer (MOET): A technology by which a single female that usually produces only one or two offspring can produce a litter of offspring. Involves stimulation of a female to shed large numbers of ova; natural mating or artificial insemination; collection of fertilized ova (either surgically, or non-surgically through the cervix); and transfer (usually non-surgical, through the cervix) of these fertilized ova to recipient females.

Multiplex: 1. The simultaneous amplification of a number of amplicons in a single polymerase chain reaction, achieved by including more than one set of primers in the reaction mix. 2. The inheritance pattern of alleles in autopolyploids.

Multiseriate: Many-rowed; in many series.

Multivalent vaccine: A vaccine designed to elicit an immune response either to more than one infectious agent or to several different antigenic determinants of a single agent.

Muriate of potash: This is a slow-acting fertilizer that adds oxide of potassium to the soil. Same as potassium chloride.

Muricate: Having a rough surface texture owing to small, sharp projections.

Mushroom: A sexually initiated phase in the life cycle of a club fungus. Usually consisting of an expanded cap and a stalk.

Mutable gene: A gene which has an unusually high rate of mutation.

Mutagen: An agent or process capable of inducing mutations (e.g. irradiation, alkylating agents).

Mutagenesis: Induction of heritable change(s) in the genetic constitution of a cell through alterations to its DNA.

Mutant: An organism or an allele bearing a mutation. Usually applied when a characteristic change in phenotype can be recognized.

Mutation: Any change in the genome with respect to a defined wild type. Can occur at the level of ploidy, karyotype, or nucleotide sequence. Most of the latter mutations are silent (i.e. cannot be associated with any change in phenotype), either because the DNA sequence affected is in the non-coding part of the genome, or because the specific change does not alter the function of a coding sequence.

Mutation pressure: A constant mutation rate that adds mutant genes to a population; repeated occurrences of mutations in a population.

Muticous: Without a vein extension, awn or hair.

Mycelial: Pertaining to mycelium.

Mycelium: Threadlike filament making up the vegetative portion of thallus fungi.

Mycology: The science of fungi; the study of mushrooms.

Mycoprotein: Fungal protein.

Mycorrhiza: A symbiotic association between fungal hyphae and a plant root.

Mycotoxin: Toxic substance of fungal origin, e.g. aflatoxin.

Myeloma: A plasma cell cancer.

Myiophily: Pollinated by diptera.

Myrmecophilous: Ant-loving, of plants inhabited by ants and offering specialised shelters and food for them.

Myrmecophily: Pollinated by ants.

Myxobacteriales: (slime bacteria) An order containing flexible creeping bacteria that lack a rigid cell wall and flagella, and move by gliding across the substrate. Most of its members are terrestrial. Myxobacters differ from other bacteria in producing resting cells, termed microcysts, that are often borne in fruiting bodies. Many are soil saprophytes, some species (e.g. of Cytophaga and Sporocytophaga) producing cellulase enzymes.

Myxomycota: A division of the Fungi containing those species that have amoeboid, plasmodial, or pseudoplasmodial thalli. It contains some 475 species in about 90 genera and is divided into the four classes Acrasiomycetes , Hydromyxomycetes, Myxomycetes , and Plasmodiophoromycetes.

NAD: (Nicotinamide Adenine Dinucleotide, coenzyme I) A pyridine-based nucleotide that functions as a coenzyme in many oxidation-reduction reactions, according to the general reaction: NAD+ + reduced substrate "!NADH + H++ oxidized substrate. An example of such a reaction is the oxidation of citrate to á-ketoglutarate in the TCA cycle. Reduced NAD can act as a reducing agent or it may be reoxidized in the respiratory chain with coupled ATP formation. NAD is not usually tightly bound to the enzyme with which it is acting but instead acts as a second substrate, binding only during the reaction and being released into the medium with the reaction products. NAD is sometimes called DPN, an abbreviation for the trivial name diphosphopyridine nucleotide.

Naked bud: A bud not protected by bud scales.

Naked: Of sporangia, not covered by an indusium; of seeds, exposed on the surface of a sporophyll (not enclosed within an ovary); of flowers, without perianth; of protoplasts or gametes, not bounded by a cell wall.

Nannandry: The existence in a species of male individuals that are considerably smaller than the females. For example, within the moss genus Homaliadelphus there is a species in which the male gametophyte is sufficiently small to grow as an epiphyte upon the leaves of the female gametophyte. The dwarf male filaments of certain members of the Oedogoniales are further examples. Species in which the male plants are of normal size are termed macrandrous.

Nanophyllous: With leaves to 225 sq. mm in size.

Narrow host-range plasmid: A plasmid that can replicate in one, or at most a few, different bacterial species.

Narrow sense heritability: The proportion of the phenotypic variance that is due to variation in breeding values; the proportion of the phenotypic variance that is due to additive genetic variance.

Nastic movement: A nondirected movement of a flat organ (e.g., petal, leaf) in which the organ alternately bends up and down.

Native protein: The naturally occurring form of a protein.

Natural selection: The action of the environment, as opposed to the actions of man, on individual organisms such that those possessing genotypes better suited to the environment will survive and reproduce more successfully than those with less favourable genotypes, which will eventually die out. By this process the characteristics of a population will change according to the nature of the environmental pressures acting on them. Over a number of generations the population may diverge into a number of distinct groups each adapted to a particular microenvironment. This process will be hastened if there are barriers to gene flow between the groups. The concept of natural selection is the cornerstone in Darwin's theory of evolution.

Naturalize: To adapt to an environment not native; of foreign origin, but established and reproducing as though native.

Navicular, naviculariform: Boat-shaped.

Neck: Narrowed portion of hypanthium, between the base and a flared limb.

Necrocoleopterophily: Pollinated by carrion beetles.

Necrosis: Death of tissue evidenced by discolouration, dehydration and loss of organization.

Nectar: The sweetish liquid in many flowers used by bees for the making of honey.

Nectar secreting glands: Sugary compound producing glands found mostly on floral parts that produce attractants for pollinators

Nectary: Gland secreting a sweet fluid (nectar) commonly in insect-pollinated flowers but not restricted there.

Needle: Acicular; slender, elongated leaf, usually over 2 in long; e.g., Pinus.

Needles or needle-like leaves: Long, narrow leaves, similar in form to the shape of a needle.

Negative autogenous regulation: Inhibition of the expression of a gene or set of co-ordinately regulated genes by the product of the gene or the product of one of the genes. Synonym: negative self-regulation.

Negative control system: A mechanism by which a regulatory protein is required to turn off gene expression.

Negative selection: Selection against individuals possessing a certain character. Opposite: positive selection.

Neighborhood: The largest population in which mating occurs at random. Generally, a small population within which individuals can be expected to be closely related. Neighbor-hoods may be created by barriers to pollen and seed movement, or other isolating factors.

Nematode: Slender, unsegmented worms, often parasitic. Also known as eelworm, especially when phytoparasitic.

Neo: Prefix meaning 'new'.

Neomorphosis: Regeneration in cases where the new part is unlike anything in the body.

Neomycin phosphotransferase II (npt-II): An enzyme which detoxifies the antibiotic neomycin, used as a marker gene to select for successfully transformed cells in plant transgenesis.

Neoplasm: Localized cell multiplication, forming a tumour. Generally the result of genetic transformation. Neoplasmic cells differ in structure and function from the original cell type.

Neoteny: The retention of juvenile body characters in the adult state, or the occurrence of adult characters in the juvenile state.

Neotrophics: The tropical areas of the 'New World', central America and the northern part of south America.

Neotype: A specimen selected to serve in place of a holotype where none of the material to which the name was originally applied is known to have been preserved.

Nerve: Strand of vascular and supporting tissue in a leaf or similar structure.

Nest leaves: Specialised sterile leaves modified for catching leaves and debris.

Net: Veins uniting to form a network.

Net photosynthesis: Photosynthetic activity minus respiratory activity, measured by the net absorption of carbon dioxide.

Net veined: Reticulate.

Neuter: Sterile (e.g. of flowers in which neither the androecium nor the gynoecium is functional in reproduction).

Neutral flower: Said of a sterile flower composed of a perianth without any sexual organs.

Neutral mutation: A mutation that changes the nucleotide sequence of a gene, but has no observable effect on the fitness of the organism.

Neutral theory: The theory that much of evolution has been primarily due to random drift of neutral mutations.

Neutron: An uncharged particle in the nucleus of an atom.

Neutrophil: A type of leukocyte involved in the early inflammatory response.

New world: The area of central America and northern south America.

NFT: Abbreviation for nutrient film technique.

Nick: To break (or a break in) a phosphodiester bond in one of the strands of a double-stranded DNA molecule.

Nick translation: A procedure for labelling DNA by treating a fragment with DNAse to produce single-stranded nicks followed by excision of a nucleotide and repair of the gaps with radiolabelled nucleotide.

Nicked circle: During the extraction of plasmid DNA from a bacterial cell, one strand of the DNA often becomes nicked. This relaxes the torsional strain which normally ensures a supercoiled structure. Synonym: relaxed circle.

Nitrate: The form of nitrogen that can be used directly by plants; a major component of inorganic fertilizers.

Nitrification: The natural process in which nitrogen in plant and animal wastes is oxidized, first to nitrites and then to nitrates, through the action of soil-borne microbes.

Nitrocellulose: A derivative of cellulose, which has the property of binding to many biological macromolecules, in particular DNA, RNA and protein. Filters made from nitrocellulose are commonly used in Southern and northern blotting experiments. Synonym: cellulose nitrate.

Nitrogen: Symbol: N. A nonmetallic element, atomic number 7, atomic weight 14, important as a macronutrient for plant growth. It is essential for the formation of amino acids and the purine and pyrimidine bases, and consequently for protein and nucleic acid synthesis. It is also found in many other compounds, e.g. porphyrins and many coenzymes. Nitrogen is absorbed by roots as the nitrate (N03-) ion or more rarely as ammonium (NH4+) or nitrite (N02-) ions. Deficiency leads to spindly growth and yellowing of the leaves. Soil nitrogen is replenished by various natural processes. It is also boosted by fertilizer applications of such compounds as urea, ammonium nitrate, ammonium sulphate, and nitrochalk. Many high-yielding crop varieties depend on high levels of nitrogen for optimum yields. However excessive nitrogen produces soft tissues with a high water content that are particularly prone to frost damage. Flowering and fruit set may also be reduced at the expense of vegetative growth, while potassium deficiency can be induced by high concentrations of nitrogen.

Nitrogen assimilation: The incorporation of nitrogen into the cells of living organisms.

Nitrogen fixation: The conversion of atmospheric nitrogen gas to oxidized forms that can be assimilated by plants, particularly by blue-green algae and some genera of bacteria (e.g. Rhizobium spp.; Azotobacter spp.). An important source of nitrogen in unfertilized soils.

Nitrogenous base: The purines (adenine and guanine) and pyrimidines (cytosine, and thymine or uracil) that are present in DNA and RNA.

Nod box: A DNA sequence that controls the transcriptional regulation of Rhizobium nodulation genes.

Nodal: At the nodes.

Nodal culture: The culture of a lateral bud and a section of adjacent stem tissue.

Node: The region of a stem between two internodes, where there is branching of the vascular tissue into leaves or other appendages.

Nodiform or nodulose: Knotty or knobby, as the roots of most of the Fabaceae.

Nodose: Knotty or knobbly (dimin. Nodulose).

Nodular: Term commonly used to describe the pebbly (rough) texture of a callus.

Nodulation: The formation of nodules on the roots of legumes following colonization by symbiotic nitrogen-fixing bacteria.

Nodule: Swollen globular structures formed on the roots of legumes, containing the nitrogen-fixing bacteria.

Nomen conservandum: A name of a family or genus (or taxon intermediate between these two) that has been formally accepted as the correct name contrary to the usual principles of botanical nomenclature.

Nomen illegitimum: A name which, at the time of its publication, was superfluous (because the taxon to which it was applied had already been named) or had already been applied to another plant.

Nomen nudum: A name published without a diagnosis or description of the entity to which it applies, and without reference to either.

Nomen rejeciendum: A name proposed for conservation but rejected by the committee.

Nomenclatural synonyms: Synonyms With the same basionym Or based on the same type, the result of the transference of a species from one genus to another.

Nomenclature: The study of the application of the names of taxa.

Non additive genetic variation: The proportion of the total genetic variation in a population that does not respond to simple mass selection and that causes specific pairwise crosses to depart from performance values predicted by the breeding values of the parents.

Non autonomous: A term referring to biological units that cannot function by themselves; such units require the assistance of another unit, or "helper". Opposite: autonomous.

Non disjunction: Failure of separation of homologous chromosomes or chromatids in mitosis or meiosis, resulting in too many chromosomes in some daughter cells and too few in others.

Non histone chromosomal protein: In chromosomes, all of the proteins except the histones.

Non repetitive DNA/RNA: A nucleotide sequence which does not include a significant proportion of repetitive sequences of nucleotides.

Non resupinate: Referring to Orchid flowers which don't twist 180 degrees during development or which twist a full 360 degrees, with the result that the labellum is uppermost.

Non target organism: An organism which is affected by a treatment (e.g. pesticide application) for which it was not the intended recipient.

Non template strand: The non-transcribed strand of DNA. Synonyms: sense strand, coding strand.

Noncoding DNA: DNA that does not code for a gene.

Nonsense mutation: A mutation which converts an amino-acid-specifying codon into a stop codon, e.g. a single base change from UAU to UAG generates the premature termination of the polypeptide chain at the position where a tyrosine was incorporated in the wild type.

NOR: Abbreviation for nucleolar organizer region.

Northern blot: A technique analogous to Southern blotting, but involving the transfer of RNA from an agarose gel to a membrane, prior to probing.

Nucellar embryo: An embryo which has developed vegetatively from somatic tissue surrounding the embryo sac, rather than by fertilization of the egg cell.

Nucellus: Ovule tissue within which an embryo develops (embryo sac); homologous with the megasporangium of a seed plant.

Nuclear transfer: A technology by which novel animals are generated by cloning a single diploid somatic cell. It involves inserting a single diploid cell from a culture of cells into an enucleated ovum. The resultant diploid ovum develops into an embryo that is placed in a recipient female, which gives birth to the cloned animal in the normal manner. Note that the term is somewhat of a misnomer, since it is a whole cell that is transferred, not just the nucleus.

Nuclease: A class of largely bacterial enzymes that degrade DNA or RNA molecules by catalysing the cleavage of the phosphodiester bonds that link adjacent nucleotides. For deoxyribonuclease (DNAse) the substrate is DNA, for ribonuclease (RNAse) the substrate is RNA, and for S1 nuclease, the substrate is single-stranded DNA or RNA. Endonu-cleases cleave at internal sites in the substrate molecule, while exonucleases progressively cleave from the end of the substrate molecule. Nucleases have varying degrees of base-sequence specificity, the most specific being the restriction endonucleases.

Nucleic acid: A macromolecule consisting of polymerized nucleotides. Two forms are found, DNA and RNA. Nucleic acids may be linear or circularized, and single- or double-stranded.

Nuclein: The term used by Friedrich Miescher to describe the nuclear material he discovered in 1869, which today is known as DNA.

Nucleo cytoplasmic ratio: In a cell, the ratio of nuclear to cytoplasmic volume. This ratio is high in meristematic cells and low in differentiated cells.

Nucleolar organizer region (NOR): A chromosomal segment containing a large array of genes that encode ribosomal RNA; located at the secondary constriction of specific chromosomes.

Nucleolus: An RNA-rich nuclear organelle in the nucleus of eukaryotic cells, produced by a nucleolar organizer. It represents the storage place for ribosomes and ribosome precursors. The nucleolus consists primarily of ribosomal precursor RNA, ribosomal RNA, their associated proteins, and some, perhaps all, of the enzymatic equipment (RNA polymerase, RNA methylase, RNA cleavage enzymes) required for synthesis, conversion and assembly of ribosomes. Subsequently the ribosomes are transported to the cytoplasm.

Nucleoplasm: The non-staining or slightly chromophilic, liquid or semi-liquid, ground substance of the interphase nucleus and which fills the nuclear space around the chromosomes and the nucleoli. Little is known of the chemical composition of this ground substance, which is not easily defined. Sometimes called "karyoplasm" when it is gel-like, and "karyolymph" when it is a colloidal fluid.

Nucleoprotein: Conjugated protein composed of nucleic acid and protein; the material of which the chromosomes are made.

Nucleoside: A base (purine or pyrimidine) that is covalently linked to a 5-carbon (pentose) sugar. When the sugar is ribose, the nucleoside is a ribonucleoside; when it is 2-deoxyribose, the nucleoside is a deoxyribonucleoside.

Nucleoside analogue: A synthetic molecule that resembles a naturally occurring nucleoside.

Nucleosome: Spherical sub-units of eukaryotic chromatin that are composed of a core particle consisting of an octamer of histones (two molecules each of histones H2a, H2b, H3 and H4) and 146 bp of DNA.

Nucleotide: A nucleoside with one or more phosphate groups linked at the 3'- or 5'-hydroxyl of a pentose sugar. When the sugar is ribose, the nucleotide is a ribonucleotide; when it is 2-deoxyribose, the nucleotide is a deoxyribonucleotide. RNA and DNA are polymers of, respectively, ribonucleoside 5'-monophosphates and deoxy-ribonucleoside 5'-monophosphates. Nucleotides containing the bases adenine, guanine and cytosine (A, G, C) occur in both DNA and RNA; thymine (T) occurs only in DNA, and uracil (U) only in RNA. Ribonucleoside mono-, di-, and triphosphates for which a specific base is not assigned are abbreviated NMP, NDP, and NTP, while deoxyribonucleoside mono-, di-, and tri-phosphates are abbreviated dNMP, dNDP, and dNTP. Otherwise, the "N" is replaced by the base letter abbreviation.

Nucleus: A dense protoplasmic membrane-bound region of a eukaryotic cell that contains the chromosomes, separated from the cytoplasm by a membrane; present in all eukaryotic cells except mature sieve-tube elements and red blood cells.

Null allele: An allele which produces no functional gene product.

Nullisomy: An otherwise diploid cell or organism lacking both members of a homologous chromosome pair.

Nurse culture: Culturing cells from a suspension culture on a raft of filter paper above a callus tissue piece (nurse tissue). The filter paper serves to prevent tissue union but allows the flow of essential substances from the nurse to the isolated cells.

Nut: A hard-shelled dry fruit or seed having a more or less distinct separatable rind or shell and interior kernel or meat; a dry indehiscent one-seeded fruit with a woody pericarp developing from an inferior syncarpous ovary.

Nutlet: A small nut.

Nutriceutical: A conventional food product that has been modified (potentially by genetic engineering) to have improved nutritional characteristics and/or pharmaceutical properties.

Nutrient: A substance that furnishes the elements and energy for the organic molecules that are the building blocks from which an organism develops.

Nutrient cycle: The passage of a nutrient or element through an ecosystem, including its assimilation and release by various organisms and its transformation into various organic or inorganic chemical forms.

Nutrient deficiency: Absence or insufficiency of an essential factor for normal growth and development.

Nutrient film technique (NFT): A hydroponic technique used to grow plants. NFT delivers a thin film of water or nutrient solution either continuously or through on-off cycles.

Nutrient gradient: A diffusion gradient of nutrients and gases that develops in tissues where only a portion of the tissue is in contact with the medium. Gradients are less likely to form in liquid media than in callus cultures.

Nutrient medium: A solid, semi-solid or liquid formulation for in vitro cell or tissue growth.

Nyctinasty: A nastic movement in which plant parts, especially leaves and flowers, assume a characteristic position at night. These sleep movements most often result in a folding together of leaflets. In certain Acacia species the process seems to be a form of photonasty, as the assumption of the night position coincides with the onset of darkness. In other species the cycle of folding continues even if the plant is kept in the dark; the process is then clearly autonomic rather than nastic.

Ob: Prefix meaning 'inverted', e.g. Obconic, oblanceolate, obcordate.

Obconic: Inversely conic, a cone attached at the narrow end.

Obconical: Cone-shaped but attached at the narrower end.

Obcordate: Inversely heart-shaped. The wider end and its deep notch at the top instead of the bottom.

Obdeltoid: Inversely deltoid. Triangular, with the apex downward.

Obdiplostemonous: Describing stamens that are inserted in two whorls with the outer opposite the petals and the inner opposite the sepals. Obdiplostemonous stamens are seen in some members of the Caryophyllaceae.

Obdiplostemony: The condition of being obdiplopstemonous.

Oblanceolate: Of a plane several times longer than wide, widest in the apical third, tapering gradually towards the base, more rapidly towards the apex.

Obligate: Mandatory, essential, unable to exist under other conditions.

Oblong: Longer than broad, with parallel margins and rounded ends.

Obovate: Inversely ovate; having the shape of the longitudinal section of an egg, with the broad end at the top, as some leaves.

Obrotund: Approaching a round form.

Obscure: Not clearly visible macroscopically, usually owing to incomplete differentiation

Obsolescent: Non-functional but not reduced to a rudiment.

Obsolete: Rudimentary or not evident; applied to a structure that is almost suppressed; vestigial.

Obtriangular: Inversely triangular.

Obtuse: Evenly narrowed into a blunt point at an angle of 90 degrees or more.

Ocean: The great body of salt water that covers mores than two thirds of the surface of the earth; any of its five principal geographical divisions, the Atlantic, Pacific, Indian, Arctic, and Antartic.

Ocellated: A broad spot of some color has another spot of a different color within it.

Ochraceus: Ochre-coloured; dull yellow with a tinge of red.

Ochrea: A tube around the stem formed by sheathing stipules at the leaf base. Ochreas are characteristic of the Polygonaceae giving the familiar swollen joints on the stems of such plants.

Ocrea: A tubelike covering around some stems, especially of plants of the Polygonaceae.

Ocreate: Having a stipular tube surrounding stem above insertion of petiole or blade.

Ocreolate: Diminutive of ocreate; usually applied to bract bases.

Octoploid: An organism, or a tissue whose cells contain eight haploid sets of chromosomes.

Odd-pinnate: Said of compound leaves having an odd number of leaflets, this is usually easily determined because there is a single terminal leaflet.

Odoriferous: Giving odor or scent, usually sweet; diffusing fragrance; fragrant, as odoriferous flowers.

Oestrogen: The generic term for a group of female sex hormones which control the development of sexual characteristics and control oestrus. AlteRNAtive spelling: estrogen.

Oestrus: In female mammals, the period of sexual excitement and acceptance of the male. Synonyms: rut, heat.

Oestrous cycle: The cycle of reproductive activity shown by most sexually mature non-pregnant female mammals. AlteRNAtive spelling: estrous.

Offshoot: Short, usually horizontal, stem produced near the crown of a plant.

Offspring: New individuals resulting from sexual or asexual reproduction. Synonym: progeny.

Oil: A fat in a liquid state.

Oil immersion: A technique used in light microscopy in which a special oil-immersion objective lens is employed to increase the resolving power of the microscope. A specimen mounted on a glass slide is covered by a drop of clear oil placed on the coverslip. The oil has the same refractive index as the glass lens. When the lens is immersed in the oil, the amount of light entering the objective increases (i.e. the effective aperture is increased). Such a technique is particularly useful at high magnifications. Oil is traditionally used but other liquids (e.g. sugar solution) may also be suitable.

Okazaki fragment: Replicated DNA fragments formed on the lagging strand in DNA synthesis from a double-stranded template. The fragments are subsequently joined together by DNA ligase.

Old world: The area of africa, se asia and the western pacific.

Oligomer: A molecule formed by the covalent joining of a small (undefined) number of monomers.

Oligomerous: With reduction in number of members within whorl.

Oligonucleotide ligation assay (OLA): A diagnostic technique for determining the presence or absence of a single nucleotide polymorphism within a target DNA sequence, often indicating whether the gene is wild type (normal) or mutant (usually defective).

Oligonucleotide: A nucleotide oligomer. Often synthesized for use as primers for in vitro DNA synthesis.

Oligosaccharide: Carbohydrate consisting of several linked monosaccharide units.

Oligotaxy: Reduction in number of whorls.

Olivaceous: Olive-coloured, a yellowish green darkened with black.

Onco mouse: A mouse that has been genetically modified to incorporate an oncogene, which acts as an animal model for studies of human cancer.

Oncogene: A gene that causes cells to grow in an uncontrolled (i.e. tumourous) manner. Oncogenes are mutant forms of normal functional genes (called proto-oncogenes) that have a role in regulating cell proliferation.

Oncogenesis: The progression of cytological, genetic and cellular changes that culminate in the development of a tumour.

Ontogeny: The development of a single organism, i.e. the sequence of stages through which it passes during its lifetime.

Oocyte: The egg mother cell; it undergoes two meiotic divisions (oogenesis) to form the egg cell. The primary oocyte refers to the state before completion of the first meiotic division; the secondary oocyte after completion of the first meiotic division.

Oogamous: Being reproduced by the fusion of a small, mobile male gamete with a large, immobile female gamete.

Oogamy: Sexual reproduction in which the female gamete, or egg, is nonmotile and larger than the male gamete, or sperm, which is motile.

Oogenesis: The formation and growth of the egg in an animal ovary.

Oogonium: A female sex organ of certain algae and fungi; it consists of a single cell that contains one to several eggs.

Oosphere: The non-motile female gamete in plants and some algae.

Oospore: A spore developing from a zygote of certain algae and fungi, following the fusion of heterogametes.

Open continuous culture: A continuous culture system, in which inflow of fresh medium is balanced by outflow of a corresponding volume of spent medium plus cells. In the steady state, the rate of cell wash-out equals the rate of formation of new cells in the system.

Open pollination: Pollination by wind, insects or other natural mechanisms.

Open reading frame (ORF): A sequence of nucleotides in a DNA molecule that has the potential to encode a peptide or protein: comprisesa start triplet (ATG), followed by a series of triplets (each of which encodes an amino acid), and ending with a stop codon (TAA, TAG or TGA). The term is generally applied to sequences of DNA fragments, for which no function has yet been determined. The number of ORFs provides an estimate of the number of genes transcribed from the DNA sequence.

Operational definition: An operation or procedure that can be carried out to define or delimit something.

Operator: The region of DNA that is upstream from a gene or genes and to which one or more regulatory proteins (repressor or activator) bind to control the expression of the gene(s).

Operculate capsule: One that dehisces through pores, each of which is covered by a flap, cap, or lid, as in papaver.

Operculum: A lid or cover becoming detached at maturity by abscission; in Eucalyptus (for example), a cap covering the bud and formed by fusion or cohesion of perianth parts.

Operon: A functionally integrated genetic unit for the control of gene expression in bacteria. It consists of one or more genes that encode one or more polypeptide(s) and the adjacent site (promoter and operator) that controls their expression by regulating the transcription of the structural genes.

Opine: The condensation product of an amino acid with either a keto-acid or a sugar, produced by the plant host as a result of Agrobacterium infection, and used exclusively by the Agrobacterium as a carbon source for growth and reproduction within the plant.

Opposite: Of leaves or bracts occurring two at a node on opposite sides of the stem. Said of flower parts when one part occurs in front of another.

Opposite leaves: Opposite refers to the arrangement of either buds or leaves along the stem. Opposite budding or leaves is two buds or leaves per node.

Orbicular: Nearly or completely circular, as an orbicular leaf. Also orbiculate.

Orchard: 1. A garden. 2. A piece of ground, usually enclosed, devoted to the cultivation of fruit trees, especially apple, pear, peach, plum, and cherry trees. A collection of cultivated fruit trees.

Organ: A tissue or group of tissues that constitute a morphologically and functionally distinct part of an organism.

Organ culture: The aseptic culture of complete living organs of animals and plants outside the body in a suitable culture medium. Animal organs must be small enough to allow the nutrients in the culture medium to penetrate all the cells.

Organellar gene: Genes located on organelles outside the nucleus.

Organelle: A membrane-bounded specialized region within a cell, such as the mitochondrion or dictyosome, that carries out a specialized function in the life of a cell.

Organic: Compounds containing carbon derived from decomposed animal or plant organisms. Is also used loosely of mulches, soil mix, etc. taken from plant materials.

Organic complex: A chemically undefined compound added to nutrient media to stimulate growth, e.g. coconut milk; malt extract; yeast extract; casein hydrolysate.

Organic gardening: A method of gardening using only organic materials, such as manure, peat moss, and compost, and rejecting inorganic material, such as rock phosphate, ammonium, insecticides, and pesticides.

Organism: An individual living system, such as animal, plant or micro-organism, that is capable of reproduction, growth and maintenance.

Organized growth: The development under tissue culture conditions of organized explants (meristem tips or shoot tips, floral buds or organ primordia). Opposite: unorganized growth.

Organized tissue: Composed of normally differentiated cells.

Organogenesis: The initiation of adventitious or de novo shoots or roots from callus, meristem or suspension cultures.

Organoleptic: Having an effect on one of the organs of sense, such as taste or smell.

Origin of replication: The nucleotide position on a DNA sequence from which DNA synthesis (replication) is initiated.

Ornithophily: Pollinated by birds.

Orphan gene: A gene or DNA sequence whose function is not known.

Orphan receptor: A receptor for which a cellular function or ligand has yet to be identified.

Ortet: The original plant from which a clone is started through rooted cuttings, grafting, or tissue culture, or other means of vegetative propagation. The original plus tree used to start a grafted clone for inclusion in a seed orchard is the ortet.

Orthologous: Homologous genes/gene products that have evolved divergently between species; many ricc genes have orthologues in other cereal genomes, because of the common ancestry of cereal species.

Orthostichous: Exhibiting orthostichy; arranged in vertical ranks.

Orthostichy: A vertical rank; an arrangement of leaves or scales at different heights on an axis so that their median planes coincide, as the vertical ranks of leaves on a stem.

Orthotropic: Of or pertaining to or exhibiting orthotropism; growing more or less vertically.

Orthotropism: Vertical growth; the tendency of plants to grow more or less vertically.

Orthotropous or atropous: With straight body so that funicular attachment is at one end and micropyle at other.

Osmophore: A gland, usually floral, which produces fragrances that attract pollinators.

Osmosis: The diffusion of water or other solvents through a differentially permeable membrane from a region of higher concentration to a region of lower concentration.

Osmotic potential: Change in the energy state of solvent brought about by dissolving a substance in the solvent - water in the biological sciences. The potential of aqueous solutions is always negative compared to pure water. Solvent flows from higher to lower osmotic potential solutions by diffusion or osmosis.

Osmotic Pressure: Most biological membranes are impermeable to many of the solutes found in the cell. If this were not so, all of the valuable biomolecules in the cell would simply diffuse out and be lost. However, the same membranes are often more or less permeable to water. Since there are many solutes trapped in the cell, the "concentration" of water is lower in the cell than outside, i.e., there are more water molecules per unit volume outside the cell than inside. Diffusion of water through the membrane works both ways and is completely random. However, water "concentration" is higher outside the cell. That is, there are more water molecules in contact with the membrane on the outside than on the inside. So, there will be a net flux of water into the cytoplasm until the concentrations equalize. The osmotic potential is the measure of the net tendency of water to enter the cell. Real cells can't usually behave in this fashion, since the cell will expand and ultimately burst. The problem is handled in numerous different ways, depending on the cell type. In plant cells (and various others), the cell membrane is confined within a semi-rigid cell wall. Water enters the cell only until the elastic reaction force of the cell wall equals the outward force caused by water molecules crowding into the cell. At steady state, the plant cell then maintains a rather high internal pressure, referred to as turgor pressure.

Turgor pressure serves as a sort of internal hydrostatic skeleton which helps to support—and even move—the plant structures.

Osmoticum: A chemical agent (e.g. polyethylene glycol, mannitol, glucose or sucrose) employed to maintain the osmotic potential of a nutrient medium equivalent to that of the cultured cells, i.e. the medium and the cells are isotonic. Because of this osmotic equilibrium, cells are not damaged in vitro.

Ostiole: An opening or pore, e.g. (in moraceae) at the apex of a fig, or (in fungi and lichens) at the apex of a perithecium.

Outbreeding: A mating system characterized by the inter-breeding of genetically unrelated or dissimilar individuals. Since genetic diversity tends to be enhanced, and vigour or fitness of individuals increased by this process, it is often used to counter the detrimental effects of continuous inbreeding.

Outcrossing: Matings (controlled or natural) among unrelated individuals. May also refer to a species that has specific barriers to selfing, or exhibits such inbreeding depression that inbred individuals never reach maturity.

Outflow: The volume of growing cells that is removed from a bioreactor during a continuous fermentation process.

Oval: Broadly elliptic, narrowing somewhat from the middle to rounded ends.

Ovary: The enlarged, rounded, ovule-producing base of the female portion (the pistil) of a flower that eventually develops into a fruit after being fertilized.

Ovate: Having the shape of a longitudinal section of an egg; egg-shaped and attached by the broader end.

Overdominance: Where heterozygote performance is superior to that of either parental genotype.

Overlapping reading frame: Start codons in different reading frames generate different polypeptides from the same DNA sequence.

Oviparous: Egg-laying; producing eggs which hatch after leaving the body of the female; germinating while still attached to the parent plant; for example, mangrove.

Ovoid: Of a solid with the form of an egg, attached at the broad end.

Ovulate: Female; bearing ovules only in the flowers.

Ovulation: The release of mammalian egg(s) from the ovary.

Ovule: A structure in seed plants which contains the megasporangium (nucellus), megaspore (embryo sac), a food store, and a coat, and develops into a seed after fertilization.

Ovuliferous scale: Highly modified lateral branch in the axil of a leaf (bract), and bearing ovules; may be flat or peltate, woody or fleshy; e.g., Pinaceae.

Ovuliferous: Bearing ovules (e.g. applied to scales in a megasporangiate cone in gymnosperms).

Ovulode: Sterile structures on the placenta.

Ovum pickup (OPU): The non-surgical collection of ova from a female.

Oxidation-reduction Reactions): chemical reactions involving gain or loss of electrons to or from a compound.

Oxidative phosphorylation: The formation of ATP from ADP and inorganic phosphate coupled to the movement of electrons down the respiratory chain. ATP formation occurs at three sites on the respiratory chain: during the transfer of electrons from NAD to coenzyme Q; during the transfer of electrons from cytochrome b to cytochrome c; and during the transfer of electrons from cytochrome aa3 to oxygen. The nature of the link between oxidative phosphorylation and the respiratory chain is not understood although there are several theories to explain it. The most widely supported theory suggests that the respiratory chain creates a pH gradient across the internal mitochondrial membrane and that the potential energy of this gradient is then utilized to convert ADP to ATP.

Oxygen electrode based sensor: Sensor in which an oxygen electrode, which measures the amount of oxygen in a solution, is coated with a biological material such as an enzyme which generates or absorbs oxygen when the appropriate substrate is present.

P

P: Denotes the shorter of the two chromosome arms, e.g. human 14p is the short arm of human chromosome 14.

P element: A Drosophila transposon.

P1, P2: Generational symbols for the two parents of a given individual.

P53 gene: A human tumour-suppressor transcription factor gene, damage or mutation to which is believed to be responsible for up to 60% of all human cancer tumours. If, in spite of the presence of p53 protein, a cell begins to divide uncontrollably following damage to its DNA, the p53 gene acts to prevent tumours by triggering apoptosis.

Pachycaul: Thick-stemmed, not 'twiggy' (unbranched, or the branches few and thick).

Pachynema: A mid-prophase stage in the first meiotic division, between zygonema and diplonema. Chromosomes appear as long, paired threads. Occasionally all four chromatids can be recognized.

Packaging cell line: A cell line designed to produce viral particles that do not contain nucleic acid. After transfection of these cells with a full size viral genome, fully infective viral particles are assembled and released.

Packed cell volume (PCV): The proportion of a cell culture volume that is occupied by cells. Cell volume is determined by sedimenting using low speed centrifugation.

Paecilomyces sp.: Commonly found in soil and dust, less frequently in air. P. variotii can cause paecilomycosis. Linked to wood-trimmers disease and humidifier associated illnesses. They are reported to allergenic. Some members of this genus are reported to cause pneumonia. It may produce arsine gas if growing on arsenic substrate. This can occur on wallpapers covered with paris green.

Painted: Colors disposed in streaks of unequal intensity.

Pair rule gene: A gene that influences the formation of body segments in Drosophila.

Pairing: The pairing of homologous chromosomes during the prophase of the first meiotic division. Pairing is the first prerequisite before crossing over and recombination can occur. Synonym: synapsis.

Palaeontology: The study of fossils. The branch dealing with the study of plant fossils is termed palaeobotany, which includes palaeoethnobotany, the study of fruit and seed remains found in archaeological sites. Palaeontology requires a knowledge of the way in which fossilization takes place and of the type of rock in which the fossil is found, a knowledge of the environmental conditions that prevailed when the rock was laid down, and an appreciation of the geological time scale so that the fossil can be dated.

Palate: The raised area in the throat of a sympetalous corolla.

Palea: The upper of the pair of bracts beneath each floret (flower) in the inflorescence of a grass, the other being the lemma. The palea is usually thin, narrow, and parallel sided. It usually has two ribs, which may project as prominent keels.

Paleaceous: With small membranous scales, chaffy.

Paleaceus: Furnished with chaffy scales.

Paleoherb: Any member of a group of basal flowering herbs which may be the closest relatives of the monocots. They include the water lilies, Piperales, and Aristolochiales.

Paleotropics: The tropical areas of the 'old world', Africa, SE Asia and the western Pacific.

Palinactinodromous: Actinodromous, the primary veins with one or more subsidiary radiations above the primary one.

Palindrome: A segment of double-stranded DNA, in which the order of bases, read 5'-3' in one strand, is the same as that in the complementary antiparallel strand, also read 5'-3'. If the sequence is written in the normal convention, on two lines with paired bases shown one above the other, the base order on one strand runs in the opposite direction to that on the complementary strand. They are often found at the ends of transposable elements, and recognition sites for type II restriction endonucleases are also palindromes. Synonym: inverted repeat.

Palisade mesophyll: Mesophyll having one or more relatively uniform rows of tightly packed, elongate, columnar parenchyma (chlorenchyma) cells beneath the upper epidermis of a leaf.

Palisade parenchyma: The palisade parenchyma is the elongated, tightly packed chlorenchyma cells in the upper region of the mesophyll of the leaf. This is where most of the trapping of light energy occurs by the chloroplasts (photosystem I). The chloroplasts circulate around the periphery (margin) of the cell by cytoplasmic streaming, carrying the chloroplasts up near the surface of the leaf and then back down again. This seems to increase the efficiency of photosynthesis.

Palmate: Radiately lobed or divided. Palmately compound - with leaflets from one point at end of petiole.

Palmate venation: A leaf with palmate venation has the main veins arising from a point at the base of the leaf.

Palmately netted/veined leaves: Palmately compound leaves are compound leaves where the leaflets are all attached to the petiole at one point. The leaflets of a pinnately compound leaf radiadiate out from that point like your fingers do from your hand. This is how the palmately compound leaf got its name.

Palmate-pinnate: With first order leaflets palmately arranged, second order pinnately arranged.

Palmatifid: Of a leaf, deeply divided into several lobes which arise (almost) at the same level.

Palmatisect: A condition intermediate between palmate and palmatifid, with the green tissue of the lamina completely divided into several segments, but the segments not fully separated at the base.

Palynology: The study of pollen and spores.

Palynomorph: A fossil spore or pollen type.

PAMP: Ampicillin-resistant plasmid.

Pandurate: Fiddle-shaped, +/- obovate but with a waist.

Panduriform: Fiddle-shaped; obovate with sinus or indentation on each side near base and with two small basal lobes.

Pangenesis: A now disregarded theory formulated by Charles Darwin that suggested a mechanism by which acquired characteristics may be inherited. He postulated that there were particles (pangenes) carried in the body fluids from all the organs of the body to the reproductive cells. These particles then influenced the gametes that in turn influenced the characteristics of the succeeding generation.

Panicle: An inflorescence, the main axis of which is branched; the branches bear loose racemose flower clusters. Rice is a prominent crop plant with a panicle inflorescence.

Panicle culture: Aseptic culture of immature panicle explants to induce microspore germination and development.

Paniculate: a. Panicled; arranged or growing in panicles.

Panmictic population: A population in which mating occurs at random.

Panmixis: Random mating in a population.

Pannose or felted: With matted, feltlike layer of trichomes.

Pantoporate: Of a pollen grain, with rounded apertures all over the surface.

Pantropic (al): Found throughout the tropics.

Papilionaceous: With large posterior petal (banner or standard) two lateral petals (wings) and usually two connate lower petals (keel); as in the Fabaceae.

Papilla: A small, elongated protuberance on the surface of an organ, usually an extension of one epidermal cell.

Papillose: Descriptive of a surface beset with short, blunt, rounded, or cylindric projections.

Pappus: A tuft (or ring) of hairs or scales borne above the ovary and outside the corolla in asteraceae and possibly representing the calyx; a tuft of hairs on a fruit.

Papulospora sp.: This fungi is found in soil, textiles, decaying plants, manure, and paper.

PAR: Abbreviation for photosynthetically active radiation.

Par gene: One of a class of genes required for faithful plasmid segregation at cell division. Initially, par loci were identified on plasmids, but have also been found on bacterial chromosomes.

Paracentric inversion: A chromosomal rearrangement in which a segment of chromosome, excluding the centromere, is rotated.

Paraffin (Wax): A translucent, white, solid hydrocarbon with a low melting point. One use is as an embedding medium to support tissue for sectioning for light microscopy observation.

Parafilma: A stretchable film based on paraffin wax; used to seal tubes and Petri dishes. Parafilmä is a proprietary name which is incorrectly applied colloquially to similar products.

Parahormone: A substance with hormone-like properties that is not a secretory product (e.g. ethylene; carbon dioxide).

Parallel: Thecae or anther cells along side of the connective or longitudinal to each other; with veins extending from base to apex, essentially parallel.

Parallel evolution: The development of different organisms along similar evolutionary paths due to similar selection pressures acting on them.

Parallelodromous: With two or more primary veins originating beside one another at the blade base and running more or less parallel to the apex where they converge.

Paralogous: Homologous genes/gene products that have duplicated and evolved divergently within a species. e.g. beta- and gamma-globulin genes.

Parameter: A value or measurement that varies with circumstances, and is used as a reference to quantify a situation or a process.

Paraphyletic: A taxon is said to be paraphyletic if it does not contain all descendants of its last common ancestor. So, for example, "seedless plants" is paraphyletic because its last common ancestor would also be the ancestor of plants with seeds. A clade must contain all descendants of its last common ancestor. It is usually fairly important to stick to a consideration of clades. However, that importance can often be outweighed by the utility of being able to discuss the earliest forms of some group. We normally signal that we are talking about such a paraphyletic group by saying "basal seedless plants" or "paraphyletic seedless plants" or by the use of some other, similar linguistic artifice.

Paraphysis: A sterile filament or hair borne among the sporangia.

Parasexual cycle: A sexual cycle involving changes in chromosome number but differing in time and place from the usual sexual cycle; occurring in those fungi in which the normal cycle is suppressed or apparently absent.

Parasite: An organism living in or on another (the host), and deriving nourishment from it.

Parasitism: The close association of two or more dissimilar organisms, where the association is harmful to the host, but beneficial to the parasite.

Parasporal crystal: Tightly packaged insect pro-toxin molecules that are produced by strains of Bacillus thuringiensis during the formation of resting spores.

Paratope: Synonym for antibody binding site.

Paratype: Specimens cited at the same time as the original description, other the holotypes and isotypes.

Parenchyma: The most common type of plant cell; thin-walled cells varying in size, shape, and function. Parenchyma cells are usually loosely packed cubed-shaped or elongated cells that contain a large central vacuole and have thin, flexible cell walls. Parenchymal cell walls are enriched in pectins and therefore stain pink with Toluidine Blue. They also have simple pits. Parenchymal cells are found in large numbers in the pith and cortex. They are the least specialized cells in the plant and normally act as a sort of reserve of stem cells. They may also serve a number of functions, including food storage (either water or nutrients), photosynthesis, as well as tissue repair.

Parent plant: Plant from which cutting material for propagation is collected.

Parichnos: An interconnected system of parenchymous strands with many air spaces that extend throughout the vegetative organs of some arborescent lycopsids. Essentially, parichnos tissue is parenchyma with lots of air space between cells. This tissue probably aided photosynthetic gas exchange in much the same way as do the lenticels of modern trees.

Parietal: Attached to the margins of a structure; of placentation, having the ovules attached to placentas on the wall of the ovary.

Paripinnate: Having an even number of pinnae by virtue of having a pair in the terminal position.

Paripinnately compound: Even-pinnately compound, without a terminal leaflet.

Parthenocarpic: Developing fruits from unfertilized ovaries; the resulting fruit is. Therefore, usually seedless.

Parthenogenesis: Production of an embryo from an unfertilized egg.

Partial digest: Incomplete reaction of a restriction enzyme with DNA, such that only a proportion of the target sites are cleaved. Partial digests are often performed to give an overlapping collection of DNA fragments for use in the construction of a gene bank. Synonym: incomplete digest. Opposite: complete digest.

Particle gun: A machine capable of changing the genetic makeup of plant tissue by shooting DNA-coated particles into it.

Particle radiation: High energy nuclear emissions, used as physical agents of mutagenesis. Three major types typically used: alpha (positively charged), beta (negatively charged), or neutrons (uncharged).

Parts per million (ppm): Unit of concentration: 1ppm = 1mg dissolved matter per litre of solution.

Parturition: The process of giving birth.

Passage: The transfer or transplantation of cells from one culture medium to another.

Passage cell: A thin-walled cell of an endodermis.

Passage number: The number of times cells in culture have been sub-cultured.

Passage time: Time interval between successive sub-cultures.

Passive immunity: 1. Natural acquisition of antibodies by the foetus or neonate (newborn) from the mother. 2. The artificial introduction of specific antibodies by the injection of serum from an immune animal. In both cases, temporary protection is conferred on the recipient.

Pat gene: A gene obtained from Streptomyces sp. encoding resistance to glufosinate-ammonium containing herbicides. (These inhibit plant synthesis of glutamine). Used widely as a means of transgenically inducing herbicide resistance in crop plants. Synonym: bar gene.

Patelliform: Knee-shaped; disk-shaped.

Patent: A legal permission to hold exclusive right - for a defined period of time - to manufacture, use or sell an invention.

Paternal: Pertaining to the father.

Pathogen free: Uncontaminated with pathogen.

Pathogen: A disease-causing organism (generally microbial: bacteria, fungi, viruses; but can extend to other organisms: e.g. nematodes etc.). Synonym: infectious agent.

Pathogenesis related protein (PR protein): One of a group of proteins that are characteristically highly expressed as part of a plant's response to pathogen attack. Many of these proteins are similarly expressed following infection with a broad range of pathogens, indicating their role in the hypersensitive response.

Pathotoxin: Substance secreted by certain pathogens, in order to attack the host tissue. Some pathotoxins are also toxic to non-hosts, especially animals or humans.

Pathovar: Strain of a plant-attacking bacterium or fungus that can be differentiated from others by their interaction with specific host cultivars.

PCR RFLP: Alternative term for cleaved amplified polymorphic sequence.

PCV: Abbreviation for packed cell volume.

Peat: Brown decomposed plant matter found in some swampy areas. It has a high water holding capacity and was once widely used in potting mixes and cutting mixes. The extraction of peat is having a damaging effect on the ecosystems from which it is taken and its use is not recommended for this reason. It is now frequently replaced by substitutes such as composted woodchip fines, coconut fibres or rice hulls.

Pectin: In plants, pectin occurs on cell walls of parenchyma and related cell types where it apparently strengthens the cell wall and assists in cell-to-cell adhesion. It is frequently extracted and used as a thickener for preserves.

Pectinase: Enzyme catalysing the hydrolysis of pectin. Used in conjunction with cellulase to solubilize plant cell walls.

Pectinate: Comb-like; deeply divided with the segments narrow and close.

Pedate: Of a palmate or palmately-lobed leaf, having the lateral segments divided again.

Pedicel: The stalk of an individual flower in an inflorescence; the stalk of a sporangium or of a conceptacle; hence pedicellate.

Pedigree: The ancestry of an individual.

Pedigree breeding: A breeding system where all the ancestors of any individual in the population are known back to the original "+" trees selected in wild stands. The system depends on control pollination for all matings.

Pedigree, full: All parents, grandparents. of a particular genotype are known all the way back to some natural population.

Pedigree, partial: Some, but not all, ancestors of a particular genotype are known, usually the female parents. Partial pedigrees are most common where open-pollinated or polycross seed is used for progeny tests.

Peduncle: The stalk of an inflorescence; in ferns, the stalk of a sporocarp.

Peg (sterigmata): Lateral stem projection to which leaf is attached and persistent after leaf dehiscence; ie., abscission layer between peg and leaf; leaf may be sessile; e.g., Picea; or petiolate; e.g. Tsuga, on the peg.

Pellucid: Transmitting light, transparent.

Peltate: Shield-shaped, leaves that are shaped like a shield and attached to the stem at the center or by some point distinctly within the margin, and having the petiole inserted into the undersurface of the lamina not far from the center.

Peltiform: Rounded with petiole attached to center of blade or apparently to laminar tissue.

Pendent: Drooping, hanging down; pendulous

Pendulous: Drooping; of ovules, attached at the top of the ovary and hanging downwards from an apical placenta.

Penetrance: The proportion of individuals in a population that express the phenotype expected from their genotype with respect to a specific gene. Measures the extent to which phenotype predicts genotype.

Penicillate: Pencil-shaped; tufted like an artist's brush.

Penicillium sp.: A wide number of organisms have placed in this genera. Identification to species is difficult. Often found in aerosol samples. Commonly found in soil, food, cellulose and grains. It is also found in paint and compost piles. It may cause hypersensitivity pneumonitis, allergic alveolitis in susceptible individuals. It is reported to be allergenic (skin). It is commonly found in carpet, wall paper, and in interior fiberglass duct insulation (NC). Some species can produce mycotoxins. Common cause of extrinsic asthma (immeadiate-type hypersensitivity: type I). Acute symptoms include edema and bronchiospasms, chronic cases may develop pulmonary emphysema.

Penniform: With ribs, the upper segments confluent at the apex.

Penninerved (penniveined): Having conspicuous lateral veins divergent from the midrib and lying approximately parallel to each other.

Pentacyclic: Five-whorled.

Pentamerous: Of a flower, having five parts in each floral whorl (not necessarily including the gynoecium).

Pepo: A fruit with firm skin, pulpy interior, many seeds and a single locule.

Peptidase: An enzyme that catalyzes the hydrolysis of a peptide bond.

Peptide: A sequence of amino acids linked by peptide bonds; a breakdown or build-up unit in protein metabolism. Typically used to describe low molecular weight species.

Peptide bond: The chemical bond holding amino acid residues together in peptides and proteins. The (CO-NH) bond is formed by the condensation, with loss of a water molecule, between the carboxyl (-COOH) group of one amino acid and the amino (-NH2) of the next amino acid.

Peptide expression library: A collection of peptide molecules, produced by recombinant cells, in which the amino acid sequences are varied.

Peptide nucleic acid (PNA): A synthetic oligonucleotide analogue, in which the sugar backbone is replaced by a peptide chain, upon which the nucleoside residues are strung. Probes made from PNA appear to have greater specificity than those made from DNA.

Peptide vaccine: A short chain of amino acids that can induce antibodies against a specific infectious agent.

Peptidyl transferase: An enzyme bound tightly to the large sub-unit of the ribosome, that catalyses the formation of peptide bonds between amino acids during translation.

Peptidyl tRNA binding site (P-site): The site on a ribosome that hosts the tRNA to which the next amino acid for the growing polypeptide chain is attached.

Per: Prefix meaning 'very' or 'all over'.

Perenate: Maintain a dormant state through the non-growing season; hence perennating buds etc.

Perennation: Survival of a plant for a number of years. To live over from season to season.

Perennial: A plant that grows for 3 or more years and usually flowers each year.

Perennial, polycarpic: Living more than two years; fruiting more than once.

Perfect flowers: Flowers possessing both the male and female reproductive organs.

Perfect or bisexual: With both stamens and carpels or pistils in the flower.

Perfoliate: Said of opposite or whorled leaves or bracts that are united into a collarlike structure around the stem that bears them.

Perianth: The outer whorl of floral leaves of a flower, when not clearly divided into calyx and corolla; collectively, the calyx and corolla, or either one if one is absent.

Pericarp: The fruit wall which has developed from the ovary wall; sometimes used for any fruit covering.

Pericarpous: Around the fruit.

Pericentric inversion: A chromosomal rearrangement in which a segment of chromosome, including the centromere, is rotated.

Pericladial: With a sheathing base, as in the apiaceae.

Periclinal: The orientation of cell wall or plane of cell division parallel to the reference surface.

Periclinal chimera: 1. Genotypically or cytoplasmically different tissues arranged in concentric layers. 2. A chimera in which one or more layers of tissue derived from one graft member enclose the central tissue derived from the other member of the graft.

Pericycle: Tissue sandwiched between the endodermis and phloem of a root; often only one or two cells wide in transverse section; the site of origin of lateral roots.

Perigynium: Sac-like bract subtending the pistillate flower, as in carex.

Perigynous: Perigynous ovaries have the flower parts (calyx, corolla, and androecium) attached to a hypanthium. The hypanthium is found only in dicots and is a fusion of the calyx, corolla, and androecium whorls forming a small cup-shaped structure that surrounds the ovary. The base of the hypanthium is typically attached to the receptacle as is the case with the members of the rose family (Rosaceae) and is therefore said to by hypogynous. The hypanthium can also be epigynous, that is, attached to the top of the ovary, as is the case with the fuschia flower.

Perigyny: The condition in which the sepals, petals, stamens are attached to the floral tube or hypanthium surrounding the ovary with the tube or hypanthium free from the ovary.

Peripheral: On the outer surface or edge.

Periplasm: The space between the cell (cytoplasmic) membrane of a bacterium or fungus and the outer membrane or cell wall. Synonym: periplasmic space.

Perisperm: Nutritive tissue in an angiosperm seed, formed from the nucellus.

Perispermous: With food reserve in perisperm, derived from diploid nucellus or integuments.

Perispore or perine: An outer covering of some fern spores, with different configuration than that of the exospore.

Peristome: A combination of Greek roots roughly meaning "stuff around the mouth." In mosses, this means the ring of peristome teeth around the orifice of the spore capsule that control spore dispersal.

Permanent wilting point (PWP): The moisture content of a soil below which plants wilt to such an extent that they fail to recover even when fully watered.

Permeable: Referring to a membrane, cell or cell system through which small molecules can diffuse.

Personate: Two-lipped with the upper arched and the lower protruding into corolla throat.

Perula: Scale of a leaf bud; hence perulate, scaly.

Pesticide: A toxic chemical product that kills harmful organisms (e.g. insecticides, fungicide, weedicides, rodenticides).

Petal: One of the outer appendages of a flower, located between the outer sepals and the stamens. Petals often display bright colors that serve to attract pollinators.

Petalantherous: With a terminal anther and distinctly petaloid filament, as in Saxifraga.

Petaliferous: Most frequently at the base of petals.

Petaloid: Like a petal; soft in texture and coloured conspicuously.

Petalostemonous: With filaments fused to corolla, anthers free.

Petiolate: With a petiole; term used to describe leaf attachment to stem.

Petiole: The stalk that attaches the leaf lamina to the stem.

Petiolulate: With a petiolule.

Petiolule: Stalk of a leaflet; hence petiolulate.

Petri dish: Flat round glass or plastic dish with a matching lid, used for small-scale culturing of organisms, germinating seeds etc. Also referred to as plates, hence to plate a culture.

PH electrode-based sensor: Sensor in which a standard pH electrode is coated with a biological material. Many biological processes raise or lower pH, and the changes can be detected by the pH electrode.

Ph: A symbol of hydrogen ion concentration indicating the degree of acidity or alkalinity.

Phage: Abbreviation for bacteriophage.

Phagemids: Cloning vectors that contain components derived from both phage and plasmid DNA.

Phagocytes: Immune system cells that ingest and destroy viruses, bacteria, fungi and other foreign substances or cells.

Phagocytosis: The process by which foreign particles invading the body are engulfed and broken down by phagocytes.

Phalaenophily: Pollinated by moths.

Phanerantherous: With stamens exserted.

Phanerocotylar or epigeous: With the cotyledons emergent from seed, usually appearing above ground.

Phanerogam: A plant with cons-picuous reproductive parts; a plant reproducing by seeds.

Pharmacokinetics: The quantitative measure-ment of how drugs move around the body, and the processes which control their absorption, distribution, metabolism, and excretion.

Phase change: The developmental change from one maturation state to another.

Phase state: The coupling or repulsion of two linked genes.

Phenocopy: An environmentally induced, non hereditary variation in an organism, resembling a genetically determined trait.

Phenolic oxidation: Common aspect of the wound response in plants. Phenolic oxidation is often indicated by blackening of tissue and it may be a precursor to growth inhibition or, in severe cases, to tissue necrosis and death.

Phenolics: Compounds with hydroxyl group(s) attached to the benzene ring, forming esters, ethers and salts. Phenolic substances produced from newly explanted tissues are liable to oxidise, and as a result form coloured compounds visible in nutrient media.

Phenology: The study of flowering or fruiting periodicity of plants.

Phenotype: The characters of an organism due to the interaction of genotype and environment, a group of individuals exhibiting the same phenotypic characters. The detectable expression of the interaction of genotype and environment constituting the visible characters of an organism.

Phenotypic: a. A set of characters arising from reaction to environmental stimulus.

Pheromone: A hormone-like substance that is secreted by an organism into the environment as a specific signal to another organism, usually of the same species.

Phil, philous: Suffix meaning 'liking' or 'preferring'.

Phloem: Conducting tissue of vascular plants. Phloem differs from xylem both structurally and functionally. Functionally, phloem transports solutes both up and down the plant, while xylem functions as a one-way transport system for moving water from the roots to the leaves (or equivalent). Phloem carries sugars and other direct or indirect products of photosynthesis to the stem and roots, generally during the day. Phloem also carries ions and soil nutrients up from the roots to the stem and leaves, generally at night. Xylem makes considerable use of the cell walls of dead or enucleated cells. Phloem uses living cells. Xylem uses capillary action and suction, like a straw, to transport water. Phloem uses osmotic pressure to move solutes. A high concentration of solute is loaded inside cells of the phloem at a source, such as a leaf where sugars are produced. This creates a diffusion gradient that draws water into the cells. The resulting pressure causes a flow to occur. If the dissolved sugars or other chemicals carried along with the sugars are removed from the phloem at another place in the tree for use (a sink such as a root or fruit), the decline in concentration of sugar causes water to move out of the phloem cells. Because water is moving in at a source and out at a sink, there is a mass flow of water and substances in the phloem. In trees, phloem is shed annually with the bark.

Phosphatase: An class of enzymes that catalyze the hydrolysis of esters of phosphoric acid, removing a phosphate group from an organic compound.

Phosphodiester (phosphor diester) bond: A bond in which a phosphate group joins adjacent carbons through ester linkages. A condensation reaction between adjacent nucleotides results in a phosphodiester bond between 3' and 5' carbons in DNA and RNA.

Phospholipase A2: An enzyme which degrades type A2 phospholipids.

Phospholipid: A class of lipid molecules in which glycerol is linked to a phosphate group and two fatty acyl groups. Contains both polar and non-polar regions. A major component of biological membranes.

Phosphorolysis: The cleavage of a bond by orthophosphate; analogous to hydrolysis referring to cleavage by water.

Phosphorylation: The addition of a phosphate group to a compound.

Photo bioreactor: Bioreactor dependent on sunlight, which is taken up by its content of plant material, usually algae.

Photon: A unit.of light energy.

Photoperiod: The length of daylight or period of daily illumination provided for growth.

Photoperiodism: The initiation of flowering and certain vegetative activities of plants in response to relative lepgths of day and night.

Photophosphorylation: The formation of ATP from ADP and inorganic phosphate using light energy harvested by photosynthesis.

Photoreactivation: A light dependent DNA repair process.

Photosynthate: The carbohydrates and other compounds produced in photosynthesis.

Photosynthesis: The conversion of light energy to chemical energy; water, carbon dioxide, and chlorophyll are all essential to the process, which ultimately produces carbohydrate, with oxygen being released as aby-product.

Photosynthetic efficiency: Efficiency of converting light energy into organic compounds.

Photosynthetic photon flux (PPF): A measure of the intensity of light utilized by plants for photosynthetic activity.

Photosynthetic unit: One of two groups of about 250 to 400 pigment molecules each that function together in chloroplasts in the light reactions of photosynthesis; the units are exceedingly numerous in each chloroplast.

Photosynthetic: Able to use sunlight energy to convert atmospheric carbon dioxide into organic compounds. Nearly all plants, most algae and some bacteria are photosynthetic.

Photosynthetically active radiation (PAR): The part of the radiant energy that is capturable by natural photosynthetic systems (approximately equivalent to the natural light spectrum of wavelengths 400-700nm).

Phototropism: The tendency of plants to direct shoot growth towards the source of light.

Phragmoplast: A complex of microtubules and endoplasmic reticulum that develops during telophase of mitosis.

Phyll, phyllo: Suffix or prefix meaning 'leaf'.

Phyllary: One of the involucral leaves subtending a capitulum, as in composites.

Phyllid: The leaf of a bryophyte. By many more exacting definitions, this does not constitute a leaf, hence the purported need for this apparently pointless addition to your vocabulary.

Phylloclade: A very leaf-like, photosynthetic stem of a plant whose true leaves are much reduced.

Phyllode: A leaf whose blade is much reduced or absent, and whose petiole and rachis have assumed the functions of the whole leaf.

Phyllodium: Flattened blade-like petiole or midrib.

Phyllopodic: With blade-bearing leaves at base of plant.

Phyllopodium: An outgrowth of the rhizome in ferns to which the frond or stipe is joined.

Phyllotaxis: Arrangement of leaves, primarily photosynthetic in function.

Phyllotaxy: The arrangement of leaves on a stem (when spiral, often expressed quantitatively as the fraction of the circumference of the stem that separates two successive leaves).

Phylogeny: The evolutionary development of a group and its derivation from ancestors and the relationship between its members; hence phylogenetic.

Phylum: A taxon of high rank, the major unit of classification.

Phyto (Prefix): To do with plants.

Phytochemical: Molecules characteristically found in plants.

Phytochrome: A pigment, found in the cytoplasm of green plants, which can exist in two forms Pr (biologically inactive) and Pfr (biologically active). Pfr is converted into Pr by exposure to light of wavelength 730 nm. Involved in the timing of many plant processes, e.g. dormancy, leaf formation, flowering and germination.

Phytomelanin: A papery "sooty" black layer over the seed of plants in the Asparagales, which includes agaves, aloes, onions and hyacinths. It is an important character for defining the group.

Phytoparasite: Parasite on plants.

Phytopathogen: A plant pathogen.

Phytoremediation: The use of plants actively to remove contaminants or pollutants from either soils (e.g. polluted fields) or water resources (e.g. polluted lakes). An example is the exploitation of the Brazil water hyacinth (Eichhornia crassipes) to accumulate in its tissues toxic metals such as lead, arsenic, cadmium, mercury, nickel, and copper.

Phytosanitary: Plant health, including quarantine.

Phytostat: Apparatus designed for the semi-continuous chemostatic culture of plant cells.

Phytosterol: One of a group of biologically active phytochemicals present in the seeds of certain plants. Evidence suggests that human consumption of certain phytosterols, such as â-sitosterol, can help to lower total serum cholesterol and low-density lipoproteins levels, thereby reducing the risk of coronary heart disease.

Pigment: Compounds that are coloured by the light they absorb. Light absorption is exploited by plants both as a means of energy capture and as a signalling mechanism.

Pileus: Umbrella-shaped structure of mushrooms or toadstools.

Pilose: Hairy; pubescence comprised of scattered long, slender, soft hairs.

Pinnae: One of the divisions of a pinnately compound leaf.

Pinnate: Compound, with the leaflets arranged on both sides of a common axis. Interruptedly pinnately compound - with smaller and larger leaflets alternating along the rachis.

Pinnately compound; pinnately veined: Having leaflets or veins on both sides of a common axis (e.g., rachis, midrib) to which they are attached.

Pinnatifid: Cut deeply into lobes that are spaced out along the axis (of the leaf).

Pinnatipartite: Pinnately lobed half to two thirds the depth of the lamina.

Pinnatisect: Dissected down to the midrib but having the segments confluent with it.

Pinnule: A secondary pinna, one of the ultimate divisions of a bipinnate or twice-pinnate leaf.

Pinnulet: As you have undoubtedly guessed, the third order of segments of a compound leaf or fern frond.

Pinocytosis: The engulfing of a minute droplet of liquid by a living cell.

Pipette: Widely used device for accurate dispensing of small volumes of liquids.

Pistil: Central organ of the flower, typically consisting of ovary, style and stigma. Usually referred to as the female part of a perfect flower.

Pistillate, carpellate, or female: Said of a flower bearing a pistil or pistils but not stamens, may refer also to a plant having only pistillate flowers.

Pistillode: A sterile pistil, often rudimentary.

Pit membrane: In many sources, the term pit refers to the absence of secondary wall, i.e. the "hole" in the secondary wall, while the primary wall is the pit membrane. The distinction becomes important in detailed xylem anatomy because vessels may have pits but usually lack pit membranes. In that case the pit is simply a hole in the vessel wall.

Pit: The thin, remnant primary wall of tracheids, i.e., primary wall which has not been covered by lignified secondary wall. Pits are involved in translocation of fluids from the xylem.

Pitcher: Ventricose to tubular insectivorous leaf, as in Sarracenia

Pith (pith): Central tissue of a dicot stem and certain roots; it usually consists of parenchyma cells that become proportionately less of the volume of woody plants as cambial activity increases the organ's girth.

Pithomyces sp.: Grow on dead grass in pastures. Causes facial eczema in ruminants.

Pitted: Having numerous small depressions in the surface.

Placenta: The part of the ovary from which the ovules arise. It generally occupies the whole or a portion of an angle of a cell.

Placentation: The arrangement of placentas, and hence of ovules, within an ovary.

Planate or plain: With lamina flat, without folds or rolls.

Plankton: Free-floating aquatic organisms that are mostly microscopic.

Plano-convex: Flat on one side and convex on the other.

Plant anatomy: The botanical discipline that pertains to the internal structure of plants.

Plant breeders' rights (PBR): Legal protection of a new plant variety granted to the breeder or his successor in title. The effect of PBR is that prior authorization is required before the material can be used for commercial purposes.

Plant cell culture: In vitro growth of plant cells.

Plant cell immobilization: Entrapment of plant cells in gel matrices so that they are protected from physical damage. The cells are suspended in liquified droplets which are then allowed to harden. Commonly used matrices are alginates, agar or polyacrylamide.

Plant community: An association (plants inhabiting a common environment and interacting with one another.

Plant ecology: The science that deals with the relationships and interactions between plants and their environment.

Plant genetic resources (PGR): The reproductive or vegetative propagating material of: 1. cultivated varieties (cultivars) in current use and newly developed varieties; 2. obsolete cultivars; 3. primitive cultivars (landraces); 4. wild and weed species, near relatives of cultivated varieties; and 5. special genetic stocks (including elite and current breeder's lines and mutants).

Plant geography: The botanical discipline that pertains to the broader aspects of the space relations of plants and their distribution over the surface of the earth.

Plant growth regulator: An organic compound, either natural or synthetic, and other than a nutrient, that modifies or controls one or more specific physiological processes within a plant.

Plant physiology/Plant morphology/Plant taxonomy: The botanical discipline that pertains to the metabolic activities and processes of plants.

Plant variety protection (PVP): Synonym for plant breeders' rights.

Plant: Any of a kingdom (Plantae) of living beings typically lacking locomotive movement or obvious sensory organs, generally making its own food, possessing cell walls, and unlimited growth.

Plantibody: An antibody expressed transgenically in an engineered plant.

Plantlet: A small rooted shoot regenerated from cell culture following embryogenesis or organogenesis. Plantlets can normally develop into normal plants when transplanted to soil.

Plaque: A clear spot on an otherwise opaque lawn of bacteria, where cells have been lysed by phage infection.

Plasma cells: Antibody-producing white blood cells derived from B lymphocytes.

Plasma: The fluid portion of the blood in which is suspended the white and red blood cells. Contains 8-9% solids, of which 85% is composed of the proteins fibrinogen, albumin, and globulin. The essential function of plasma is the maintenance of blood pressure and the transport of nutrients and waste.

Plasmalemma: The lipid bilayer and associated proteins and other molecules that surrounding the protoplast, within the cell wall. Synonyms: cell membrane; plasma membrane.

Plasmid: An circular self-replicating non-chromosomal DNA molecule found in many bacteria, capable of transfer between bacterial cells of the same species, and occasionally of different species. Antibiotic resistance genes are frequently located on plasmids. Plasmids are particularly important as vectors for genetic engineering.

Plasmodesma: Fine protoplasmic thread that connects adjacent plant cells by passing through the plant cell wall. Exploited by viruses as a conduit for cell to cell movement.

Plasmodium: The multinucleate, semiviscous liquid. Active form of slime mold; it moves in a.crawling-flowing" motion.

Plasmolysis: The shrinking in volume of the protoplasm of a cell and the separation of the protoplasm from the cell wall due to loss of water via osmosis.

Plastid: A general term for a number of plant cell organelles which carry non-nuclear DNA. Includes the pigment-carrying bodies: 1. chloroplasts in leaves, 2. chromoplasts in flowers, and 3. the starch-synthesizing amyloplasts in seeds.

Plastoquinone: One of a group of compounds involved in the transport of electrons as part of the process of photosynthesis.

Plating efficiency: The percentage of inoculated cells which give rise to cell colonies when seeded into culture vessels.

Platycanthous: With flat and usually large spines.

Platyspermic: Having seeds which are flattened and disc-like. Contrast with radiospermic.

Plectostele: A complex stele with the vascular bundles arranged in several parallel ribbons.

Pleiochasium: Compound dichasium in which each cymule has three lateral branches.

Pleiomerous: With increase in number of members within whorl.

Pleiotaxy: Increase in number of whorls.

Pleiotropy: The simultaneous effect of a given gene on more than one apparently unrelated trait.

Plesiomorphic: A plesiomorphic character of a taxon is one which it shares with an ancestral group. It is not a unique, derived character (synapomorphy or apomorphy), but a primitive character which tells us nothing about its evolutionary position.

Pleurogamy: Pollen tube entrance through side of ovule.

Plicate: Folded like a paper fan, as in the leaves of palms, cyclanthoids, and some orchids.

Pliestesial or multiperennial: Monocarpic but living several to many years before flowering, as in Agave.

Plinerved: Of a leaf with lateral nerves similar to the midrib arising near the insertion of the petiole, eg. Triplinerved, 5-plinerved etc.

Ploidy: The number of complete sets of chromosomes per cell, e.g. one set: haploid, two sets: diploid, etc.

Plumose: Like a feather; with fine hairs branching from a central axis.

Plumule: The portion of an embryo that gives rise to the shoot system (as distinct from the root system) of a plant.

Pluri: Prefix meaning 'several.'

Pluricellular: Of a hair of several cells and opposed to unicellular.

Plus tree: A phenotypically superior but untested tree.

PNA: Abbreviation for peptide nucleic acid.

Pneumathodes: Bands or pores or aerating tissue, especially along the stipes of ferns.

Pneumatophore: Spongy root extending above the surface of the water, produced by a plant growing in water; pneumatophores facilitate oxygen absorption.

Pneumatophorous: With spongy, aerating roots, usually found in marsh plants.

Pocosin: A bog that has formed in a shallow, undrained depression, the surrounding land being somewhat elevated, the vegetation predominantly evergreen shrubs or small trees. Pocosins vary greatly in size.

Point mutation: A change in DNA sequence at a specific locus. The smallest change involves the substitution, deletion or insertion of a single nucleotide.

Polar bodies: In female animals, the products of a meiotic division that do not develop into a functional ovum. The first polar body comprises one of the two products of the first meiotic divisions, which may fail to divide at the second division. The second polar body comprises one of the products of the second division.

Polar mutation: A mutation that influences the functioning of genes that are downstream from the site of mutagenesis but are in the same transcription unit.

Polar nuclei: Two centrally located nuclei in the embryo sac that unite with a second sperm cell in a triple fusion. In some plant species (particularly the monocotyledons), the product of this fusion develops into the endosperm.

Polar transport: A directed movement within plants of compounds (usually endogenous plant growth regulators) mostly in one direction; polar transport overcomes the tendency for diffusion in all directions.

Polarity: The observed differentiation of an organism, tissue or cell into parts having opposed or contrasted properties or form.

Pole (pohl): An invisible focal point toward each end of a cell from which spindle fibers extend in arcs during mitosis or meiosis.

Pole cells: A group of cells in the posterior of Drosophila embryos that are precursors to the adult germ line.

Pollen: The male or fertilizing element of seed plants, consisting of fine yellowish powder formed within the anther of the stamen.

Pollen culture: The in vitro culture and germination of pollen grains to generate haploid plants.

Pollen grain: The mature microspore, produced in the pollen sac of angiosperms or the microsporangium of gymnosperms. Unicellular, with variable shape and size, and an elaborately structured wall.

Pollen tube: In seed plants, the extension of the male gametophyte as it emerges from the pollen grain in search of the female gametophyte.

Pollination: Process of transferring the pollen from its place of production to the place where the egg cell is produced. This may be accomplished by the use of wind, water, insects, birds, bats, or other means. Pollination is usually followed by fertilization, in which sperm are released from the pollen grain to unite with the egg cell.

Pollinium: A cohesive mass of pollen grains commonly found in members of the Orchid Family (Orchidaceae) and the Milkweed Family (Asclepiadaceae).

Poly (A) polymerase: Enzyme that catalyses the addition of adenine residues to the 3' end of mRNA molecules, forming the characteristic poly-(A) tail.

Polyacrylamide gel: Inert electrophoresis matrix, formed by the polymerization of acrylamide monomer in the presence of the cross-linker N,N'-methylene-bis-acrylamide. Gels are usually supported between two glass plates, which need to be removed for post-electrophoresis manipulations. Sometimes referred to incorrectly as acrylamide gels.

Polyacrylamide gel electrophoresis (PAGE): Ubiquitous method for separating nucleic acids and proteins on the basis of their molecular size. The method relies on the migration through an inert matrix (polyacrylamide gel) of electrically charged molecules as a result of the imposition of an electric field.

Polyadenylation: Post-transcriptional addition of multiple adenine residues to the 3' end of eukaryotic mRNA. Also called poly-(A) tailing. The adenine-rich 3' terminal segment is called a poly (A) tail.

Polyanthous: Having different states in several to many (more than three) different sets of flowers, only one state present in each set.

Polycarpellate: Many-carpellate.

Polycephalous: Many-headed, as in composites

Polycistronic: A single mRNA that contains the information necessary for the production of more than one polypeptide. Particularly characteristic of prokaryotic mRNAs.

Polyclonal antibody: A serum sample that contains a mixture of distinct immu-noglobulin molecules, each recognizing a different antigenic determinant of a given antigen.

Polycross test: A progeny test to assess general combining ability from crosses among selected parents. Identities can be maintained only for the seed parents. A mixture of pollen is artificially applied to each female parent, or the selections naturally and randomly open-pollinate themselves.

Polydelphous: With several groups of stamens connate by their filaments.

Polyembryony: The production of more than one embryo from a single egg cell (in animals) or from a range of embryogenic cell types (in plants). These embryos are genetically identical to one another.

Polyethylene glycol (PEG): A polymer having the general formula HOCH2 (CH2OCH2)nCH2OH and available in a range of molecular weights. Thus PEG 1000 is a polyethylene glycol of average molecular weight 1000. PEG 4000 and 6000 are commonly used to promote cell or protoplast fusion, and to facilitate DNA uptake in the transformation of organisms such as yeast. Also used to concentrate solutions by withdrawing water from them via osmosis.

Polygalacturonase (PG): An enzyme which catalyses the breakdown of pectin. A tomato engineered to contain an antisense-PG gene succeeded in delaying the onset of softening, by inhibiting the expression of PG. This allowed the fruit to be picked at a riper stage than is conventionally possible, and represented the first commercialized genetically engineered crop plant.

Polygamodioecious: Having bisexual and male flowers on some plants, and bisexual and female flowers on others.

Polygamo-monoecious: Plant monoecious, but with some perfect flowers.

Polygamous: Having bisexual, pistillate, and staminate flowers on the same individual plant.

Polygene: One of a number of genes, each of small effect, which together act to determine the phenotype of a quantitative trait. The result is continuous variation in the trait and a seemingly non-Mendelian mode of inheritance.

Polygenic: Character controlled by many genes of small effect.

Polyhedral: Having many faces or planes.

Polyheterophytous: Having different states in several to many (more than three) different individuals or sets of plants, only one state present in each set.

Polyhphyletic: Composed of members that descended independently from two or more ancestral lines.

Polyhydroxybutyrate (PHB): A biopolymer, with physical properties similar to polystyrene, originally discovered in the bacterium Alcaligenes eutropus. The gene coding for this compound has since been transformed into both other bacteria and into some crop plants in order to produce a source of renewable raw material for the plastics industry. It is rapidly degraded by soil micro-organisms.

Polylinker: A synthetic segment of DNA, designed to include a number of different restriction endonuclease sites. When ligated to a DNA fragment that is to be cloned, this enables a wide choice of restriction endonucleases to be used for the cloning process.

Polymer: A macromolecule synthesized by the chemical joining of many identical or similar monomers. For example, amino acids, monosaccharides and nucleotides give rise to proteins, polysaccharides and nucleic acids respectively. Water is eliminated between the monomers as they link to form chains. The individual monomer units condensed within a chain are often referred to as residues, a term which is also employed for the bases incorporated in polynucleotides.

Polymerase: An enzyme that catalyses the formation of polymers from monomers. A DNA polymerase synthesizes DNA from deoxynucleoside triphosphates using a complementary DNA strand and a primer. An RNA polymerase synthesizes RNA from ribonucleoside triphosphates and a complementary DNA strand.

Polymerase chain reaction (PCR): A widespread molecular biology procedure that allows the production of multiple copies (amplification) of a specific DNA sequence, provided that the base pair sequence of each end of the target is known. It involves multiple cycles of DNA denaturation, primer annealing, and strand extension, and requires a thermostable DNA polymerase, deoxyribonucleotides, and specific oligonucleotides (primers).

Polymerization: The chemical fusion of a number of identical or similar monomers to form a polymer. Common biological polymers are starch (polymerized monosaccharides), DNA (deoxyri-bonucleotides) and proteins (amino acids).

Polymery: The phenomenon whereby a number of genes at different loci (which may be polygenes) can act together to produce a single effect.

Polymorphic (polymorphous): Existing in several or many forms.

Polymorphism: 1. The occurrence of allelic variation at a locus. Polymorphism in nucleotide sequences has provided powerful diagnostic tools. 2. The occurrence of two or more forms in a population.

Polypeptide: A linear polymer composed of covalently linked amino acids. Each link is formed by a single peptide bond. Sometimes used as a synonym for protein, but also describes non-natural and low-molecular-weight polymers.

Polypetalous: With many separate petals.

Polyphore: A receptacle or torus bearing many distinct carpels, as in Rosa.

Polyphyletic: Composed of members that originated, independently, from more than one evolutionary line.

Polyploid: A cell, tissue, individual, population, or whole species having more than twice the basic number oex" of chromosomes of the ancestral species.

Polyploidy: may lead to increased growth rates (Populus) or severe dwarfing (Pinus). Three sets of chromosomes is called triploid, four sets-tetraploid, six sets-hexaploid, etc.

Polysaccharide: A linear or branched polymer (e.g. starch, cellulose, etc.) composed of covalently linked monosaccharides, including cellulose, pectin and starch. Synonym: carbohydrate.

Polysome: A multi-ribosomal structure representing a linear array of ribosomes held together by mRNA.

Polyspermy: The entry of several sperm nuclei into the egg during fertilization, although only one actually fuses with the egg nucleus.

Polystelic: Having more than one stele.

Polystichous: Leaves or other structures in many rows.

Polytene chromosome: Giant chromosomes produced by interphase replication without division, and consisting of many identical chromatids arranged side by side.

Polytypic: Containing more than one taxon of the next lower rank.

Polyunsaturates: Oils in which some of the carbon-carbon bonds are not fully hydrogenated - i.e. of the form -CH=CH-, rather than -CH2-CH2-.

Polyvalent vaccine: A recombinant organism into which antigenic determinants have been cloned from a number of pathogens, for use as a vaccine.

Polyvinylpyrrolidone (PVP): An occasional constituent of plant tissue culture isolation media. PVP is of variable molecular weight and of general formula (C6H9NO)n. Its antioxidant properties are used to prevent oxidative browning of excised plant tissues.

Pome: A fleshy (false) fruit, formed from an inferior ovary, in which the receptacle or hypanthium has enlarged to enclose the true fruit.

Pond: A body of standing water smaller than a lake, often artifically formed.

Population: A group of individual trees having some characteristics in common, either location, family ancestry, or intended use.

Population density: Number of cells or individuals per unit. The unit could be an area, or a volume of medium.

Population genetics: The branch of genetics that deals with frequencies of alleles and genotypes in breeding populations.

Porate: Of a pollen grain, with rounded apertures only.

Porcine endogenous retrovirus (PERV): The provirus of a porcine retrovirus. The possibility that PERVs could be activated after xenotransplantation of pig organs into humans has raised concern that xenotransplantation may result in the transter of novel infections to the human population.

Poricidal: Dehiscing through a pore at apex of theca.

Porogamy: Pollen tube entrance through the micropyle.

Porrect: Directed outward and forward.

Positional candidate gene: A gene known to be located in the same region as a DNA marker that has been shown to be linked to a single-locus trait or to a QTL, and whose deduced function suggests that it could be the source of genetic variation in the trait in question.

Positional cloning: A strategy for gene cloning that relies on the identification of closely linked markers to the target trait, and then uses chromosome walking to identify, isolate and characterize the gene(s) responsible for the trait. The strategy is particularly appropriate when the biochemical basis of the target trait is unclear, thus precluding the use of a candidate gene approach.

Positive control system: A mechanism in which a regulatory protein(s) is required to turn on gene expression.

Positive selection: A method by which cells that carry a DNA insert integrated at a specific chromosomal location can be selected, since this integration confers a predictable phenotype.

Post replication repair: A recombination-dependent mechanism for repairing damaged DNA.

Post translational modification: The addition of specific chemical residues to a protein after it has been translated. Common residues are phosphate groups (phosphorylation) and sugars (glycosylation).

Posterior: Lobe The lobe next to axis, away from the subtending bract; adaxial lobe. Posterior Ridges, Lines, Grooves - The lines, grooves, ridges in or on the ventral side, adaxial, within the perianth.

Potting on: This is the process of transferring rooted cuttings from the cutting mix into pots of potting mix for growth before hardening off. Potting on enables the plant to establish a good root system.

Pouch or sac: A bag-shaped structure.

PR protein: Abbreviation for pathogenesis related protein.

Praemorse: Appearing bitten off at the end.

Pre filter: A coarse filter used to screen out large particles from a fluid or gas, before it is passed through a much finer filter.

Pre transplant: A stage in micropropagation - the rooting and hardening process prior to transfer to soil.

Precautionary principle: The approach whereby any possible risk associated with the introduction of a new technology is avoided, until a full understanding of its impact on health, environment etc. is available. Particularly applied to the release of genetically modified organisms, since unlike many technologies, these cannot be recalled if problems arise.

Precocious germination: Early germination of a seed or embryo, prior to the full maturation of the embryo.

Preformed shoots: Normal shoots that develop from winter buds which contain primordia of all leaves that will expand during the season.

Pressure potential: The pressure generated within a cell, being the net difference between the cell's osmotic potential and the water potential of the external environment.

Pressure-flow hypothesis: The theory that food substances in solution in plants flow along concentration gradients between the sources of the food and sinks (places where the food is utilized).

Pre-treatment: one method of pre-treatment involves lightly damaging the seed coat to allow water uptake necessary for germination. Usually heat or abrasion (rubbing the seed coat with sandpaper) are used - e.g. with Acacia seeds. Pre-treatment for seeds of some plants involves chilling seeds (cold, moist stratification).

Preventive immunization: Infection with an antigen to elicit an antibody response that will protect the organism against future infections. Synonym: vaccination.

Pribnow box: Consensus sequence near the mRNA start-point of prokaryotic genes.

Pricking out: the process of transferring seedlings from the seed mix into pots of potting mix for growth before hardening off and planting out.

Prickle: A sharp pointed emergence arising from the epidermis or bark of a plant.

Primary antibody: In an ELISA or other immunological assay, the antibody that binds to the target molecule.

Primary cell wall: The cell wall layer formed during cell expansion. Plant cells possessing only primary walls may divide or undergo differentiation.

Primary cell: A cell or cell line taken directly from a living organism, which is not immortalized.

Primary consumer: Organism that feeds directly on producers.

Primary culture: A culture started from cells, tissues or organs taken directly from organisms. A primary culture may be regarded as such until it is sub-cultured for the first time. It then becomes a cell line.

Primary growth: 1. Apical meristem-derived growth; the tissues of a young plant. 2. Explant growth during the initial culture period.

Primary immune response: The immune response that occurs during the first encounter of a mammal with a given antigen.

Primary meristem: Meristem of the shoot or root tip giving rise to the primary plant body.

Primary pinna: Leaflet of first subdivision of a fern frond or compound leaf.

Primary production: The quantity of new organic matter created by photosynthesis.

Primary structure: The linear sequence of residues making up a polymer such as a nucleic acid, polysaccharide or protein.

Primary tissue: A tissue produced by an apical meristem (e.g., epidermis, cortex, primary xylem and phloem, pith).

Primary transcript: The RNA molecule produced by transcription prior to any post-transcriptional modifications; also called a pre-mRNA in eukaryotes.

Primary xylem: Xylem is found in leaves and young stems or in young roots it is referred to as primary xylem. Primary xylem is xylem derived from apical meristem, rather than cambium. It contains fiber cells and tracheids (pipe-like) elements which progressively develop secondary, lignified walls until little of the primary wall is left except at pits. These pits operate to permit fluids to move between tracheids. The precise centrifugal series of secondary wall structures, and the shape and pattern of mature pits are useful in taxonomic and forensic work.

Primer walking: A method for sequencing long (>1 kbp) cloned pieces of DNA. The initial sequencing reaction reveals the sequence of the first few hundred nucleotides of the cloned DNA. Using this, a new primer of about 20 nucleotides is synthesized, which is complementary to a sequence near the end of sequenced DNA, and used to sequence the next few hundred nucleotides of the cloned DNA. This procedure is repeated until the complete nucleotide sequence of the cloned DNA is determined.

Primer: A short oligonucleotide annealed to a template of single-stranded DNA, providing a doubled stranded structure from which DNA polymerase will synthesize a new DNA strand to produce a duplex molecule.

Primocane: The first year non-flowering stem, as in most blackberries; a turion.

Primordium: Cells in embryo or bud giving rise to roots, leaves or flowers. Protected primordium—shoot and/or flower primordia surrounded by scales. Naked Primordium—shoot and/or flower primordia not surrounded by scales.

Primosome: A protein-replication complex that catalyses the initiation of synthesis of Okazaki fragments during discontinuous replication of DNA. It involves DNA primase and DNA helicase activities.

Pro embryo: A group of cells arising from the division of the fertilized egg cell or somatic embryo before those cells which are to become the embryo are recognizable.

Pro meristem: The embryonic meristem that is the source of organ initials or foundation cells.

Pro nuclear micro-injection: An early, low success-rate method to achieve transgenesis in animals, involving the micro-injection of many gene copies into one of the two pro-nuclei of a fertilized egg. Now being replaced by micro-injection into a culture of cloned embryos produced by nuclear transfer, which can be tested for expression of the transgene before transfer to recipient females.

Pro nucleus: Either one of the two haploid gamete nuclei, just prior to their fusion in the fertilized egg.

Pro phage: The genome of a bacteriophage integrated into the chromosome of a lysogenic bacterial cell, and replicated along with its host chromosome.

Pro toxin: A latent, non-active precursor form of a toxin.

Probability: The frequency of occurrence of an event.

Proband: The individual in a family in whom an inherited trait is first identified.

Probe: A labelled DNA or RNA sequence used to detect the presence of a complementary sequence by hybridization with a nucleic acid sample.

Probract: Small, leaf-like structure at the base of an inflorescence in cucurbitaceae, usually arising opposite a tendril.

Procambium: A primary meristem that gives rise to primary vascular tissues and, in most woody plants, to the vascular cambium.

Process: A projecting appendage.

Processed pseudo-gene: A copy of a functional gene which has no promoter, no introns and which, consequently, is not itself transcribed.

Procumbent, prostrate, or reclining: Trailing or spreading along the ground but not rooting at the nodes.

Producer: An organism that manufactures food through the process of photosynthesis.

Production: The weight of new organic material formed over a period of time, plus any losses during that time period. Losses may be due to respiration, excretion, secretion, injury, death, or grazing.

Production environment: All input-output relationships, over time, at a particular location. The relationships include biological, climatic, economic, social, cultural and political factors, which combine to determine the productive potential of a particular enterprise. Production environments are classified as high-, medium- and low-input.

Production traits: Characteristics of animals, such as the quantity or quality of the milk, meat, fibre, eggs, work, etc., they (or their progeny) produce, which contribute directly to the value of the animals for the farmer, and that are identifiable or measurable at the individual level.

Productivity: The amount of economically significant product generated within a given period of time from a specified quantity of resource.

Progeny testing: With respect to discrete loci, the inference of the allelic state of an individual from the pattern of segregation among its offspring. For a quantitative trait, the use of progeny performance to estimate the breeding value of an individual.

Progesterone: A hormone produced primarily by the corpus luteum, but also by the placenta. Its function in mammals is to prepare the inner lining of the uterus for the implantation of a fertilized egg. Also made by non-placental animals, including fish.

Prokaryote: A member of the large group of organisms, including bacteria and blue-green algae, in which the chromosome is not enclosed within a nucleus, but instead exists as a linear or circular strand. Prokaryotes do not undergo meiosis and do not have functional organelles such as mitochondria and chloroplasts.

Prokaryotic: Having a cell or cells that lack a distinct nucleus and other membrane-bound organelles (e.g., bacteria).

Prolactin: A hormone, produced by the anterior pituitary gland, that stimulates and controls lactation in mammals.

Proleptic shoots: Abnormal late season shoots that develop from the lateral buds immediately beneath the terminal.

Proliferation: Increase by frequent and repeated reproduction; growth by cell division.

Proliferous: Bearing supplementary structures such as buds or flowers, either in an abnormal manner or in a manner that is normal but from adventitious tissue.

Promeristem: Apical growing or meristematic tissue that gives rise to other bud parts.

Prominent: Standing out beyond some other part.

Promoter region: The DNA sequence to which RNA polymerase binds to initiate transcription.

Promoter: 1. A short DNA sequence, usually upstream of (5' to) the relevant coding sequence, to which RNA polymerase binds before initiating transcription. This binding aligns the RNA polymerase so that transcription will initiate at a specific site. The nucleotide sequence of the promoter determines the nature of the enzyme that attaches to it and the rate of RNA synthesis. 2. A chemical substance that enhances the transformation of benign cells into cancerous cells.

Proofreading: The scanning of newly-synthesized DNA for structural defects, such as mis-matched base pairs. A functional activity of most DNA polymerases.

Propagation: The duplication of a whole plant from a range of vegetative materials; adapted for in vitro culture as micropropagation.

Propagule: A structure with the capacity to give rise to a new plant, e.g. a seed, a spore, part of the vegetative body capable of independent growth if detached from the parent.

Propagulum/propagule: A runner or sucker used in the asexual propagation of plants. pl. propagula or propagules.

Prophase: The first stage of nuclear division. The stage during which chromosome pairing occurs in the first division of meiosis. In mitosis and the second division of meiosis, the chromosomes shorten and thicken as a result of coiling.

Prophyll: A leaf formed at the base of a shoot, usually smaller than those formed subsequently.

Proplastid: A tiny, undifferentiated organelle that can duplicate itself and that may develop into a chloroplast, leucoplast, or other type of plastid.

Prostrate: Flat, spreading; growing low along the ground.

Protamine: A class of small basic proteins that replace the histones in the chromosomes of some sperm cells.

Protandrous: Having the male sex organs maturing before the female; of a flower, shedding the pollen before the stigma is receptive.

Protease: An enzyme that catalyses the hydrolysis of proteins, cleaving the peptide bonds that link amino acids in protein molecules. Synonym: peptidase.

Protein crystallization: The production of a pure preparation of a protein. In this form, the three-dimensional structure of the molecule can be determined.

Protein engineering: Generating proteins with modified structures that confer novel properties such as higher catalytic specificity or thermal stability.

Protein kinase: An enzyme that catalyses the addition of a phosphate group(s) to a protein molecule at the sites of serine, threonine or tyrosine residues.

Protein metabolic step: One step in the chain of reactions that take place in an organism and dictate the composition of that organism.

Protein sequencing: The process of determining the amino acid sequence of a protein. Usually achieved following initially partial hydrolysis of the protein into smaller peptides by enzymatic digestion.

Protein synthesis: The creation of proteins from their constituent amino acids, in accordance with the encoding gene DNA sequence.

Protein: A macromolecule composed of one or more polypeptides, each comprising a chain of amino acids linked by peptide bonds.

Proteinaceous infectious particle: Believed to be the agent responsible for the class of diseases called spongiform encephalo-pathies, including scrapie in sheep, bovine spongiform encephalopathy (BSE; mad cow disease) in cattle and CJD in humans. It is an abnormal form of a brain protein, and has no detectable nucleic acid content. Synonym: prion.

Proteolysis: Enzymatic degradation of a protein.

Proteolytic: Having the ability to degrade protein molecules.

Proteome: The complete complement of proteins made by a given species in all its tissues and growth stages.

Proteomics: An approach that seeks to identify and characterize complete sets of protein, and protein-protein interactions in a given species.

Proto oncogene: A normal gene that can be mutated to an oncogene. Synonym: cellular oncogene.

Protoclone: Regenerated plant derived from protoplast culture or a single colony derived from protoplasts in culture.

Protocol: The step-by-step experiments proposed to describe or solve a scientific problem, or the defined steps of a specific procedure.

Protocorm: A tuberous structure, formed following the germination of orchid seeds, from which develops a complete plant. It develops from an unorganized embryo in the seed, comprising only a few hundred cells. In culture, vegetative explants of several orchid species form round, smooth protocorms which can be multiplied indefinitely or induced to regenerate into a whole plant.

Protogynous: Having the female sex organs maturing before the male; of a flower, shedding the pollen after the stigma has ceased to be receptive.

Protogyny: The condition in which the female reproductive organs (carpels) of a flower mature before the male ones (stamens), thereby ensuring that self-fertilization does not occur.

Protologue: The original or first publication of a taxonomic name.

Protonema: A green, usually branched, threadlike or sometimes platelike growth from a bryophyte spore; it gives rise to "leafy" gametophytes.

Protoplasm: The essential, complex living substance of cells, upon which all vital functions of nutrition, secretion, growth and reproduction depend.

Protoplast culture: The culturing in vitro of plant protoplasts. Where protoplasts can be regenerated into whole plants, they represent an attractive target for genetic manipulation.

Protoplast fusion: The induced or spontaneous coalescence of two or more protoplasts of the same or different species origin. Where fused protoplasts can be regenerated into whole plants, the opportunity exists for the creation of novel genomic combinations.

Protoplast: A bacterial or plant cell for which the cell wall has been removed either chemically or enzymatically, leaving its cytoplasm enveloped by a peripheral membrane. Protoplasts are spherical and smaller than the elongate, angular shaped and often vacuolated cells from which they have been released.

Protostele: When a plant's vascular tissue develops in a solid central bundle, it is said to have a protostele.

Prototroph: A nutritionally independent cell. Opposite: auxotroph.

Protoxylem: The first formed primary xylem, consisting of annular and spiral (helical) vessels.

Protozoan: A microscopic, single-cell organism.

Protuberance: A swelling or bump on the surface.

Provenance test: A test comparing trees grown from seed or cuttings collected in many parts of a species range.

Provenance: The geographical and/or genetic origin of an individual.

Provirus: A double stranded DNA copy of the single RNA strand of a retrovirus, which has been integrated into a host genome.

Pruning: Removal of portions of plants for aesthetic purposes, for improving quality and size of fruits or flowers, or for elimination of diseased tissues.

Pseudanthium: Several flowers simulating a simple flower but composed of more than a single axis with subsidiary flowers.

Pseudo affinity chromatography: A chromatographic technique in which a ligand is immobilized selectively to retain enzymes or other proteins.

Pseudo autosomal region: A section at one end of the X and Y chromosomes for which there is sufficient homology that there is synapsis between them during meiosis.

Pseudocarp: A fruit that incorporates, in addition to the ovary wall, other parts of the flower, such as the receptacle (e.g. strawberry).

Pseudodichotomous: Apparently dichotomous with a dormant terminal bud and two equal lateral branches.

Pseudodrupe: Two-four loculed nut surrounded by a fleshy involucre, as in Juglans.

Pseudoelaters: Moisture-sensitive cells produced in the sporangium of hornworts.

Pseudogene: An incomplete or mutated copy of a gene which is not transcribed because it lacks a continuous open reading frame. Those that lack introns are called processed pseudogenes and are most likely cDNA copies synthesized from mRNA by reverse transcriptase.

Pseudolamina: The extended apical portion of a phyllode.

Pseudomonas spp: A widely distributed Gram-negative bacterial genus. Many of the soil forms produce a pigment that fluoresces under ultraviolet light, hence the descriptive term fluorescent Pseudomonas.

Pseudomonomerous: Whorl seemingly with one member which is a fusion product of two or more parts.

Pseudomonopodial: Branching a type of branching characterized by the presence of a main branch which has outgrown the other of the dichotomous pair, resulting in a main axis with smaller lateral branches. A type of branching where the apical meristem appears to divide to form two branches, one of which is dominant resulting in an upright main axis with distinct side branches.

Pseudo-terminal: Bud appearing apical but is lateral near apex, developing with death or nondevelopment of terminal bud

Pseudovivipary: A condition where vegetative propagules replace some or all of the normal sexual flowers in the inflorescence.

Psychophily: Pollinated by butterflies.

Psychrophile: A micro-organism that can grow at temperatures below 30 °C and as low as 0 °C.

Pteridophyte: Plant in which the sporophyte generation is the larger phase and in which the gametophyte lives an existence independent of its parent sporophyte. Pteridophytes are almost all vascular plants, and include the lycophytes, trimerophytes, sphenophytes, and ferns.

Pteridosperm: An extinct group of seed plants which bore fern-like leaves.

Pterophytes: Ferns; members of the division pterophyta.

Puberulent: Covered with fine, short, and nearly imperceptable down; minutely pubescent, the hairs soft, straight, erect, but scarcely visible to the unaided eye.

Puberulous: Covered with minute, soft, erect hairs.

Pubescent: A general term for hairiness; covered with soft hair or down.

PUC: A widely used plasmid, containing as a marker a galactosidase gene.

Pulsed field gel electrophoresis (PFGE): A procedure used to separate very large (50 kbp to several Mbp) DNA molecules by alternating the direction of electric current in a pulsed manner across a gel.

Pulverulent: Covered with fine, powdery wax granules.

Pulvinus: Swelling at the base of a stalk or leaf or leaflet, sometimes glandular or responsive to touch; hence pulvinate.

Punctate: Covered with minute impressions or depressions.

Puncticulate: Minutely dotted.

Punctiform: Reduced to a mere dot or point.

Punctuated equilibrium: The occurrence of speciation events in bursts, separated by long intervals of species stability.

Punctum: A dot or pit; hence punctate, covered with dots or pits.

Pungent: Ending in a stiff, sharp point; having an acrid taste or smell.

Pure line: A strain in which all members are genetically nearly identical and are indistinguishable by phenotype. Usually created by repeated generations of self-fertilization or close inbreeding.

Purine: A double-ring, nitrogen-containing base present in nucleic acids. Adenine (A) and guanine (G) are the two purines normally present in DNA and RNA molecules.

Pustulate hair: Hair with an enlarged base.

Pustulate: Covered with small pustule- or blister-like elevations.

Pustule: A low projection like a blister or pimple, larger than a papilla; hence pustular, pustulate.

Putative: Reputed, generally regarded as such, supposed; eg. Putative hybrids.

Pycnoxylic: Wood in which there is little or no parenchyma tissue among the xylem is called pycnoxylic. Conifers and flowering plants have pycnoxylic wood. Contrast with mannoxylic.

Pyrene: The 'stone' (endocarp plus seed) of a succulent fruit.

Pyrenoid: A small body found on the chloroplasts of certain green algae and homworts; pyrenoids are associated with starch accumulation; they may occur singly on a chloroplast, or they may be numerous.

Pyrenulales: (pyrenolichens) An order of the Ascolichenes or of the Pyrenomycetes containing lichens in which the fungal partner produces perithecia (pyrenocarps). These are buried in the thallus and only visible as dots on the surface. There are over 1500 species in the Pyrenulales, common genera including Dermatocarpon, Pyrenula, and Verrucaria. Lichens with fungi that form bitunicate rather than unitunicate perithecia may be placed in a separate order, the Pseudosphaeriales.

Pyrethrins: Active constituents of pyrethrum (Tanacetum cinerariifolium) flowers, used as insecticides.

Pyridoxine: (vitamin B6) A pyridine derivative, essential in its activated forms, pyridoxal phosphate and pyridoxanine, as a coenzyme in various transamination reactions.

Pyrimidine: A single-ring, nitrogen-containing base present in nucleic acids. Cytosine (C) and thymine (T) are present in DNA, whereas uracil (U) replaces T in RNA. Thymine is a synonym for 5-methyluracil.

Pyrogen: Bacterial substance that causes fever in mammals.

Pyrophosphate: A phosphate ion dimer; may be released on hydrolysis of ATP.

Pyruvic acid: A three-carbon carboxylic keto acid with the formula CH3COCO OH. In glucose metabolism pyruvate is an intermediate in glycolysis. Under anaerobic conditions it is reduced to form ethanol or some other fermentation product, while in aerobic conditions it is decarboxylated to form acetyl CoA. In C4 plants pyruvate is an intermediate of the Hatch-Slack pathway. In amino acid metabolism pyruvate is the degradation product of several amino acids, including alanine and cysteine, while other amino acids are synthesized from pyruvate. Pyruvate can also be carboxylated to form oxaloacetate or malate, both intermediates in the TCA cycle. These reactions, known as anaplerotic reactions, replenish TCA cycle intermediates.

Q beta replicase: A viral RNA polymerase secreted by a bacteriophage that infects E. coli. It has the property of being able to copy RNA sequences at a rapid rate.

QSAR: Abbreviation for quantitative structure-activity relationship.

QTL: Abbreviation for quantitative trait locus.

Quadrat: A small area, usually 0.5 or 1.0 m2, marked out with a frame that can be used in an ecological survey to study in detail the distribution and abundance of different species. It can be used for random sampling within an area or for systematic sampling at regular intervals. A permanent quadrat can be used to record changes in the distribution and numbers of species over a number of years. A quadrat may be used in conjunction with a metal 'comb' with teeth at regular intervals that allows detailed sampling at equally spaced points. A hundred such points would estimate the percentage of a particular species present.

Quadri: Prefix meaning 'four'.

Quadrifarious: Arranged in four close-set rows along the stem.

Quadrifid: Cut or divided into four lobes or parts.

Quadriseriate: In four ranks or rows.

Quadrivalent: The structure formed by the pairing of four homologous chromosomes in a tetraploid during prophase and metaphase of the first division of meiosis.

Quadruplex: The inheritance of alleles in autotetraploids. A genotype AAAa will produce gametes AA, Aa in the ratio 3:1.

Qualitative trait: A trait that shows discontinuous variation—i.e. individuals can be assigned to one of a small number of discrete classes.

Quantitative genetics: The area of genetics concerned with the inheritance of quantitative traits that show continuous variation, as opposed to qualitative traits. Since many of the critical targets in both plant and animal breeding are of this type, most practical improvement programs involve the application of quantitative genetics.

Quantitative inheritance: Inheritance of measurable traits that depend on the cumulative action of many genes and/or involve a significant proportion of non-genetic determination.

Quantitative structure activity relationship (QSAR): A computer modelling technique that enables the prediction of the likely activity of a molecule before it is synthesized. QSAR analysis relies on recognizing associations of molecular structures and activity from historical data.

Quantitative trait locus (QTL): A locus where allelic variation is associated with variation in a quantitative trait. The presence of a QTL is inferred from genetic mapping, where the total variation is partitioned into components linked to a number of discrete chromosome regions.

Quantitative trait: A measurable trait that shows continuous variation (e.g. height, weight, colour intensity, etc.) - i.e. the population cannot be classified into a few discrete classes.

Quantum speciation: The rapid formation of new species, primarily by genetic drift.

Quarantine: Isolation for a period after arrival in a new location, to allow any pre-existing disease symptoms to appear. Used in the context of regulations restricting the sale or shipment of living organisms, usually to prevent disease or pest invasion of an area.

Quaternary structure: A level of protein structure where several individual molecules assemble together and form a functional cluster. A classic example is haemoglobin, a complex of four myoglobin-like units.

Quiescence: A state in which a seed or other plant part will not germinate or grow unless environmental conditions normally required for growth are present.

Quiescent: A temporary suspension or reduction in the rate of activity or growth, while retaining the potential to resume prior activity. Applies particularly to cell division.

Quincuncial: Having five structures, two of which are exterior, two interior, and a fifth with one margin covering interior structure and other margin covered by that of one of the exterior structures.

Quinone fungicide: Any fungicide developed from chlorinated quinones, such as chloranil, which is used as a seed dressing, and dichlone, which is used as a foliar fungicide.

R

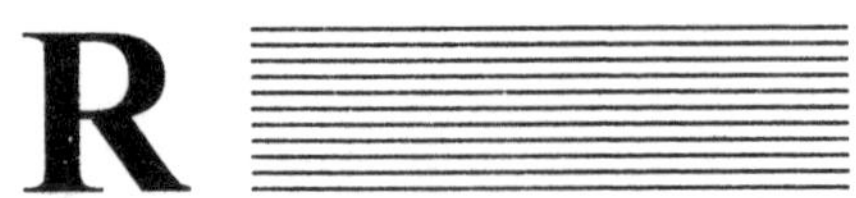

R1: The first-generation offspring of a recombinant (genetically modified) organism. Not standard terminology.

R loops: Single-stranded DNA regions in RNA-DNA hybrids formed in vitro under conditions where RNA-DNA duplexes are more stable than DNA-DNA duplexes.

Race: In taxonomic classification, an in-fraspecific category of uncertain position but occasionally used in floras in place of, or subordinate to, form. The term is also used in lieu of ecotype, implying a category between subspecies and variety covering geographical groupings of plants. Races are often uniform in respect of ecological preference, physiological requirements, and topographical distribution.

Raceme: An indeterminate inflorescence in which a main axis produces a series of flowers on lateral stalks, the oldest at the base and the youngest at the top.

Racemose: An inflorescence whose growing points continue to add to the inflorescence and in which there are no terminal flowers, and the branching is monopodial, as racemes, or spikes.

Racemose inflorescence: An inflorescence in which meristematic activity continues at the apex of the main stem and primary laterals and flowers are developed from the axillary meristems. The inflorescence is often pyramidal in shape with older flowers at the base or, in the case of a flat-topped arrangement, on the outside.

Rachidian: Of or pertaining to a rachis.

Rachilla: The zigzag center upon which the florets are arranged in the spikelet of grasses or in some sedges.

Rachis: Main axis of a spike; axis of fern leaf (frond) from which pinnae arise; in compound leaves, the extension of the petiole corresponding to the midrib of an entire leaf.

Radial symmetry: The arrangement of parts in an organ or organism such that any cut taken through the centre divides the structure into similar halves. Most stems and roots exhibit such symmetry. Radial symmetry in flowers is usually termed actinomorphy. The flowers of relatively primitive angiosperm families, e.g. Ranunculaceae, are usually actinomorphic. In a floral formula, actinomorphy is represented by the symbol.

Radially: Arranged or having parts arranged like rays developing uniformly around a central axis.

Radially symmetrical: Said of a flower or set of flower parts which can be cut through the center into equal and similar parts along two or more planes; actinomorphic.

Radiation hybrid cell panel (RH): A somatic cell hybrid panel in which the chromosomes from the species of interest have been fragmented by irradiation prior to cell fusion. The resultant small fragments of chromosomes greatly increase the power of physical mapping in the species of interest.

Radical: Of leaves arising at the base of the stem and forming a rosette or tuft.

Radicant: Rooting, usually appplied to stems and leaves.

Radicate: 1. To take root. 2. To cause to take root; to plant deeply and firmly.

Radicicolous: Living upon or in roots.

Radicle: The portion of an embryo that gives rise to the root system of a plant.

Radiculose: Producing numerous rootlets.

Radioimmunoassay (RIA): An assay based on the use of a radioactively labelled antibody, where the amount of radiation detected indicates the amount of target substance present in the sample.

Radioisotope: An unstable isotope that emits ionizing radiation. Synonym: radioactive isotope.

Radiospermic: Having seeds which are round or ovoid. Contrast with platyspermic.

Radix: The root of a plant.

Rainforest: A complex community dominated by trees, with high rainfall, many epiphytes and lianes.

Raised bed: A raised area for growing plants, usually enclosed by landscape timbers, in which the growing medium can be accurately determined.

Ramentaceous: Covered with, consisting of, or resembling ramentum.

Ramentum: A thin, brownish, fringed scale that appears on the young shoots or leaves of many ferns.

Ramet: A vegetatively reproduced copy of a plant. Each ramet will have almost precisely the same genotype as the original parent tree, known as the ortet.

Ramicaul: The leafy stem of some sympodial Orchids, such as those in subtribe Pleurothallidinae; distinguished from the rhizome.

Ramuliferous: Having many small branches.

Ramulus: A small branch or branchlet.

Random amplified polymorphic DNA (RAPD): A PCR-based genotyping technique in which genomic template is amplified with single, short (usually 10-mer) randomly chosen primers. Typical patterns consist of a small number of amplified products of up to 2 kbp in length, which are separated by electrophoresis.

Random mutagenesis: A non-directed change of one or more nucleotide pairs in a DNA molecule.

Random primer method: A method for labelling DNA probes, mainly for Southern hybridization experiments. A mixture of short oligonucleotides is hybridized to a single-stranded DNA probe. In the presence of DNA polymerase and deoxyribonucleotides - one of which is labelled - DNA synthesis then generates labelled copies of probe DNA.

Randomized complete-block design: The most common experimental design used in progeny, provenance and clonal field tests. Each entry in the test is replicated once in each block. All the entries are arranged randomly within a block and a new randomization pattern is used for each block.

Raphides: Needle-like crystals that occur in bundles in the vacuoles of some plant cells.

Rate limiting enzyme: The enzyme whose activity controls the output of final product from a multi-enzyme metabolic pathway.

Rational drug design: A systematic method of creating compounds by analysing their structure, function and stereochemical interactions.

Ray (ray): Radially oriented tiers of parenchyma cells that conduct food. Water. And other materials laterally in the stems and roots of woody plants; they are generally continuous across the vascular cambium between the xylem and the phloem: the portion within the wood is called a xylem ray, while the extension of the same ray in the phloem is called a phloem ray.

Ray flower: One of the petal-like parts of the flowers of many of the Compositae (Daisy family), such as the Sunflower and Aster.

Read through: Transcription or translation that proceeds beyond the normal stopping point because of the absence of the usual transcription or translation termination signal of a gene.

Reading frame: The reading frame defines which sets of three nucleotides are read as triplets, and hence as codons, in DNA transcription. The start point is usually determined by the initiation codon, AUG. Thus the sequence AUGGCAAAA would be read as AUG/GCA/AAA not as A/UGC/CAA/AA.

Reca: A protein, found in most bacteria, that is essential for DNA repair and DNA recombination.

Recalcitrant: Of seeds, unable to survive drying and subsequent storage at low temperature.

Receptacle or torus: The region at end of pedicel or on axis to which flower is attached; point on a leaf where sporangia are attached.

Receptacle: The commonly expanded tip of a peduncle or pedicel to which the various parts of a flower (e.g., calyx, corolla) are attached.

Receptaculum: A fleshy structure below the seed formed from the bases of bracts and the swollen receptacle or cone axis; e. g., Acmopyle, and some Podocarpus spp.

Receptor: A trans-membrane protein located in the plasma membrane that can bind with a ligand on the extracellular surface, as a result of which it induces a change in activity on the cytoplasmic surface.

Receptor binding screening: A biotechnology-based method for drug discovery, which relies on the fact that many drugs act by binding to specific receptors on or in cells. Since receptors in vivo bind to hormones or to other cells, and thereby control the cell's behaviour, a receptor bound with a drug will likely affect the normal activity of the cell.

Recessive: A condition in which the phenotypic expression of one allele of a gene is masked by the phenotypic expression of another (dominant) allele.

Recessive allele: Allelic state of a gene, where homozygosity is required for the expression of the relevant phenotype.

Recessive oncogene: A single copy of this gene is sufficient to suppress cell proliferation; the loss of both copies of the gene contributes to cancer formation.

Reciprocal cross: The repetition of a cross where the sexual function of the parents is reversed, i.e., female B x male A is the reciprocal of female A x male B.

Reciprocating shaker: A platform shaker used for agitating culture flasks, with a back and forth action at variable speeds.

Reclinate: Reclining, turned or bent downwards upon some other part.

Reclined: Descending at 106-135° angle of divergence.

Recognition site: A nucleotide sequence, typically 4-8bp long and often palindromic, that is recognized by, and at which a restriction endonuclease binds to the DNA. For some restriction endonucleases, the presence of a methylated residue within the recognition site abolishes recognition. Synonym: recognition sequence; restriction site.

Recombinant DNA technology: A set of techniques for manipulating DNA, including: the identification and cloning of genes; the study of the expression of cloned genes; and the production of large quantities of gene product.

Recombinant human (Abbreviation rh): A prefix denoting molecules made through the use of recombinant DNA technology.

Recombinant protein: A protein encoded by a cloned gene. Synonym: heterologous protein.

Recombinant RNA: RNA molecules joined in vitro by T4 RNA ligase.

Recombinant toxin: A single multifunctional toxic protein encoded by a recombinant gene.

Recombinant type: An individual offspring that due to recombination has a combination of alleles different from either of its parents.

Recombinant vaccine: A vaccine produced from a cloned gene.

Recombinant: A term used in both classical and molecular genetics. 1. In classical genetics: An organism or cell that is the result of meiotic recombination. 2. In molecular genetics: A hybrid molecule made up of DNA obtained from different organisms. Typically used as an adjective, e.g. recombinant DNA.

Recombinase: A class of enzymes that are able to alter the arrangement of DNA sequences in a site-specific way.

Recombination fraction: The proportion of recombinant (with respect to two loci) gametes arising from meiosis. Linkage maps are based on estimates of recombination fraction between all pair-wise combinations of loci. Synonyms: recombination frequency, crossing-over unit.

Recombination frequency: Synonym: recombination fraction.

Recombination: The production of a DNA molecule with segments derived from more than one parent DNA molecule. In eukaryotes, this is achieved by the reciprocal exchange of DNA between non-sister chromatids within an homologous pair of chromosomes during prophase of the first meiotic division.

Recombinational hot spot: A chromosomal region where recombination appears to occur more frequently than expected.

Reconstructed cell: A viable transformed cell resulting from genetic engineering.

Recurrent: Running or proceeding backwards towards the axis or costa.

Recurrent selection: Selection of individuals or families and intermating them or allowing them to interpollinate to produce the next generation. Usually the process is repeated several times (for long-lived perennials such as trees) or many times (for annuals.) The technique is used to improve the overall performance of the population rather than to select outstanding varieties for immediate use.

Recurved: Curved downwards or to the abaxial (lower) side.

Red tide: (red tyd) The marine phenomenon that results in the water becoming temporarily tinged with red due to the sudden proliferation of certain dinoflagellates that produce substances poisonous to animal life and humans.

Reduction: division The first division of meiosis in which the chromosome number is reduced from the somatic to the gametic number.

Refugium: An area set aside to provide protection/escape from ecological consequences occurring elsewhere.

Regeneration: The growth of new tissues or organs to replace those injured or lost. In plant tissue culture, regeneration refers to the development of organs or plantlets from an explant.

Regulator: Substance regulating growth and development of cells, organs, etc.

Regulatory gene: A gene with the primary function of controlling the rate of synthesis of the products of one or several other genes or pathways.

Regulatory sequence: A DNA sequence involved in regulating the expression of a gene, e.g. a promoter or operator region (in the DNA molecule).

Rejuvenation: 1. Reversion from adult to juvenile stage. 2. The process of regular reproduction of seed stocks or collections in gene banks, in order to ensure continued viability.

Relaxed plasmid: A plasmid that replicates independently of the bacterial chromosome and is present in 10-500 copies per cell.

Release factor: 1. A soluble protein that recognizes termination codons in mRNAs and terminates translation in response to these codons. 2. A hormone, produced by the hypothalamus, which stimulates the release of a hormone from the anterior pituitary gland into the bloodstream.

Remediation: The cleanup or containment of a hazardous waste disposal site to the satisfaction of the applicable regulatory agency. This can sometimes be accomplished with naturally occurring or engineered micro-organisms or plants.

Remote: Separated from one another; separated by intervals or spaces greater than the ordinary.

Renascent: Springing up afresh each year.

Renaturation: Of DNA, the reforming of two complementary molecules into a double-stranded structure, following heat or chemical induction of dissociation (denaturation). Of protein, the resumption of three-dimensional conformation, allowing the molecule to function normally. Denaturation of many proteins is irreversible, but denatured DNA molecules will renature readily under appropriate chemical and physical conditions.

Reniform: Having the form or shape of a kidney.

Rennin: An enzyme, secreted by cells lining the stomach in mammals, responsible for the clotting of milk. Used in the manufacture of certain dairy products.

Repand: Sinuate with indentions less than 1/16 distance to midrib or midvein.

Repeat unit: A sequence of nucleotides that occurs repeatedly, often in a head-to-tail arrangement (tandemly).

Repent: Said of a stem that is prostrate and rooting at the nodes.

Repetitive DNA: DNA sequences that are present in a genome in many copies, some of it originating from retrotransposon activity. A substantial proportion of all eukaryotic genomes is composed of this class of DNA, whose biological function is uncertain. Sometimes referred to as 'junk DNA'.

Replacement therapy: The administration of metabolites, co-factors or hormones that are deficient as the result of a genetic disease.

Replica plating: Duplicating a population of bacterial colonies growing on agar medium in one Petri plate to agar medium in another Petri plate.

Replicase: A viral enzyme necessary for the replication of the virus in the host cell.

Replicate: With lamina folded once abaxially along midrib or midvein.

Replication fork: Y shaped structure associated with DNA replication. It represents the point at which the strands of double-stranded DNA are separated so that replication can proceed.

Replication: In a genetics test a replication contains one plot of each entry in the test.

Replicative form (RF) : The molecular configuration of viral nucleic acid that is the template for replication in the host cell.

Replicon: The portion of a DNA molecule which can be replicated from a single origin of replication. Plasmids and the chromosomes of bacteria, phages and other viruses usually have a single origin of replication so that their entire genome constitutes a single replicon. Eukaryotic chromosomes have multiple origins of replication, so comprise several replicons. Also used to describe a DNA molecule capable of independent replication.

Replisome: The complete replication apparatus, present at a replication fork, that carries out the replication of DNA.

Replum: A longitudinal partition in an ovary, formed between parietal placentas.

Reporter gene: A gene that encodes a product that can be readily assayed. Used as a marker to confirm the incorporation of a transgene into a cell, organ or tissue, and as a means of testing the efficiency of specific promoters.

Repressible enzyme: An enzyme whose activity can be diminished by the presence of a regulatory molecule.

Repressible gene: A gene whose expression can be diminished or extinguished by the presence of a regulatory molecule.

Repulsion: A double heterozygote in which the dominant (or wild-type) allele at one locus and the recessive (or mutant) allele at a second linked locus occur on the same chromosome (genetic constitution Ab/aB). Synonym: trans configuration.

Residue: 1. Materials remaining after degradation and/or attempted removal, e.g. pesticide residues in food.

Resilience: The ability of a population to persist in a given environment despite disturbance or reduced population size. The resilience of a population is based upon the ability of individuals within the population to survive (fitness) and reproduce (fecundity) in a changed environment and the genetic variability of the population which allows the production of new genotypes.

Resin canal: A tubular duct of many conifers and some angiosperms that is lined with resin-secreting cells.

Resin: Semisolid or viscous substance secreted by conifer wood or bark.

Resinous: Having a yellowish, sticky, exudate.

Resistance: The ability to withstand abiotic (high temperature, drought etc.) or biotic (disease) stress, or a toxic substance. Often in the context of genetic determination of resistance.

Resistance factor: A plasmid that confers antibiotic resistance to a bacterium.

Respiration: The process by which living things breakdown energy containing organic molecules in the presence of oxygen to supply energy for growth and reproduction. Respiration produces carbon dioxide as waste product.

Rest period: A physiological condition of viable seeds, buds or bulbs that prevents growth even in the presence of otherwise favourable environmental conditions. Synonym: dormancy.

Restitution nucleus: A single nucleus arising from a failure of nuclear division, either during meiosis, in which a gamete is formed with the unreduced chromosome number; or at mitosis to give a cell with a doubled chromosome number.

Restriction endonuclease: A class of enzymes that cut DNA after recognizing a specific sequence. The three types of restriction endonuclease are: I. Where the cut occurs within a random sequence at sites >1kbp from the recognition sequence, and has both restriction and methylation activities. II: Cuts within, or near a short, usually palindromic recognition sequence. A separate enzyme methylates the same recognition sequence. III: Cuts 24-26bp downstream from a short, asymmetrical recognition sequence, requires ATP and has both restriction and methylation activities. Type II enzymes are the class used for most molecular biology applications.

Restriction enzyme: An enzyme capable of severing a DNA molecule at a specific site.

Restriction exonuclease: A class of enzymes that degrade DNA or RNA, starting from either the 5'- or the 3'-end.

Restriction fragment length polymorphism (RFLP): A class of genetic marker based on the detection of variation in the length of restriction fragments generated when DNA is treated with restriction endonucleases. Differences in fragment lengths arise due to genetic variation with respect to the presence or absence of specific recognition site(s). RFLPs were initially detected by Southern hybridization but are now detected by electrophoresis of digested PCR product.

Restriction fragment: A shortened DNA molecule generated by the cleavage of a larger molecule by one or more restriction endonucleases.

Restriction map: The linear arrangement of restriction endonuclease recognition sites along a DNA molecule.

Restriction site: Synonym of recognition site.

Resupinate: Inverted or twisted 180°, as in pedicels in the Orchidaceae.

Reticulocyte: A slightly immature red blood cell.

Reticulodromous: With a single primary vein, the secondary veins not terminating at the margin and losing their identities near the margin by repeated branching, yielding a dense reticulum.

Retinaculum: The hook-like funicle of a seed of a plant of the family Acanthaceae; a band or band-like structure that holds an organ in place.

Retroposon: A transposable element that moves via reverse transcription but lacks the long terminal repeat sequences necessary for autonomous transposition. Much of the repetitive DNA that makes up a large proportion of eukaryotic genomes consists of silenced (i.e. inactive) retroposons. Synonym: retro-transposon.

Retrorse: Bent or directed downward. Retrorsely crenate - rounded teeth directed toward base. Retrorsely serrate-sharp or pointed teeth directed toward base.

Retroviral vectors: Gene transfer systems based on viruses that have RNA as their genetic material.

Retrovirus: A class of eukaryotic RNA viruses that, by using reverse transcription, can form double-stranded DNA copies of their genomes, which can integrate into the chromosomes of an infected cell. Pathogenic retroviruses include HIV and the causative agents of many vertebrate animal cancers.

Reversal transfer: Transfer of a culture from a callus-supporting medium to a shoot-inducing medium.

Reverse transcriptase: An enzyme that uses an RNA molecule as a template for the synthesis of a complementary DNA strand. Synonym: RNA-dependent DNA polymerase.

Reversion: Restitution of a mutant gene to the wild-type condition, or at least to a form that gives the wild-type phenotype; more generally, the appearance of a trait expressed by a remote ancestor. Synonym: reverse mutation.

Revolute: Margins or outer portion of sides rolled outward or downward over lower or dorsal surface.

Rhachilla: The secondary axis of a decompound leaf or inflorescence.

Rhachis: The axis of a compound leaf or inflorescence.

Rheophyte: A flood persistent plant, living between the high and low water levels of rivers.

Rhipidium: An inflorescence of cymose units, the lateral branches developed alternately in opposite directions.

Rhizobium: Prokaryotic species which are able to establish a symbiotic relationship with leguminous plants, as a result of which elemental nitrogen is fixed or converted to ammonia.

Rhizocarpic: Plants having the roots living for many years with the stems dying annually.

Rhizoid: A delicate root- or roothair-like structure of algae, fungi, the gametophytes of bryophytes, and certain structures of a few vascular plants; functions in anchorage and absorption but have no xylem of phloem.

Rhizome: A (usually) underground stem that is horizontally oriented; rhizomes may appear like roots, but have a definite node and internode architecture.

Rhizomucor sp.: The Zygomycetous fungus is reported to be allergenic. It may cause mucorosis in immune compromised individuals. It occupies a biological niche similar to Mucor sp. It is often linked to occupational allergy. May cause mucorosis in immune compromised individuals. The sites of infection are the lung, nasal sinus, brain, eye and skin. Infection may have multiple sites.

Rhizophore: A specialised leafless stem which bears roots, as in selaginella.

Rhizopus sp.: The Zygomycetous fungus is reported to be allergenic. It may cause mucorosis in immune compromised individuals. It occupies a biological niche similar to Mucor sp. It is often linked to occupational allergy. May cause mucorosis in immune compromised individuals. The sites of infection are the lung, nasal sinus, brain, eye and skin. Infection may have multiple sites.

Rhizosphere: The soil region in the immediate vicinity of growing plant roots.

Rhizotaxis: Arrangement of roots.

Rhodotorula sp.: A reddish yeast typically found in moist environments such as carpeting, cooling coils and drain pans. In some countries it is the most common yeast genus identified in indoor air. This yeast has been reported to be allergenic. Positive skin tests have been reported. It has colonized terminally ill patients.

Rhombic: With widest axis at midpoint of structure, and with straight margins; elliptic but margins straight and middle angled.

Rhomboid: A plane of diamond shape.

Rhombus: An outline like a rhomboid, a parallelogram with equal sides, having two oblique angles and two acute angles.

Ri plasmid: A class of large conjugative plasmids found in the soil bacterium Agrobacterium rhizogenes, which can infect certain plants and cause hairy root disease. Like Ti plasmids, Ri plasmids include sequences that are transferred to plant cells and inserted into the plant's DNA as part of the infection process.

RIA: Abbreviation for radioimmunoassay.

Ribonuclease (RNAse): Any enzyme that catalyses the hydrolysis of RNA.

Ribonucleic acid (RNA): An organic acid polymer composed of adenosine, guanosine, cytidine and uridine ribonucleotides. The genetic material of some viruses, but more generally is the molecule, derived from DNA by transcription, that either carries information (messenger RNA), provides sub-cellular structure (ribosomal RNA), transports amino acids (transfer RNA), or facilitates the biochemical modification of itself or other RNA molecules.

Ribose: A monosaccharide found in all ribonucleosides, ribonucleotides and RNA. Its close analogue, 2-deoxyribose, is similarly found in all deoxyribonucleosides, deoxyribonucleotides and DNA.

Ribosomal binding site: A sequence of nucleotides near the 5' end of a bacterial mRNA molecule that facilitates the binding of the mRNA to the small ribosomal sub-unit. Also called the Shine-Delgarno sequence.

Ribosomal DNA: The coding locus for ribosomal RNA. This is generally a large and complex locus, typically composed of a large number of repeat units, separated from one another by the intergenic spacer. A repeat unit comprises a gene copy for each individual ribosomal RNA component, separated from one another by the internal transcribed spacer.

Ribosomal RNA (rRNA): The RNA molecules that are essential structural and functional components of ribosomes, where protein synthesis occurs. Different classes of rRNA molecule are identified by their sedimentation (S) values. E. coli ribosomes contain one 16S rRNA molecule (1541 nucleotides long) in one (small) ribosomal sub-unit, and a 23S rRNA (2904 nucleotides) and a 5S rRNA (120 nucleotides) in the other (large) sub-unit. These three rRNA molecules are synthesized as part of a large precursor molecule which also contains the sequences of a number of tRNAs. Special processing enzymes cleave this large precursor to generate the functional molecules. Constitutes about 80% of total cellular RNA.

Ribosome: A granular particle composed of two subunits consisting of RNA and proteins; ribosomes lack membranes, are the sites of protein synthesis, and are very numerous in living cells.

Ribosome-inactivating protein (RIP): A class of plant proteins that inhibit normal ribosome function, and are thus highly toxic. Type 1 RIPs consist of single polypeptide chain proteins; type 2 (e.g. ricin) consist of two proteins linked by a disulphide bridge, one the toxin and the other a lectin that attaches to recognition sites on a target cell.

Ribozyme: An RNA molecule that can catalyse chemical cleavage of itself or of other RNAs. Synonyms: catalytic RNA, gene shears.

Ribulose: A keto-pentose sugar (C5H11O5) involved in the carbon dioxide fixation pathway of photosynthesis.

Ribulose biphosphate (RuBP): A five-carbon sugar combined with carbon dioxide to form a six-carbon intermediate in the first stage of the dark reaction of photosynthesis.

Rinderpest: Cattle plague; a viral infection of cattle, sheep and goats.

Ringed: With old bud scale scar rings.

RNA: The standard abbreviation for ribonucleic acid, an important cellular molecule that occurs in three forms, all involved in communication between the nucleus and the cytoplasm and in the synthesis of proteins.

RNA editing: Post-transcriptional processes that alter the information encoded in RNAs.

RNA polymerase: A polymerase enzyme that catalyses the synthesis of RNA from a DNA template.

Rogue: To remove trees that have an undesirable phenotype, or that have been shown through progeny tests to have a less desirable genotype from a seed orchard, seed production area, or nursery bed.

Rol genes: A family of genes, present on the Ri plasmid of Agrobacterium rhizogenes, that when transferred to a plant upon infection by the bacterium, induce the formation of roots. Used as a means of root induction on different species and cultivars of micropropagated fruit trees.

Rolled: Sides enrolled, usually loosely, over upper or lower surfaces.

Root: An absorbing and anchoring organ, usually initially developed from the radicle and growing downward. Root cap - parenchymatous, protective apex of root. Root hair - lateral, absorbing outgrowth of the epidermal cell.

Root apex: The apical meristem of a root; very similar to the shoot apical meristem in that it forms the three meristematic areas: the protoderm (develops into the epidermis); the procambium (the stele); and the growth meristem (the cortex).

Root cap: A thimble-shaped mass of cells at the tip of a growing root; functions primarily in protection.

Root culture: The culture of isolated apical or lateral root tips to produce in vitro root systems with indeterminate growth habits. Used to study mycorrhizal, symbiotic and plant-parasitic relationships.

Root cutting: Cutting made from sections of roots alone.

Root hair (root hair): A delicate protuberance that is part of an epidermal cell of a root; root hairs occur in a zone behind the growing tip.

Root nodule: A small round mass of cells attached to the roots of leguminous plants, containing symbiotic nitrogen-fixing bacteroids, particularly Rhizobium spp.

Root pressure: Pressure in the roots which, when the shoot is cut off, will cause liquid to secrete from the root stump; the mechanisms and tissues involved in this process are not clearly understood.

Root tuber: Thickened root that stores carbohydrates.

Root zone: The volume of soil or growing medium containing the roots of a plant. In soil science, the depth of the soil profile in which roots are normally found.

Rootstock: A swollen root and/or part of all of a very short stem, sometimes partly above the ground.

Roridulate or dewy: Covered with waxy platelets, appearing dewy.

Rostellum: A beak-like upward extension of the stigma in orchidaceae.

Rotary shaker: Rotating apparatus with a platform on which liquid media or cultures can be continuously shaken.

Rounded: Margins and apex forming a smooth arc.

Roundup-readya: Describing transgenic crop varieties that carry the bacterial gene which detoxifies the herbicide glyphosate, thereby making them resistant to its application.

RRNA: Abbreviation for ribosomal RNA.

RuBP: Abbreviation for ribulose biphosphate.

Ruderal: Growing in waste places.

Rudimentary: Basal, small nonperipheral embryo in small to large seed; relatively undifferentiated; endosperm copious.

Rufous: Reddish, of all shades.

Ruminate: Describing endosperm that is irregularly grooved or ridged and so appears chewed as, for example, seen in many members of the Myristicaceae.

Runcinate: Pinnatified, with the lobes convex before and straight behind, pointing backward, like the teeth of a saw, as in the dandelion leaf.

Runner: A specialized stolon consisting of a prostrate stem rooting at the node and forming a new plant which eventually becomes detached from the parent plant as in a strawberry plant.

Rupestral: Growing among rocks or on rock walls.

Russetting: The development of brown corky patches on certain fruits, especially apple varieties, in response to various chemicals. Russetting of leaves, tubers, and other plant organs may also occur in response to damage or infection.

Rusts: Plant diseases caused by fungi of the order Uredinales. Rust diseases are easily recognized by streaks of dark pustules on the leaves or stems. Autoecious rusts complete their life cycle on one host whereas heteroecious rusts have an alternate host for some of their spore stages. Many rust fungi cause economically important diseases. Rust of currant is caused by the heteroecious rust Cronartium ribicola whose alternate host is pine. Black stem rust of cereals (Puccinia graminis) has barberry (Berberis) as an alternate host.

S alleles: A multiple allelic series governing incompatibility reactions in certain plant species. Plants possessing the same two S alleles are incompatible. Plants sharing one S allele are semicom-patible in that about half the pollen grains will be able to germinate on the style and subsequently achieve pollination. Such plants are usually indistinguishable from fully compatible plants (plants possessing two different pairs of S alleles) since pollen is usually produced in sufficient quantity to mask the fact that 50% is inviable. S alleles have been found in many fruit crops (e.g. Primus avium), in several grasses, in clover, and in brassicas. There may be more than 40 such alleles in a species and complex dominance relationships are found.

S phase: The phase in the cell cycle during which DNA synthesis occurs.

S1 mapping: A method to characterise post-transcriptional modifications in RNA (removal of introns etc.) by hybridizing RNA with single-stranded DNA and treating with S1 nuclease.

S1 nuclease: An enzyme obtained from the filamentous fungus Aspergillus oryzae which specifically degrades RNA or single-stranded DNA into its constituent mononucleotides, and cleaves nicked double-stranded DNA at the nick.

Sabadilla: A broad-spectrum, short residual (2 days in sunlight) botanical insecticide derived from a South American lily. It can be very toxic to humans in purified form.

Saccate pollen: Pollen with a saccus or sacci; characteristic of many conifers.

Saccate: Furnished with or having the form of a bag, pouch, or sac, as a saccate petal.

Saccharomyces sp.: Reported to be allergenic. Baker's Yeast.

Sacciform: Resembling a pouch.

Saccus: A wing-like or bladder-like extension on a pollen grain.

Safranin: A histological stain that stains lignified cells red.

Sagenoid: Of anastomosing venation with regular areoles with included, free, often branched veinlets pointing in all directions; like species of Tecaria.

Sagittate: Describing a structure shaped like an arrowhead. Sagittate leaves have two barbs extending back behind the point where the petiole is joined to the leaf. They are characteristic of the genus Sagittaria. The marsh arrow-grass (Triglochin palustris) is so named because of its sagittate dehisced fruits.

Sagittiform: Triangular-ovate with two straight or slightly incurved basal lobes.

Salient, porrect, or projected: Pointed outward, usually said of teeth.

Saline resistance: Synonym for salt tolerance.

Salmonella: A genus of rod-shaped, Gram-negative bacteria that are a common cause of food poisoning.

Salsuginous: Growing naturally in soils with a high salt content; halophytic.

Salt: A substance produced by the bonding of ions that remain after hydrogen and hydroxyl ions of an acid and a base combine to form water.

Salt tolerance: The ability of a plant in soil or in culture to withstand a concentration of common salt (sodium chloride) which is damaging or lethal to most other plants. Breeding and selection for increased tolerance and resistance in crop plants is of great current interest. Synonym: saline resistance. An organism with extreme salt tolerance is a halophyte.

Saltation: The movement of soil and mineral particles by intermittent leaps from the ground when particles are being moved by wind or water.

Salverform: Said of a corolla in which the tube is essentially cylindrical, the lobes abruptly spreading; a gamopetalous corolla.

Samara: A type of achene with a pericarp extended into a membranous wing, which aids wind dispersal of the seed. The winged fruits or keys of the ash (Fraxinus excelsior) are an example. The double samara, typical of sycamores and maples (Acer), is a kind of schizocarp.

Samaracetum: An aggregation of samaras, as in Liriodendron.

Samariform: Having the form of a samara.

Sap: Fluid content of the xylem and phloem cells of plants. Fluid content of the vacuole generally referred to as cell sap.

Saponin: Any of a class of bitter-tasting glycosides in which the aglycone portion (the sapogenin) is a steroid alcohol. Saponins are soluble in water, characteristically producing a foam, hence their name. Many are toxic to animals and have been used as fish poisons. Some saponins are important in the commercial production of steroid hormones, notably diosgen, obtained from various yam (Dioscorea) species. The function of saponins in the plant is obscure though they may serve to deter predators.

Saprobe: An organism that obtains its food directly from nonliving organic matter.

Sapromyiophily: Pollinated by carrion or dung flies.

Saprophyte: A plant which obtains all its nutrients from decaying matter; this may be an animal or vegetation. Saprophpytic flowering plants usually have no green color in their leaves, which are usually reduced to scales. The roots of these plants are covered by a cobweb-like growth called fungus mycelium. This isn't harmful to the plant, but helps it obtain nutrients from the decaying matter. There are a few flowering plants that are saprophytic; Monotropa and Ericceae are two. There are many saprophytic bacteria and fungi that obtain their nutrients from decaying matter and help the decaying process. The cultivated Mushroom is an example of a saprophyte as it derives its nourishment from decaying manure. A few saprophytic fungi are the causes of disease in plants.

Sapwood: Outer layers of wood that transport water and minerals in a tree trunk; sapwood is usually lighter in color than heartwood.

Sarcocarp: The fleshy part of certain fruits, between the epicarp and the endocarp; mesocarp; the part of fleshy fruits usually eaten, as in the peach, plum, etc.

Sarment: A runner; a slender running stem, as that of the strawberry.

Sarmentose: Producing slender prostrate branches or runners.

Sartage: The clearing of woodland for agricultural purposes, as by setting fire to the trees.

Satellite DNA: Highly repetitive DNA in plant and animal genomes, consisting of millions of copies of sequences typically in the range 5-500 bp long. Thousands of copies occur tandemly (head-to-tail) at each of many sites. It can be isolated from the rest of the genomic DNA by density gradient centrifugation.

Satellite RNA: A small, self-splicing RNA molecule that accompanies several plant viruses, including tobacco ringspot virus. Synonym: viroid.

Satiny: Of an indumentum of fine haris closely apprese to form a complete, very smooth, more or less shiny cover.

Savanna: A community dominated by species of grass with scattered trees; mostly strongly seasonal.

Saxifragous: Growing in the crevices of rocks and eventually splitting the rock.

SC: Abbreviation for synaptonemal complex.

SCA: Abbreviation for specific combining ability.

Scaberulent: Approaching scabrous.

Scabrid, scarbrous: Rough to touch due to minute, hard projections (dimin. Scabridulous, scaberlous).

Scabridulous: Slightly rough; diminutive of scabrous.

Scabrous a. (L. scabrosus, rough): With small points or knobs, like a file; scaly, scabby, rough.

Scaffold: The central proteinaceous core structure of condensed eukaryotic chromosomes. The scaffold is composed of non-histone chromosomal proteins.

Scalariform: Ladder-like, the markings suggestive of a ladder, eg. Venation.

Scale up: Conversion of a process, such as fermentation of a micro-organism, from a small laboratory scale to a larger industrial scale.

Scales or scale-like leaves: Leaves in the shape of small, flat or thickened triangles.

Scandent: Climbing plant of a creeping or scandent nature.

Scanning electron microscope (SEM): An electron-beam-based microscope used to examine, in a three dimensional screen image, the surface structure of prepared specimens.

Scape: A stem growing from the crown of the root, bearing the blossom without leaves.

Scapose: With a solitary flower on a leafless peduncle or scape, usually arising from a basal rosette.

Scarification: The chemical or physical treatment given to certain seeds having hard, impermeable seed coats in order to puncture or weaken the seed coat sufficiently to permit water uptake and germination.

Schizocarp: A dry fruit, as in the maple, that splits at maturity into two or more one seeded carpels which remain closed.

Science: A branch of study involved with the systematic observation, recording, organization, and classification of facts from which natural laws are derived and used predictively.

Scion stock interaction: The effect of a rootstock on a scion (and vice versa) in which a particular scion grafted onto a specific s performs differently than it would either on its own roots or on a different rootstock.

Scion: A twig, bud, or other vegetative cutting to be grafted onto the root-system of another plant.

Sclereid: A sclerenchyma cell that usually has one axis not conspicuously longer than the other; it may vary in shape and is heavily lignified.

Sclerenchyma: Strengthening tissue composed of relatively short cells (sclereids) and/or relatively long ones (fibres) with secondarily thickened cell walls of lignin and usually lacking a living protoplast at maturity.

Sclerids: Sclerids are classified as sclerenchyma, thick-walled and star-shaped. Sclerids are strengthening cells that are used for strengthening and are dead when functioning. The lumen is very small and the cell wall contains lignin and thus stains red.

Sclerocauly: Hard, dryish stems.

Scleromorph: A plant whose leaves (or stems, if leafless) are hard in texture, usually having thick cuticle and containing many fibres.

Sclerophyllous: With leaves stiffened by sclerenchyma.

Sclerotesta: The middle, fibrous layer of the integument in some seeds.

Scopulariopsis sp.: It may produce arsine gas if growing on arsenic substrate. This can occur on wallpapers covered with paris green. It has been found growing on a wide variety of materials including house dust. It is associated with type III allergy.

Scorpioid: Resembling a scorpion; said of a circinnately coiled determinate inflorescence in which the flowers are two-ranked and borne alternately at the right and left.

Scrapie: A spongiform encephalopathy disease of sheep.

Screening: Selecting for a particular trait, often used when referring to the application of a specific treatment such as white pine blister rust spores or a herbicide, and then looking for resistant individuals. Usually implies checking large number of individuals at one time.

Scribble: Irregular lines on the bark of some eucalypts, being the old tunnels burrowed by moth larvae between bark layers and exposed when the outer layer falls.

Scrobiculate: Marked with minute depressions.

Scurfy or lentiginous: With exfoliating scaly incrustations.

Scutellum: A shield; hence scutate, scutelliform, shield-shaped.

SDS PAGE: Abbreviation for sodium dodecyl sulphate polyacrylamide gel electrophoresis.

Secondary antibody: In an ELISA or other immunological assay system, the antibody designed to bind to the primary antibody, and to which a label is generally attached.

Secondary cell wall: The innermost layer of cell wall, giving rigidity to the cells. Characterized by its highly organized microfibrillar structure, and only formed in certain cells after cell elongation has ceased.

Secondary consumer: An organism that feeds on other consumers.

Secondary growth: Growth in width initiated and maintained by the vascular cambium and cork cambium. The vascular cambium surrounds the core of the stem, branch or root. It creates xylem medially and phloem radially. If present, the cork cambium, a second, outer layer of cambium, creates a new outer layer (typically bark) radially.

Secondary immune response: The rapid immune response that occurs during the second (and subsequent) encounters of the immune system of a mammal with a specific antigen.

Secondary messenger: A chemical compound within a cell that is responsible for initiating the response to a signal from a chemical messenger (such as a hormone) that cannot enter the target cell itself.

Secondary metabolism: The production by living organisms of substances not essential for primary metabolic functions or physiology. Their role is associated with interaction with the environment, for example for defence, as elicitors or as attractants. Some of these have useful pharmacological or nutritional properties, while others are toxic.

Secondary phloem: Phloem tissue formed by the vascular cambium during secondary growth in a vascular plant.

Secondary root: Lateral root with root cap and hairs, derived from the pericycle.

Secondary structure: Localized three dimensional conformations adopted by macromolecules, in particular nucleic acids and polypeptides. These arise as a result of the action of non-covalent forces generated by interactions between residues which are brought into close contact with one another. Examples are alpha-helix regions and beta-pleated sheets in proteins, and hairpin loops in nucleic acids.

Secondary thickening: Of cells, the deposition of lignin or cellulose onto the primary cell wall to give rise to sclerenchyma and collenchyma cells respectively.

Secondary tissue: A tissue produced by the vascular cambium or the cork cambium (e.g., virtually all the xylem and phloem in a tree trunk).

Secondary vascular tissue: Vascular tissue (xylem and phloem) formed by the vascular cambium during secondary growth in a vascular plant.

Secondary xylem: Xylem derived from the vascular cambium in plants exhibiting secondary growth. Wood is secondary xylem.

Secretion: The transport of a molecule from the inside of a cell through the cell membrane.

Secretory cell, tissue: Cell or tissue producing a substance or substances that are moved outside the cells.

Section: A subgroup of a genus used to identify closely related species.

Secund: Arranged or growing on one side only, as flowers or leaves on a stem.

Seed: A fertilized ovule; megasporangium that contains an embryo enclosed in an integument. A seed has been described as "a baby sporophyte in a jacket with a lunch sack." Gymnosperm Evolution. The advantage of a seed is that it can combine the dispersal functions of a spore with sexual reproduction.

Seed coat: The outer boundary layer of a seed; it is developed from the integument(s).

Seed fern: Any of a number of extinct seed-bearing plants with fern-like leaves.

Seed orchard, seedling: A seed orchard established from seedlings (as opposed to grafts). Usually seedling seed orchards are established with multiple-tree plots so that selection can take place first among families and then among the individuals within each family plot, reducing each plot to a single tree.

Seed plants: A monophyletic clade of plants that reproduces by seeds; megagametophyte is retained on the parent sporophyte and enclosed in an integument; microga-metophyte is transferred to the megagametophyte.

Seed production area: A stand or plantation not originally planted to produce seed, but rogued of inferior trees and treated in such a manner as to produce large quantities of seed. Usually the stand or plantation is from a known origin or selected seedlot.

Seed storage proteins: Proteins accumulated in large amounts in protein bodies within seeds. They act as a source of amino acids during germination. Of interest in biotechnology: 1. As a major source of human and animal nutritional protein. 2. As a model expression system. Since they are produced in large amounts relative to other proteins, and are stored in stable, compact bodies in the plant seed, it may be possible to engineer transgenes which are expressed in the same way as seed storage proteins - i.e. in large amounts and in a convenient form.

Seed transfer guide: A set of rules for collecting seed and planting seedlings so that genotypes are not moved to microclimates or soils within which they will be mis-adapted. Usually seed transfer guides describe the maximum movement from the point of collection in miles east and west, north and south as well as feet in elevation.

Seed zone: An area within which seed can be collected from any natural stand and planted in any new site without fear of mis-adaptation.

Seedlot: A designation of a group of seeds with some factor in common, i.e., year of collection, stand or seed orchard, individual "+" trees, point of origin in a provenance test, a half or full-sib family.

Segment polarity gene: A gene that functions to define the anterior and posterior components of body segments in Drosophila.

Segment: A part or sub-division of a divided organ; one of a group of similar organs named collectively, e.g. one petal = a segment of a corolla.

Segregant: An individual derived from a cross between two unlike parents.

Segregation: For genes, the separation of allele pairs from one another and their resulting assortment into different cells at meiosis. For chromosomes, the separation and re-assortment of the two homologues in anaphase of the first meiotic division. For individuals, the occurrence of different genotypes and/or phenotypes among offspring, resulting from chromosome or allele separation in their heterozygous parents.

Selectable marker: A gene whose expression allows the identification of a specific trait or gene in an organism.

Selectable: Having a gene product that, when present, enables the identification and preferential propagation of a particular genotype.

Selection: Choosing individual trees or populations with desirable characters to obtain genetic improvement.

Selection coefficient: A measure of the intensity of selection at a locus, commonly abbreviated as s. It represents the proportionate reduction in the gametic contribution of a particular genotype, compared with the (generally most favoured) standard genotype.

Selection culture: A selection based on difference(s) in environmental conditions or in culture medium composition, such that preferred variant cells or cell lines (presumptive or putative mutants) are favoured over other variants or the wild type.

Selection differential: The difference between the mean of the individuals selected to be parents and the mean of the overall population; it represents the average superiority of the selected parents; commonly abbreviated as S.

Selection pressure: The intensity of selection acting on a population of organisms or on cells in culture. Its effectiveness is measured in terms of differential survival and reproduction, and consequently in changes in allele frequency in a population.

Selection response: The difference between the mean of the individuals selected to be parents and the mean of their offspring. Predicted response is calculated as the product of narrow-sense heritability and selection differential.

Selection, clonal: Choosing the best clones from a clonal test.

Selection, index: Choosing parents on the basis of a weighted score which combines economic value and heritability of several desirable traits.

Selection, mass: (phenotypic selection) Choosing trees on the basis of their phenotypes (appearance) alone.

Selection, recurrent: Choosing individuals out of families, making crosses, then progeny testing. The process is usually repeated several to many times. Most tree improvement programs are based on recurrent selection.

Selection, tandem: Selecting for two or more traits sequentially rather than simultaneously. The technique is useful when one trait can be evaluated early and a second trait only after a number of years, or when one trait is much more expensive to measure.

Self incompatibility: In plants, the inability of the pollen to fertilize ovules (female gametes) of the same plant.

Self pollination: The natural or artificial pollination of a female flower with pollen from the same genotype.

Self replicating elements: Extrachromosomal DNA elements that have origins of replication for the initiation of their own DNA synthesis.

Self sterility: Synonym of self-incompatibility.

Semataxis: Arrangement of semaphylls (petals, sepals, tepals), primarily advertising (pollinator attracting) in function.

Semen sexing: Synonym of sperm sexing.

Semi conservative replication. During DNA duplication, each strand of a parent DNA molecule acts as a template for the synthesis of a new complementary strand. Thus, one half of a pre-existing DNA molecule is conserved during each round of replication.

Semi continuous culture: Cells in an actively dividing state which are maintained in culture by periodically draining off the medium and replenishing it with fresh medium.

Semi permeable membrane: A natural or synthetic material which selectively allows the passage of certain ions or molecules.

Semi sterility: The condition of partial fertility. Often associated with chromosomal aberrations or the result of mutagenesis.

Semicarpous: With ovaries of adjacent carpels partly fused, stigmas and styles separate.

Semiconservative replication: DNA replication mechanism that ensures each daughter molecule has one parental strand and one new strand.

Semicraspedodromous: With a single primary vein, the secondary veins branching just within the margin, one branch from each terminating at the margin and the other forming a marginal loop and joining the superadjacent secondary vein.

Senescence: A late stage in the development of multicellular organisms, during which irreversible loss of function and degradation of biological components occur. The physiological ageing process in which cells and tissues deteriorate and finally die.

Sense RNA: The RNA transcript of the coding strand DNA (often represented as the (+)-strand). Opposite: antisense RNA. When both sense and antisense transcripts of a gene are present simultaneously, gene silencing is often the result.

Sensitivity: In diagnostic tests, the smallest amount of the target molecule that the assay can detect.

Sepal: Any of the leaf divisions of the calyx. When a calyx consists of but one part, it is said to be monosepalous; when of two parts, it is said to be disepalous; when of a variable and indefinite number of parts, it is said to be polysepalous; and when the parts are more or less united, it is said to be gamosepalous.

Sepaliferous: Most frequently at the base of sepals.

Sepaloid: Looking like sepals, e.g. of bracts, usually green and arranged in a ring beneath a flower.

Sepsis: Destruction of tissue by pathogenic micro-organisms or their toxins, especially through infection of a wound.

Septicidal: Dividing through middle of ovary septa; dehiscing or breaking open at a natural dividing line.

Septifragal: Of the dehiscence of a fruit, when the valves or backs of the carpels break away leaving the septa intact.

Septum: A partition separating two cavities or masses of tissue, as in fruits.

Sequence characterized amplified region (SCAR): A molecular marker obtained by the conversion to a sequence-tagged site of a single random amplified polymorphic DNA product.

Sequence divergence: The percent difference in the nucleotide sequence between related nucleic acid sequences, or in the amino acid sequence in a comparison between related proteins.

Sequence hypothesis: The concept that genetic information exists as a linear DNA code, and that DNA and gene product sequence are collinear.

Sequence: The linear order of nucleotides along a DNA or RNA molecule, and the process of obtaining this. Genome sequencing aims to generate the linear order of all nucleotides present in the nuclear DNA of an organism.

Sequence-tagged site (STS): Short unique DNA sequence (200-500 bp long) that can be amplified by PCR and is thus tagged to the site on the chromosome from which it was amplified.

Serial division: Splitting of excised shoot-tip material growing in vitro, in order to induce the development of greater numbers of plantlets.

Serial float culture: A technique whereby immature anthers are floated on a liquid medium, and continue their development through to the release of pollen.

Serology: The study of serum reactions between an antigen and its antibody. Mainly used to identify and distinguish between antigens, such as those specific to particular micro-organisms or viruses.

Serotinal: Opening late; appearing in late summer.

Serpula lacrymans: Common cause of extrinsic asthma (immeadiate-type hypersensitivity: type I). Acute symptoms include edema and bronchiospasms, chronic cases may develop pulmonary emphysema.

Serrate: Notched on edge like a saw; having sharp notches along the edge pointing toward the apex; as, a serrate leaf. When a serrate leaf has small serratures upon the large ones, it is said to be double serrate, as in the elm. A serrate-ciliate leaf is one having fine hairs, like eyelashes, on the serratures. A serrate-dentate leaf has the serratures toothed.

Serrulate: Diminutive of serrate, but cut to 1/16 distance to midrib or midvein.

Serum albumin: A globular protein obtained from blood and body fluids. Bovine and human serum albumins are abbreviated BSA and HSA respectively.

Serum: Blood plasma that has had its clotting factor removed.

Sessile: Sitting directly on base without support, stalk, pedicel, or peduncle; attached or stationary as opposed to free living or motile.

Seta: This incredibly over-used anatomical term is simply Latin for a bristle or a stiff hair. It is used in a variety of contexts, not only for things that look like bristles (or, to be sure, stiff hairs), but also for things like the stalk of the sporophyte in mosses, which looks nothing like a bristle (or, for that matter, a stiff hair).

Sewage treatment: A widespread biotechnological processes in developed economies. Methods vary widely, but all are designed for the biological break-down of human and animal waste in order to allow safe discharge into the environment.

Sex chromosome: Differentiated chromosome which is responsible for the determination of sex of the individual. For all mammals, a small number of flowering plants and many insects, female individuals carry a pair of X chromosomes, and males carry one X and one Y. For birds, reptiles and most amphibians, male individuals carry a pair of W chromosomes, and females carry one W and one Z. In some insects there is only one sex chromosome, X, and sex is determined by the number of these present. Synonym: allosome. Opposite: autosome.

Sex determination: Any method by which the distinction between males and females is established in a species, particularly at an early stage of foetal development.

Sex duction: The incorporation of bacterial genes into F factors and their subsequent transfer, by conjugation, to a recipient cell.

Sex factor: A bacterial episome (e.g. the F plasmid in E. coli) that enables the cell to be a donor of genetic material. The sex factor may be propagated in the cytoplasm, or it may be integrated into the bacterial chromosome.

Sex hormones: Steroid hormones that control sexual development in animals.

Sex influenced dominance: The tendency for gene action to vary between the sexes within a species. For example, the presence of horns in some breeds of sheep appears to be dominant in males but recessive in females.

Sex limited: Expression of a trait in only one sex; e.g. milk production in mammals; egg production in chickens.

Sex linkage: Referring to genes present on one of the sex chromosomes, thus genetically linked to the sex of the individual.

Sex mosaic: Synonym of gynandromorph.

Sexed embryos: Embryos separated according to sex.

Sexual reproduction: The process whereby two gametes fuse to form one fertilized cell (zygote).

Sexual: Concerned with reproduction through the union of male and female gametes to form a zygote which develops into a new plant.

Shake culture: An agitated suspension in culture providing adequate aeration for cells in the liquid medium. Usually achieved using platform shakers, or by constant stirring with a magnetic stirrer.

Shaker: A platform, with set or variable speed control, used to agitate vessels containing liquid cell cultures. Also described as a platform shaker.

Shear: Literally the sliding of one layer across another, with deformation and fracturing in the direction parallel to the movement. In the present context, used to describe 1. the forces that cells are subjected to in a bioreactor or a mechanical device used for cell breakage. 2. the intentional or unintentional fragmentation of large DNA molecules, achieved commonly by passing a concentrated DNA solution through a hypodermic needle. This treatment generates random breaks in the DNA, and the average size of fragments can be manipulated by varying the bore of the needle.

Sheath: Any more or less tubular portion of the leaf surrounding the stem or culm, as in the poaceae.

Shine dalgarno sequence: A conserved sequence of prokaryotic mRNAs that is complementary to a sequence near the 5' terminus of the 16S ribosomal RNA and is involved in the initiation of translation.

Shoot: A young branch which shoots out from the main stock.

Shoot differentiation: The development of growing points, leaf primordia and finally shoots from a shoot tip, axial bud, or callus surface.

Shoot tip graft: A shoot tip or meristem tip grafted onto a prepared seedling or micropropagated rootstock in culture. Meristem tip grafting is mainly used for in vitro virus elimination from Citrus spp. and other plants.

Shoot tip: The terminal bud (0.1 - 1.0 mm) of a plant, which consists of the apical meristem (0.05 - 0.1 mm) and the immediately surrounding leaf primordia and developing leaves, and adjacent stem tissue.

Short day plant: A plant which will not flower until triggered to do so by exposure to one or a number of dark periods equal to or longer than its critical period. Other plant species are long-day and some are daylength neutral. Genetic variation for daylength sensitivity is present in many crop species.

Short-day plant (short-day plant): A plant in which flowering is initiated when the days are shorter than its critical photoperiod.

Shotgun genome sequencing: A strategy for sequencing a whole genome, in which the genomic DNA is initially fragmented into pieces small enough to be sequenced. Specialized computer software is then used to piece together the individual sequences to create long contiguous tracts of sequenced DNA.

Shrub: A woody plant less than 5 metres high, either without a distinct main axis, or with branches persisting on the main axis almost to its base.

Shuttle vector: A plasmid capable of replicating in two different host organisms because it carries two different origins of replication and can therefore be used to transfer genes from one to the other. Synonym: bifunctional vector.

Sib (sibling): A term meaning brother or sister. Half sibs have one parent in common. Full sibs have both parents in common.

Sib mating: The deliberate crossing of siblings. Generally done where self-incompatibility prevents the production of self-fertilized progeny.

Siderophore: A low molecular weight entity that binds very tightly to iron. Siderophores are synthesized by a variety of soil micro-organisms to ensure that the organism is able to obtain sufficient amounts of iron from the environment.

Sieve cell: A long and slender sieve element in vascular plants, characterized by relatively unspecialized sieve areas and tapering end walls that lack sieve plates.

Sieve element: The phloem cell concerned with longitudinal conduction of food materials.

Sieve plate: An area of the wall of a sieve tube member that contains several to many perforations that permit cytoplasmic connec1ions between similar adjacent cells, the cytoplasmic strands being larger than plasmodesmata.

Sieve tube member: A single cell of II sieve tube.

Sieve tube: Of phloem, a continuous longitudinal tube characterised by sieve plates, non-lignified secondary cell walls and a living protoplast.

Sieve-plates: Of sieve tubes; a perforated modification of the end walls between adjacent elongated sieve tube elements.

Sigma factor: The sub-unit of prokaryotic RNA polymerases responsible for the initiation of transcription at specific initiation sequences.

Signal sequence: A stretch of 15-30 amino acid residues at the N terminus of a protein, which is thought to enable the protein to be secreted (pass through a cell membrane). The signal sequence is removed as the protein is secreted. Synonyms: signal peptide, leader peptide.

Signal to noise ratio: A specifically produced response (signal) compared to the response level (noise) when no specific stimulus (activity) is present.

Signal transduction: The biochemical events that conduct the signal of a hormone or growth factor from the cell exterior, through the cell membrane, and into the cytoplasm. This involves a number of molecules, including receptors, ligands and messengers.

Silencing: Loss of gene expression either through an alteration in the DNA sequence of a structural gene, or its regulatory region; or because of interactions between its transcript and other mRNAs present in the cell.

Siliceous: Containing crystals of silica.

Silicle: A dry, dehiscent fruit derived from two or more carpels that dehisce along two sutures and which has a persistent partition after dehiscence and is as broad as, or broader, than long.

Silicula: A short siliqua, not more than twice as long as its width.

Siliqua: A dry, dehiscent fruit formed from a superior ovary of two carpels, with two parietal placentas and divided into two loculi by a false septum between the placentas.

Silique: The long, narrow pod of plants of the mustard family, Cruciferae, with valves which fall away from a frame bearing the seeds.

Silky: With a covering of very fine, more or less appressed, lustrous hairs.

Single copy: A gene or DNA sequence which occurs only once per (haploid) genome. Many structural genes are single copy.

Single node culture: Culture of separate lateral buds, each carrying a piece of stem tissue.

Single nucleotide polymorphism (SNP): A genetic marker resulting from variation in sequence at a particular position within a DNA sequence. SNPs are commonly the result of transition changes (A for G, T for C), but also transversions (G or A for T or C) and single base deletions. Such variation is extensive throughout all genomes, and offers the particular advantage of being detectable without the need for gel electrophoresis.

Single primer amplification reaction (SPAR): A PCR-based genotyping technique in which genomic template is amplified with a single primer.

Single strand conformational polymorphism (SSCP): A technique for detection of mutations in a defined DNA sequence. Single-stranded polynucleotides are electrophoretically separated on non-denaturing gels. Intrachain base pairing results in a limited number of conformers stabilized by intrachain loops, and mutated DNA shows on electrophoresis an altered assortment of such conformers.

Single strand DNA binding protein: A protein that coats single-stranded DNA, preventing renaturation and so maintaining the DNA in an extended state.

Single stranded nucleic acid: Nucleic acid molecules consisting of only one polynucleotide chain. The genomes of many viruses are single-stranded DNA molecules, as are most biologically effective RNAs. Many RNA molecules do include double-stranded regions formed by the intra-strand base-pairing of self-complementary sequences, and these determine the 3-dimensional shape (conformation) that they adopt in vivo.

Sinistrorse: Rising helically from left to right, a characteristic of twining stems.

Sinuate: Long horizontal curves in the body of the structure parallel to the central axis.

Sinus membrane: A hyaline flap of tissue occurring in the base of the sinus in some ferns.

Sinus: The rounded depression between two consecutive lobes. as of a leaf. pl. sinuses, sinus.

Siphonestele: A cylindrical stele with a hollow parenchymatous centre; amphiphloic siphonostele (solenostele) has phloem on both the inside and outside of the cylinder, an ectophloic siphonostele (medullated protostele) has phloem on the outside only.

Sister chromatid exchange (SCE): Reciprocal interchanges of the two chromatid arms within a single chromosome.

Site specific mutagenesis: The induction of mutations, by molecular biology techniques, in one or more specific nucleotides within a defined coding sequence in order to create altered forms of the gene product. Used to define the active sites of proteins and for protein engineering.

Site specific: A term used to describe any process or enzyme which acts at a defined sequence within a DNA or RNA molecule.

Six base cutter: Type II restriction endonucleases whose recognition site and cleavage site consist of a characteristic sequence of six nucleotide pairs.

Slime mold: A simple organism that moves like an amoeba but resembles a fungus when reproducing.

Slime-plugs: Of phloem sieve-tubes, where the sieve-tube contents are deposited at sieve plates and a thin strand extends through the centre of the tube element. Caused by damage to the sieve-tubes.

Slough: A wet place of deep mud or mire; a sluggish channel; a swamp, bog, or marsh, especially one that is part of an inlet or backwater.

Small nuclear ribonucleoprotein (snRNP): A complex of small nuclear RNA and nuclear protein, heavily involved in the post-transcriptional processing of mRNA, especially the removal of introns. snRNPs are a major component of spliceosomes.

Small nuclear RNA (snRNA): RNA transcripts of 100-300 bp that associate with proteins to form small nuclear ribonucleoprotein particles. Most snRNAs are components of the spliceosomes.

Soboliferous: With loosely clumped shoots arising some distance apart from rhizomes or under ground suckers.

Sodium dodecyl sulphate (SDS): A detergent used to solubilize protein and DNA from biological materials. Specific use in sodium dodecyl sulphate polyacrylamide gel electrophoresis.

Sodium dodecyl sulphate polyacrylamide gel electrophoresis (SDS-PAGE): A widely employed electrophoretic method for the separation of proteins from biological samples. The sodium dodecyl sulphate gives a uniform charge density to the surface of proteins or nucleic acids, so that their rate of migration through the gel is determined largely by their molecular weight.

Soil amelioration: The improvement of poor soils. Includes the fungal and bacterial break down of plant organic matter, to form humus; the release of minerals - such as phosphates - to the soil, making them available to plants; the fixation of nitrogen. Can sometimes include an element of bioremediation.

Soil less culture: Growing plants in nutrient solution without soil. Synonym: hydroponics.

Solenostele: A siphonostele having phloem both internal and external to the xylem.

Solid medium: Nutrient medium solidified by the addition of a gelling agent, commonly agar.

Solitary: Occurring singly and not borne in a cluster or group, such as a solitary lily flower.

Solute: Anything dissolved in a solvent. In salt water, the water is the solvent, and the salts are solutes.

Solvent: A substance (usually liquid) capable of dissolving another substance.

Somaclonal variation: Epigenetic or genetic changes induced during the callus phase of plant cells cultured in vitro. Sometimes visible as changed phenotype in plants regenerated from culture.

Somatic cell: Cells not involved in sexual reproduction, i.e. not germ cells.

Somatic cell embryogenesis: The process of differentiation of somatic embryos either from explant cells (direct embryogenesis), or from callus generated from explants (indirect embryogenesis). Synonym: asexual embryogenesis.

Somatic cell gene therapy: The delivery of a transgene(s) to a somatic tissue in order to correct a physiological defect.

Somatic cell hybrid panel: A panel of cells created by cell fusion, typically involving a reference species (e.g. hamster) and the species of interest (e.g. sheep) with each member of the panel containing a different mixture of chromosomes from the two species. By relating the presence or absence of cloned fragments (via in situ hybridization) or PCR products to the presence or absence of particular chromosomes from the species of interest, such panels can be used for physical mapping.

Somatic cell variant: A somatic cell with unique characters not present in the other cells, and which could be selected for by an appropriate screen.

Somatic embryo: An organized embryo-like structure. Although morphologically similar to a zygotic embryo it is initiated from somatic plant cells. Under in vitro conditions, somatic embryos go through developmental processes similar to embryos of zygotic origin. Each somatic embryo is potentially capable of developing into a normal plantlet.

Somatic hybrid: A plant produced by protoplast fusion.

Somatic hybridization: Naturally occurring or induced fusion of somatic protoplasts or cells of two genetically different parents. The difference may be as wide as interspecific. Wide synthetic hybrids formed in this way (i.e. not via gametic fusion) are known as cybrids. Not all cybrids contain the full genetic information (nuclear and non-nuclear) of both parents.

Somatic hypermutation: The high frequency of mutation that occurs in the gene segments encoding the variable regions of immunoglobulins during the differentiation of B lymphocytes into antibody producing plasma cells.

Somatic mutation: A mutation in a somatic (body) cell; such a mutation is not passed on to offspring.

Somatic reduction: Halving of the chromosomal number of somatic cells; a possible method of producing "haploids" from somatic cells and calli by artificial means.

Somatocrinin: Growth hormone-releasing hormone.

Sonication: Disruption of cells or DNA molecules by high frequency sound waves.

Sori: Clusters of sporangia on the undersides of fern fronds.

Sorophore: Specialised sporangia-bearing lobes of the leaf margin in species of Schizaeaceae.

Sorosis: Fruits on a common axis that are usually coalesced and derived from the ovaries of several flowers, as in morus.

Sorus: A cluster or group of sporangia of a fern; most frequently applied to clusters of fern sporangia attached to the bottom of fern leaves.

SOS response: The synthesis of a whole set of DNA repair, recombination and replication proteins in bacteria suffering severe DNA damage (e.g. following exposure to UV light).

Source DNA: The DNA from an organism that contains a target gene, and used as the starting material in a cloning experiment.

Source organism: A bacterium, plant or animal from which DNA is purified and used in a cloning experiment.

Southern blot: A nitrocellulose or nylon membrane to which DNA fragments previously separated by gel electrophoresis, have been transferred by capillary action.

Southern hybridization: A procedure in which a cloned, labelled segment of DNA is hybridized to DNA restriction fragments on a Southern blot.

Spacer sequence: A DNA sequence separating neighbouring genes; spacer sequences are not usually transcribed.

Spadix: A racemose inflorescence with elongated axis, sessile flowers, and an enveloping spathe; a succulent spike; a fleshy spike of flowers, usually enclosed in a spathe.

SPAR: Abbreviation for single primer amplification reaction.

Sparger: A device that introduces, into a bioreactor, air in the form of fine bubbles.

Spathaceous: Having a spathe, or having the nature of a spathe.

Spathe: A large leaflike part or pair of such enclosing a flower cluster (especially a spadix).

Spathella: A closed membranous sac which envelopes the immature flower in some podostemaceae, rupturing irregularly as the pedicel elongates at anthesis.

Spathulate: Spoon-shaped; broad at the tip and narrowed towards the base.

Spatial autocorrelation statistics: A set of statistical parameters aimed to depict the spatial (geographical) pattern of genetic diversity in a population.

Spatulate: Shaped like a spatula or spoon, gradually widening distally and with a rounded tip, as some leaves.

Speciation: The evolutionary differentiation of a pre-existing species into one or more distinct species.

Specific combining ability (SCA): A component of genetic variance calculable where a number of genotypes are intercrossed in all possible combinations. The SCA measures the deviation of the performance of a particular cross from the average general combining ability of its two parents.

Sperm competition: Competition between different spermatozoa to fertilize the egg cell of a single female.

Sperm sexing: The separation of mammalian sperm into those bearing an X chromosome and those bearing a Y chromosome, in order to be able to produce, via artificial insemination or in vitro fertilization, animals of a specified sex. Methods for achieving this include the inactivation of X-bearing or Y-bearing sperm by antibodies recognizing sex-specific sperm surface peptides, and fluorescence-activated cell sorting.

Sperm: A male gamete; except for those of red algae and angiosperms. Sperms are frequently motile and are usually smaller than the corresponding female gametes.

Spermatid: Immature spermatozoon. One of the four cells formed at the end of the second meiotic division in spermatogenesis.

Spermatocyte: The premeiotic parental cell of the spermatids; the primary spermatocyte before the initiation of the first meiotic division; the secondary spermatocyte after completion of the first meiotic division, but before the initiation of the second division. Synonym: sperm mother cell.

Spermatogenesis: The series of cell divisions in the testis as a result of which the formation and the maturation of the male gametes (i.e. sperm) are achieved.

Spermatogonium: Primordial male germ cell. These can either divide by mitosis to produce daughter cells, or enter a growth phase and differentiate into a primary spermatocyte.

Spermatophyta: A major division of the plant kingdom, characterized by reproducing by seed and subdivided into the Gymnos-permae and Angiospermae.

Spermatophyte: A seed plant.

Spermatozoon: The mature, mobile gametic cell of male animals, produced in the testis.

Sphagnum moss: A type of moss which retains moisture well and is sometimes used in propagation such as in aerial layering. Its use is not recommended, as serious damage is caused during its extraction from the fragile areas in which it grows.

Spharoblast: Nodule of wood which can give rise to adventitious shoots with juvenile characteristics.

Spherical: With multi-dimensional radial symmetry.

Spheroplast: A microbial or plant cell from which most of the cell wall has been removed, usually by enzymatic treatment. Strictly, in a spheroplast, some of the cell wall remains, while in a protoplast the cell wall has been completely removed. In practice, the two words are often used interchangeably.

Sphingophily: Pollinated by hawk moths and nocturnal lepidoptera.

Spicate: Having the form of a spike.

Spice: An aromatic organic plant product used to season or flavor food or drink.

Spiculate: With crystals in or on the surface.

Spicule: A small, slender, sharp-pointed piece, usually on a surface; a small spike of flowers.

Spike: 1. An inflorescence in which the main axis is elongated and the flowers are sessile. 2. The deliberate addition of a known quantity of a known substance to an analytical sample, used to validate the analytical technique.

Spikelet or locusta: A unit of the inflorescence in grasses, sedges and some other monocotyledons, consisting of one to many flowers and associated glumes.

Spindle: An aggregation offiberlike threads (microtubules) that appears in cells during mitosis and meiosis; some threads are attached to the centromeres of chromosomes, whereas other threads extend directly or in arcs between two invisible points designated as poles.

Spine: A stiff sharp-pointed plant process as a modified leaf, leaf part, petiole, or stipule.

Spinescent: Terminated by a spine; modified to form a spine.

Spinose or pungent: Acuminate but coriaceous and stiff.

Spiral: Of leaves or floral organs, borne at different levels on the axis, in an ascending spiral.

Spirolobal: With incumbent cotyledons folded once.

Spliceosome: A complex of small nuclear ribonucleoproteins and other proteins that assemble on an immature mRNA and catalyse the excision of an intron.

Splicing: 1. During the maturation of eukaryotic mRNA, the process that removes intron sequences and covalently joins exon sequences. Synonym: editing. 2. In recombinant DNA technology, the term refers to the ligation of two fragments of DNA together.

Splicing junction: The DNA sequence immediately surrounding the boundary between an exon and an intron. There is a degree of sequence conservation in these regions, allowing the identification of introns in newly sequenced genes.

Split gene: In eukaryotes, the encoding DNA of many structural genes is made up of exons and introns. This commonly found pattern of interruption in the coding sequence is referred to as a 'split gene'.

Spongy: Cellular; sponge-like

Spontaneous mutation: A mutation occurring in the absence of any known mutagen.

Sporangia: Spore-producing structures in ferns.

Sporangiophore: The umbrella-shaped sporangium-bearing unit of the strobilus, as in Equisetum.

Sporangium: A reproductive structure in plants that produces spores. A megasporangium produces megaspores, which give rise to the female gametophyte; in seed plants it is represented by the ovule. A microsporangium produces microspores, which give rise to the male gametophyte; it is represented in seed plants by the pollen sac.

Spore mother cell: Synonym of sporocyte.

Spore: A reproductive cell or aggregation of cells capable of developing directly into a gametophyte or other body without uniting with another cell; sexual spores formed as a result of meiosis are often called meiospores; spores produced by mitosis may be referred to as vegetative spores.

Sporeling: A very young fern plant developing from the prothallas after fertilization.

Sporobolomyces sp.: Reported to be allergenic.

Sporocarp: A hard, nut-like structure containing the sporangia in heterosporous ferns.

Sporocyte: A diploid cell that becomes four haploid spores or nuclei as a result of undergoing meiosis.

Sporogenous: Of cells or tissues, in which spores are formed.

Sporophyll: Leaf-like or foliaceus organ bearing reproductive parts or organs (particularly spores).

Sporophyte: The diploid (2n) spore-producing phase of the life cycle of an organism exhibiting Alternation of Generations.

Sporopollenin: The highly resistant material making up the exine of spores and pollen grains. It is a polymerized carotenoid, capable of withstanding temperatures approaching 300°C and strong acids.

Sporotrichum sp.: Reported to be allergenic. This genera does not cause sporotrichosis.

Sport: An individual plant, or portion thereof, showing a recognizably different phenotype from the parent, presumably as a result of spontaneous mutation. Novel traits displayed by some sports can become of great agricultural worth, but generally they are disadvantageous.

Spotted: The color disposed in small spots.

Spur: A slender, tubelike structure formed by an extension of one or more petals or sepals; also refers to a very short branch with closely spaced leaves.

Squamose: Scaly or scale-like (dimin. Squamulose).

Squamule: A small papery scale; hence squamulose.

Squarrose: Usually sharply curved downward or outward in the apical region, as the bracts of some species of Aster.

Stachybotrys sp.: Several strains of this fungus may produce a trichothecene mycotoxin- Satratoxin H - which is a poisonous by inhalation. The toxins are present on the fungal spores. This is a slow growing fungus on media. It does not compete well with other rapidly growing fungi. The dark colored fungi grows on building material with a high cellulose content and a low nitrogen content. Areas with relative humidities above 55% and are subject to temperature fluctuations are ideal for toxin production. Individuals with chronic exposure to the toxin produced by this fungus reported cold and flu symptoms, sore throats, diarrhea, headaches, fatigue, dermatitis, intermittent local hair loss and generalized malaise. The toxins produced by this fungus will suppress the immune system affecting the lymphoid tissue and the bone marrow. Animals injected with the toxin from this fungus exhibited the following symptoms, necrosis and hemorrhage within the brain, thymus, spleen, intestine, lung, heart, lymph node, liver, and kidney. Affects by absorption of the toxin in the human lung are known as pneumomycosis. This organism is rarely found in outdoor samples. It is usually difficult to find in indoor air samples unless it is physically disturbed or if there is (speculation- a drop in the relative humidity). The spores are in a gelatinous mass. Appropriate media for the growth of this organism will have a high cellulose content and a low nitrogen content. The spores will die readily after release. The dead spores are still allergenic and toxigenic. Percutaneous absorption has caused mild symptoms.

Stacked genes: Refers to the insertion of two or more genes into the genome of an organism. An example would be a plant carrying a Bt transgene giving insect resistance, and a bar transgene giving resistance to a specific herbicide.

Staggered cuts: Symmetrically cleaved phosphodiester bonds that lie on both strands of double-stranded DNA, but are not opposite one another.

Stalk: The stem or main axis of a plant, which supports the leaves, flowers, and fruit. Any lengthened support on which an organ grows, as the petiole of a leaf or the peduncle of a flower.

Stamen: The male reproductive organs in flowers; it is situated immediately within the petals, and is composed, in most cases, of two parts, the filament, and the anther, which is filled with pollen.

Staminal: Most frequently at base of filament.

Staminate: a. Producing or consisting of stamens; flowers with stamens but not pistils.

Staminode: A sterile stamen, often rudimentary.

Staminodial: Frequently entire structure is nectariferous.

Staminodium: Sterile stamen, may be modified as a nectary or petaloid structure. Staminal Disc - A fleshy, elevated cushion formed from coalesced staminodia or nectaries

Staminophore: A band of tissue around the apex of the hypanthium in a eucalypt flower on which the stamens are inserted.

Standard deviation: A statistical measure of variability in a population of individuals or in a set of data.

Standard error: A statistical measure that indicates the predictive accuracy over all individuals of a mean value derived from a sample population.

Standard, banner, or vexillum: The upper, usually wide petal in a papilionaceous corolla.

Standing crop: Weight or organic material that can be sampled or harvested at any one time from a given area, but may not necessarily include the entire plant. Usually refers to normal harvesting procedures, unless specified, for the particular plant under consideration.

Starch: The major plant carbohydrate storage substance, particularly but not exclusively found in seeds, and used both as food and feed source and for various industrial processes. A large water-insoluble heterogenous group of polysaccharides, consisting of various proportions of the two glucose polymers, amylose and amylopectin. Starch is broken down into simple metabolisable sugars in vivo by the action of amylases.

Start codon: The codon which specifies the first amino acid of a polypeptide chain and at which the ribosome starts the process of translation. In bacteria, this is either AUG (translated as n-formyl methionine) or, rarely, GUG (valine). In eukaryotes, it is always AUG and is translated as methionine. The start codon sets the reading frame for translation. Synonym: initiation codon.

Starter culture: Micro-organisms that are deliberately added to foods to alter flavour, colour, texture, smell, or taste.

Stationary phase: The plateau of the growth curve, during which cell number remains relatively constant, following the logarithmic phase.

Steady state: In a continuous fermentation process, the condition under which the number of cells removed with the outflow is exactly balanced by the number of newly synthesized cells.

Stele: The central primary vascular system of the stem and associated tissues delimited from the cortex by endodermis and pericycle, Delimited from the cortex by endodermis and pericycle.

Stellate: Starlike; said of hairs that branch in such a manner as to radiate from a central point.

Stem cell: An undifferentiated somatic cell that is capable of either division to give rise to daughter stem cells, or differentiating into any specialized cell type given the appropriate signals. Cultured stem cells are critical to the concept of therapeutic cloning.

Stem tuber: Swollen structures produced by stolons and runners which remain dormant during adverse conditions and later grow into new plants when the conditions become favorable for growth.

Stem: Main axis of a plant typically above the soil surface, having leaves or scales, and a characteristic arrangement of the vascular tissue.

Stemphylium sp.: Reported to be allergenic. Isolated from dead plants and cellulose materials.

Stereomorphic: Flowers 3-dimensional with basically radial symmetry; parts many or reduced, and usually regular; e.g., Narcissus, Aquilegia.

Sterile room: Dedicated space for the carrying out of activities that require sterile conditions. Can usually be achieved more economically with a laminar air-flow cabinet.

Sterile: Barren, not producing seed, pollen or spores capable of germination; of a plant lacking reproductive organs.

Sterility: Complete or partial failure of an individual to produce functional gametes or viable zygotes under a given set of environmental conditions.

Sterilize: 1. The elimination of micro-organisms, using heat, irradiation, filtration or chemicals. 2. The operation of making an animal incapable of producing offspring.

Steward bottle: Flask developed for the growth of cells and tissues in a liquid medium, in which they can be periodically submerged during rotation.

Stigma: The distal part of the pistil, the organ that receives the pollen.

Stigmata may be quite varied in shape and structure. They are often button-shaped and studded with hair-like papillae ("dry" stigmata) or coated with a sticky film ("wet" stigmata) to capture pollen.

Stilt-roots: Oblique adventitious roots from the stem.

Stinging urent: With erect, usually long trichomes that produce irritation when touched

Stipe, podogyne, carpopodium: The stalk-like basal part of an ovary, or of a fruit such as an achene; the stem bearing pileus in mushrooms and toadstools.

Stipel: A small secondary stipule at the base of a leaflet.

Stipellate: With stipels.

Stipels: Paired scales, spines, or glands at the base of petiolule

Stipitate: Stalked; borne on a stipe; of an ovary, borne on a gynophore.

Stipule: One of two foliaceous or membranaceous processes developed at base of a leaf petiole, sometimes in tendril or spine form, sometimes fused.

Stirred tank fermenter: A growth vessel in which cells or micro-organisms are mixed by mechanically-driven impellers.

Stock: The lower portion of a graft.

Stock plant: The source plant from which cuttings or explants are obtained. Stock plants should be well maintained to optimize explant and cutting quality.

Stock solution: Pre-prepared solution of commonly used reagents.

Stolon: Stolons are modified stems whose purpose is to spread the plant over the surface of the ground. Stolons in strawberries will run out from a given strawberry plant, form a single node in the middle and then at the second node it will form a new plant will form.

Stoloniferous: Having stolons; trailing over the soil surface and rooting at the nodes.

Stoma: 1. Any of various small openings or pores in an animal body, especially an opening resembling a mouth in various invertebrates. 2. A pore in the epidermis of the leaf or stem of a plant, which allows the exchange of gases, including water vapour, to and from the intercellular spaces. Sometimes used loosely to refer to the pore along with its associated pair of guard cells.

Stomatal complex: Includes the stoma, together with its guard cells and, when present, any related subsidiary cells.

Stomatal index: A measurement of the surface density of stomata. This parameter has been found useful in comparing leaves of different sizes. Relative humidity and light intensity during leaf development affect the value of stomatal index.

Stomium: The opening of the annulus in a sporangium through dehiscence occurs and the spores are shed, often marked by thin-walled, enlarged cells.

Stop codon: A set of three nucleotides for which there is no corresponding tRNA molecule to insert an amino acid into the polypeptide chain. Protein synthesis is hence terminated and the completed polypeptide released from the ribosome. Three stop codons are known: UAA (ochre), UAG (amber) and UGA (opal). Synonyms: chain terminator; nonsense codon, termination codon.

STR: Abbreviation for sequence tandem repeat.

Strain: A group of individuals derived by descent from a single individual within a species.

Stramineous: Straw coloured.

Stratification: Subjection of moist seeds to a period of low temperature (+2 to +4 °C) to break dormancy.

Streptavidin: A microbial protein with a high affinity for the B complex vitamin biotin. The specific interaction of these two molecules has been exploited in labelling technology and in applications where a specific molecule needs to be captured or purified.

Streptophytes: The clade consisting of the plants plus their closest relatives, the charophytes.

Stress: Non-optimal conditions for growth. Stresses may be imposed by biotic (pathogens, pests) or abiotic (environment, such as heat, drought etc.) factors.

Stria: A fine longitudinal line or ridge; hence striate (pl. Striae).

Striate: Striped with parallel longitudinal lines or ridges.

Striated: (L. striatus, grooved) Marked by narrow lines or grooves, usually parallel.

Strict: Upright, straight and rigid.

Strigillose: Diminutive of strigose.

Strigose: Covered with stiff hairs; ridged; marked by small furrows; surface clothed with stiff, often appressed hairs, these usually pointing in one direction.

Stringency: Reaction conditions (notably temperature, salt concentration and pH) that affect the annealing process of single-stranded DNA or RNA to make double-stranded DNA or RNA, or DNA/RNA hybrids. At high stringency, duplexes form only between strands with perfect complementarity; lower stringency allows the annealing of strands with some degree of mismatch.

Stringent plasmid: A plasmid that can only replicate at the same time as does the main bacterial chromosome, and is present as a single or, at most, several copies per cell.

Striped: Longitudinal stripes of one color crossing another.

Strobilus: An aggregation of sporophylls on a common axis; it usually resembles a cone or is somewhat conelike in appearance.

Strombiform: Elongate snail-shaped.

Strophiolate: With elongate aril or strophiole in the hilum region.

Structural gene: A gene that encodes a polypeptide, with either enzymatic or structural functions, and that is required for the normal metabolism and growth of a cell or organism.

Structure functionalism: The scientific tradition that stresses the relationship between a physical structure and its function, e.g. the related disciplines of anatomy and physiology.

Struma: A cushion-like swelling, e.g. at the apex of staminal filaments in dianella.

Stylocarpellous: With a style and without a stipe, the normal carpel.

Stylopodic: With a stylopodium or discoid base, as in the Apiaceae.

Stylopodium: The fleshy support at the base of the style in flowers of the carrot family, Umbelliferae.

Sub acrocaulous: With branches at or near tip of main stem.

Sub apical: At one side near apex of ovary.

Sub basicaulous: With branches at or near base of main stem.

Sub basifixed: Anther attached near its base to apex of filament.

Sub culture: Division and transfer of a portion of a culture to fresh medium. Sometimes used to denote the adding of fresh liquid to a suspension culture. Synonym: passage.

Sub culture interval: The time between consecutive sub-cultures of cells.

Sub culture number: The number of times cells, etc., have been sub-cultured.

Sub strain: Derived from a strain by the isolation of an individual or group of individuals having properties or markers not shared by the strain as a whole.

Sub unit vaccine: One or more immunogenic proteins, either purified from the pathogen itself or produced from a cloned pathogen gene. A vaccine composed of a purified antigenic determinant that is separated from the virulent organism.

Suberin: Waxy, waterproof chemical in some plant cells, notably cork (in stems) and endodermis cells (in roots). Suberin is an extremely complex and irregular material, like lignin—with which it shares some similarities. Suberin is composed of two physically separated domains the aliphatic and phenolic. The phenolic domain is rather lignin-like, but with even greater variability, and built on the same basic unit of a di- or tri-hydroxyphenyl group attached to a three-carbon chain, variously oxidized and integrated with the carbohydrates of the cell walls. Perhaps the most common building block is ferulic acid formally, 3-(2'-methoxy-3'-hydroxyphenyl)-propenoic acid. Distally, the phenolic domain is attached at points by ester linkages to glycerol. The remaining hydroxyls of the glycerol molecule are ester-linked to some strange-looking C-18 to C-30 lipids. These lipids are substituted at C9-10 with one or two hydroxyls, or even with an epoxide link between the two carbons.

Subfamily: A grouping of similar genera within a family, a category above tribe.

Subgenomic promoter: A promoter added to a virus for a specific heterologous gene, resulting in the formation of mRNA for that gene alone.

Subglabrate: Almost glabrous.

Subglobose: Almost round or spherical.

Sublining: Dividing a breeding population into several to many smaller populations. All controlled crosses for forward selection are made within a subline, leading to inbreeding within sublines. Production seed orchards are planted with clones or seedlings from several to many sublines to minimize inbreeding in the production orchard.

Submerge: To sink or plunge beneath the surface of water.

Submersed plants: Plants growing with their root, stems, and leaves completely under the surface of the water.

Submersed: Beneath the surface of the water.

Submersicaulous: With submersed stems.

Suborbicular: Approximately circular.

Subspecies: Population(s) of organisms sharing certain characteristics that are not present in other populations of the same species.

Substrate: 1. A compound that is altered by an enzyme. 2. Food source for growing cells or micro-organisms. 3. Material on which a sedentary organism lives and grows.

Subtend: To occur immediately below as in a bract subtending a flower.

Subterminal: Near the apex.

Subterranean or hypogeous: Below the surface of the ground.

Subulate: Awl-shaped, narrow and gradually tapering to a fine point.

Succession: An orderly progression of changes in the composition of a community from the initial development of vegetation to the establishment of a climax community.

Succulent: A plant that is able to store water in its tissues and then withdraw it during times of drought. e.g. a cactus. The water storage tissue may be found in the stem, leaves, or roots depending on the species. Stem succulents, leaf succulents, and root succulents are types of growth forms.

Sucker shoots: Shoots that develop from adventitious buds on old stumps or roots, usually after cutting or injury, which have elongate internodal lengths and intervals.

Sucker: A shoot that arises from an underground root or stem. Of particular significance to grafted plants, since the sucker will be genotypically rootstock, rather than scion.

Suckering: Type of vegetative propagation where lateral buds grow out to produce an individual that is a clone of the parent.

Sucrose density gradient centrifugation: A procedure used to fractionate nucleic acids on the basis of their size.

Sucrose: A disaccharide composed of glucose and fructose; the primary form in which sugar produced by photosynthesis is transported throughout a plant.

Sulcus: A furrow or groove (pl. Sulci.); hence sulcate, longitudinally grooved.

Summer annual: Germinating in spring or early summer and flowering and fruiting in late summer or early fall, then dying.

Sun/shade leaves: Leaves exposed to full sun tend to have thicker cuticles and more layers of palisade tissue than leaves of the same plant growing in shade.

Superbug: Jargon for a particular engineered strain of Pseudomonas, in which various hydrocarbon-degrading genes, derived from different plasmids, were combined into one genotype. This provided the basis for the precedent-setting legal decision that declared that genetically engineered organisms were patentable.

Supercoil: The conformation of a double-stranded DNA molecule placed under torsional stress as a result of interactions with proteins. The stress is accommodated by a twist imposed on the duplex. A left-handed supercoil favours unwinding of the double helix; a right-handed supercoil favours tighter winding.

Supercoiled plasmid: The predominant in vivo form of most plasmids, in which the DNA is coiled around histone-like proteins. When supporting proteins are stripped away during DNA extraction from the bacterial cell, the plasmid molecule also tends to supercoil around itself in vitro.

Supergene: A group of tightly linked genes that are co-inherited, and may be functionally related.

Superior: Of an ovary, borne above the level of attachment of the other floral parts, or above the base of a cup (hypanthium) that is free from the ovary and bears the perianth segments and stamens.

Superior ovary: An ovary that is free from the calyx, corolla, and other floral parts, so the sepals and petals appear to be attached at its base.

Supernatant: The liquid phase remaining after insoluble materials are pelleted by centrifugation or precipitation.

Supervolute: With lamina with one edge tightly enrolled and with the other loosely enrolled covering the first, loosely convolute.

Supine: Prostrate, with parts oriented upward.

Suppressor mutation: A mutation that reverses the effect of an earlier mutation, e.g. a mutation in a gene for a tRNA that permits it to read and override an amber mutation.

Suppressor sensitive mutant: An organism that can grow in the presence, but not in the absence of a second genetic factor (the suppressor).

Supra: Prefix meaning 'higher than'.

Suprafamilial: Above the rank of family; similarly supra generic etc.

Suprafoliar: On the stem above the leaves, as in the Arecaceae.

Suprarhizous: On top of the root.

Surcarpous: With fruits on surface of ground.

Surcurrent: Extending along stem upward from leaf base.

Surficial or epigeous: Upon or spread over the surface of the ground.

Susceptible: Inability to withstand injury due to biotic or abiotic stress. Opposite: resistance, tolerance.

Suspension culture: A type of culture in which cells and/or clumps of cells grow and multiply while suspended in a liquid medium.

Suture: A seam formed when two parts unite; a seam or line or groove; usually applied to the line along which a fruit dehisces; any lengthwise groove that forms a junction between two parts.

Swale: A hollow or depression, especially one in wet, marshy ground.

Swamp: Spongy land; low ground filled with water; a wooded area having surface water much of the time.

Syconium: A syncarp with the achenes borne on the inside of a hollowed-out receptacle or peduncle, as in Ficus.

Syleptic shoots: Abnormal shoots that develop from lateral buds before they have reached maturity.

Symbiosis: The close association of two different kinds of living organisms where there is benefit to both or where both receive an advantage from the association. A prominent example is the colonization of Rhizobium spp. inside the roots of leguminous plants.

Sympatric: Of two or more species having coincident or overlaping ranges of geographic distribution.

Sympatric speciation: The evolution of new species by populations that inhabit the same or overlapping geographic regions.

Sympodial: A type of plant development in which the terminal bud of the stem stops growing due either to its abortion, or to its differentiation into a floral meristem. Frequently, the uppermost lateral bud then takes over the further axial growth of the stem.

Sympodium: An axis made up of the basal portions of several branches, the apex of each branch dying and growth continued by an axillary bud; hence sympodial.

Synangium: A sorus-like structure formed by the fusion of two or more sporangia, a single body divided internally into several locules each bearing spores.

Synantherous: With leaves and flowers appearing at same time.

Synapomorphy: A unique character which is shared by all basal members of a clade and is derived from their common ancestor, but not shared with ancestral groups. A synapomorphy may be secondarily lost in later descendants. Only a synapomorphy may be used to infer phylogeny.

Synaptonemal complex (SC): A ribbon-like proteinaceous structure formed between paired homologous chromosomes at the end of the first meiotic prophase. The SC binds the chromatids along their length, and facilitates crossing over.

Syncarp: A multiple or aggregate fruit derived from numerous separate ovaries of a single flower; a collective unit, as a blackberry.

Syncarpous: Of a flower, having two or more carpels, all fused together.

Syncephalastrum: Can cause a respiratory infection characterized by a solid intracaitary fungal ball.

Synchronous culture: A culture in which the cell cycle is synchronized for the majority of the cells present. Synchrony can be induced by the addition of drugs which arrest the cell cycle at specific stages.

Syncotyly: Cotyledons coalesced, forming a funnel or trumpet.

Syncytium: A group of cells in which cytoplasmic continuity is maintained; the effect is of a multinucleate cell.

Syndrome: A group of specific characters that occur together, and are characteristic of a particular disease or genetic condition (e.g. Down's syndrome).

Synergid: One of the two haploid nuclei at the micropylar end of the embryo sac of higher plants. The third nucleus is the egg.

Synergidae: The two haploid nuclei at the micropylar end of the embryo sac that do not participate in the fertilization process. Together with the egg nucleus they constitute the egg apparatus. Their function is not known and they abort soon after fertilization.

Synergism: An interaction between two organisms (e.g. Rhizobium and legumes) in which the growth of one is helped by the other.

Syngenesious: Of the stamens of one flower, fused together by the anthers e.g. in asteraceae.

Synkaryon The initial hybrid nucleus of the zygote, formed by the fusion of the gametic nuclei upon fertilization. A hybrid nucleus formed by the fusion of two different somatic cells during somatic cell hybridization is called a heterokaryon.

Synonym: Another name for the same taxon, either the result of independent description, or the transference or combination of different taxa.

Synovarious: With ovaries of adjacent carpels completely fused, styles and stigmas separate.

Synteny: The occurrence of two or more loci on the same chromosome, without regard to their genetic linkage. Increasingly used to describe the conservation of gene order between related species.

Syntepalous: Flowers in which the tepals are fused.

Syntepalum: In musaceae, a unilaterally split tube formed by the coherence of 3 sepals and 2 anterior petals in flowers of some species.

Syntropous: With radicle pointing toward hilum.

Syntype: Any one of two or more specimens or other material designated by an author in the original publication of the name of a taxon. As a taxon can only have one type, a lectotype can subsequently be chosen from a group of syntypes to serve as the nomenclatural type.

Systematics: The study of the identification (taxonomy) and evolutionary relationships among plant species.

T: Abbreviation for thymine.

T0, T1 and T2: Successive generations of plants following a transformation event. The parent transformed plant is T0, its immediate progeny is T1, and the progeny of the T1 are T2 plants etc. Of particular interest is the stability of transgene expression from T0 to T2, and beyond.

T4 DNA ligase: An enzyme, present in bacteria infected with bacteriophage T4, which catalyses the joining (ligation) of, and repairs nicks in, duplex DNA molecules. Ligation activity requires that one DNA molecule has a 5'-phosphate group, and that the other has a free 3'-hydroxyl group.

T cell: Lymphocytes which pass through the thymus gland during maturation. Different kinds of T cells play important roles in the immune response. Synonym: T lymphocyte.

T distribution: The ratio of the deviation, d, to the estimated standard deviation, s. It is used in experiments where the number of observations is small (31 or less and hence 30 or less degrees of freedom) and consequently the estimated standard deviation may differ widely from the true standard deviation. To find whether any deviation is significant, its probability is looked up in 'Student's' t tables, which take the number of degrees of freedom (N) into account. The greater the value of TV, the smaller the value of t for any given level of probability.

T DNA: The DNA segment of the Ti plasmid, present in pathogenic Agrobacterium tumefaciens, that is transferred to plant cells and inserted into the plant's DNA as part of the infection process. Wild type T-DNA encodes enzymes that induce the plant to synthesize specific opines that are required for bacterial growth. In engineered T-DNAs, these genes are replaced by a transgene(s).

Tailing: The in vitro addition, to the 3'-hydroxyl ends of a double-stranded DNA molecule, of multiple copies of a single nucleotide by the enzyme terminal transferase.

Take-all: A disease of grasses and cereals caused by the fungus Gaeumannomyces (Ophiobolus) graminis. The pathogen survives in the soil on crop debris and can infect the crop at any stage. The dense mycelium on the roots and stem bases gives them a typical blackened appearance. If the plants survive until ear emergence the ears have little grain and appear bleached and are therefore called 'whiteheads'.

Tandem repeat: Two (or more) contiguous identical DNA sequences. The orientation can be either head-to-tail, or head-to-head. Synonyms: tandem array, sequence tandem repeat.

Tangential section: A tangential section is a longitudinal section of a stem where the section is perpendicular to the tangent or radius of the stem. The section will be perpendicular to the vascular rays, so therefore only the ends of the rays will be visible.

Tank bioreactor: A fermentation vessel designed to grow large scale quantities of a micro-organism (bacteria, yeast or fungi). Most tank bioreactors are designed to be stirred mechanically, since this allows effective distribution throughout the culture of gas and nutrients. Alternative bioreactors use fibre or membrane surfaces to immobilize the cultured cells.

Tannin bearing glands: Tannin producing glands found in various parts of the plant, presumably protective in some structures.

Tannins: Complex aromatic compounds some of which are glucosides, possibly giving protection or concerned with pigment formation.

Tap: Persistent, well-developed primary root.

Tap root: Root system in which the primary root has a much larger diameter than any lateral roots (e.g. carrot). Opposite: fibrous root.

Taq polymerase: A heat-stable DNA polymerase isolated from the thermophilic bacterium Thermus aquaticus, widely used in PCR.

Target: In diagnostic tests, the molecule or nucleic acid sequence assayed in a sample. In mutagenesis, the gene sequence that needs to be altered to generate the desired change in phenotype.

Target site duplication: A short sequence of DNA duplicated when a transposable element inserts at a new locus; usually found at each end of the insertion.

Targeted drug delivery: A method of delivering the activated form of a drug molecule to the site in the body where it is needed, rather than allowing it reach the target by uncontrolled diffusion.

Targeting vector: A cloning vector carrying a DNA sequence capable of participating in a recombinational event at a specified chromosomal location in the host cell.

TATA box: A widely conserved adenine- and thymine-rich DNA sequence found 25-30 bp upstream of the transcription initiation point of many eukaryotic genes. The TATA box is implicated in the promotion of gene transcription as it acts as a binding site for RNA polymerase. Analogous to the Pribnow box in prokaryotic promoters. Synonym: Hogness box.

Tautomeric shift: The transfer of a hydrogen atom from one position in an organic molecule to another position. Tautomers can have widely different biological activities, as the shift can induce a significant change in the conformation of the molecule.

Tautomerism: A type of isomerism in which the two isomers arising from a tautomeric shift are in equilibrium.

Tautonym: A specific or infraspecific name that exactly repeats the generic name, e.g. Magnolia magnolia. This is not allowed in botanical nomenclature but is, however, acceptable in zoology.

Taxon: A group of plants of the same type, eg. Species, genus, family, order etc; hence taxonomy, the study of taxa.

Taxonomic synonyms: With different basionyms Or based on different types.

Taxonomy: A science that includes identification, nomenclature, and classification of objects, and is usually restricted to objects of biological origin; orderly classification of plants according to their presumed natural relationships forming a basic biological discipline involving during its Linnean period the firm establishment of binomial nomenclature and acceptance of the static concept of fixity of the species, during its Darwinion period the dynamic concept of speciation by natural selection, and during its modern Mendelian epoch an expansion to include study of the mechanisms underlying speciation and related processes.

Telomerase: An enzyme that maintains the structure of the telomere by adding the required repetitive sequences to the ends of eukaryotic chromosomes.

Telomere: The structure found at the end of eukaryotic chromosomes containing specialized repetitive (and widely conserved across species) DNA sequences, which are necessary to assure the completion of a cycle of DNA replication.

Telophase: The last stage in each mitotic or meiotic division, in which the chromosomes coalesce at each pole of the dividing cell.

Temperate phage: A phage (virus) that invades but does not normally destroy (lyse) the host bacterial cell. Under specific circumstances, the lytic cycle is induced, resulting in the release of infective phage particles.

Temperate: Pertaining to the cooler areas of the world with moderate climates.

Temperature sensitive protein: A protein that is functional at one temperature but loses function at another (usually higher) temperature.

Tendril: A slender structure that coils on contact with a support of suitable diameter; it usually is a modified leaf or leaflet and aids the plant in climbing.

Tentacular: Glandular-haired or tentacle-bearing insectivorous leaf, as in drosera.

Tenuiexenous: Of a pollen grain, with a thin exine.

Tepal: When the sepals and petals of a flower are indistinguishable, they are referred to as tepals. Tepals are common in many groups of monocots.

Terete: Nearly cylindrical in cross-section, as stems.

Tergeminate: With three orders of leaflets, each bifoliolate, or with geminate leaflets ternately compound.

Terminal: At apex or end of stem. Terminal Bud Scale Scar rings - several marks in a ring indicating former places of attachment of bud scales.

Terminal bud: A branch tip, an undeveloped shoot containing rudimentary floral buds or leaves, enclosed within protective bud scales.

Terminal transferase: An enzyme that catalyses the addition of nucleotides to the 3' end of a DNA molecule.

Terminalization: Repelling movement of the centromeres of bivalents in the diplotene stage of the meiotic prophase, that appears to move visible chiasmata toward the ends of the bivalents.

Termination signal: In transcription, a nucleotide sequence that specifies RNA chain termination.

Terminator: 1. A DNA sequence just downstream of the coding segment of a gene, which is recognized by RNA polymerase as a signal to stop synthesizing mRNA. 2. A term used in GMO technology for a transgenic method which genetically sterilizes the progeny of the planted seed, thereby preventing the use of farm-saved seed.

Terminator gene: A specific variety-level genetic use restriction technology. A patented technique.

Terminator region: A DNA sequence that signals the end of transcription.

Ternate: In groups of three; of leaves, arranged in whorls of three; of a single leaf, having the leaflets arranged in groups of three.

Ternately compound: With leaflets in three's.

Terrestrial: Of or on the ground; of the habitat of a plant, on land as opposed to in water, or on the ground as opposed to on another plant.

Tertiary structure: The three-dimensional conformation taken up by complete macromolecules as a result of intramolecular interactions, such as hydrogen-bonding.

Tesselate: Of a checker-work pattern or divided into squares or squarish pieces.

Tessellated: Color arranged in small squares, so as to have some resemblance to a checkered pavement.

Testa: The hard outer covering or integument of seed.

Testcross: A cross between a genetically unknown individual and a recessive tester to determine whether the individual in question is heterozygous or homozygous for a certain allele. It can also used as a method to test for linkage, i.e. to estimate recombination fraction.

Testis: Male sex organ where spermatozoa mature and are stored.

Testosterone: Male hormone, synthesized in the testis of mammals; used to induce sex reversal in fish.

Tetra: Prefix meaning 'four'.

Tetracyclic: Four-whorled.

Tetracycline: An antibiotic that interferes with protein synthesis in prokaryotes. A gene encoding resistance to tetracycline has been widely used as a marker to distinguish between transformed and non-transformed cells in the production of transgenic plants.

Tetrad: The four haploid cells formed after the second meiotic division in plants (pollen tetrads) or fungi (ascospores).

Tetradynamous: Of an androecium, consisting of four stamens of the same length and two of a different length.

Tetragonous: Having four angles.

Tetrahedral: Having the form of a tetrahedron

Tetralocular: Four-locular.

Tetramerous: Of a flower, having four segments in each perianth whorl, and usually in each whorl of stamens also.

Tetraploid: An organism, or a tissue whose cells contain four haploid sets of chromosomes.

Tetrasomic: Pertaining to a nucleus or an organism with four members of one of its chromosomes, whereas the remainder of its chromosome complement is diploid. Chromosome formula: $2n + 2$.

Tetrastichous: Leaves or other structures in four rows.

Tetratype: In fungi, a tetrad of spores that contains four different types; e.g. AB, aB, Ab and ab.

TGGE: Abbreviation for thermal gel gradient electrophoresis.

Thalloid: Plants which have no roots, stems, or leaves are called thalloid, such as liverworts and hornworts.

Thallophyta: A primary division of plants including all forms consisting of one cell and cell aggregates not clearly differentiated into root, stem, and leaf, including bacteria, algae, fungi, and lichens.

Thallus: Term given to the body of a lower plant which has no recognizable shoot, root, leaf regions. Most of the things this term is used to describe are not even plants, e.g. lichen.

Theca: One half of anther containing two pollen sacs or male sporangia.

Therapeutic agent: A compound used for the treatment of a disease or for improving the well-being of an organism. Synonyms: pharmaceutical agent, drug.

Therapeutic cloning: The potential use of stem cells to grow, in vitro, tissue or organs for use in transplantation. Because these cells would be obtained from, and would therefore be genetically identical to the patient's own cells, problems of transplant rejection would be overcome. The technique would also remove the difficulty of identifying an organ donor.

Thermal gel gradient electrophoresis (TGGE): A method for separating DNA fragments according to their mobility under increasingly denaturing conditions imposed by heat.

Thermal shock: Exposure to reduced or increased temperature for a significant period.

Thermolabile: Not resistant to heat, often in the context of a molecule which is unstable upon heating. Opposite: thermostable.

Thermophile: An organism which is adapted to high temperatures, such as in hot springs and geysers, smoker vents on the sea floor, and domestic hot water pipes. A wide range of bacteria, fungi and simple plants and animals can grow at temperature up to 50 °C; thermophiles grow and reproduce at above 50 °C. They can be classified, according to their optimal growth temperature, into simple thermophiles (50-65 °C); thermophiles (65-85 °C), and extreme thermophiles (>85 °C).

Thermosensitivity: Loss of biological activity of a molecule at high temperature.

Thermostable: A molecule which retains its biological activity at some specified higher temperature. Opposite: thermolabile.

Thermotherapy: Exposure to elevated temperatures, a technique mainly used for virus or mycoplasma elimination, taking advantage of the higher thermostability of the host over its pathogen. Synonym: heat therapy.

Therophytes: An annual plant that overwinters as a seed.

Thorn: A sharp rigid process on a plant; specif., a short, indurated, sharp-pointed, and leafless branch developed from a bud in a manner typical to a leafy branch.

Throat: Term applied to an expanded part of a corolla tube just below the lobes.

Thylakoid: Coin-shaped membranes whose contents include chlorophyll; they are arranged in stacks that form the grana of chloroplasts.

Thymidine kinase (tk): An enzyme that allows a cell to utilize an alternate metabolic pathway for incorporating thymidine into DNA. Used as a selectable marker to identify transfected eukaryotic cells.

Thymidine triphosphate: TTP; dTTP is strictly correct but rarely used.

Thymidine: The deoxyribonucleoside resulting from the combination of the base thymine (T) and the sugar 2-deoxy-D-ribose.

Thymidylic acid (TMP or dTMP): Synonym for thymidine 5'-monophosphate, a deoxyribonucleotide containing the nucleoside thymidine.

Thymine (T): One the bases found in DNA.

Thyrseus: panicle-like inflorescence consisting of a slender indeterminate main axis with lateral axes determinate, i.e., cymose.

Ti plasmid: Tumour-inducing plasmid. A large plasmid present in pathogenic Agrobacterium tumefaciens, responsible for the induction of tumours in plant with crown gall disease. Engineered forms of this plasmid are central to the production of transgenics in many crop species.

Tiller: Sprout, stalk, especially one from the base of a plant or from the axils of its lower leaves.

Tip layering: Asexual propagation involving the burying of the tip of a flexible stem in soil to induce the formation of adventitious roots; the rooted portion is then cut from the parent plant and grown separately.

Tissue: A group of cells of similar structure which sometimes performs a special function.

Tissue culture: A technique for cultivation cells, tissues, or organs of plants in a sterile, synthetic medium; includes the tissues excised from a plant and the culture of pollen or seeds.

Titre: 1. The concentration of infectious virus particles present in a suspension. 2. A measure of antibody concentration, given by the highest dilution of the sample that results either in a useable immunoassay, or in the formation of visible precipitate when challenged by the appropriate antigen.

TK: Abbreviation for thymidine kinase.

TMP: Abbreviation for the deoxyribonucleotide thymidine 5'-monophosphate.

Tolerance: Incomplete resistance to a given biotic or abiotic stress. Tolerant genotypes are less inhibited by the stress, but are not immune.

Toluidine-blue: A histological stain. Lignified walls stain greenish-blue, bright blue or white. Most primary (non-lignified) walls stain pinkish-purple (e.g. Parenchyma).

Tomentum: A dense woolly or matted covering of +/- appressed hairs; hence tomentose.

Tonoplast: The cytoplasmic membrane bordering the vacuole of plant cells. It plays a prominent role in regulating the osmotic pressure exerted by the cell sap.

Toothed margin: Margin having projections or serrations with pointed apices, indented less than one quarter of the distance to the midvein or long axis of the leaf; compare entire margin and lobed margin leaves.

Topotype: A specimen collected from near the locality of the type.

Torose: Cylindrical with contractions at intervals.

Totipotency: The potential of a cell to develop into a complete plant.

Toxicity: The extent to which a toxic compound negatively affects a given trait.

Toxin: A compound produced by one organism, which is deleterious to the growth and/or survival of another organism of the same or different species.

Trabecula: A transverse partition dividing or partly dividing a cavity; hence trabeculate.

Tracer: A substance (typically a radioactive isotope or a fluorescent dye) that can be detected by physical means, and which is used to analyse the progress of a chemical reaction or a biological process.

Tracheophyta: A division of plants comprising green plants with a vascular system that contains tracheids or tracheary elements, being the Pteridophyta and Spermatophyta, commonly called vascular plants.

Tracheophyte: Plants with true vascular tissue, i.e. xylem and phloem;. Includes all land plants higher than bryophytes (mosses) and liverworts.

Trailing: Sprawling on ground, usually with adventitious roots

Trait: One of the many characteristics that define an organism. The phenotype is a description of one or more traits. Synonym: character.

Trans acting factor: Any of the multiple ancillary DNA-binding proteins that interact with the cis-regulatory DNA sequences to control gene expression.

Trans acting: 1. A term describing substances that are diffusable and that can affect spatially separated entities within cells. 2. A genetic element (e.g. a promoter sequence) that is effective only when present in the trans configuration.

Trans heterozygote: A double heterozygote that contains two mutations arranged in the trans configuration.

Transcapsidation: The partial or full coating of the nucleic acid of a virus particle with the coat protein of a different virus.

Transcript: An RNA molecule that has been synthesized from a specific DNA template. In eukaryotes, the primary transcript produced by RNA polymerase is often processed or modified in order to form functional mRNA, rRNA or tRNA.

Transcription: The copying of a sequence of DNA nucleotides into an RNA sequence.

Transcription factor: A protein that regulates the transcription of genes.

Transcription unit: A segment of DNA that contains signals for the initiation and termination of transcription, and is transcribed into one RNA molecule.

Transcriptional anti-terminator: A protein that prevents RNA polymerase from terminating transcription at specific transcription termination sequences.

Transcriptional roadblock: A DNA-binding protein which affects the rate at which RNA polymerases transcribe genes. The protein/DNA complex interferes with the passage of the elongation complex. In some cases these obstacles are readily bypassed, but in others a significant level of pausing or termination occurs, and this can then act as a control point for gene expression.

Transduction: 1. Genetic: the transfer by means of a viral vector of a DNA sequence from one cell to another. 2. Signal: any process that helps to produce biological responses to events in the environment (e.g. transduction of hormone binding into cellular events by hormone receptors).

Transfection: The infection of a cell with isolated viral DNA (or RNA), resulting in the production of intact viral particles.

Transferase: A class of enzymes that catalyses the transfer of a group of atoms from one molecule to another.

Transformant: A cell or organism that has been genetically altered through the integration of a transgene(s). Primary: the first generation following the transformation event. Secondary: progeny of the primary transformant.

Transformation: 1. The uptake and integration of DNA in a cell, in which the introduced DNA is intended to change the phenotype of the recipient organism in a predictable manner. 2. The conversion, by various means, of cultured animal cells from controlled to uncontrolled cell growth, typically through infection with a tumour virus or transfection with an oncogene.

Transformation efficiency or frequency: The fraction of a cell population that takes up and integrates the introduced transgene; expressed as the number of transformed cells recovered divided by the total number of cells in a population.

Transforming oncogene: A gene that, upon transfection, converts a previously immortalized cell to the malignant phenotype.

Transgene: An isolated gene sequence used to transform an organism. Often, but not always, the transgene has been derived from a different species than that of the recipient.

Transgenesis: The introduction of a gene or genes into animal or plant cells, which leads to the transmission of the input gene (transgene) to successive generations.

Transgenic plant: A plant containing recombinant DNA.

Transgenic: An individual in which a transgene has been integrated into its genome. In transgenic eukaryotes, the transgene must be transmitted through meiosis to allow its inheritance by the offspring.

Transgressive variation: The appearance, in a segregating generation, of individuals showing expression of a trait outside the extremes defined by the parent of the cross that was used to generate the population.

Transient expression: Short-term activity of a transgene following its introduction into target tissue. Transient expression usually implies non-integration of the transgene into the host genome.

Transition: The substitution in DNA or RNA of one purine by another purine, or of one pyrimidine by another pyrimidine.

Transition stage: The period between juvenile and reproductive stages of growth.

Transition-state intermediate: In a chemical reaction, an unstable and high-energy configuration assumed by reactants on the way to making products. Enzymes are thought to bind and stabilize the transition state, thus lowering the energy of activation needed to drive the reaction to completion.

Translocation: The process whereby solutes are transported through the phloem. Unlike xylem, phloem is essentially a chain of living cells. The most widely accepted explanation for translocation of substances in the phloem is the Münch pressure flow hypothesis. The proposed mechanism is as follows a high concentration of solute (e.g., sugars) is loaded into cells of the phloem, presumably by active transport, at locations, such as a leaf, where sugars are produced by photosynthesis. The high solute concentration in the phloem cell creates an osmotic gradient which draws water into the phloem. The resulting high turgor pressure causes flow to occur. If the dissolved sugars or other chemicals carried along with the sugars are removed from the phloem at another place in the tree for use (a sink such as a root or fruit), the decline in concentration of sugar causes water to move out of the phloem cells. Because water is moving in at a source and out at a sink, there is a mass flow of water and substances in the phloem.

Translucent: Letting light through, almost transparent.

Transpiration: Loss of water in vapor form; most transpiration takes place through the stomata.

Transposable genetic element: A DNA sequence transpasan) capable of being moved from one chromosomal location to another.

Transposase: An enzyme encoded by a transposon gene that catalyses the movement of a DNA sequence to a different site in a DNA molecule.

Transposition: The process whereby a transposon or insertion sequence inserts itself into a new site on the same or another DNA molecule. The exact mechanism is not fully understood and different transposons may transpose by different mechanisms. Transposition in bacteria does not require extensive DNA homology between the transposon and the target DNA.

Transposon: Synonym of transposable genetic element.

Transposon tagging: A method of gene isolation that exploits the disruption of normal gene expression that is the result of an insertion of a transposon within, or close to the target. Since the sequence of the transposon is known, this can be used as a DNA probe to define the DNA fragment containing the target gene. Large-scale experiments to generate populations of gene mutations are colloquially referred to as gene machines.

Transverse or explanate: At rightangles to long axis.

Transverse section: Cross section. A section perpendicular to the main axis of the plant or organ.

Transversion: The substitution in DNA or RNA of one purine by a pyrimidine or vice versa.

Trapezoid: Trapezium-shaped, a four-sided figure with the opposite sides parallel.

Tree: Any tall plant, including many conifers and flowering plants, as well as extinct lycophytes and sphenophytes.

Tri hybrid: The hybrid offspring of a cross between parents carrying contrasting alleles at three loci.

Tri: Prefix meaning 'three'.

Triangular: With three sides and three angles.

Triarch: Consisting of three; for example a triarch stele has three lobes.

Tribrid protein: A fusion protein that has three segments, each encoded by parts of different genes.

Trichoderma: It is commonly found in soil, dead trees, pine needles, paper, unglazed ceramics. It often will grow on other fungi. It produces antibiotics which are toxic to humans. It has been reported to be allergenic. It readily degrades cellulose.

Trichome: An outgrowth from an epidermis; a hair or scale which may be unicellular or multicellular, branched or unbranched, secretory, absorbing or non-functional.

Tridynamous: With stamens in two equal groups of three.

Triflorous: Three-flowered.

Trifoliolate: Of a compound leaf with three radial leaflets.

Trifurcate: Divided into three forks or branches; three-forked.

Trigonous: With three angles, of a solid body, triangular in cross-section with rounded corners.

Triheterophytous: Having different states in three different sets of plants, only one state present in each set.

Trilete spore: Basically tetrahedral, but often appearing round or triangular, with three scar lines forming a Y.

Trilete: Of a pore with a radial, three-armed scar.

Trimerous: Of a flower, having three segments in each perianth whorl and usually in each whorl of stamens also.

Trimorphic: Having three different shapes and/or sizes within the same species.

Trinucleotide repeat: Tandem repeats of three nucleotides that are present in many genes. Commonly trinucleotide repeats have undergone variable expansion in copy number, forming the basis of microsatellite markers, and occasionally resulting in the formation of alleles giving rise to genetic disease.

Trioecious: Plants staminate, pistillate or perfect.

Tripalmately compound: With three orders of leaflets, each palmately compound.

Tripartite mating: A process in which conjugation is used to transfer a plasmid vector to a target cell when the plasmid vector is not self-mobilizable.

Tripinnately Compound: With three orders of leaflets, each pinnately compound.

Triplet: A sequential group of three nucleotides in DNA or RNA.

Triplinerved: With three main veins.

Triploid: Having or being a chromosome number three times the monoploid number.

Triquetrous: Triangular in cross-section and acutely-angled; with three distinct longitudinal ridges.

Trisomy: The presence in a diploid cell or organism of an extra chromosome of one homologue.

Tristylous: Heterostylous species having three style lengths (short, mid, long), the flowers of any one plant having styles of the same length.

Triternate: With three orders of leaflets, each ternately compound.

Triticale: The hybrid man-made species formed by the crossing of tetraploid or hexaploid wheat with diploid rye.

Tritirachium: Reported to be allergenic.

TRNA: Abbreviation for transfer RNA. Small RNA molecules that transfer amino acids to the ribosome during protein synthesis. Each tRNA binds just one species of amino acid and recognizes a specific codon in the mRNA, thus implementing the genetic code.

Tropism: Plant response to an external stimulus, resulting in the bending/ turning of stem or root growth. Typical tropisms are phototropism (light), geotropism (gravity) or hydrotropism (water).

True to type: Conforming to the phenotype of the breed/variety.

Trullate: With widest axis below middle and with straight margins; ovate but margins straight and angled below middle, trowel-shaped.

Truncate: Terminating abruptly, as if tapering end were cut off; cut squarely across, either at the base or apex of an organ.

Trunk: The main stem or body of a tree, considered apart from its roots and branches.

Tryma (involucre): Two-four loculed nut surrounded by a dehiscent involucre at maturity, as in most species of carya.

Trypsin: A proteolytic enzyme used in vivo for the digestion of peptides. It acts by hydrolysing peptide bonds on the carboxyl side of the amino acids arginine and lysine.

Trypsin inhibitor: Substances inactivating trypsin, typically found in seed tissue of certain plants, where they are thought to have evolved as anti-feedant agents against insect predators.

TTP: Abbreviation for thymidine 5'-triphosphate. TTP is required for DNA synthesis since it is a direct precursor molecule.

Tube: Any hollow elongate body of an organ; hence tubular.

Tuber: A tuber is a modified stem that contains nodes and internodes. It is underground and is attached to a rhizome. It is really the swollen portion of a rhizome where large amounts of food are stored, generally starch. A good example of a tuber is a potato. It is possible to find the terminal bud and the lateral buds. The eyes of the potato are these buds. When potatos are planted, the potato is cut up in pieces so that each piece has an eye. Each eye will sprout a new stem and the portion of attached potato will provide the food necessary to get the plant started growing.

Tubercle: A small rounded protuberance; root swelling or nodule; bubil; a surficial nodule; a thickened, solid, spongy crown or cap, as on an achene; a small tuber or tuberlike growth.

Tuberculate: With hard, swollen, persistent base or tubercle. Tuberculate or Verrucose - With a warty surface.

Tubercules: Silica deposits on the stem ridges, as in equisetum.

Tuberous: Fleshy roots resembling stem tubers

Tubular: Cylindrical.

Tubulin: The major protein component of the microtubules of eukaryotic cells.

Tufted: Growing in small clumps.

Tumble tube: A glass tube mainly used in vitro to agitate and consequently aerate suspension cultures. The tube, which is commonly attached to a slowly revolving platform, is closed at both ends, with a side-neck opening.

Tumid: Swollen; inflated.

Tumor-suppressor gene: A gene that regulates cell growth. If such a gene becomes dysfunctional, and potentiating damage occurs to the cell, then uncontrolled growth and a cancer may result.

Tumour virus: A virus capable of transforming a cell to a malignant phenotype.

Tunic: Thin membranous or fibrous outer layers of a bulb or corm.

Tunica: The outer one- to four-cell layer region of the apical meristem, where cell division is anticlinal, i.e. perpendicular to the surface.

Turbidostat: An open continuous culture in which a pre-selected biomass density is uniformly maintained by automatic removal of excess cells. The fresh medium flows in response to an increase in the turbidity (usually corresponding to cell density) of the culture.

Turbinate: Inversely conical; shaped like a cone resting on its apex.

Turgid: Swollen, distended; referring to a cell that is extended as a result of adequate water uptake. Loss of turgidity in plant cells is a sign of water deficit.

Turgor movement: The movement that results from changes in internal water pressures in a plant part.

Turgor pressure: Force exerted outward on a cell wall by the water contained in the cell. This force gives the plant rigidity, and may help to keep it erect.

Turion: (a) A type of perennating bud formed by certain aquatic plants, e.g. frogbit (Hydrocharis morsusranae), that is shed from the plant and lies dormant on the pond or river bed until the spring. (b) Any vegetative shoot or sucker.

Twig: A small shoot or branch of a tree or other plant.

Twin: One of two individuals originating from the same zygote.

Twiner: A climbing plant supporting itself by winding spirally around an object.

Twining: Twisted around a central axis

Tyloses: Bladder-like ingrowths that protrude into the tracheary elements of older wood eventually causing blockage. They originate from adjacent parenchyma cells via paired pits in the cell walls. Tyloses often become filled with tannins, resins, gums, or various pigments, so giving the heartwood its characteristic darker colour. These substances also help to preserve and strengthen the wood, while some of the pigments are important commercially as dyes (e.g. haematoxylin). Tyloses are sometimes found in the vessels of herbaceous plants, in which their function is unclear. They may act to seal off damaged vessels.

Type genus: The genus to which the name of a genus is permanently attached

Type species: The species to which the name of a genus is permanently attached.

Type subspecies, type variety: The variety or subspecies of the species that contains the nomenclatural type of the species.

Type, type specimen: The nomenclatural type or specimen to which the name of a taxon is always attached.

U

Ulocladium: Isolated from dead plants and cellulose materials. Found on textiles.

Ulotrichales: An order of the Chlorophyceae containing simple unbranching filamentous algae (e.g. Ulothrix). Each cell of the filament contains one bandlike chloroplast around its periphery and cell division is in one direction only. Asexual reproduction is by zoospores of various kinds while sexual reproduction varies from isogamy to the well developed oogamy seen in Cylindrocapsa.

Ultrastructure: (fine structure) Structural details of cells below the limit of resolution of the light microscope and only revealed by the electron microscope.

Umbellate: Bearing umbels; consisting of umbels; forming an umbel or umbels.

Umbilicate: Depressed in the center.

Umbo: A rounded protuberance or elevation in the centre; hence umbonate, bearing a protuberance in the center.

Umbonate: Round with a projection in center.

Umbraculate: Umbrella-shaped, as in Sarracenia

Umbraculiform: Umbrella-shaped.

UMP: Abbreviation for the (ribo)nucleotide uridine 5'-monophosphate.

Unbalanced: In experimental design, refers to an experiment or set of data in which all treatments or treatment combinations are not equally represented. The most common cause of unbalanced experiments is unequal mortality among entries in a test. Also used to describe any plant breeder specializing in an organism with nearly as long a life cycle as his or her own.

Uncinate: Terminating in a hooked point.

Understock: Host plant for a grafted scion, a branch or shoot from another plant; an understock may be a fully grown tree or a stump with a living root system.

Understory: Trees, shrubs and other plants located beneath and in the shade of larger trees.

Undifferentiated: Undifferentiated cells are those which have not been committed to become part of a specialized tissue.

Undulate: Corrugated or with the margin waved in a plane perpendicular to the surface.

Unencapsidated: A virus not enclosed by a coat protein or capsid.

Unequal crossing over: Abnormal meiotic event, in which one chromatid contains a duplication and the other a deletion. Often arises in a region containing repeated DNA sequences, which can pair out of register.

Uni: Prefix meaning 'one' or 'solitary'.

Unicarpellous or stylodious: With solitary, free carpel in gynoecium.

Unicellular: Tissues, organs or organisms consisting of a single cell.

Unifoliate: Having one leaf.

Unifoliolate: With a single leaflet with a petiolule distinct from the petiole of the whole leaf, as in Cercis.

Unilateral: Of stamens, with anthers grouped to one side of the style.

Unilocular: Of an ovary, anther or fruit, having only one internal cavity.

Uninodal shoot: Spring shoot developing from the terminal winter bud and producing only one internode with one whorl of branches at the end; the cones are subterminal at the end of the shoot; e.g., pinus resinosa.

Uniparental inheritance: The inheritance of genes exclusively from one parent, e.g. chloroplast DNA is inherited either maternally (many angiosperms) or paternally (most gymnosperms).

Uniseriate, uniserial: Arranged in a single row.

Unisexual: Higher organisms (animals or plants) possessing either male or female reproductive organs, but not both.

Univalent: An unpaired chromosome at the first division of meiosis.

Universal donor cell: Cells that, after introduction into a recipient, will not induce an immune response that leads to their rejection.

Unorganized growth: In vitro formation of tissues with few differentiated cell types and no recognizable structure; typical structure of calli formed in tissue culture. Opposite: organized growth.

Upstream: 1. The stretch of DNA lying in the 5' direction from the site being considered. Where the reference point is the initiation of transcription, the first transcribed base is designated +1 and upstream nucleotides are marked with minus signs, e.g. -1, -10; 2. In chemical engineering, those phases of a manufacturing process that precede the biotransformation step. Refers to the preparation of raw materials for a fermentation process. Also called upstream processing.

Uracil (U): One the bases found in RNA.

Urceolate: Shaped like a pitcher or urn.

Uridine: The (ribo)nucleoside resulting from the combination of the base uracil (U) and the sugar D-ribose.

Uridine triphosphate (uridine 5'-triphosphate) (UTP): Required for RNA synthesis since it is a direct precursor molecule.

Uridylic acid: Synonym for uridine 5'-monophosphate (UMP), a (ribo)nucleotide containing the base uracil.

Urn: A term used for anything even vaguely vase- or gourd-shaped, e.g. the sporangium in mosses.

Uronic acids: A class of sugar acids in which the carbon atom j carrying the primary hydroxyl group (i.e. the CH2OH end of the molecule) is oxidized to a carboxyl group (COOH). Uronic acids are biologically the most important group of the sugar acids and are common constituents of polysaccharides. For example, glucuronic acid, derived from glucose, is a common constituent of gums and mucilages. Galacturonic acid is a component of pectic substances while mannuronic acid is found in the seaweed gum alginic acid.

Utilization of farm animal genetic resources: The use and development of animal genetic resources for the production of food in a sustainable system of agriculture.

Utricle: An air bladder of aquatic plants; membranous indehiscent 1-celled fruit.

V

V/v: Abbreviation for volume per volume. The relative proportion of each liquid in a mixture.

Vaccine: A preparation of dead or attenuated (weakened) pathogens, or of derived antigenic determinants, that can induce the formation of antibodies in a host, and thereby produce host immunity against the pathogen.

Vaccinia: The cowpox virus used to vaccinate against smallpox and, experimentally, as a carrier of genes for antigenic determinants cloned from other disease organisms.

Vacuolar membrane: The delimiting membrane of a cell vacuole; also called tonoplast.

Vacuole: A fluid-filled cavity within the cytoplasm and separated from it by a membrane, the tonoplast . In newly formed cells, when division has ceased, vacuoles are formed from small detached parts of the endoplasmic reticulum. As fluid (cell sap) accumulates they enlarge and coalesce to form a single vacuole, pushing the protoplasm against the cell wall. The surface area of the wall is increased, by stretching and the formation of additional material, to accomodate the increased volume of the cell. The vacuolar sap is a solution of organic and inorganic compounds. These may include sugars, soluble polysaccharides, soluble proteins, amino acids, carboxylic acids, red, blue, and purple anthocyanins, and mineral salts. Starch grains, oil droplets, and crystals of various kinds may also be present. These constituents of the sap probably represent metabolic by-products and reserve food material.

Vaginula: In mosses, a derivative of the archegonium forms a hard, protective epigonium around the developing sporophyte. Later the epigonium breaks up, but the sporophyte retains a conical "dunce cap" or calyptra over its distal end and sometimes a ring around the base. The term calyptra refers to the "dunce cap," and the piece of the epigonium retained around the base (if any) is the vaginula.

Valine: A nonpolar amino acid with the formula (CH3)2CHCH(NH2) COOH. Valine is synthesized from pyruvate via á-ketoisovalerate. The degradation of valine is extremely complex, leading eventually to proprionyl CoA and thence to succinyl CoA. Methionine, leucine, and isoleucine also degrade to proprionyl CoA; the last sequence of reactions to succinyl CoA is thus common to all four amino acids.

Vallecular canal: A longitudinal channel in the stem internode of Equisetum and some of its fossil relatives, positioned radially opposite a longitudinal furrow (valley) between the stem ridges. The vallecular canals are arranged roughly between the vascular bundles.

Valvate: Meeting at the edges without overlapping; opening as if by doors or valves.

Valve: A portion of an organ that has fragmented; of a capsule, the teeth-like portions into which the dehiscing part of the pericarp splits at maturity.

Valvular: Dehiscing through a pore covered by a flap of tissue. Valvular or septifragal capsule - one with valves breaking away from the septa, as in Ipomoea.

Variable domain: Regions of antibody molecules that have different amino acid sequences in different antibody molecules. These regions are responsible for the antigen-binding specificity of the antibody.

Variable expressivity: Variation in the phenotype caused by different alleles of the same gene and/or by the action of other genes and/or by the action of non-genetic factors.

Variable number tandem repeat (VNTR): A DNA sequence, present as tandem repeats, for which the number of copies varies greatly between unrelated genotypes.

Variable surface glycoprotein (VSG): One of a battery of antigenic determinants expressed by a micro-organism to elude immune detection.

Variance: A statistical term representing a measure of the dispersion of data from the overall mean. Used to quantify the variability of a population.

Variant: An individual that is genetically distinct from others in the population.

Variation: Differences between individuals within a population or among populations.

Variegated: The color disposed in various irregular, sinuous, spaces.

Variegation: The occurrence, within a single tissue, organ or organism, of mosaicism. Usually referring to plants showing either both green and albino colouration in a leaf, or flecks of contrasting colour in a flower. The origin of variegation can be through viral infection, nutritional deficiency, or genetic instability caused by transposon activity.

Vascular: Relating collectively to the conductive plant tissues, xylem and phloem. Analogous vascular tissues in bryophytes are referred to as hydroids and leptoids, respectively.

Vascular bundles: Vascular bundles are clusters of xylem and phloem conducting elements that conduct food, water, and minerals throughtout the plant. Plants are able to live on land because they have the vascular tissue for the nourishment of the cells as does the vascular tissue of animal cells.

Vascular cambium: A narrow cylindrical sheath of cells that produces secondary xylem and phloem in sterns and roots.

Vascular plant: A plant having xylem and phloem.

Vascular system: 1. A specialized network of vessels for the circulation of fluids throughout the body tissue of an animal. 2. The system of vascular tissue in plants.

Vector: 1. An organism, usually an insect, that carries and transmits pathogens. 2. A small DNA molecule (plasmid, virus, bacteriophage, artificial or cut DNA molecule) that can be used to deliver DNA into a cell. Vectors must be capable of being replicated and contain cloning sites for the introduction of foreign DNA.

Vegetation: The total aggregation of plant communities within an area.

Vegetative: Of a plant lacking reproductive organs.

Vegetative frond: Frond lacking sporangia.

Vegetative growth: Growth of a plant by division of cells, without sexual reproduction.

Vegetative propagation: Propagation of a plant by asexual means, as in budding, dividing, grafting, rooting, and air layering.

Vein: A term applied to any of the vascular bundles that form a branching network within leaves.

Velamen: A membrane; water-storing tissue in the outer layer of some roots.

Velamen root: An aerial root with a multilayered epidermis believed to function in retarding moisture loss.

Velocity density gradient centrifugation: A procedure used to separate macromolecules based on their rate of movement through a density gradient.

Velogenetics: The combined use of marker-assisted selection and embryo technologies such as OPU, IVM and IVF, in order to increase the rate of genetic improvement in animal populations.

Velum: The membranous flap covering the sporangium, as in Isoetes.

Velutinous: Covered with dense, straight, long and soft trichomes; pile-like.

Venation: The pattern formed by the veins of a leaf, as viewed from above or below. The many different types of venation are useful diagnostically, especially in identifying fragmentary material. As a very general rule, the leaves of monocotyledons tend to have many parallel veins of more or less equal width while those of dicotyledons may be divided into one or a few primary veins, with secondary and tertiary veins branching off giving a net-veined or reticulate pattern.

Venter: Swollen basal region of the archegonium where the sporophyte develops in bryophytes.

Ventral: Pertaining to the surface nearest the axis; inner face of an organ; the upper surface of the leaf; adaxial. Ventral side - top side or upper side of a perianth part.

Ventricose: Inflated on one side near the middle

Ventristipular: On ventral side of stipule.

Vermiculite: Material made from expanded mica used as a rooting medium and as a soil additive.

Vernalization: Chilling juvenile plants for a minimum period in order to induce flowering. Some plants require veRNAlization to flower, but others have no such requirement.

Verrucose: Warty; having little warts or wartlike growth on the surface.

Verruculose: Covered with closely spaced, minute wart-like outgrowths.

Versatile: Turning freely on its support, as an anther attached near the middle and capable of swinging freely on the filament.

Verticil: An arrangement of leaves, flowers, inflorescences, or other structures which surround the stem in a circle upon the same plane about the same point on the axis.

Verticillaster: Whorled dichasia at the nodes of an elongate rachis.

Verticillate: Growing in a whorl or arranged on the same plane around an axis, as flowers, leaves, branches, etc.; arranged in verticils, whorled.

Verticillium: Conidia dimensions 2.3-10 x 1-2.6 microns. Found in decaying vegetation, on straw, soil and arthropods. A rare cause of corneal infections.

Vespertine: With flowers opening in the evening or night; appearing or expanding in the evening.

Vessel element: A type of cell occurring within the xylem of flowering plants. Many are water-conducting vessels.

Vessel: One of usually very numerous cylindrical "tubes" whose cells have lost their cytoplasm; occur in the xylem of most angiosperms and a few other vascular plants; each vessel is composed of vessel members laid end to end; the perforated or open-ended walls of the vessel members permit water to pass through freely.

Vestigial: Reduced from the ancestral condition and no longer functional.

Vestiture: That which covers a surface, as hairs, scales, etc.

Vexillate: Having one structure larger than others which is folded over smaller enclosed structures.

Viability test: Assay of the number or percent of living cells or plants in a population following a specific treatment. Often used to describe quality of seed following long-term storage.

Viability: A populations ability to live, grow and develop. It is affected by physical habitat factors (climate, geology, topography, and aquatic features) and by biotic habitat factors (plant and animal populations and communities).

Villous: Pubescent; shaggy; covered with fine long hairs, but the hairs not matted.

Vine or liana: An elongate, weak-stemmed, often climbing annual or perennial plant, with herbaceous or woody texture.

Vir genes: A set of genes on a Ti plasmid that prepare the T-DNA segment for transfer into a plant cell.

Viral coat protein: A protein present in the layer surrounding the nucleic acid core of a virus.

Viral oncogene: A viral gene that promotes tumour development in a host.

Viral pathogen: A disease-causing virus.

Viral vaccine: Vaccine consisting of live viruses, genetically engineered to avoid causing the disease itself.

Virgate: Twiggy, elongate, straight and slender.

Virion: A complete infectious virus particle.

Viroid: A plant pathogenic agent, composed of an infectious single-stranded low molecular weight RNA, and no coat protein.

Virulence: The degree of ability of an organism to cause disease. The relative infectiousness of a bacterium or virus, or its ability to overcome the resistance of the host metabolism.

Virus: A minute particle consisting of a core of nucleic acid, usually surrounded by a protein coat; it is incapable of growth alone and can reproduce only within, and at the expense of, a living cell.

Virus tested: Description of a organism or a cell stock certified as being free of certain specified viruses following recognized procedures of virus diagnosis.

Viscid: Thick, sirupy, and sticky, viscous; covered with a viscid substance as of leaves.

Viscous: Of a liquid, not pouring freely; having the consistency of syrup or honey.

Vitamin: Any compound, essential in trace amounts for the normal functioning of an organism, but not synthesized by some heterotrophs, which thus need to obtain it from plants or microorganisms. All vitamins with the exceptions of vitamins C (ascorbic acid), Å (tocopherol), and K, function as coenzymes. They can be divided into two groups, the water-soluble vitamins, which contain all the B-group vitamins and vitamin C, and the fat-soluble vitamins, including vitamins A, D, E, and K.

Vitrified: Cultured tissue having leaves and sometimes stems with a glassy, transparent or wet and often swollen appearance. The process of vitrification is a general term for a variety of physiological disorders that lead to shoot tip and leaf necrosis. Synonym: water soaked.

Viviparous: Producing young alive rather than in eggs, as in most mammals; multiplying by vegetative means such as buds or bulbils in the position of flowers.

Vivipary: (a) The differentiation of young plants or bulbils at the floral axils, instead of flowers. This is seen, for instance, in viviparous fescue (Festuca vivipara) and in the spider plant (Chlorophytum comosum). (b) The premature germination of seeds or spores in situ on the maternal plant before they have been released. This occurs in the mangroves where seeds may develop into sizeable seedlings before they are shed from the parent tree.

Vmax: The maximal rate of an enzyme-catalysed reaction. Vmax is the product of Eo (the total amount of enzyme) and Kcat (the catalytic rate constant).

VNTR: Abbreviation for variable number tandem repeat.

Volatilization: The conversion of a solid or liquid into a gas or vapour.

Volva: The cuplike structure that encircles the base of the fruiting bodies of many basidiomycete fungi. It is part of the remnants of the universal veil.

VSG: Abbreviation for variable surface glycoprotein.

W/v: Abbreviation for weight per volume. The relative proportions of solid and liquid in a solution.

Wall pressure: The force exerted upon cell contents by the cell wall. It is equal and opposite to the turgor pressure.

Wallemia: Conidia dimensions 2.5-3.5 microns. Found in sugary foods, salted meats, dairy products, textiles, soil, hay and fruits.

Water potential: Symbol Ø. A measure of the energy available in an aqueous solution to cause the migration of water molecules across semipermeable membranes during osmosis. Values of water potential cannot be calculated absolutely but are highest in pure water, which for convenience is given the value zero, and fall with increasing solute concentration. Water always tends to move from areas of high (less negative) to areas of low (more negative) potential. This principle governs water conduction in plants. Water potential is the sum of osmotic potential , pressure potential , and matric potential. The term is replacing the concept of osmotic pressure and differs from osmotic pressure in taking capillary and imbibitional forces into account.

Water stress: Occurs when plants are unable to absorb enough water to replace that lost by transpiration. Short-term water stress leads to turgor loss (wilting). Prolonged stress leads to cessation of growth, and eventually plant death.

Water-splitting (photolysis): A process in photosystem II of photosynthesis whereby water molecules are split with the release of oxygen.

Wax: Water-insoluble esters of long-chain acids with long-chain alcohols. Waxes form protective waterproof layers on leaves, stems, fruits, animal fur and integuments of insects.

Weed: A plant growing where it is not wanted. Generally used to describe plants which colonize readily, and can compete for resources with a planted crop.

Weediness: The ability of a plant to colonize a disturbed habitat and compete with cultivated species.

Western blot: A technique whereby a complex mixture of size-separated proteins is fixed to a solid support, and then probed with a labelled antibody. Useful, for example, for the measurement of levels of production of a specific protein in a particular tissue or at particular developmental stage.

Wet rot: A plant disease in which there is disintegration of tissues and release of cell fluids. Brown rot of stored fruits, such as plums and apples, is caused by fungi of the genus Sclerotinia. Wet rot of structural timber is caused by various fungi including Coniophora puteana and Poria vaillantii.

Wet woodland: A wooded area having surface water some of the time, for intermittent short periods.

Whorl: An arrangement of appendages, such as branches or leaves, such that all are equally spaced around the stem at the same point, much like the spokes of a wheel or the ribs of an umbrella.

Whorled, radiate, or verticillate: When three or more leaves are arranged at the same level on a stem, typical of such plants as hydrilla.

Wild type: The most frequent allele or genotype found in nature, or a specified organism against which mutants are defined.

Wilting point: The moisture content of soil at which plants start to wilt, but not to the extent that they fail to recover when placed in a humid atmosphere.

Wing: A membranous expansion of a fruit or seed, which aids dispersal; a thin flange of tissue extended beyond the normal outline of a stem or petiole; a lateral petal of a flower in fabaceae.

Winged: With flattened blade-like margins. Winged Nut (Bract) - Nut enclosed in a winglike bract, as in Carpinus.

Wobble hypothesis: An explanation of how one tRNA may recognize more than one codon. The first two bases of the mRNA codon and anticodon pair properly, but the third base in the anticodon has some flexibility that permits it to pair with either the expected base or an alternative.

Wood ray: A radially oriented tier of parenchyma cells that conducts food, water, waste products and other materials laterally in stems and roots of woody plants; rays are usually continuous across the vascular cambium between the secondary phloem and xylem.

Wound hormone: Any substance produced by damaged cells, that diffuses into nearby undamaged cells and there stimulates meristematic activity, resulting in the formation of a protective callus. Auxins, gibberellins, and certain products of wounding have been implicated in the wounding reaction.

Wrinkled: Creased, folded up irregularly in every direction.

X: The basic number of chromosomes in a polyploid series, monoploid/ haploid = x; diploid = 2x; triploid = 3x; etc.

X linked: The presence of a gene on the X-chromosome.

X linked disease: A genetic disease caused by an allele at a locus on the X-chromosome.

Xanthophylls: Any of a class of oxygenated hydrocarbons derived from the carotenes. Xanthophylls function mainly as photosynthetic accessory pigments, and are found in many different plant species. However the xanthophylls fucoxanthin and peridinin of the brown algae are of especial interest, because they are the primary light absorbing pigments for these organisms. They absorb light at frequencies where chlorophyll has only poor absorption and transfer the absorbed energy to chlorophyll.

Xanthophyta: A division consisting mainly of freshwater and terrestrial algae, including unicellular, colonial (palmelloid), filamentous, and siphonaceous forms. They are characterized by having disclike yellow-green plastids (due to the large amounts of carotenoids present) and by accumulating oil and leucosin rather than starch. The motile stages have two unequal flagella (one flimmer and one smooth flagellum) hence the older name Heterokontae. The cell wall is divided into two halves but this character is not obvious except in the filamentous forms, where disruption results in a number of Ç-shaped fragments.

Xenobiotic: A chemical compound that is not produced by, and often cannot be degraded by, living organisms.

Xenogeneic: Refers to organs, genetically engineered ("humanized") todecrease the chance of rejection, that have been grown in an animal of another species for potential transplant to humans.

Xenotransplantation: The transplantation of tissue or organs from one species to another species, typically from pigs to humans. Zoonoses are an important issue.

Xeric: Characterized by a scanty supply of moisture, tolerating, or adapted to, arid conditions.

Xeromorph: A plant having structural features usually associated with plants of arid habitats (such as hard or succulent leaves) but not necessarily drought-tolerant.

Xerophilous: Growing in dry places.

Xerophytes: A plant that is adapted to living in dry conditions caused either by lack of soil water or by heat or wind bringing about excessive transpiration. Many xerophytes are found in deserts, on sand dunes, and on exposed moors and heaths. Some xerophytes, e.g. the succulent desert cacti, store water in swollen stems and leaves. Many species reduce the rate of transpiration by having permanently rolled leaves, e.g. cross-leaved heath (Erica tetralix) or by having leaves that are rolled in dry weather, e.g. marram grass (Ammophila arenaria). Some have hairy leaves to trap moist air, e.g. great mullein (Verbascum thapsus) while others have stomata sunken into grooves producing pockets of moist air, e.g. Pinus. The leaves of many species are leathery with a thick cuticle and epidermis to reduce cuticular transpiration. Some species have stomata that close during the day and open at night.

Xerosere: A primary succession that initiates with bare rock.

X-ray diffraction analysis: A technique used to determine the three-dimensional pattern of large molecules such as proteins or DNA. A beam of x-rays is fired at a crystal and the resulting diffraction pattern is recorded on a photographic plate behind the crystal. The crystal is rotated slightly and is subjected to more x-rays. By repeating this, the three-dimensional pattern can be determined. It was work of this nature that showed DNA to be a regular double helix.

Xylem: Vascular tissue whose principal function is the upward translocation of water and solutes. It is composed mainly of vessels, tracheids, fibre-tracheids, libriform fibres, and parenchyma cells. It should be noted, however, that all these cell types may not be present in any one wood sample. Wood anatomy is often very important taxonomically, the presence or absence of the various cell types and their distribution within the xylem being important diagnostic characters. The xylem occurs in association with, and usually internal to, the phloem.

Xylose: An aldopentose sugar widely found in plants, particularly in woody tissues. It occurs mainly in its polymerized form xylan. It is also a constituent of the rare disaccharide primeverose.

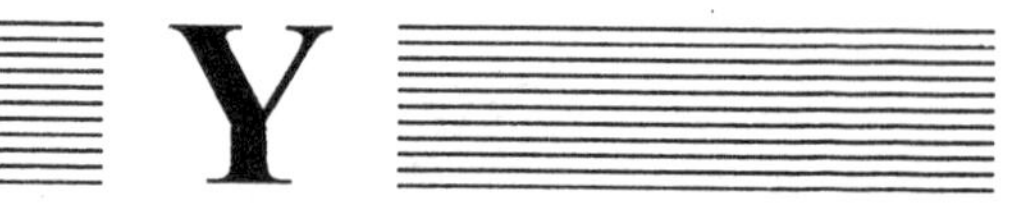

Y

Yeast: Various yeasts are commonly identified on air samples. Some yeasts are reported to be allergenic. They may cause problems if a person has had previous exposure and developed hypersensitivity's. Yeasts may be allergenic to susceptible individuals when present in sufficient concentrations.

Yeast artificial chromosome (YAC): A vector which can be propagated in budding yeast (Saccharamyces pombe), consisting of the minimal elements required for a chromosome to replicate, and allowing for the cloning of large DNA fragments (hundreds of kilobase pairs).

Yeast episomal vector (YEp): A cloning plasmid vector for the yeast Saccharomyces cerevisiae maintained as an extrachromosomal nuclear DNA molecule.

Yeast extract: A mixture of substances from yeast.

Yellows: (a) A plant disease, caused by mineral deficiency or a virus or mycoplasma, in which there is yellowing of the foliage. Yellowing is a common symptom when there is a deficiency of elements important in chlorophyll production, namely, iron, magnesium, manganese, nitrogen, or sulphur. Barley yellow dwarf and beet yellows are caused by viruses and coconut lethal yellowing is caused by a mycoplasma. (b) A disease of cabbage caused by Fusarium conglutinans.

Yield: Standing crop expressed as a rate, i.e., g dry weight per meter square per day.

Z DNA: A form of DNA, in which the double helix is wound in a left-hand, instead of a right-hand, manner. DNA adopts the Z conformation when purines and pyrimidines alternate on each strand, e.g. 5'CGCGCGCG 3' or 3'GCGCGCGC5'. Synonym: zig-zag DNA.

Zeatin: (6-(4-hydroxy-3-methyl but-2-enyl)aminopurine) The first plant growth substance of the cytokinin type to be isolated from plant tissues. It was obtained from the kernels of sweet corn (Zea mays) hence its name. Subsequently other cytokinins similar in structure to zeatin (i.e. an adenine molecule substituted with an isoprenoid derivative) have been isolated. Some of these are found as minor bases in transfer RNA molecules.

Zein: A low-molecular-weight simple protein found as a major storage protein in maize grains.

Zinc finger: A DNA-binding protein motif, characterized by two closely spaced cysteine and two histidine residues that serve as ligands for a single Zn^{2+} ion. When bound, the structure takes on a conformation in which amino acid side chains protrude in a way that allows interaction with the DNA major groove.

Zone of elongation: The section of the young root or shoot just behind the apical meristem, in which the cells are enlarging and elongating rapidly.

Zoned: The same as ocellated, but the concentric bands more numerous.

Zonocaulous: With branches intermittently spaced along main stem.

Zoo blot: Hybridization of cloned DNA from one species to DNA from a range of other organisms to determine the extent to which the cloned DNA is evolutionarily conserved.

Zoo FISH: Fluorescence in situ hybridization technique, probing metaphase chromosomes of one species with DNA from another species. The technique allows inferences to be made regarding the evolutionary relationships between species.

Zoonosis: A disease that is communicable from animals to humans.

Zoospore: A motile usually nSaked spore with one or more flagella. It may be produced either by a zygote or a zoo-sporangium and is dependent on water for dispersal. In some species, e.g. the green alga Ulothrix, two types of zoospore may be developed. In Ulothrix large macrozoospores with four flagella and small microzoospores with two flagella are seen. Zoospores may encyst under adverse conditions.

Zygomorphic: Said of the corolla or calyx when divisible into equal halves in one plane only bilaterally symmetrical, with only one plane of symmetry.

Zygonema: Stage of meiotic prophase during which chromosome synapsis occurs.

Zygote: The product of the fusion of two gametes, before it has undergone mitosis or meiosis. In lower algae and fungi it may retain the motile nature of the gametes. More usually the zygote is immobile and may develop a thickened resistant wall to form a zygospore. In higher plants the zygote is typically protected by maternal tissue, and divides immediately after fertilization forming a proembryo.

● ● ●